Corporate Hacking and Technology-Driven Crime:
Social Dynamics and Implications

Thomas J. Holt
Michigan State University, USA

Bernadette H. Schell
Laurentian University, Canada

Information Science
REFERENCE

INFORMATION SCIENCE REFERENCE
Hershey · New York

Director of Editorial Content:	Kristin Klinger
Director of Book Publications:	Julia Mosemann
Acquisitions Editor:	Lindsay Johnston
Development Editor:	Joel Gamon
Production Editor:	Jamie Snavely
Cover Design:	Lisa Tosheff

Published in the United States of America by
Information Science Reference (an imprint of IGI Global)
701 E. Chocolate Avenue
Hershey PA 17033
Tel: 717-533-8845
Fax: 717-533-8661
E-mail: cust@igi-global.com
Web site: http://www.igi-global.com

Library of Congress Cataloging-in-Publication Data

Corporate hacking and technology-driven crime : social dynamics and implications / Thomas J. Holt and Bernadette H. Schell, editors. p. cm.
Includes bibliographical references and index. Summary: "This book addresses various aspects of hacking and technology-driven crime, including the ability to understand computer-based threats, identify and examine attack dynamics, and find solutions"--Provided by publisher. ISBN 978-1-61692-805-6 (hbk.) -- ISBN 978-1-61692-807-0 (ebook) 1. Computer crimes. 2. Computer hackers. I. Holt, Thomas J., 1978- II. Schell, Bernadette H. (Bernadette Hlubik), 1952- HV6773.C674 2011
364.16'8--dc22

2010016447

British Cataloguing in Publication Data
A Cataloguing in Publication record for this book is available from the British Library.

List of Reviewers

Michael Bachmann, *Texas Christian University, USA*
Adam M. Bossler, *Georgia Southern University, USA*
Dorothy E. Denning, *Naval Postgraduate School, USA*
Thomas J. Holt, *Michigan State University, USA*
Max Kilger, *Honeynet Project, USA*
Miguel Vargas Martin, *University of Ontario Institute of Technology, Canada*
Robert G. Morris, *University of Texas at Dallas, USA*
Gregory Newby, *University of Alaska Fairbanks, USA*
Johnny Nhan, *Texas Christian University (TCU), USA*
Bernadette H. Schell, *Laurentian University, Canada*
Orly Turgeman-Goldschmidt, *Bar-Ilan University, Israel*

Table of Contents

Section 3
Empirical Assessments

Section 4
Macro-System Issues Regarding Corporate and Government Hacking and Network Intrusions

Section 5
Policies, Techniques, and Laws for Protection

Detailed Table of Contents

Section 3
Empirical Assessments

While the societal threat posed by malicious hackers motivated to cause harm to property and persons utilizing computers and networks has grown exponentially over the past decade, the field of cyber criminology has not provided many insights into important theoretical questions that have emerged—such as who are these network attackers, and why do they engage in malicious hacking acts? Besides a lack of criminological theories proposed to help explain emerging cyber crimes, the field has also suffered from a severe lack of available data for empirical analysis. This chapter tries filling the gap by outlining a significant motivational shift that seems to occur over the trajectory of hackers' careers by utilizing data collected at a large hacker convention held in Washington, D.C. in 2008. It also suggests that more effecting countermeasures will require ongoing adjustments to society's current understanding of who hackers are and why they hack over the course of their careers, often making hacking their chosen careers.

Besides the growth in creative computer applications over the past two decades has come the opportunity for cyber criminals to create new venues for committing their exploits. One field that has emerged but has received relatively scant attention from scholars is carding—the illegal acquisition, sale, and exchange of sensitive information online. Also missing from scholarly undertakings has been the study of the language, or argot, used by this special group of cyber criminals to communicate with one another using special codes. This chapter provides valuable insights into this emerging cyber criminal domain, detailing key values that appear to drive carders' behaviors. It also suggests policy implications for more effective legal enforcement interventions.

The media and the general population seem to consistently view all computer hackers as being mal-inclined and socially, emotionally, and behaviorally poorly adjusted. Little has been done by scholars to outline the different motivations and behavioral predispositions of the positively motivated hacker segment from those of the negatively motivated hacker segment. Also, few empirical investigations have been completed by scholars linking possible social and behavioral traits of computer hackers to those found in individuals in coveted careers like mathematics and science. This chapter focuses on hacker conference attendees' self-reported Autism-spectrum Quotient (AQ) predispositions and examines whether hackers themselves feel that their somewhat odd thinking and behaving patterns—at least the way the media and the general population see it—have actually helped them to be successful in their chosen fields of endeavor.

Section 4
Macro-System Issues Regarding Corporate and Government Hacking and Network Intrusions

Since the beginning of time, land-based warfare has been inherently social in nature. Soldiers have trained and operated in units, and they have fought for and died in units where their commitment to their comrades has been as strong as their commitment to their countries for which they were fighting. Do these same social forces exist in the virtual world, where cyber warriors operate and relate in virtual spaces? This chapter examines the emergence of social networks of non-state warriors motivated to launch cyber attacks for social and political causes. It not only examines the origin and nature of these networks, but it also details the objectives, targets, tactics and use of online forums to carry out the mission in cyber space.

Over the past year or two, the United States, Canada, and other developed nations have become extremely concerned about the safety of critical infrastructures and various Supervisory Control and Data Acquisition (SCADA) systems keeping the nations functioning. To this end, various national Cyber Security Strategies and action plans have been proposed to better secure cyber space from tech-savvy individuals motivated to wreak significant social and financial havoc on targeted nation states. This chapter not only highlights this important and seemingly under-researched area but provides a review and discussion of the known weaknesses or vulnerabilities of SCADA systems that can be exploited by Black Hat hackers and terrorists intent on causing harm to property and persons. Suggested remedies for securing these systems are also presented.

Preface

This book takes a novel approach to the presentation and understanding of a controversial topic in modern-day society: *hacking*. The term *hacker* was originally used to denote positively-motivated individuals wanting to stretch the capabilities of computers and networks. In contrast, the term *cracker* was a later version of the term, used to denote negatively-motivated individuals wanting to take advantage of computers and networks' vulnerabilities to cause harm to property or persons, or to personally gain financially. Most of what the public knows about hackers comes from the media—who tend to emphasize the cracker side in many journalistic pieces. In the academic domain, content experts from computer science, criminology, or psychology are often called in to assess individuals caught and convicted of computer-related crimes—and their findings are sometimes published as case studies.

In an age when computer crime is growing at a exponential rate and on a global scale, industry and government leaders are crying out for answers from the academic and IT Security fields to keep cyber crime in check—and to, one day, be ahead of the "cyber criminal curve" rather than have to react to it. After all, the safety and security of nations' critical infrastructures and their citizens are at risk, as are companies' reputations and profitable futures. According to 2009 Computer Security Institute report, the average loss due to IT security incidents per company exceeds the $230,000 mark for the U.S., alone. Given the 2009 financial crisis worldwide, a looming fear among IT Security experts is that desperate times feed desperate crimes, including those in the virtual world—driving the cost factor for network breaches upward.

To answer this call for assistance, we approached content experts in Criminal Justice, Business, and Information Technology Security from around the world, asking them to share their current research undertakings and findings with us and our readers so that, together, we can begin to find interdisciplinary solutions to the complex domain of cyber crime and network breaches. In our invitation to potential authors, we said, "Your pieces, we hope, will focus on the analysis of various forms of attacks or technological solutions to identify and mitigate these problems, with a view to assisting industry and government agencies in mitigating present-day and future exploits." Following a blind review of chapters submitted, we compiled the best and most exciting submissions in this book, entitled, *Corporate Hacking and Technology-Driven Crime: Social Dynamics and Implications.*

The chapters in this book are meant to address various aspects of corporate hacking and technology-driven crime, including the ability to:

Define and understand computer-based threats using empirical examinations of hacker activity and theoretical evaluations of their motives and beliefs.

Provide a thorough review of existing social science research on the hacker community and identify new avenues of scholarship in this area.

Identify and examine attack dynamics in network environments and on-line using various data sets.

Explore technological solutions that can be used to proactively or reactively respond to diverse threats in networked environments.

Outline a future research agenda for the interdisciplinary academic community to better understand and examine hackers and hacking over time.

There are 12 great chapters in this book, grouped into the following five sections: (1) Background, (2) Frameworks, (3) Empirical Assessments, (4) Corporate and Government Hacking and Network Intrusions, and (5) Policies, Techniques, and Laws for Protection.

Section 1 provides background information and an overview of hacking—and what experts say is the breadth of the problem. In **Chapter 1**, Robert Morris explores malicious hacking from a criminological perspective, while focusing on the justifications, or neutralizations, that cyber criminals may use when engaging in computer cracking—an act that is illegal in the United States and other jurisdictions worldwide.

In **Chapter 2**, Orly Turgeman-Goldschmidt notes that scholars often view hacking as one category of computer crime, and computer crime as white-collar crime. He affirms that no study, to date, has examined the extent to which hackers exhibit the same characteristics as white-collar offenders. This chapter attempts to fill this void by looking at empirical data drawn from over 50 face-to-face interviews with Israeli hackers, in light of the literature in the field of white-collar offenders and concentrating on their accounts and socio-demographic characteristics. While white-collar offenders usually act for economic gain, notes the author, hackers act for fun, curiosity, and opportunities to demonstrate their computer virtuosity. But is this assertion validated by the data analyzed by this researcher?

In **Chapter 3**, Adam Bossler and George Burrus note that though in recent years, a number of studies have been completed on hackers' personality and communication traits by experts in the fields of psychology and criminology, a number of questions regarding this population remain. One such query is, Does Gottfredson and Hirschi's concept of low self-control predict the unauthorized access of computer systems? Do computer hackers have low levels of self-control, as has been found for other criminals in mainstream society? Their chapter focuses on proffering some answers to these questions.

In **Chapter 4**, David Wall notes that over the past two decades, network technologies have shaped just about every aspect of our lives, not least the way that we are now victimized. From the criminal's point of view, networked technologies are a gift, for new technologies act as a force multiplier of grand proportions, providing individual criminals with personal access to an entirely new field of "distanciated" victims across a global span. This chapter looks at different ways that offenders can use networked computers to assist them in performing deceptions upon individual or corporate victims to obtain an informational or pecuniary advantage.

Section 2 consists of one chapter offering frameworks and models to study inhabitants of the Computer Underground. In **Chapter 5**, Johnny Nhan and Alesandra Garbagnatti look at policing of movie and music piracy in a U.S. context, applying the utility of a nodal governance model. This chapter explores structural and cultural conflicts among security actors that make fighting piracy extremely difficult. In addition, this chapter considers the role of law enforcement, government, and industries—as well as the general public—in creating long-term security models that will work.

Section 3 includes research studies from around the globe that report empirical findings on who hacks and cracks—why and how. In **Chapter 6**, Michael Bachmann notes that the increasing dependence of modern societies, industries, and individuals on information technology and computer networks renders them ever more vulnerable to attacks. While the societal threat posed by malicious hackers and other types of cyber criminals has been growing significantly in the past decade, mainstream criminology has only begun to realize the significance of this threat. In this chapter, the author attempts to provide answers to questions like: Who exactly are these network attackers? Why do they engage in malicious hacking activities?

In **Chapter 7**, Thomas J. Holt looks at a particular segment of the dark side of the Computer Underground: Carders. Carders engage in carding activities—the illegal acquisition, sale, and exchange of sensitive information—which, the author notes, are a threat that has emerged in recent years. In this chapter, the author explores the argot, or language, used by carders through a qualitative analysis of 300 threads from six web forums run by and for data thieves. The terms used to convey knowledge about the information and services sold are explored.

In **Chapter 8**, Bernadette H. Schell and June Melnychuk look at the psychological, behavioral, and motivational traits of female and male hacker conference attendees, expanding the findings of the first author's 2002 study on hackers' predispositions, as detailed in the book *The Hacking of America.* This chapter looks at whether hackers are as strange behaviorally and psychologically as the media and the public believe them to be, focusing, in particular, on hackers' autism-spectrum traits. It also focuses on hacker conference attendees' self-reports about whether they believe their somewhat odd thinking and behaving patterns (as the world stereotypically perceives them) help them to be successful in their chosen field of endeavor.

Section 4 focuses on macro-system issues regarding corporate and government hacking and network intrusions. In **Chapter 9**, Dorothy E. Denning examines the emergence of social networks of non-state warriors launching cyber attacks for social and political reasons. The chapter examines the origin and nature of these networks; their objectives, targets, tactics, and use of online forums. In addition, the author looks at their relationship, if any, to their governments. General concepts are illustrated with case studies drawn from operations by Strano Net, the Electronic Disturbance Theater, the Electrohippies, and other networks of cyber activists. The chapter also examines the concepts of electronic jihad and patriotic hacking.

In **Chapter 10**, Robert Radzinoski looks at present-day fears regarding the safety and integrity of the U.S. national power grid, as questions have been raised by both political and executive-level management as to the risks associated with critical infrastructures, given their vulnerabilities and the possibility that hackers will exploit them. This chapter highlights the importance of preventing hack attacks against SCADA systems, or Industrial Control Systems (abbreviated as ICS), as a means of protecting nations' critical infrastructures.

Section 5 deals with policies, techniques, and laws for protecting networks from insider and outsider attacks. In **Chapter 11**, Max Kilger notes that the future paths that cybercrime and cyber terrorism will take are influenced, in large part, by social factors at work, in concert with rapid advances in technology. Detailing the motivations of malicious actors in the digital world—coupled with an enhanced knowledge of the social structure of the hacker community, the author affirms, will give social scientists and computer scientists a better understanding of why these phenomena exist. This chapter builds on the previous book chapters by beginning with a brief review of malicious and non-malicious actors, proceeding to a comparative analysis of the shifts in the components of the social structure of the hacker subculture over the last decade, and concluding with an examination of two future cybercrime and national-security-related scenarios likely to emerge in the near future.

In **Chapter 12,** Walid Hejazi, Alan Lefort, Rafael Etges, and Ben Sapiro—a study team comprised of Canadian IT Security experts and a Business academic--examined Canadian IT Security Best Practices, with an aim to answering the question, Compared to the United States, how well is the Canadian industry doing in thwarting network intrusions? This chapter describes their 2009 study findings, focusing on how 500 Canadian organizations with over 100 employees are faring in effectively coping with network breaches. The study team concludes that in 2009, as in 2008, Canadian organizations maintained that they have an ongoing commitment to IT Security Best Practices; however, with the global 2009 financial crisis, the threat appears to be amplified, both from outside the organization and from within. Study implications regarding the USA PATRIOT Act are discussed at the end of this chapter.

In closing, while we cannot posit that we have found all of the answers for helping to keep industrial and government networks safe, we believe that this book fills a major gap by providing social science, IT Security, and Business perspectives on present and future threats in this regard and on proposed safeguards for doing a better job of staying ahead of the cyber criminal curve.

Thomas J. Holt
Michigan State University, USA

Bernadette H. Schell
Laurentian University, USA

Acknowledgment

We are grateful to the many individuals whose assistance and contributions to the development of this scholarly book either made this book possible or helped to improve its academic robustness and real-world applications.

First, we would like to thank the chapter reviewers for their invaluable comments. They helped to ensure the intellectual value of this book. We would also like to express our sincere gratitude to our chapter authors for their excellent contributions and willingness to consider further changes once the chapter reviews were received.

Special thanks are due to the publishing team of IGI Global and, in particular, to our Managing Development Editor, Mr. Joel A. Gamon. A special word of thanks also goes to Ms. Jamie Snavely, Production Senior Managing Editor.

Thomas J. Holt
Michigan State University, USA

Bernadette H. Schell
Laurentian University, USA

Section 1
Background

Chapter 1
Computer Hacking and the Techniques of Neutralization:
An Empirical Assessment

Robert G. Morris
University of Texas at Dallas, USA

ABSTRACT

Nowadays, experts have suggested that the economic losses resulting from mal-intended computer hacking, or cracking, have been conservatively estimated to be in the hundreds of millions of dollars per annum. The authors who have contributed to this book share a mutual vision that future research, as well as the topics covered in this book, will help to stimulate more scholarly attention to the issue of corporate hacking and the harms that are caused as a result. This chapter explores malicious hacking from a criminological perspective, while focusing on the justifications, or neutralizations, that cyber criminals may use when engaging in computer cracking--which is in the United States and many other jurisdictions worldwide, illegal.

INTRODUCTION

The impact on daily life in westernized countries as a result of technological development is profound. Computer technology has been integrated into our very existence. It has changed the way that many people operate in the consumer world and in the social world. Today, it is not uncommon for people to spend more time in front of a screen than they do engaging in physical activities (Gordon-Larson, Nelson, & Popkin, 2005). In fact, too much participation in some sedentary behaviors (e.g., playing video/computer games; spending time online, etc.) has become a serious public health concern that researchers have only recently begun to explore. Research has shown that American youths spend an average of nine hours per week playing video games (Gentile, Lynch, Linder, & Walsh, 2004). Video gaming and other similar forms of sedentary behavior among youth may be linked to obesity (e.g., Wong & Leatherdale, 2009), aggression (stemming from violent video gaming—see Anderson, 2004, for a review), and may increase the probability of engaging in

DOI: 10.4018/978-1-61692-805-6.ch001

some risky behaviors (Nelson & Gordon-Larsen, 2006; Morris & Johnson, 2009). In all, it is difficult to say whether increased screen time as a result of technological development is good or bad in the grand scheme of things; the information age is still in its infancy and it is simply too early for anyone to have a full understanding of how humans will adapt to technology and mass information in the long-run. However, we do know that people are spending considerable amounts of time participating in the digital environment, and the popularity of technology has spawned a new breed of behaviors, some of which are, in fact, criminal. One such criminal act is that of malicious computer hacking.[1]

Scholarly attention to cyber-related crimes has gained much popularity in recent years; however, much of this attention has been aimed at preventing such acts from occurring through Information Technology and information assurance/security developments. To a lesser extent, criminologists have focused on explaining the etiology of malicious cyber offending (e.g., malicious computer hacking) through existing theories of criminal behavior (e.g., Hollinger, 1993; Holt, 2007; Morris & Blackburn, 2009; Skinner & Fream, 1997; Yar, 2005a; 2005b; 2006). This reality is somewhat startling, considering the fact that economic losses resulting from computer hacking have been conservatively estimated in the hundreds of millions of dollars per year (Hughes & DeLone, 2007), and media attention to the problem has been considerable (Skurodomova, 2004; see also Yar, 2005a). Hopefully, future research, this chapter included, will help to stimulate more scholarly attention to the issue. The goal of this chapter is to explore malicious hacking from a criminological perspective, while focusing on the justifications, or neutralizations, that people might use when engaging in criminal computer hacking.

Caution must be used when using the term *hacking* to connote deviant or even criminal behavior. Originally, the term was associated with technological exploration and freedom of information; nowadays, the term is commonly associated with crime conduct. In general, hacking refers to the act of gaining unauthorized/illegal access to a computer, electronic communications device, network, web page, data base or etc. and/or manipulating data associated with the hacked hardware (Chandler, 1996; Hafner & Markoff, 1993; Hannemyr, 1999; Hollinger, 1993; Levy, 1994; Roush, 1995; Yar, 2005a). For the purposes of this chapter, I will use the term hacking as a reference to illegal activities surrounding computer hacking. Such forms of hacking have been referred to in the popular media and other references as "black hat" hacking or "cracking" (Stallman, 2002). Again, the primary demarcation here is criminal and/or malicious intent. However, before we fully engage understanding hacking from a criminological perspective, it is important to briefly discuss the history of computer hacking.

The meaning of computer hacking has evolved considerably since the term was first used in the 1960s, and as many readers are surely aware, there still remains a considerable debate on the connotation of the word hacking. The more recent definition of hacking surrounds the issue of understanding technology and being able to manipulate it. Ultimately, the goal is to advance technology by making existing technology better; this is to be done through by freely sharing information. This first definition is clearly a positive one and does not refer to criminal activity in any form.

As time progressed since the 1960s and as computer and software development became less expensive and more common to own, the persona of a hacker began to evolve, taking on a darker tone (Levy, 1984; Naughton, 2000; Yar, 2006); Clough & Mungo, 1992). Many hackers of this "second generation" have participated in a tightly-knit community that followed the social outcry and protest movements from the late 1960s and early 1970s (Yar, 2006). In this sense, second-generation hackers appear to be "anti-regulation" as far as the exchange of information is concerned. As one might expect (or have witnessed), this view typically runs counter to the views of governmental and corporate stakeholders. These second-generation hackers believe that information can and should be free to anyone interested in it, and that by showing unrestrained interest, technology will advance more efficiently and effectively since there will be less "reinventing of the wheel" and, thus, more rapid progress (Thomas, 2002).

Clearly, there is some logic to this more recent wave of hacker argument, which serves as the foundation for the "hacker ethic." Indeed, many hackers of this generation have argued vehemently that such exploration is not for malicious purposes but for healthy "exploration."

Nowadays, as publicized by the media, the term *hacking* refers to a variety of illegitimate and illegal behaviors. The definitional debate continues, and many "old school" hackers contest the current negative label of what it is to be a hacker (see Yar, 2005). The reality is that malicious hacking, or cracking, causes much harm to society. The primary difference between classical hacking and modern hacking is that with the latter, being a skilled programmer is not a requirement to cause harm or to be able to do *hacks*. For example, any neophyte computer user can simply download malicious pre-written code (e.g., viruses, worms, botnet programs, etc.) and conduct simple Internet searches to find literature on how to use the code for harmful or illegal purposes. Thus, it seems that the hacker ethic is a double-edged sword; the open sharing of information may very well stimulate technological progression, but it also opens the door to harm committed by those with, presumably, a lack of respect for and/or skill for the technology behind the code. This difference is critical to our understanding of why some users engage in malicious computer hacking and to our basic understanding that, notwithstanding the various motives behind hacker activities, today, there are simply more hackers globally than there were in the past few decades—with increased opportunities to cause harm to property and to persons.

THIS CHAPTER'S FOCUS

The primary goal of this chapter is to explore why some individuals engage in illegal computer hacking, certainly, most moderately experienced computer users could develop some anecdote that might explain why some people hack. For example, some suggest that people hack because it is an adrenaline rush. In other words, hackers get a thrill out of hacking and enjoy solving problems or understanding how a program operates and how it can be manipulated (see Schell, Dodge, with Moutsatsos, 2002). Anyone who enjoys computing technology and problem-solving might be sensitive to this explanation, and it may very well be the case some of the time. However, this point does not explain why some people go beyond simply exploring computer code to actually manipulating code for some alternative purpose. Perhaps the purpose is simply for kicks, akin of juvenile vandalism, or perhaps, the goal is financially motivated. Whatever the case, simple anecdotes developed "from the hip" are not very systematic and may not go too far in explaining the motivations behind hacking, in general.

In understanding something more thoroughly, we need a strong theoretical foundation to develop our understanding of the issue. Established criminological theories provide us with a systematic basis to begin our evaluation of the etiology of hacking. However, as discussed below, the transition into the digital age has serious implications for crimes and the theories that best explain the onset, continuity, and desistance of participating in cyber-related crimes. It is hoped that this chapter will shed some light (both theoretically and empirically) as to why some people engage in some types of malicious computer hacking.

For over a century, criminologists have been concerned with the question "Why do people commit crimes?" Several theories of crime are suggestive of the idea that an individual's environment plays a large role in the development of individual beliefs and attitudes toward moral and immoral behavior, and that such are likely to play a strong role in behavior. Some individuals may develop attitudes favorable to crime, while others may not, depending on their particular situation. However, varying theories of crime present varying explanations with regard to the nature of such attitudes and beliefs (Agnew, 1994). One theory of crime that focuses explicitly on the nature of beliefs in the process of becoming delinquent or, worse, criminal, is referred to as the *techniques of neutralization* (Sykes & Matza, 1957; Matza; 1964).

THE TECHNIQUES OF NEUTRALIZATION

The techniques of neutralization theory (Sykes & Matza, 1957; Matza; 1964) attempt to explain part of the etiology of crime, while assuming that most people are generally unopposed to conventional (i.e., non-criminal) beliefs most of the time. Even so, they may engage in criminal behavior from time to time (Sykes & Matza, 1957; Matza, 1964). Sykes and Matza focused only on juvenile delinquency, arguing that people become criminal or deviant through developing rationalizations or neutralizations for their activities *prior* to engaging in the criminal act. In this sense, attitudes toward criminality may be contextually based. Sykes and Matza developed five techniques of neutralization argued to capture the justifications that a person uses prior to engaging in a criminal or deviant act. This assertion was made to allow the individual to *drift* between criminality and conventionality (Matza, 1964).

The techniques of neutralization include the following: 1) denial of responsibility, 2) denial of an injury, 3) denial of a victim, 4) condemnation of the condemners, and 5) appeal to higher loyalties. Each of these five techniques is discussed in some detail below.

Some Examples of How Neutralization is Used

In using the denial of responsibility to justify engaging in a crime, an individual may direct any potential blame to an alternative source or circumstance. In other words, blame is shifted to a source other than oneself. The individual may also conclude that no harm (to property or to another individual) will result from the action (i.e., the denial of injury)—thus, participation in 'the behavior' is harmless. For example, Copes (2003) found that joy-riding auto thieves regularly felt that since the car was eventually brought back, there was no harm in joy-riding. The denial of a victim may be particularly apparent in cyber-related crimes. This technique might be used when the victim is not physically visible or is unknown or abstract. This view suggests that if there is *no* victim, there can be *no* harm. As another example, Dabney (1995) found that employees tended to use this neutralization technique to justify taking items found on company property if there were no clear owner (i.e., another employee or the company).

A condemnation of the condemners refers to an expression of discontent with the perception of authority holders; for example, holding the view that those opposed to the action are hypocrites, deviants in disguise, or impelled by personal spite (Skyes & Matza (1957, p. 668). In other words, the critics are in no position to judge my actions, thus my actions are not inappropriate.

Sykes and Matza's (1957) final technique of neutralization, an appeal to higher loyalties, refers to justifying actions as being a part of an obligation to something equal to or greater than one's own self-interest. For traditional crimes, an example would be the rationalization of embezzling from a company to pay for a child's college tuition or medical costs.

Recent Expansions of the List of Five

After reading the above passages, readers may be thinking of types of justifications, or neutralizations, that were not explicitly covered in the original five points presented by Sykes and Matza (1957)—at least one should be doing so! The original five techniques do not account for every possible justification. Several criminologists have expanded the list through more recent research studies. An example developed by Minor (1981) was termed the *defense of necessity*. According to this technique, "if an act is perceived as necessary, then one need not feel guilty about its commission, even if it is considered morally wrong in the abstract" (Minor, 1981, p. 298).

Morris and Higgins (2009) found modest support for this technique of neutralization and others in predicting self-reported and anticipated digital piracy (i.e., illegal downloading of media). Other extensions of the techniques of neutralization include, but are not limited to, the metaphor of ledgers (Klockers, 1974) and justification by comparison and postponement (Cromwell & Thurman, 2003). [For greater detail and a full review of neutralization theory, see Maruna & Copes, 2005.]

To this point, the discussion on neutralization theory has surrounded the idea that neutralizations of criminal conduct precede the actual conduct, as argued by Sykes and Matza (1957). However, neutralizations may occur *after* the crime takes place, and there is some research that is suggestive of this finding. For example, Hirschi (1969) argued that neutralizations may begin after the initial criminal acts take place, but post-onset may be used as a pre-cursor to the act. Either way, continued research is needed to hash out whether neutralizations occur before or after a crime is committed (see Maruna & Copes, 2005).

The fact is that several studies have found a significant link between neutralizations and crime, including digital crimes (e.g., Ingram & Hinduja, 2008; Hinduja, 2007; Morris & Higgins, 2009). However, no study, to date, has quantitatively assessed the relationship between techniques of neutralization and computer hacking. One study sought to explain computer hacking through the lens of moral disengagement theory, complementing the techniques of neutralization. This study found that hackers possessed higher levels of moral disengagement compared to non-hackers (Young, Zhang, & Prybutok, 2007).

THE PRESENT STUDY

The remainder of this chapter is devoted to addressing this gap in the literature by examining the findings of the author's recent study using college students. Based on the extant neutralization literature, it was hypothesized that neutralization will explain some variation in participation in computer hacking.

Methods

To address this issue, data were used from a larger project aimed at assessing computer activities among college students. During the fall of 2006, a total of 785 students participated in a self-report survey delivered to ten college courses at a university located in the southeastern United States. The students who participated were representative of the general university demographic with regard to individual characteristics (e.g., age, gender, and race) and their academic majors. Specifically, fifty-six percent of respondents were female; seventy-eight percent were White; and most (eighty percent) were between 18 and 21 years of age.

Measures

Dependent variables. Several indicators of participation in computer hacking were used to measure malicious hacking. Such indicators included guessing passwords, gaining illegitimate access to a computer or network, and manipulating another's files or data. Specifically, students were asked to report the number of times during the year prior to completing the questionnaire that they had tried to guess a password to gain access to a system other than their own. Second, they were asked to report the number of times they had gained access to another's computer without his/her permission to look at files or information. Finally, students were asked to report the number of times that they had had added, deleted, changed, or printed any information in another person's computer without the owner's knowledge or permission. For each type of hacking (without authorization), students were asked to report the number of times that they had engaged in the behavior using university-owned hardware, as well as the number of times that they had done so using a non-university computer. Responses were recorded on a five-point scale (Never, 1-2 times, 3-5 times, 6-9 times, and 10 or more times).

To provide the most complete analysis possible, each of the hacking indicators (i.e., password guessing, illegitimate access, and file manipulation) was explored individually and in an aggregated fashion (i.e., all types combined to represent general hacking). First, each of the three hacking types, as well as a fourth "any of the three" hacking variable, was explored as a prevalence measure. In other words, a binary indicator was created for each type that identified whether the student had engaged in the activity, or not. Next, a variable was created to represent the level of hacking frequency among all three hacking types together. This assessment was done by calculating factor scores based on each hacking variable, where higher scores represented increased frequency of participation in hacking (alpha = .91). Finally, a measure of hacking diversity was created by counting the number of different forms of hacking reported (zero, one, two, or all three forms reported).

In all, analyzing reports of hacking in this manner provided a more complete analysis of the outcome measure, hacking, than has typically been done in the past. Here, whether respondents participated in a particular form of hacking, how much they participated (if at all), and how versatile they are in various hacking acts were assessed, while statistically controlling for several demographic and theoretical predictors of offending.

As shown in Table 1, twenty-one percent of respondents reported at least minimal participation in computer hacking within the year prior to the date of the survey. Fifteen percent of respondents reported gaining illegal access or guessing passwords, respectively. Of all students reporting at least one type of hacking, seventy-four percent reported password guessing, seventy-three percent reported unauthorized access, and twenty-four percent reported file manipulation. Clearly, there is some versatility in hacking, as defined here. With regard to hacking versatility, forty-nine percent of those reporting hacking reported only one type, twenty-seven percent reported two types, and twenty-four percent reported all three types of hacking.

Independent variables. As discussed above, the main goal of this chapter is to explore participation in computer hacking from a *techniques of neutralization* perspective. Since the available data were secondary in nature, neutralization was limited to eight survey items, each reflecting varying, but not all, techniques of neutralization. The items asked respondents to report their level of agreement with a series of statements on a four-point scale (strongly disagree=4; strongly agree=1), and all items were coded in a manner so that higher scores were representative of increased neutralizing attitudes.

It is important to note that each of the neutralization items reflects neutralizations toward cybercrime. Unfortunately, no items appropriately reflected the denial of responsibility. However, three items captured the denial of injury: 1) "Compared with other illegal acts people do, gaining

Table 1. Self-report computer hacking prevalence

	n	Overall %	% of hackers
Any hacking	162	20.6%	100.0%
Guessing passwords	120	15.3%	74.1%
Unauthorized access	118	15.0%	72.8%
File manipulation	46	5.9%	28.4%
Diversity Index			
None reported	627	79.5%	0.0%
1 Type	79	10.0%	48.8%
2 Types	44	5.6%	27.2%
3 Types	39	4.9%	24.1%

unauthorized access to a computer system or someone's account is not very serious," 2) "It is okay for me to pirate music because I only want one or two songs from most CDs," and 3) "It is okay for me to pirate media because the creators are really not going to lose any money."

The denial of a victim was assessed via these items: 1) "If people do not want me to get access to their computer or computer systems, they should have better computer security," 2)" It is okay for me to pirate commercial software because it costs too much, and 3)" People who break into computer systems are actually helping society."

Condemnation of the condemners was not directly represented but could be argued through the second indicator from the denial of a victim, above. An appeal to higher loyalties was represented by the third statement, above, from the denial of a victim category and from one additional item, "I see nothing wrong in giving people copies of pirated media to foster friendships."

Clearly, there is substantial overlap among the available neutralization items. For this reason, neutralization was assessed as a singular construct by factor analyzing each of the eight items. A similar approach was taken by Morris and Higgins (2009). Factor scores were calculated to represent the techniques of neutralization, in general. where higher scores represent increased neutralization (alpha = .80). However, the neutralization indicators were also explored as individualized variables as a secondary analysis, discussed below.

It was also important to control for other important theoretical constructs to insure that the impact from neutralization on hacking was not spurious. Differential association with deviant peers and cognitive self-control were each incorporated into the analysis. "Differential association" refers socializing with people who engage in illegal activities; it is one of the most robust predictors of criminal and deviant behavior (see Akers & Jensen, 2006).

In theory, increased association with peers who are deviant increases the probability that an individual will become deviant (i.e., engage in crime). Recent research has shown that increased association with deviant peers is significantly linked with participation in a variety of forms of computer hacking (see Morris & Blackburn, 2009).

Differential association was operationalized via three items asking students to report how many times in the past year their friends had guessed passwords, had gained unauthorized access to someone's computer, and had modified someone's files without their permission. Responses were recorded on a five-point scale (5 = all of my friends; 1 = none of my friends). Factor score were calculated based on the three indicators, where higher scores represent increased differential association. The internal consistency of the differential association measure was strong (alpha = .88).

"Self-control" refers to one's "tendency to avoid acts whose long-term costs exceed their momentary advantages" (Hirschi & Gottfredson, 1993, p. 3). Research has consistently found that low self-control has a significant positive link with a variety of criminal behaviors; see Pratt & Cullen (2000) for a review. Here, self-control was operationalized via the popular twenty-three item self-control scale developed by Grasmick, Tittle, Bursik, & Arneklev (1993). Again, factor scores were calculated based on the self-control items. Items were coded so that higher scores on the self-control scale reflect lower self-control. The internal consistency of the scale was also strong (alpha = .89).

Control variables. In staying consistent with the extant literature on the topic of computer hacking, several control variables were incorporated into the analysis. As for individual demographics, the analysis controls were as follows for gender (female = 1), age (over 26 years old = 1), and race (White = 1). Also controlled for were each individual's computer skill and a variable representing cyber-victimization. Computer skill was operationalized through a variable assessing computer skill. This variable was dichotomized, where 1 represented computer skill at the level of being able to use a variety of software and being able to fix some computer problems, or greater. Cyber-victimization was operationalized through four items asking respondents to report the number of times during the past year that someone had accessed their computer illegally, modified their files, received a virus or worm, and/or harried them in a chat room. Factor scores were calculated to represented the victimization construct, where higher scores represent increased victimization. The factor analysis suggested a singular construct; however, internal consistency was only modest (alpha = .54).

Models used for analysis. In all, six regression models were developed to address the statistical analysis and content goals of this chapter. Each model contains the same independent variables, as described above; however, each dependent variable is different, also described above. Each variable's metric determined the type of regression model utilized. For the hacking frequency model, ordinary least squares regression (OLS) was employed, as the outcome variable is continuous. For the hacking versatility model, the outcome is an over-dispersed count variable, with a substantial proportion of cases reporting a zero count. To this end, zero-inflated negative binomial regression was used (ZINB). The remainder of the models, all of which are based on varying binary dependent variables, used logistic regression (Logit). It is important to note that collinearity among the independent variables was deemed non-problematic. This phenomenon was assessed by examining bi-variate correlation coefficients among independent variables (see Appendix) and by calculating variance inflation factors. Further, residual analyses of each model suggested reasonable model fit, and robust standard errors were calculated to determine coefficient significance levels. Table 2 provides the summary statistics for each variable used in the analysis.

Results

The regression model results are presented in Table 3. To start, note the model assessing the predictors of the "any type of hacking" model. The results suggest that both techniques of neutralization and association with hacking peers significantly predict whether someone reported some type of hacking, as defined here. It appears that in predicting hacking participation, in general, association with peers who hack plays a stronger role than neutralizing attitudes, but both have a uniquely substantive impact on hacking. Also, for hacking, in general, being female and having been a victim

Table 2. Summary statistics of model variables

Variable		Mean	S.D.	Minimum Value	Maximum Value
Hacking frequency *(log)*		-0.16	.45	-0.35	2.23
Hacking involvement		0.53	1.28	0	6
Any type of hacking		0.21	.40	0	1
	1 = yes; 0 = no				
Guessing passwords		0.15	.36	0	1
	1 = yes; 0 = no				
Illegal access		0.15	.36	0	1
	1 = yes; 0 = no				
File manipulation		0.06	.24	0	1
	1 = yes; 0 = no				
Neutralization		0.00	.92	-1.38	2.72
Differential association		0.00	.93	-0.54	5.40
Low self-control		0.00	.96	-2.21	3.99
Victimization		0.00	.79	-0.39	7.07
Female		0.56	.50	0	1
	1 = female; 0 = male				
White		0.78	.41	0	1
	1 = yes; 0 = no				
Over 26 years old		0.06	.24	0	1
	1 = yes; 0 = no				
Advanced user		0.62	.49	0	1
	1 = yes; 0 = no				

of a cybercrime modestly increased the odds of reporting hacking.

For each of the specific hacking prevalence models (i.e., predicting password guessing, illegal access, and file manipulation individually), differential association was significant in predicting the outcome measure, as expected. However, neutralization was significant in predicting only password guessing and illegal access, but not for file manipulation. In each case, the odds ratio (i.e., the change in the odds of reporting hacking) for differential association was greater than that of neutralization; however, the difference was modest. As with the general prevalence model, the illegal access model suggested that being female increased the odds of reporting illegal access. Further, being an advanced computer user double the odds of reporting illegal access, as one might expect.

The hacking versatility model produced similar results to the binary models, in that both neutralization and differential association were significant. However, for versatility, the impact from the techniques of neutralization was stronger than that of differential association. Similarly, for hacking frequency, both neutralization and differential association significantly predict increased participation in hacking, but the impact from differential association is stronger. For each regression model, the amount of explained vari-

Table 3. Model results (robust standard errors)

Dependent variable	**Hacking Frequency**			**Hacking Versatility**			**Guessing Passwords (Logit)**	
	Beta	SE		OR	SE		OR	SE
Neutralization	0.20	**.023****		1.28	**.126***		1.83	**.315****
Differential Assoc.	0.39	**.040****		1.09	**.088***		2.25	**.542****
Low self-control	0.00	.021		0.96	.100		1.01	.164
Victimization	0.14	.033		1.06	.049		1.26	.170
Female	0.06	.035		1.04	.207		1.71	.496
White	0.02	.037		1.27	.324		0.88	.283
Over 26	0.02	.043		1.37	1.090		0.30	.295
Advanced user	0.04	.033		1.01	.194		1.27	.362
R Square		.39			.31			.20
Dependent variable	Illegal Access			File Manipulation			Any Type	
	OR	SE		OR	SE		OR	SE
Neutralization	2.23	**.419****		1.62	.439		1.82	**.284****
Differential Assoc.	2.55	**.541****		2.13	**.393****		2.49	**.538****
Low self-control	0.98	.168		1.32	.338		1.10	.165
Victimization	1.28	.190		1.31	.283		1.44	**.207****
Female	2.29	**.711****		1.35	.615		1.92	**.521***
White	1.09	.382		1.17	.661		0.88	.256
Over 26	0.80	.540		3.19	.265		0.76	.455
Advanced user	2.02	**.645***		1.71	.823		1.51	.400
R Square		.25			.23			.31

*$p < .05$; **$p < .01$
Legend:
Hacking Frequency: OLS; Hacking Versatility: ZINB; Guessing Passwords: Logit; Illegal Access: Logit; File Manipulation: Logit; Any Type: Logit

ance in the dependent variable was good, ranging between twenty and thirty-nine percent.

As a secondary analysis, each model was rerun with each neutralization indicator as its own independent variable (output omitted), producing some noteworthy findings. Two neutralization indicators stood out. Representing the denial of injury, the item worded "compared with other illegal acts people do, gaining unauthorized access to a computer system or someone's account is not very serious" was significant in each binary model, as well as the hacking frequency model. Further, one indicator representing the denial of a victim ("If people do not want me to get access… they should have better computer security") was significant in the general hacking model and in the file manipulation model. The impact from differential association remained unchanged here. Interestingly, when the neutralization variable was itemized, cyber-victimization was significant in four of the six models.

Limitations of Study

Before we delve into discussing the relevance of the model results further, it is important to recognize several methodological limitations of the above analysis. The primary limitation is that the data were cross-sectional, not longitudinal, and the hacking variables only account for twelve months of time for a limited number of types of hacking. Thus, causal inferences cannot be made from the above results. Second, the results cannot be used to determine whether the neutralizations occur before or after hacking act takes place. That being said, it is more likely that the results are a better reflection of continuity in hacking. Third, the sample was not random; it was a convenience sample of college students attending one university. Fourth, as with any secondary data analysis, the theoretical constructs developed here are by no means complete; however, they do offer a fair assessment of each of the three theories incorporated into the analysis.

DISCUSSSION

Overall, the findings from the above analysis lend modest support to the notion that techniques of neutralization (i.e., neutralizing attitudes) are significantly related to some, but not all, types of malicious computer hacking, at least among the college students who participated in the survey. Clearly, constructs from other theories, particularly social learning theory, may play a role in explaining some computer hacking behaviors. However, the significant findings for neutralization held, despite the inclusion of several relevant theoretical and demographic control variables (i.e., social learning and self-control). The results were not supportive of self-control, as defined by Hirschi and Gottfredson (1990), in predicting any type of computer hacking. Finding significant, but non-confounding, results for the neutralization variables supports Skyes and Matza's (1957) theory, in that the techniques of neutralization are more of a complement to other theories of crime rather than a general theory of crime (Maruna & Copes, 2005). Again, it is important to note here that the above analysis was not a causal modeling approach. Rather, the regression models used here were more for exploring the relationship of neutralizations with malicious hacking, while controlling for other relevant factors.

Focusing on the techniques of neutralization as a partial explanatory factor in malicious computer hacking is particularly salient, considering the current state of social reliance on technology. The primary difference here, as compared to attempts at explaining more traditional crimes (e.g., street crimes), is that many factors that may be involved in a terrestrially-based crime do not come into play when a crime is committed via a computer terminal (see Yar, 2005b). Unlike many other crimes, the victim in a malicious hacking incident is often ambiguous or abstract. There will likely be no direct interaction between the victim and the offender, and opportunities to engage in hacking are readily available at any given time. This removal of face-to-face interactions changes the dynamic of criminal offending and, thus, may require us to rethink how existing theories of crime might explain digital crimes. We still only know very little about the dynamic behind what is involved in the onset and continuity in computer hacking. Certainly, more research with quality longitudinal data is warranted.

In considering the above results, Akers (1985, 1998) social learning theory provides plausible theoretical framework for explaining some of this process; however, the theory does not explicitly account for the importance of the digital environment for which the crimes take place. Social learning theory argues that crime and deviance occur as a result of the process of learning, and this theory has been supported by many studies of crime (e.g., Akers, Krohn, Lanza-Kaduce, & Radosevich, 1979; Krohn, Skinner, Massey, & Akers, 1985; Elliot, Huizinga, & Menard, 1989; see Akers & Jensen, 2006, for a review).

This theory posits that crime and deviance occur as a result of the learning process, where increased exposure to deviant peers (i.e., differential association) is exaggerated. Through such exposure, a person may develop attitudes, or neu tralizations/justifications, favorable to crime. Of course, all of this depends on the quality, duration, and frequency of exposure to such views and, to a large extent, on exposure to, or the witnessing of positive versus negative outcomes as a result of engaging in the act (i.e., the balance between rewards and punishments). This study, and others (e.g., Morris & Blackburn, 2009; Skinner & Fream, 1997) lend modest support to the social learning theory approach for explaining the etiology of computer hacking but leave many questions unanswered.

Beyond the dispositional theoretical explanations outlined above, situational theories, for example, should be considered when attempting to understand cybercrime, in general (see Yar, 2005b). Yar (2005b) makes a case for the applicability for routine activities theory (Cohen & Felson, 1979), albeit limited, in explaining cybercrime.

It is currently unknown if neutralizations play a different role in justifying, or neutralizing, computer crimes as compared to traditional crimes. Certainly, much between-individual variation exists in why any given individual becomes involved in computer hacking, or any crime for that matter. Some of this variation is individual-specific, but some variation may be a result of environmental, or contextual, factors. The problem is that elements of the digital environment are not fully understood and have yet to be explicitly incorporated into any general theory of crime and deviance.

Indeed, research has suggested that young hackers are commonly represented by a troubled or dysfunctional home life (Verton, 2002)--complementing work by developmental criminologists (e.g., Loeber & Stouthamer-Loeber, 1986). However, research assessing this issue with regard to hacking is limited. Furthermore, we do not know if exposure to deviant virtual peers (i.e., cyber friends) has the same impact on one's own cyber deviance as exposure to terrestrial peers might have on traditional deviance. Clearly, more research is needed with regard to virtual peer groups (see Warr, 2002). Holt's (2007) research suggests that hacking may take place, in some part, through group communication within hacking subcultures, and such relationships may exist both terrestrially as well as digitally in some cases.

The above results may provide us with more questions than answers. Indeed, future researchers have their work cut out for them. For one observation, we do not know if the impact from neutralizing attitudes on cybercrime is stronger than neutralizing attitudes toward traditional crimes/delinquency. Much work remains in the quest for understanding the origins of computer hacking and how best to prevent future harms as a result. For example, the findings here modestly suggest that cyber-victimization and participation in computer hacking are positively correlated. It is possible that having been a victim of computer hacking, or other cybercrimes, may play some role in developing pro-hacking attitudes or in stimulating retaliatory hacking. It is clear, however, that the virtual environment provides abundant opportunities for training in hacking and for networking with other hackers, which may ultimately promote malicious behavior (Denning, 1991; see also Yar, 2005). One need only do a quick Internet search to find specific information on how to hack.

As scholars continue to develop research and attempt to explain the origins of computer hacking and related cybercrimes, action can be taken to reduce the occurrence of malicious computer hacking. Regarding practical solutions that should be considered, administrators and policy makers can consider providing quality education/training for today's youth in reference to ethical behavior while online. School administrators should consider providing in-person and online ethical training to parents as well as students, beginning at a very early age. Any proactive attempt to curb neutralizing attitudes toward hacking would be beneficial. Universities can also contribute by providing, or even requiring, ethical training to students.

In fact, at my home university, which is by and large a science and engineering university, all engineering and computer science majors are required to complete an upper-level course on social issues and ethics in computer science and engineering. I have taught this course for over two years and each semester, one of the more popular sections is on computer crime and hacking. I regularly get comments from students about how evaluating all sides of computer hacking got them to understand the importance of ethical behavior in computing. Although most of my students end up voting in favor of offering a course specific to teaching hacking (as part of a formal debate we hold each term), they generally agree that there are ethical boundaries that all computer users should consider; malicious hacking or cracking (as defined in this chapter) is unethical, but the knowledge behind true hacking can be a good thing and something that ethical computer experts should be familiar with. Again, computer science majors are not the only potential malicious hackers out there; malicious hacking today does not require that level of skill. Ethical training and evaluation should be a requirement for all computer users.

The bottom line is that the digital environment should not be taken for granted, and we have to be mindful of the fact that as time goes on, we will increasingly rely on such technology for everyday activities. Victimization does occur online, and we have a responsibility to understand and respond to it in an ethical manner. One way to respond is to try to quash neutralizing attitudes that might make hacking justifiable for some users. People must understand that just because there is no face-to-face interaction and the risk of getting in trouble might be low, such behavior causes harm and is, therefore, absolutely unethical. Simultaneously, people should not be discouraged from learning the skills that fall in line with what could be referred to as computer hacking. This is especially salient, considering plausible threats of cyber-terrorism (see Furnell & Warren, 1999).

CONCLUSION

The goal of this chapter was to assess participation in computer hacking from a criminological perspective, specifically through Sykes and Matza's (1957) techniques of neutralization theory. This activity was done to contribute to the debate surrounding the issue of why some individuals engage in malicious computer hacking with intent to cause harm to persons or property. It is hoped that the findings presented here contribute in a positive manner to this debate. Relying on a series of regression modes stemming from self-reported survey data from 785 college students, the study results outlined here suggest that rationalizing, or neutralizing, attitudes are significantly linked to participation in hacking--even when controlling for other important predictors of criminal/deviant behavior. Mal-inclined hacking (or cracking), in general, may be explained in part through existing theories of crime, such as social learning theory--directly incorporating neutralizing attitudes to explain the process of engaging in deviant behavior.

Continued theoretical and empirical exploration is critical as we increasingly rely on technology as a society, spending more of our lives in front of a computer screen. For this reason, it is important that we strongly consider the ethics of online behavior and refrain from taking the digital environment for granted. It is plausible to assume that crimes committed behind a computer terminal are more readily justified than crimes committed in person; the findings presented in this chapter lend some support to this notion. Unfortunately, because both terrestrial and digital crimes cause a variety of substantial social and individual harms, all computer users should be aware of this reality and take computing ethics very seriously.

A good first step in any social response devoted to curtailing computer crimes would be to provide, or even require, ethical training for everyone who engages in the digital environment, regardless of whether they are a computer scientist, an engineer, or a general computer user. Hopefully, the research presented here will help to stimulate such initiatives in addition to the issuing of a call for an increased focus from scholars on this important topic.

REFERENCES

Agnew, R. (1994). The techniques of neutralization and violence. *Criminology*, *32*, 555–580. doi:10.1111/j.1745-9125.1994.tb01165.x

Akers, R. L., & Jensen, G. F. (2006). The empirical status of social learning theory of crime and deviance: The past, present, and future. In F. R. Cullen, J. P. Wright, & K. Blevins (Ed.): *Vol. 15. Advances in criminological theory.* New Brunswick, N.J.: Transaction Publishers.

Akers, R. L., Krohn, M. D., Lanza-Kaduce, L., & Radosevich, M. (1979). Social learning and deviant behavior: A specific test of a general theory. *American Sociological Review*, *44*, 636–655. doi:10.2307/2094592

Anderson, C. A. (2004). An update on the effects of playing violent video games. *Journal of Adolescence*, *27*, 113–122. doi:10.1016/j.adolescence.2003.10.009

Chandler, A. (1996). The changing definition and image of hackers in popular discourse. *International Journal of the Sociology of Law*, *24*, 229–251. doi:10.1006/ijsl.1996.0015

Clough, B., & Mungo, P. (1992). *Approaching zero: Data crime and the computer underworld.* London: Faber and Faber.

Cohen, L., & Felson, M. (1979). Social change and crime rate trends: A routine activity approach. *American Sociological Review*, *44*, 588–608. doi:10.2307/2094589

Copes, J. H. (2003). Societal attachments, offending frequency, and techniques of neutralization. *Deviant Behavior*, *24*, 101–127. doi:10.1080/01639620390117200

Cromwell, P., & Thruman, Q. (2003). The devil made me do it: Use of neutralizations by shoplifters. *Deviant Behavior*, *24*, 535–550. doi:10.1080/713840271

Dabney, D. A. (1995). Neutralization and deviance in the workplace: Theft of supplies and medicines by hospital nurses. *Deviant Behavior*, *16*, 313–331. doi:10.1080/01639625.1995.9968006

Elliott, D. S., Huizinga, D., & Menard, S. (1989). *Multiple problem youth.* New York: Springer-Verlag.

Furnell, S. M., & Warren, M. J. (1999). Computer hacking and cyber terrorism: The real threats in the new millennium. *Computers & Security*, *18*, 28–34. doi:10.1016/S0167-4048(99)80006-6

Gentile, D. A., Lynch, P. J., Linder, J. R., & Walsh, D. A. (2004). The effects of violent video game habits on adolescent hostility, aggressive behaviors, and school performance. *Journal of Adolescence*, *27*, 5–22. doi:10.1016/j.adolescence.2003.10.002

Gordon-Larsen, P., Nelson, M. C., & Popkin, B. M. (2005). Meeting national activity and inactivity recommendations: Adolescence to adulthood. *American Journal of Preventive Medicine*, *28*, 259–266.

Gottfredson, M. R., & Hirschi, T. (1990). *A general theory of crime.* Stanford, CA: Stanford University Press.

Grasmick, H. G., Tittle, C. R., Bursik, R. J. Jr, & Arneklev, B. J. (1993). Testing the core empirical implications of Gottfredson and Hirschi's general theory of crime. *Journal of Research in Crime and Delinquency*, *30*, 5–29. doi:10.1177/0022427893030001002

Hafner, K., & Markoff, J. (1993). *Cyberpunk: Outlaws and hackers on the computer frontier*. London: Corgi Books.

Hannemyr, G. (1999). Technology and pleasure: Considering hacking constructive. *Firstmonday, Peer-Reviewed Journal on the Internet, 4*.

Hinduja, S. (2007). Neutralization theory and online software piracy: An empirical analysis. *Ethics and Information Technology*, *9*, 187–204. doi:10.1007/s10676-007-9143-5

Hirschi, T. (1969). *Causes of delinquency*. Berkeley, CA: University of California Press.

Hirschi, T., & Gottfredson, M. R. (1993). Commentary: Testing the general theory of crime. *Journal of Research in Crime and Delinquency*, *30*, 47–54. doi:10.1177/0022427893030001004

Hollinger, R. C. (1993). Crime by computer: Correlates of software piracy and unauthorized account access. *Security Journal*, *4*, 2–12.

Holt, T. J. (2007). Subcultural evolution? Examining the influence of on- and off-line experiences on deviant subcultures. *Deviant Behavior*, *28*, 171–198. doi:10.1080/01639620601131065

Hughes, L. A., & DeLone, G. J. (2007). Viruses, worms, and Trojan horses: Serious crimes, nuisance, or both? *Social Science Computer Review*, *25*, 79–98. doi:10.1177/0894439306292346

Ingram, J. R., & Hinduja, S. (2008). Neutralizing music piracy: An empirical examination. *Deviant Behavior*, *29*, 334–366. doi:10.1080/01639620701588131

Jordan, T., & Taylor, P. (2008). A sociology of hackers. *The Sociological Review*, *28*, 757–780.

Klockars, C. B. (1974). *The professional fence*. New York: Free Press.

Krohn, M. D., Skinner, W. F., Massey, J. L., & Akers, R. L. (1985). Social learning theory and adolescent cigarette smoking: A longitudinal study. *Social Problems*, *32*, 455–473. doi:10.1525/sp.1985.32.5.03a00050

Levy, S. (1994). *Hackers: Heroes of the computer revolution*. Harmondsworth, UK: Penguin.

Loeber, R., & Stouthamer-Loeber, M. (1986). Family factors as correlates and predictors of juvenile conduct problems and delinquency . In Tonry, M., & Morris, N. (Eds.), *Crime and justice: An annual review of research* (*Vol. 7*). Chicago, Ill.: University of Chicago Press.

Maruna, S., & Copes, J. H. (2005). What have we learned from five decades of neutralization research? *Crime and Justice: An Annual Review of Research*, *32*, 221–320.

Matza, D. (1964). *Delinquency and drift*. New York: John Wiley and Sons, Inc.

Minor, W. W. (1981). Techniques of neutralization: A re-conceptualization and empirical examination. *Journal of Research in Crime and Delinquency*, *18*, 295–318. doi:10.1177/002242788101800206

Morris, R. G., & Blackburn, A. G. (2009). Cracking the code: An empirical exploration of social learning theory and computer crime. *Journal of Criminal Justice*, *32*, 1–32.

Morris, R. G., & Higgins, G. E. (2009). (in press). Neutralizing potential and self-reported digital piracy: A multi-theoretical exploration among college undergraduates. *Criminal Justice Review*, *34*. doi:10.1177/0734016808325034

Morris, R. G., & Johnson, M. C. (2009). Sedentary activities, peer behavior, and delinquency among American youth. *University of Texas at Dallas*. Working Paper.

Naughton, J. (2000). *A brief history of the future: The origins of the internet*. London, UK: Phoenix.

Nelson, M. C., & Gordon-Larsen, P. (2006). Physical activity and sedentary behavior patterns are associated with selected adolescent health risk behaviors. *Pediatrics*, *117*, 1281–1290. doi:10.1542/peds.2005-1692

Roush, W. (1995). Hackers: Taking a byte out of computer crime. *Technology Review*, *98*, 32–40.

Schell, B. H., Dodge, J. L., & Moutsatos, S. (2002). *The Hacking of America: Who's Doing It, Why, and How*. Westport, CT: Quorum Books.

Skinner, W. F., & Fream, A. M. (1997). A social learning theory analysis of computer crime among college students. *Journal of Research in Crime and Delinquency*, *34*, 495–518. doi:10.1177/0022427897034004005

Skorodumova, O. (2004). Hackers as information space phenomenon. *Social Sciences*, *35*, 105–113.

Stallman, R. (2002). *Free software, free society: Selected essays of Richard M. Stallman*. Boston: Free Software Foundation.

Thomas, D. (2002). *Notes from the underground: Hackers as watchdogs of industry*. Retrieved April 20, 2009, from http://www.ojr.org/ojr/business/1017969515.php

Warr, M. (2002). *Companions in crime: The social aspects of criminal conduct*. Cambridge, MA: Cambridge University Press.

Wong, S. L., & Leatherdale, S. T. (2009). Association between sedentary behavior, physical activity, and obesity: Inactivity among active kids. *Preventing Chronic Disease*, *6*, 1–13.

Yar, M. (2005a). Computer hacking: Just another case of juvenile delinquency? *The Howard Journal*, *44*, 387–399. doi:10.1111/j.1468-2311.2005.00383.x

Yar, M. (2005b). The novelty of cybercrime. *European Journal of Criminology*, *2*, 407–427. doi:10.1177/147737080556056

Yar, M. (2006). *Cybercrime and society*. Thousand Oaks, CA: Sage.

Young, R., Zhang, L., & Prybutok, V. R. (2007). Hacking into the minds of hackers. *Information Systems Management*, *24*, 271–28. doi:10.1080/10580530701585823

ENDNOTE

1. Yar (2005b) contends that cybercrimes represent a distinct form of criminality, worthy of focused attention.

APPENDIX

Table 4. Correlation Matrix

		1.	2.	3.	4.	5.	6.	7.	8.	9.	10.	11.	12.	13.	14.
1.	Hacking frequency	1													
2.	Hacking involvement	.87	1												
3.	Any type of hacking	.60	.82	1											
4.	Guessing passwords	.64	.81	.83	1										
5.	Illegal access	.65	.83	.82	.62	1									
6.	File manipulation	.72	.73	.49	.48	.52	1								
7.	Neutralization	.25	.29	.26	.24	.26	.17	1							
8.	Differential Assoc.	.45	.50	.45	.41	.46	.37	.27	1						
9.	Low self-control	.19	.19	.19	.14	.18	.15	.45	.25	1					
10.	Victimization	.28	.25	.25	.21	.22	.19	.09	.36	.15	1				
11.	Female	-.06	-.05	-.02	-.03	-.01	-.06	-.18	-.10	-.28	-.03	1			
12.	White	.04	.02	.00	.00	.03	.02	.02	.04	.05	-.01	-.07	1		
13.	Over 26 years old	-.05	-.07	-.07	-.09	-.06	-.01	-.09	-.11	-.17	-.05	-.07	-.12	1	
14.	Advanced user	.07	.09	.07	.06	.09	.08	.07	.06	.13	.04	-.21	.07	.01	1

Note: All correlation coefficients greater than ±.07 are significant at $p < .05$.

Chapter 2
Between Hackers and White-Collar Offenders

Orly Turgeman-Goldschmidt
Bar-Ilan University, Israel

ABSTRACT

Scholars often view hacking as one category of computer crime, and computer crime as white-collar crime. However, no study to date has examined the extent to which hackers exhibit the same characteristics as white-collar offenders. This chapter looks at empirical data drawn from 54 face-to-face interviews with Israeli hackers, in light of the literature in the field of white-collar offenders, concentrating on their accounts and socio-demographic characteristics. Hackers and white-collar offenders differ significantly in age and in their accounts. White-collar offenders usually act for economic gain; hackers act for fun, curiosity, and opportunities to demonstrate their computer virtuosity. Hackers, in contrast to white-collar offenders, do not deny their responsibility, nor do they tell a "sad tale."

INTRODUCTION

Today, the falsified ledger, long the traditional instrument of the embezzler, is being replaced by corrupted software programs. The classic weapons of the bank robber can now be drawn from a far more sophisticated arsenal containing such modern tools as automatic teller machines and electronic fund transfers. In short, white-collar crime has entered the computer age. (Rosoff, Pontell, & Tillman, 2002, p. 417)

The National Institute of Justice defines "computer crime" as any violation of criminal law that involves the knowledge of computer technology for their perpetration, investigation, or prosecution (NIJ, 2000). Computer crime is usually classified as white-collar crime (WCC), in which the perpetrators gain from offenses committed against individual victims or organizations and is usually done as part of someone's occupational activity (Clinard & Quinney, 1973). According to Bequai (1987), computer crime is a part of WCC, since WCC is defined as unlawful activities characterized by fraud and deception, and no

DOI: 10.4018/978-1-61692-805-6.ch002

direct violence. McEwen (1989) claims that the advent and proliferation of computer crimes have become as costly as WCC, equally obscure in the public's mind, and similarly underreported. Duff and Gardiner (1996) state that, due to the advent of computers, WCC has become more visible, with the media having an important role in presenting computer crimes as an acute social problem in the new information age. Recent publicized scandals in major corporations have increased public awareness to WCC (Holtfreter, Slyke, Bratton & Gertz, 2008). Duff and Gardiner claim that the "criminalizing of unauthorized access to computer systems, hacking, is one step in this process to the city of surveillance" (p. 212). Recently, Pontell and Rosoff (2009) labeled the term "white-collar delinquency" as the committing of computer crimes (such as piracy, securities fraud, auction fraud, espionage, and Denial of Service attacks) by middle and upper-class youthful offenders.

In this chapter, I view the phenomenon of hacking with regard to that of WCC to learn whether hacking should really be included in the same category. Duff and Gardiner (1996) argued that hacking should not be considered as criminal, and that most forms of hacking cannot be seen as WCC (p. 214). Other scholars, however, view hacking as one of the categories of computer crime (e.g., Rosoff et al., 2002), and computer crime generally as WCC (Bequai, 1987; Clinard & Quinney, 1973; Parker, 1989; Rosoff et al., 2002). No study to date, has been completed pairing hackers and white-collar offenders.

This chapter looks at empirical data drawn from interviews with Israeli hackers in light of the literature in the field of white-collar offenders, concentrating on socio-demographic characteristics and accounts. The roots of the term 'account' can be traced back to Mills' work (1940), who claimed that vocabularies of motives are used to determine behaviors and expectations when faced by other people's responses, regarding different situations (p. 911). "Account" is a statement made by a social actor to explain unanticipated or untoward behavior. An account is not called for when people engage in routine, commonsense behavior in a cultural environment that recognizes the particular behavior as such (Scott & Lyman, 1968, p. 46-7).

I refer to hackers as possible white-collar offenders on three dimensions: content, form, and structure. In the first dimension, the content of the accounts is examined; that is, the language offenders use to explain and justify their behavior to themselves and to others. The second dimension of form relates to whether hackers, as in WCC, employ the "techniques of neutralization" (Sykes & Matza, 1957; Scott & Lyman, 1968). The third dimension of structure deals with the construction of identity (i.e., the way hackers that structure their self-identity and their formation, relative to white-collar offenders).

WHITE-COLLAR CRIME

The term "WCC" can be traced as far back as the works of Sutherland (1940), who defined white-collar crime as "a crime committed by a person of respectability and high social status in the course of his occupation" (p. 9). For sociologists and criminologists, claimed Sutherland, crime is a phenomenon found mainly among the lower social classes, driven by poverty or personal and social characteristics, and statistically linked to poverty, psychopathic deviance, destitute living conditions, and dysfunctional families. But there is evidence that the criminal use of force and fraud exists in all social classes. WCC can be found in every occupation--money laundering, insurance, banking, the financial market, and the oil industry, among others.

Including the offender's social status and level of respectability in the definition of WCC has created a problem in researching and analyzing the terms "high" or "respected status" (Croall, 1992; Green, 1990; Nelken, 1994). Edelhertz (1975) solved this significant problem in Sutherland's definition by suggesting an alternative definition, calling WCC "*an illegal act or series of illegal acts committed by nonphysical means and by concealment or guile, to obtain money or property, to avoid the payment or loss of money or property, or to obtain business or personal advantage*" (p. 3, emphasis in original).

Indeed, there is conceptual confusion in criminological discourse around concepts such as WCC, corporate crime, occupational crime, organizational crime, and organized crime (Ruggiero, 1996), as well as who should be considered to be a white-collar criminal (Tappan, 1947). Legal experts point out that there is no such definition in the law (Geis, 1992). The appropriate definition depends on the purpose of the study (Braithwaite, 2000, p. 17). The term "white-collar crime" continues to be controversial (Pontell & Rosoff, 2009).

In this chapter, the focus is on the "occupational crime" (Green, 1990) from the point of view of the nature of the crime rather than on the person committing it. *Occupational crime* is defined as "any act punishable by law that is committed through opportunity created in the course of an occupation which is legal" (p. 12). Using Green's typology, this chapter refers specifically to professional occupational crime and individual occupational crime. According to Croall (1992), the main categories of occupational crime are employee theft, fraud, computer crimes, and tax evasion.

HACKING AND HACKERS: WHAT WE KNOW

Cybercrime represent the emergence of a new and distinctive form of crime (Yar, 2005). Rosoff et al., (2002, p. 417-8) view computer crime as a kind of WCC, and they have conceptualized computer crime specifically as: (1) Electronic embezzlement and financial theft; (2) Computer hacking; (3) Malicious sabotage, such as viruses; (4) Utilization of computers and computer networks for the purposes of espionage; and, (5) Use of electronic devices and computer codes for making unauthorized long distance telephone calls (known as phreaking). Tavani (2000) developed a more specific categorization that separates genuine computer crimes from criminal activities in which computer technology is merely present or is used as another tool. He defined three categories of computer crimes: piracy, break-ins, and sabotage in cyberspace--all of which concern hackers' activities. This chapter is focuseS on hackers, per se.

Hackers began to emerge as a group with the dawning of the computer age at MIT in the 1960s. From the start, hacking raised serious concerns regarding misuse of the powerful new electronic technology (Bequai, 1987). Yet, while originally the term "hacker" implied the honorable motive of programmers' virtuosity in overcoming obstacles, currently it has acquired negative connotations of "computer criminals" and "electronic vandals" (Chandler, 1996; Halbert, 1997; Hollinger, 1991; Levy, 1984; Roush, 1995).

Hackers focus on gaining unauthorized access to personal computers or to computer networks. Although they violate the law, sometimes with a clear-cut malicious intent, hackers have their own ethics, prominent among them, which is the principle that all information should be free (Levy, 1984). Denning (1990) claimed that the "hacker ethic" is shared by many hackers. Hackers themselves contend that sharing information is a social responsibility, while information hoarding and misinformation are the real crimes (Sterling, 1992).

Hacking is usually categorized as one particular type of computer-related crime (Bequai, 1990; Parker, 1989; Sieber, 1986; Stewart, 1990). Hacking is also used as a general term denoting various activities, the severity of which varies. Sometimes the label "hackers" is used in its original meaning, as users who master the technology (e.g., Upitis, 1998), while at other times, it is used in its current meaning, as electronic criminals (e.g., Jordan & Taylor, 1998). There are different moral expressions of hacking (Coleman

& Golub, 2008). A hacker may be a programmer who explores, tests, and pushes computers to their limits, as well as someone whose activities could also include destruction or sabotage of important data (Stewart, 1990).

There are differences between subgroups, depending on their expertise and behavior patterns (Holt & Kilger, 2008; Schell, Dodge, & Moutsatsos, 2002; Voiskounsky & Smyslova, 2003). For example, Schell, Dodge, with Moutsatsos (2002) distinguish between "white hat" (good hackers), "black hat" (malevolent hackers) and "scriptkiddies" (young individuals with little hacker knowledge and skills). Holt and Kilger (2008) propose two neutral terms that identify differential use of technology across hacker culture: "makecraft" and "techcraft". "Craft" is used as a referent to the magic way in which hackers control technology. The makecraft hackers are producers of materials who develop new scripts, tools and products, beneficial or malicious, depending on the users. The techcraft hackers apply their knowledge to repair systems or to complete a task with known tools.

Hackers sustain a distinct subculture (e.g. Holt, 2007). Holt and Kilger (2008, p. 68) claim that three subcultural values have constantly been found across studies: (i) technology (intimate connection to technology facilitating the ability to hack); (ii) secrecy (avoiding unwanted attention from government and law enforcement agencies, coupled with a desire to brag and share accumulated knowledge); and (iii) mastery (continual learning of new skills and the mastering of one's social and physical environment).

Social learning theory, as well, has been utilized to demonstrate the way peer relations and definition in favor of deviant behavior affect individual practices of hackers (Holt & Kilger, 2008; Skinner & Fream, 1997). A process of social learning takes place in the context of social interaction in order to commit a computer illegal act (Skinner & Fream, 1997). In examining the utility of social learning theory on hacking behavior, Holt and Kilger (2008) found that those in the "wild" (makecraft) indeed have a greater numbers of hackers within their peer networks and spend more time communicating in on-line environments than the control group, as expected.

SIMILARITIES BETWEEN WHITE-COLLAR OFFENDERS AND HACKERS

Probably the fact that computer crime is often classified as WCC is, in part, due to the apparent similarity between hackers and white-collar offenders. There is a sense of a social double standard toward these two types of crime. Hackers are often presented as geniuses or heroes (Turkle, 1984; Voiskounsky & Smyslova, 2003). In a survey of public attitudes toward computer crimes, Dowland et al. (1999) found that only the theft of computer equipment was considered to be entirely criminal, while a high proportion of respondents were indifferent or unconcerned about such activities as the unauthorized copying of data/software, or viewing someone else's data.

WCC is also not always presented as "real" crime, although not to the same extent, and it varies according to the forms of WCC (Braithwaite, 1985). Friedrichs (1996) noted that different studies have reported that many people do not perceive tax evasion as a serious crime, but as something much less serious than embezzlement, or on the same level of criminality as stealing a bicycle. According to Weisburd and Schlegal (1992), most public attention is directed toward street crime, even though WCCs are no less unlawful; they are just not crimes that make us feel insecure in our houses or neighborhoods. Parker (1989) claimed that, in general, the public perceives WCC as less serious than violent crime, with the exception of extreme cases of customer fraud. "Many white-collar crimes are characterized by diffuse victimization, making it difficult for persons to know when and if they are victimized" (Pontell & Rosoff, 2009, p. 148). Furthermore, the public perception of WCC is one of the reasons why the government pays so little attention to it (Rosoff et al., 2002, p. 26). Recent surveys, however, show that this is changing; the public increasingly believes that WCC is serious and wrong, but this has not yet translated into legislative attention (Meier 2000, p. 15). Recently, a research examination of public perception concerning white-collar and street crime found that the majority of participants felt that violent offenders are more likely to be apprehended and receive harsher punishment. Furthermore, the majority of participants felt violent offenders should receive harsher punishments, although over one-third expressed the opposite opinion (Schoepfer, Carmichael, & Piquero, 2007).

Although both hackers and white-collar offenders perform illegitimate and illegal practices, it seems that they do not fully perceive themselves, nor do others perceive them, as "real criminals." Moreover, they often enjoy the privilege of sympathy from society. This can be understood as a consequence of our perception of the term "criminal" as a "different" kind of person. As Weisburd, Waring and Chayat (2001, p. 138) put it:

Like nationality, culture, or religion, the criminal label is intended to convey a great deal about those to whom it is applied. Criminals are generally viewed as dangerous to society, as products of bad genes or bad parenting or broken communities. Crime is not merely an incident in such peoples' lives. The criminal label summarizes a vast array of behaviors and activities, and it communicates something very meaningful about who such people are and where they are going. Most importantly, criminals are different. This is a very comfortable moral position, and one that helps the rest of us to define what we have in common with each other.

However, one should remember that:

Everyone commits crime...Criminality is simply not something that people have or don't have; crime is not something some people do and others don't. Crime is a matter of who can pin the label on whom, and underlying this socio-political process is the structure of social relations determined by the political economy (Chambliss, 1975, p. 165).

According to Weisburd et al. (2001), many criminological theories explore the offender's past in order to understand their involvement in crime (p. 140). Further, they found in their research that the lives of white-collar criminals do not seem so different from those of law-abiding citizens. In fact, Rosoff et al. (2002) contend that white-collar offenders are not significantly different from other people in personality or psychological make-up. We, therefore, need to inspect more the relationships of these offenders with society instead.

The similarity between hackers and white-collar offenders lies also in the difficulties that law enforcement authorities face in dealing with their crimes. WCC is difficult to detect (Clinard & Yeager, 1980), and there is a lack of resources to investigate and prosecute WCC (Holtfreter et al., 2008). Weisburd and Schlegal (1992) believe that there are three main concepts that separate WCC from regular crime: (i) the organization, (ii) the victims (who are mostly not aware of their being victims), and (iii) the penal system. These problems are also relevant to defining and prosecuting criminal hacking.

As more and more computers in the business community are connected via the Internet and private networks, they become exposed to intrusion. As of today, there are hardly any large computer networks in the United States that have not been breached-- including the networks of the CIA, NATO, NASA, the Pentagon, universities, industrial and military research centers, banks, hospitals, etc. Almost all of the intrusions remain undetected (about 95%), according to the FBI. Among those that are exposed, only about 15% are reported to law enforcement authorities (Behar, 1997). Data from a survey conducted by the Computer Security Institute and the FBI (Computer Security

Institute, 2006) detected that negative publicity from reporting intrusions to law enforcement is still a major concern of respondents (primarily large corporations and government agencies). In addition, even if the offenders are caught, it is not always easy to prosecute them (Michalowski & Pfuhl, 1991).

WCC is also not that scarce (Steffensmeier, 1989), and its damages are immensely costly. Financial losses from WCC continue to exceed those of street crime (Holtfreter et al., 2008). Edelhertz (1975, p. 11) claimed that there are enormous costs, both social and economic, for various white-collar offenses such as tax violations, self-dealing by corporate employees and bank officials, adulteration or watering of foods and drugs, charity fraud, insurance frauds, price fixing, frauds arising out of government procurement, and trust abuses. Thus, the categorization of hacking as white-collar crime, as well as the apparent similarities between these kinds of offenses, led me to examine whether hacking does, indeed, resemble WCC, or if it should be viewed as a different and unique phenomenon.

In this chapter, I will show that hackers represent a new category of crime that should be examined separately from other types of computer crime in which the computer is simply used as a new and effective tool for more traditional crimes. Specifically, the activities of hackers should not be conceptualized as a sub-category of WCC, because they challenge it on the basis of content, form, and structure dimension of their accounts. This chapter will imply that a new theory is needed--one based on the vocabularies of motives.

STUDY METHOD

Research on both hackers and white-collar offenders is limited. Entering the Computer Underground community poses certain organizational and procedural difficulties for researchers (Jordan & Taylor, 1998; Voiskounsky & Smyslova, 2003; Yar, 2005). Most studies of the Computer Underground have relied mainly on discreet exposés by the media (Hollinger & Lanza-Kaduce, 1988; Parker, 1989; Skinner & Fream, 1997).

White-collar offenders do not tend to talk about "how I did it" or "how it felt," as do "traditional" criminals (Katz, 1988). Moreover, the growing literature on corporate crime is mostly descriptive or theoretical (Simpson, 1987). Croall (1992) claimed that much of the research on WCC focuses on the law and law enforcement, rather than on patterns of criminality. Croall also contends that, in general, researchers have tended to examine fields in which offenses are more visible, offenders are more accessible, and findings are more readily available — all of which are not the case among either hackers or white-collar offenders.

In the current study, data gathering was based on unstructured, in-depth, face-to-face interviews with 54 Israeli self-defined hackers, who were asked to tell their life stories. Finding interviewees was the result of snowball or "chain referrals"--that is one subject was asked to recommend other participants. Potential interviewees were located through advertisements placed in various media (7), at hacker conferences (5), at a conference on information security (1), through the Internet (2), and among employees of computer companies (6). In addition, two interviewees approached me when I was lecturing on computer crime, and acquaintances and family members were the source of six others.

The interviews lasted an average of three hours apiece, but took anywhere from two to eight hours, three hours being the most common. In a few cases, more than one meeting was required to complete the interview. A full methodology is available in Turgeman-Goldschmidt (2005). Basically, I compared my data on hackers with the literature on white-collar criminals according to the socio-demographic characteristics and accounts categories to examine whether differences exist between hackers and white-collar criminals.

Most of the interviewees were men (51 of 54). Of the total interviewees, six reported that they had criminal records (five of whom said their crimes were computer-related). The interviewees tended to be young (ranging between 14 to 48.5 years old, average age 24, with the most common age group being between 20 to 30), single (78%), educated (76% with 12 years or more of schooling, and 41% with higher education), with higher-than-average incomes (74%), of European or American origin (74%), secular (83%), left-wing (54%), and living in the center of the country (56%). This profile is congruent with the literature, in which hackers have been found to be mostly non-violent, white, young, middle- or upper-class men with no criminal record (e.g., Hollinger, 1991).

Voiskounsky and Smyslova (2003, p. 173) stated that: "We take as granted that hacking is a universal activity with few (if any) ethnic/geopolitical differences," and no data collected for the present study suggest that Israeli hackers are different from others. Furthermore, the different ways by which I located interviewees, the fact that the participants included hackers who were members of various social networks with varying aims, were of different ages, and lived in different areas (from the north to the south of Israel), as well as the fact that relative to this unique population, the number of interviews is large (54), with few refusals (four), all lead me to believe that the sample appears to be representative.

SOCIO-DEMOGRAPHIC CHARACTERISTICS: HACKERS VERSUS WHITE-COLLAR OFFENDERS

Looking at the socio-demographic characteristics of hackers in the present study demonstrated that they are very similar to those of white-collar offenders. The Israeli hackers, as well as those described in the literature, have been found to be predominantly male (Ball, 1985; Forester & Morrison, 1994; Gilbora, 1996; Hollinger, 1991; Jordan & Taylor, 1998; Taylor, 1999; Turkle, 1984), usually white, young (the average age of the Israeli hackers was 24), non-violent, from a middle-high class background, with no prior criminal record. In other words, hackers belong to the middle- to upper- middle classes of society (Hollinger, 1991).

White-collar offenders generally differ from traditional criminals in demographic parameters; age, sex, and ethnicity (Steffensmeier, 1989). More men break the law than women, and this is also the case among white-collar offenders (Weisburd, Wheeler, Waring, & Bode, 1991). Most offenders convicted are white (Weisburd et al., 1991). White-collar offenders are relatively older than regular criminals, the average age being 40 (Weisburd et al., 1991). This age factor can be directly attributed to their positions and occupations, as reflected in different studies; e.g., doctors (Jesilow, Pontell, & Geis, 1996) and people in key positions who have committed securities and exchange fraud, antitrust violations, false claims, and tax evasion (Benson, 1996). In sum, with the exception of the age difference, there are no substantial identified socio-demographic differences between hackers and white-collar offenders.

ACCOUNTS; HACKERS VERSUS WHITE-COLLAR OFFENDERS

The Content Dimension

From the content perspective, there exist significant differences between the accounts given by hackers and those of white-collar offenders. While some elements seem to be shared between hackers and white-collar offenders, such as low deterrence factor, lack of malicious intent, and non-tangibility of the offense, the most common and significant accounts used by hackers are essentially different from those used by white-collar offenders.

Israeli hackers used their accounts to justify the wide range of computer offenses they commit in software piracy (unauthorized duplication of pirated software, unauthorized distribution of pirated software, cracking software or games, selling cracked and pirated software); hacking (unauthorized accessing of computer systems, using illegal internet accounts, development and/or distribution of viruses, browsing or reading other users' files, stealing computer-stored information, causing computer systems to crash, using stolen credit cards from the internet); and phreaking (making phone calls without paying).

Hackers' prevalent accounts (see also Turgeman-Goldschmidt, 2005) in descending order of frequency, from the most frequently mentioned to the least, were:

1. Fun, thrill, and excitement ("it's so much fun; it [creating viruses] was fun, I was satisfied, creating something so perfect, working, multiplying");
2. Curiosity for its own sake and a need to know ("the desire to learn and to know as much as possible; to be the most up to date, to know a lot about everything. For me, it's about communication");
3. Computer virtuosity--power, dominance and competitiveness ("to break the boundaries, to be smarter than someone else; taking a software I don't know, and take control over it; to show that I can");
4. Economic accounts--ideological opposition, lack of money, monetary rewards ("the software giants are unrealistic. Instead of saying 'you're criminals,' do something about it; the prices charged by the software companies are too high and unfair; I don't have the money; I think it's crazy to pay");
5. Deterrent factor ("it depends on the chances of someone actually knocking on my door; once it became dangerous, and I became aware of the danger, I saw the ground burning, so I decided to stop");
6. Lack of malicious or harmful intentions ("the power isn't used for causing harm; "I was never into destruction, it never interested me");
7. Intangible offenses ("the term stealing in cyberspace assumes a meaning; it's not that I'm stealing somebody else's cucumber. The cucumber stays there");
8. "Nosy" curiosity, voyeurism ("it's like voyeurism, whose the person who's house I broke into?; I want to have access to all of the things people do all the time");
9. Revenge ("don't forgive, get back, get even; they kicked you out, as if you are not good enough. Now you have to make them realized what a mistake they made. It is a form of revenge");
10. Ease of execution ("you have to actually ring bells to make a racket; if I got in there [computer system], it was open, I don't enter closed places").

Thus, the primary accounts are: Fun, thrill and excitement; curiosity for its own sake; and computer virtuosity (as Gili said, "many break-ins are for learning purposes. It is fun because it is as if you are solving some kind of puzzle"). These accounts were given, in general, for a variety of computer offenses.

In this study, Interviewee Mor (this name is fabricated, as are all other interviewees' names) well exemplifies these common accounts:

- Mor: "I started with it [hacking] when I was 13 or 14. I used to go to the Tel-Aviv University, write a program, and after a week I'd get all of the account entrance codes. I did it for the fun of it, breaking into places, doing illegal things."
- Q: "What did you feel?"
- Mor: "I felt... I liked the feeling that they might catch me, the feeling that you're communicating with somebody and you know you're smarter than he is, and he

doesn't know it. It gives you the feeling of superiority and control. That's the feeling. Basically, it all comes from the same place — you're doing something that nobody else thought of. You have the power to do things that are more sophisticated, it's a competition with the world, to do things that others think I can't. Stealing students' computer access codes is one thing, but I'm talking about much harder things."

- Q: "Such as?"
- Mor: "It's hard to say now… for instance, I helped friends get good jobs in the army, it gave me the sense of ego trip, like a girl going down the street and everybody's looking at her even if she doesn't want anything. Computers gave me an ego trip, everyone knew I was the best, I proved it to everybody and to myself. A real ego trip."
- Q: "What's so much fun about it?"
- Mor: "The thrill in hiding. Voyeurs like prying. It's about curiosity. It's one of the strongest human urges. When I discovered my sexuality, I would go to the university dorms, to see if somebody is doing something. We would watch through binoculars for hours. My friend had a neighbor, a great looking girl. It's about watching her and knowing she can't see you, the same with hpc (hacking, phreaking, cracking)."

Other studies have found similar accounts among hackers. For example, the desire and ability to learn and discover (Mitnick & Simon, 2002), the knowledge and devotion to learn (Holt, 2007), the adventure and desire to gain recognition (Jordan & Taylor, 1998, 2004; Taylor, 1999). Woo, Kim, & Dominick (2004) found that 70% of web defacement incidents by hackers were pranks, while the rest had more political motives. They found that hackers are eager to demonstrate their hacking accounts; they often leave calling cards, greetings, etc. The sites that were hacked due to political motivation contained more aggressive expressions and greater use of communication channels than those who hacked for fun or self-aggrandizement.

Turning to the difference between hackers and white-collar offenders, requires, first, the description of the main accounts of white-collar offenders. According to the literature, there is no doubt that the economic motive makes up a significant account among white-collar offenders. Weisburd et al. (1991), in a comprehensive study of convicted white-collar criminals, examined eight categories: securities fraud; antitrust violations; bribery; bank embezzlement; postal and wire fraud; false claims and statements; credit and lending institutions fraud; and tax fraud. They reported that a recurring characteristic found among white-collar offenders was the sense of financial need. Two distinct paths were identified. The first path was taken by those offenders who learned early how to use techniques such as deceit for economic success, and who, once the competition grew, could not maintain their success without breaking the rules. The second was taken by those who would have been more than happy to remain in the same position, using legitimate means, if they could. As financial and economic pressures grew, however, they felt that they might lose the lifestyle to which they had become accustomed. The motivation was not satisfying a selfish ego, therefore, but rather the fear of crashing and loosing what they worked hard to achieve. This led them to the same illegitimate means used by those in the first path. Those in the second group, however, felt more regretful when they were caught.

Friedrichs (2002) contends that the term "occupational crime" should be restricted to illegal and unethical activities committed for individual financial gain, or to avoid financial loss, within the context of a legitimate occupation. The economic motive among white-collar offenders appears in different variations, as greed or necessity, or as a legitimate reward for services not properly paid for (Croall, 1992). Coleman (1987) developed a theory for understanding WCC that combines motivation and opportunity. According to Coleman, the motivation in most cases is the desire for economic gain and the need to be perceived as a "success" by others, or the fear of loosing what one already has. The political economics of the industrialized society have made competition that increases these desires and fears a part of its culture. Coleman (1994) called it the "culture of competition" in American society. Langton and Piquero (2007, p. 4) claim that WCC scholars suggest that white-collar offenders are frequently preoccupied by a desire for more money. General strain theory argues that strains increase the likelihood of negative emotions like anger and frustration, creating pressure for corrective action. Crime is one optional response (Agnew, 1992). Thus, in examining the ability of general strain theory to explain white-collar offenses, Langton and Piquero (2007) were not surprised to find that strain was associated with feelings of financial concern among white-collar offenders.

White-collar offenders also use some of the accounts that were found among hackers. For example, both groups shared a low deterring factor. In the case of hackers, both the probability of being caught and the severity of the punishment are low (Ball, 1985; Bloom-Becker, 1986; Hollinger, 1991; Michalowski & Pfuhl, 1991), and they take that into consideration (as Interviewee Roy said, "when I cracked software it was at home, so why should I be afraid? It was a pride, fun, satisfaction when you are succeeding"). In the case of WCC, the potential rewards also outweigh the risks (Rosoff et al., 2002, p. 463).

Another example concerns the intangibility account (as Interviewee Mor said, "If I cracked software, I am not taking money from someone, it is not stealing from him, he would have just earned more"). Hacking is an offense in which the offender may not feel that he or she has caused any harm in the physical sense; as Michalowski and Pfuhl (1991, p. 268) put it: "Information, documents, and data reside inside computers in a form that can be 'stolen' without ever being removed, indeed without ever being touched by the would-be thief." Likewise, Green (1990) reported that employees who commit WCC would steal from the organization but not from other people, and that they also prefer stealing from large organizations. This is often referred to as "victimless crime."

Considering the main driving forces, while hackers are driven mostly by fun, curiosity, and an opportunity to demonstrate their computer virtuosity, white-collar offenders aim primarily at improving or sustaining their own economic welfare.

The Form Dimension

Both hackers and white-collar offenders use the form of "techniques of neutralization" (Sykes & Matza, 1957). The neutralization approach to criminality is a theory that attempts to explain why people who, for the most part, are law-abiding citizens are swept into criminality. The theory assumes that they feel some guilt and have to defend themselves against recognizing their own responsibility. Neutralizations are necessary for to give themselves permission to commit the crime and to deal with their subsequent self-images. Sykes and Matza (1957) defined five neutralization techniques: (i) denial of responsibility, (ii) denial of injury, (iii) denial of victim, (iv) condemnation of condemners, and (v) appeal to higher loyalties. Scott and Lyman (1968) have added two other justifications: the "sad tale" and "self-fulfillment."

Neutralizing attitudes include such beliefs as, "Everybody has a racket," "I can't help myself, I was born this way," "I am not at fault," "I am not responsible," "I was drunk and didn't know what I was doing," "I just blew my top," "They can afford it," "He deserved it," and other excuses and justification for committing deviant acts and victimizing others (Akers, 2000, p. 77).

Hackers interviewed for the present study, although they used a variety of neutralization techniques, did not use the denial of responsibility or the sad tale. Indeed, Sykes and Matza (1957:670) noted: "Certain techniques of neutralization would appear to be better adapted to particular deviant acts than to others." Interviewee Ran used the "denial of injury;" for example, "Everybody's doing it, myself included — [you] enter (into the cracked system), experience whatever is there, and move on. No harm is done using the power." Interviewee Ben used the "denial of the victim" to explain why he sent a virus to someone, which, in his mind, made his offenses guilt-free; he said, "he deserved it, you feel a cool kind of satisfaction." Interviewee Yoram used the condemnation of the condemners to explain his unauthorized access to computer systems, noting, "The most accessible and easiest to penetrate were the academic institutions, and everything that's connected to them... Wow, what an idiot is this system manager--he could have easily closed this hole." And Interviewee Oren used the "appeal to higher loyalties," affirming, "We're the only ones that can confront the giant corporations, we have the knowledge and knowledge is power." (see also Turgeman-Goldscmidt, 2008).

Furthermore, hacking for fun, curiosity for knowledge, and computer virtuosity all can be seen as different aspects of the "self-fulfillment" technique of neutralization (Scott & Lyman, 1968), used to justify behaviors seen by others as undesirable, as in the case of a person taking drugs who claims that it expands his consciousness. Interviewee Aviram, for instance, said, "There's some kind of a thrill in copying software." When Interviewee Ben says, "to be the most up-to-date, to know a lot about everything; For me, it's about communication, to find out things, also about people... it's like a library," he justifies himself by making his desire to fulfill his knowledge as his pre-eminent concern, while ignoring the practices he uses to obtain the information.

White-collar offenders also use neutralization techniques. Cromwell (1996) claimed that occupational offenders prepare detailed justifications, excuses, and rationalizations to fend off accepting personal responsibility over their criminal behavior. In his opinion, this justification can be attributed to the fact that their initial identity is not criminal: they are doctors, lawyers, shareholders, etc. As such, they tend not to perceive themselves as criminals. According to Coleman (1995), a crucial element in the motivation of most white-collar offenders is the neutralization of the society's ethical restraints. This neutralization is achieved by using a variety of rationalizations that justify the offender's behavior.

Jesilow, Pontell, and Geis (1996), for example, examined 42 doctors who were involved in medical fraud cases and found that each of the subjects used at least one neutralization technique to justify the acts. This study team found that while the doctors they studied did not deny their responsibility for white-collar offenses, they tended to refer to their acts as "mistakes," and some blamed themselves for not being cautious enough, or blamed a wide array of other people, but not themselves. Friedrichs (1996) presented the techniques white-collar offenders use to confront their consciences and other people's criticism, claiming, for instance, that tax violators employ a wide array of rationalizations, including claims that the laws are unfair, that the government wastes the taxes collected, and that everybody does it. Another example is found in a study conducted by Benson (1996), who examined thirty white-collar offenders.

The most consistent pattern throughout his interviews was denial of any criminal intent. One of the most common claims is denying the damage. Individuals involved in organizational crimes tend to justify their acts by claiming that the law they broke was unnecessary, unjust, or constitutes "governmental intervention in the free market," etc. Another claim is that certain criminal practices are necessary for achieving essential economic goals or even for surviving. Yet another technique is shifting the responsibility from the offender to the large, and often, abstract group he belongs to, claiming that "everyone does it." Finally, many occupational offenders justify their offenses by claiming that they deserve the money; this technique is especially frequent among embezzlers. Piquero, Tibbetts, and Blankenship (2005), who evaluated the decisions of MBA students to commit corporate offenses in the promotion of a hypothetical pharmaceutical drug, found that the "denial of responsibility" technique had positive effects on the intention to commit corporate crime.

To conclude, both hackers and white-collar offenders are using techniques of neutralization. While white-collar offenders often use the denial of responsibility and sad tale forms of neutralization (Rothman & Gandossy, 1982), hackers do not appear to use the denial of responsibility, nor the sad tale. This current study finding suggests a meaningful and interesting dissimilarity between white-collar criminals and hackers in the specific form of use of the neutralization techniques, which I will discuss later.

The Structural Dimension

An examination of the structural aspect reveals significant differences between hackers and white-collar offenders, as is evident in the hackers' message "we are different." (For example, Interviewee Menash claimed, "the fun is to be a bit smarter, to invent something new"), as opposed to the white-collar offenders' message of "we are just like you."

Hackers identify themselves and are identified by others as a distinct group, with its own networks. Hackers maintain a deviant subculture (Holt, 2007, Meyer & Thomas, 1990; Rosoff et al., 2002); that is, the hacking culture is based upon its sense of community (Jordan & Taylor, 1998). Holt (2007) found that five normative orders of computer hacker subculture-- technology, knowledge, commitment, categorization, and law--impact the attitudes, actions, and relationships of hackers; they provide justifications, interests, and values that can be used to gain status and respect among their peers both on- and off-line.

Computer Underground cultures exist around the world, with members operating in social settings that provide support, expertise, professional development, literature, web sites, and conferences (Jordan & Taylor, 1998). Hackers are a distinct group with its own ethics (although diverse), culture, lifestyle, dialect, philosophy, etc. They see themselves as different, special, and even superior. They operate in groups, and there are many Internet sites devoted to hackers' philosophy and activities. A good example to this sense of self-distinction and community is the hacking jargon book, which is updated constantly via the net (The on-line hacker Jargon File, at: http://www.tuxedo.org/~esr/jargon/html/index.html) and published as a printed book (see Raymond & Steele, 1994, 1996). As Holt (2008, p. 352) established: "The on- and offline social ties between hackers were used to share information, tools, and introduce sub-cultural norms to new hackers." Hackers, then, have developed a social identity, which they construct themselves. As social networks, they have succeeded in creating a unique, distinct, and positive identity, which they "sell" to others.

In the following paragraph are quotations from the current study interviewees, illustrating that hackers work in groups and that they have shared interests, quality, ideology, and methods of action:

- Viruses, we'd write viruses. Now I recall it as being the most fun of all. (Meir)
- We entered their data site, took all their accommodation tests (Boaz)
- It's all about vandalism, like when we broke into the Knesset's [the Israeli parliament] website. (Ben)
- We wouldn't buy a TV set [with someone else's credit card numbers], because that would be too risky, and we didn't need one anyway. (Or)

- We are not very nice people. Everyone has some nonsense actions that he does. (Bar)
- There's that thing [that hackers have] about deducing conclusions. (Ilan)
- We're the only ones that can confront the giant corporations, we have the knowledge and knowledge is power. Because of Microsoft's dominance, we see it as our enemy. (Oren)

There is no reason to believe that white-collar offenders, specifically occupational offenders, identify themselves and/or are identified by others as a distinct group. As opposed to hackers, they do not develop a culture or a network around their criminal practices. On the contrary, they try to conceal their activities. Weisburd et al. (1991) found that white-collar offenders are not committed by the affluent and the influential, but rather by "ordinary people." They are, for the most part, regular, non-distinct people. They are neither lower-class offenders who use violence to achieve their ends nor upper-class offenders. They are mostly middle-class people interested in moving ahead fast.

White-collar offenders are, thus, a part of the society; they are perceived as such, and they try to emphasize their belonging to the normative society. This point is exemplified by their claims: "anybody could have done it," "everybody does it," or "it is the values of competitiveness and achievement in Western societies that are to blame." In addition, the white-collar offenders' desire for non-distinction can be seen by the fact that they do not have their own ethics or communal awareness, and they definitely do not try to "sell" themselves as a different or distinct group.

As opposed to white-collar offenders, hackers do structure their identity as different and unique; they network with other hackers and sustain a subculture. These characteristics indicate the different sense of cohesion and legitimacy that hackers experience, as opposed to white-collar offenders.

DISCUSSION

This study sought to examine the extent to which hackers exhibit the same characteristics as white-collar offenders on three dimensions: content, form and structure of their accounts. Most hackers break the law without an economic motive, claiming to act in the name of common social values, such as the pursuit of pleasure, knowledge, curiosity, control, and competitiveness, and achieving their goals (even if they distort these values) through computer wizardry. White-collar offenders, on the other hand, break the law mostly for the sake of individual gain (e.g., Ben-Yehuda, 1986; Rosoff et al., 2002) and are mainly driven by money or money equivalents; sometimes committing their offenses to keep what they have, and at other times to advance economically. They describe their situation as "having no choice", or " as an irresistible opportunity that arises," which can be seen as "defense of necessity" (Minor, 1981), in which some actions are unavoidable.

The difference between hacking and WCC regarding the content of the accounts is, therefore, very significant. "Money is a conspicuous feature of modern society that plays a key role in almost all economic crime." (Engdahl, 2008, p. 154). Yet even if hackers do sometimes profit monetarily (or gain monetary equivalents)--such as using somebody else's Internet account free of charge, using free "cracked" software, or even landing a better job based on their "proven" skills--this is not their main account. those who break the law not for greed but for a passion for knowledge, in their opinion, should be appreciated. For example, Interviewee Ronen says, "the software giants are unrealistic. Their software is copied. Instead of saying 'you [the hackers] are criminals,' do something about it." As Interviewee Bar says, "If there is a software that can make someone in the world do something good, why should he be deprived of it?"

Concerning the form dimension, hackers use *internal justifications*, attributing their actions to internal forces, while white-collar offenders use *external justifications*, attributing their actions to external forces (Turgeman-Goldschmidt, 2008). The term "locus of control" (Rotter, 1954) refers to the specific type of expectations regarding the individual's belief as to who or what determines the continuum between behavior and reward. When a person believes that he can more or less control the outcomes of the events he takes part in, his locus of control is internal. On the other hand, when he believes that external forces, such as luck, fate or other powerful forces determine his actions, his locus of control is external.

The findings of this research showed that hackers provide internal justifications rather than external justifications. They tend not to deny their responsibility over their actions or to tell a "sad tale," but rather accept the responsibility, attribute it to themselves, and are interested in being given the credit. They are often proud of who they are and what they are doing. Every now and then hackers' actions reach the media headlines, and we read at length as hackers tell their stories. To exemplify, when Oren said, "We're the only ones that can confront the giant corporations, we have the knowledge and knowledge is power," he provides internal justification and actually declares responsibility.

In contrast to hackers, white-collar offenders tend to use external justifications. They attribute the responsibility of their actions to external factors over which they have no control, thus denying their own responsibility. Claims such as, "I didn't know it was against the law" are common. they often tell a "sad tale" about the need to maintain their present status. For instance, Weisburd et al. (2001) concluded that white-collar offenders often presented their behavior as a reaction to a crisis. Willott et al. (2001) found that one of the "sad tales" used by upper middle-class offenders to justify money-related crime was that they were the victims of circumstances beyond their control.

In relation to the structure dimension, hackers' use of internal justifications is the way that enables them to structure their own identities; they provide accounts that refer to their "self," and these self presentations are based upon their claims that they are smart, knowledgeable, and anti-establishment. The most frequently used accounts are those referring to internal justifications such as: fun, enjoyment and thrill; curiosity for the sake of knowledge; and computer virtuosity--which seem fit to the "self-fulfillment" technique (Scott & Lyman, 1968). Hackers structure their social identities around their computer hacking practices, in contrast to white-collar offenders who are not constructing their social identities distinctly different from us.

There are numerous theoretical approaches based on the concept that deviants do not have actual control over entering the criminal realm, but, rather, are driven by external forces. For instance, Matza's theory (1964, 1969) attempts to explain how people become criminals. Are people free to choose a deviant career or are they passive, driven by forces over which they have little, if any, control? The term "drift" that describes a state in which the individual detaches from a specific social group or from the moral codes of the general society appears to be the beginning of the process. The "desire" to deviate depends on two conditions—preparation and desperation—which enable the individual to make the decision whether to commit a crime. Preparation is when a crime is committed once the person believes that it is possible. Desperation is when the driving force for committing a crime is an external event, or the sense of fatalism and loss of control. In general, it seems that hackers, as opposed to Matza's approach, do not "drift" into deviance, and, surely, do not become deviants due to lack of control; on the contrary, they need to go through a serious social learning process to become a hacker. This conscious process is voluntary, and the hacker is aware of the time and energy needed, regarding both the technical and the ideological aspects (in the sense of acquiring the justifications and rationalizations). the process of becoming a hacker is not something that one is "swept into" or "ends up" doing in times of crisis.

Gottfredson and Hirschi (1990, 1994) developed a theory of crime based solely on self-control. They presented a general theory that explains individual differences in committing crimes, covering all kinds of crime and deviance, in all ages and all circumstances. Accordingly, all types of crime and deviance can be explained through the concept of self-control. People with high self-control would tend to engage in criminal activity less often throughout their lifetimes, while people with low levels of self-control would have strong tendencies toward criminal activity. This theory had a great deal of impact. "Just as impressive as the number of tests is the consistency of their findings (Hay, 2001, p. 707). With few exceptions, these studies indicate that low self-control, whether measured attitudinally or behaviorally, positively affects deviant and criminal behavior." Hay also contends, however, that there are questions concerning the extent to which this general theory can explain WCC.

SUMMARY OF KEY STUDY FINDINGS

The current study, as described in this chapter, was not designed to test the general theory, nor to examine the presumed low levels of self-control among hackers. My research, while not examining self-control directly, suggests that hackers are not low in self-control. This assertion is supported by the findings of Holt and Kilger (2008), who reported no significant differences in the level of self-control between hackers and a control group of information security students. Obviously, a further study that would systematically inquire into levels of self-control among both hackers and white-collar offenders and drawn from samples of convicted or non-convicted offenders would contribute to our knowledge. For now, the insights derived from the present study lead me to argue the possibility that the case of hackers challenges the general theory to the causation of crime. Thus, I tend to concur with Weisburd et al. (1991), who cautioned that while not all offenses require special understanding, it would be a mistake to go to the opposite extreme of finding a single explanation for all types of offenses.

One of the implications of this study is that future research is required to explore the relationship between WCC and other types of computer crime. In the latter, the relationships could be different for using the computer for embezzlement and financial theft, or for the purposes of espionage (Rosoff et al., 2002). For example, using the computer for embezzlement probably involves categorically different accounts from hackers, one that could be viewed as a subcategory of WCC.

Apparently there are indications that hackers, especially in the advanced stages in their careers, could be appropriately considered as white-collar offenders, even if they continue to perceive themselves as hackers or ex-hackers. An "ex-hacker" who engages in industrial espionage, for instance, can be considered a bona fide white-collar criminal. For instance, Interviewee Eran, a founder of a hi-tech start-up, said: "If I have a powerful competitor in the market, then many times I utilize my knowledge in order to know about him as much as I can in order to achieve a competitive advantage over him." In that sense, the hacker of today may be the white-collar offender of tomorrow.

The implications of this research may also interest the business community. Weisburd et al. (1991) contend that, contrary to public assumption, the majority of white-collar criminals are not wealthy but come from the middle-class. This assertion is accurate for hackers as well. There are reciprocated relations between hackers and computer professionals, both of who come from the same strata. Further, the outsider hackers may eventually become inside workers (Hollinger, 1993). The information security professionals should be cautious not only with closing breach and preventing intrusion opportunities, but also in understanding whom they employ. The employer who is hiring ex-hackers should be concerned with fostering a sense of belonging and a feeling of superiority, and with the recognition of their technological mastery--all of this reducing the likelihood of the ex-hacker's engaging in illegitimate computer behavior.

This chapter highlights the complexity of the relationships between hacking and white-collar crime. As Benson and Moore (1992) contend, the rejection by the general theory of motives as causal forces is misguided. In that sense, perhaps, it is time for scholars to develop a theory based on motivation, as it seems relevant to differentiate types of crimes and their perpetrators on the basis of differential motivations.

CONCLUSION

To summarize, similarity was found between hackers and white-collar offenders with regard to socio-demographic characteristics (sex, ethnicity, social status, non violence), although the two groups differed in terms of average age. Considerable differences, however, were found in the accounts used by the two groups throughout the content, form and structural dimensions analysis Thus, with regard to the question about whether hackers can be considered as white-collar offenders, the answer seems to be "no." While both groups are, indeed, driven to commit crimes by the same characteristics, the acts themselves are different and are committed, for the most part, for different accounts. While white-collar offenders usually "act" for economic gain, hackers "act" in the name of fun, curiosity, and demonstrating their computer virtuosity. While white-collar offenders use external justifications, hackers use internal justifications. Finally, their social formations are completely different; white-collar offenders do not structure their personal or social identities around their criminal activities, and thus do not cohere to a subculture identity. In contrast, hackers are a subculture that has formed around their activities as a whole culture, a distinct community, a sense of belonging, and a sense of superiority. To this end, hacking is definitely a unique type of crime.

REFERENCES

Agnew, R. (1992). Foundation for a general strain theory of crime and delinquency. *Criminology*, *30*(1), 47–87. doi:10.1111/j.1745-9125.1992.tb01093.x

Akers, R. L. (2000). *Criminological theories: Introduction, evaluation, and application*. Los Angeles: Roxbury Publishing Company.

Ball, L. D. (1985). Computer crime. In F. Tom (Ed.), *The information technology revolution* (pp. 532-545). Oxford, UK: Basil Blackwell and Cambridge, MA: MIT Press.

Behar, R. (1997). Who's reading your e-mail? *Fortune*, *147*, 57–70.

Ben Yehuda, N. (1986). The sociology of moral panics: Toward a new synthesis. *The Sociological Quarterly*, *27*(4), 495–513. doi:10.1111/j.1533-8525.1986.tb00274.x

Benson, M. L. (1996). Denying the guilty mind: Accounting for involvement in a white-collar crime . In Cromwell, P. (Ed.), *In their own words, criminals on crime* (pp. 66–73). Los Angeles: Roxbury Publishing Company.

Benson, M. L., & Moore, E. (1992). Are white-collar and common offenders the same? An empirical and theoretical critique of a recently proposed general theory of crime. *Journal of Research in Crime and Delinquency*, *29*(3), 251–272. doi:10.1177/0022427892029003001

Bequai, A. (1987). *Technocrimes*. Lexington, MA: Lexington.

Bequai, A. (1990). *Computer-related crime*. Strasburg, Germany: Council of Europe.

Bloom-Becker, J. (1986). *Computer crime law reporter*. Los Angeles: National Center for Computer Crime Data.

Braithwaite, J. (1985). White collar crime. *Annual Review of Sociology*, *11*, 1–25. doi:10.1146/annurev.so.11.080185.000245

Braithwaite, J. (1989). *Crime, shame and reintegration*. Cambridge, UK: Cambridge University Press.

Brezina, T. (2000). Are deviants different from the rest of us? Using student accounts of academic cheating to explore a popular myth. *Teaching Sociology*, *28*, 71–78. doi:10.2307/1319424

Chambliss, W. J. (1975). Toward a political economy of crime. *Theory and Society*, *2*(2), 149–170. doi:10.1007/BF00212732

Chandler, A. (1996). The changing definition and image of hackers in popular discourse. *International Journal of the Sociology of Law*, *24*(2), 229–251. doi:10.1006/ijsl.1996.0015

Clinard, M. B., & Quinney, R. (1973). *Criminal behavior systems: A typology*. New York: Holt, Rinehart and Winston.

Coleman, E. G., & Golub, A. (2008). Hacker practice: Moral genres and the cultural articulation of liberalism. *Anthropological Theory*, *8*, 255–277. doi:10.1177/1463499608093814

Coleman, J. W. (1987). Toward an integrated theory of white-collar crime. *American Journal of Sociology*, *93*(2), 406–439. doi:10.1086/228750

Coleman, J. W. (1995). Constructing white-collar crime: Rationalities, communication, power. *American Journal of Sociology*, *100*(4), 1094–1096. doi:10.1086/230631

Computer Security Institute and Federal Bureau of investigations. (2006). *CSI/FBI Computer crime and security survey*. Retrieved 2006 from http://i.cmpnet.com/gocsi/db_area/pdfs/fbi/FBI2006.pdf

Croall, H. (1992). *White-collar crime*. Philadelphia and Buckingham, PA: Open University Press.

Cromwell, P. (Ed.). (1999). *In their own words, criminals on crime*. Los Angeles: Roxbury Publishing Company.

DeLamater, J. (1978). On the nature of deviance . In Farrel, R. A., & Lynn Swigert, V. (Eds.), *Social deviance*. Philadelphia, PA: J.B. Lippincott.

Denning, D. E. (1990). *Concerning hackers who break into computer security systems*. Paper presented at the 13th National Computer Security Conference, October 1-4, Washington, D.C.

Dowland, P. S., Furnell, S. M., Illingworth, H. M., & Reynolds, P. L. (1999). Computer crime and abuse: A survey of public attitudes and awareness. *Computers & Security*, *18*(8), 715–726. doi:10.1016/S0167-4048(99)80135-7

Duff, L., & Gardiner, S. (1996). Computer crime in the global village: Strategies for control and regulation--in defence of the hacker. *International Journal of the Sociology of Law*, *24*(2), 211–228. doi:10.1006/ijsl.1996.0014

Edelhertz, H. (1975). *The nature, impact and prosecution of white collar crime*. Washington, DC: LEAA.

Engdahl, O. (2008). The role of money in economic crime. *The British Journal of Criminology*, *48*(2), 154–170. doi:10.1093/bjc/azm075

Forester, T., & Morrison, P. (1994). *Computer ethics: Cautionary tales and ethical dilemmas in computing*. London: MIT Press.

Friedrichs, D. O. (1996). *Trusted criminals in contemporary society*. Belmont, CA: Wadsworth Publishing Company.

Friedrichs, D. O. (2002). Occupational crime, occupational deviance, and workplace crime: Sorting out the difference. *Criminal Justice*, *2*, 243–256.

Garfinkel, H. (1978). Conditions of successful degradation ceremonies . In Farrell, R. A., & Swigert, V. L. (Eds.), *Social deviance* (pp. 135–142). Philadelphia, PA: J.B. Lippincott Company.

Geis, G. (1992). White-collar crime: What is it? In Kip, S., & Weisburd, D. (Eds.), *White-collar crime reconsidered* (pp. 31–52). Boston, MA: Northeastern University Press.

Gilbora, N. (1996). Elites, lamers, narcs and whores: Exploring the computer underground . In Cherny, L., & Weise, E. R. (Eds.), *Wired women: Gender and new realities in cyberspace*. Seattle, WA: Seal Press.

Gottfredson, M. R., & Hirschi, T. (1990). *A general theory of crime*. Stanford, CA: Stanford University Press.

Green, G. S. (1990). *Occupational crime*. Chicago, IL: Nelson-Hall.

Halbert, D. (1997). Discourses of danger and the computer hacker. *The Information Society*, *13*, 361–374. doi:10.1080/019722497129061

Hirschi, T., & Gottfredson, M. R. (Eds.). (1994). *The generality of deviance*. New Brunswick, NJ: Transaction Publishers.

Hollinger, R. C. (1991). Hackers: Computer heroes or electronic highwaymen. *Computers & Society*, *2*, 6–17. doi:10.1145/122246.122248

Hollinger, R. C. (1993). Crime by computer: Correlates of software piracy and unauthorized account access. *Security Journal*, *4*, 2–12.

Hollinger, R. C., & Lanza-Kaduce, L. (1988). The process of criminalization: The case of computer crime laws. *Criminology*, *26*(1), 101–126. doi:10.1111/j.1745-9125.1988.tb00834.x

Holt, T., & Kilger, M. (2008). Techcrafters and Makecrafters: A comparison of two populations of hackers. WOMBAT *Workshop on Information Security Threats Data Collection and Sharing*, pp.67-78.

Holt, T. J. (2007). Subcultural evolution? examining the influence of on- and off-line experiences on deviant subcultures. *Deviant Behavior*, *28*(2), 171–198. doi:10.1080/01639620601131065

Holt, T. J. (2008). Lone Hacks or Group Cracks: Examining the Social Organization of Computer Hackers . In Schmalleger, F., & Pittaro, M. (Eds.), *Crimes of the Internet* (pp. 336–355). Upper Saddle River, NJ: Prentice-Hall.

Holtfreter, K., Slyke, S. V., Bratton, J., & Gertz, M. (2008). Public perceptions of white-collar crime and punishment. *Journal of Criminal Justice*, *36*(1), 50–60. doi:10.1016/j.jcrimjus.2007.12.006

Jesilow, P., Pontell, H. M., & Geis, G. (1996). How doctors defraud medicaid: Doctors tell their stories . In Cromwell, P. (Ed.), *In their own words, criminals on crime* (pp. 74–84). Los Angeles: Roxbury Publishing Company.

Jordan, T., & Taylor, P. (1998). A sociology of hackers. *The Sociological Review*, *46*(4), 757–780. doi:10.1111/1467-954X.00139

Jordan, T., & Taylor, P. (2004). *Hacktivism and cyberwars: Rebels with a cause?* London, UK: Routledge.

Katz, J. (1988). *Seductions of crime: Moral and sensual attractions in doing evil*. New York: Basic Books.

Levy, S. (1984). *Hackers: Heroes of the computer revolution*. New York: Dell.

Matza, D. (1964). *Delinquency and drift*. New York: John Wiley and Sons.

Matza, D. (1969). *Becoming deviant*. Upper Saddle River, NJ: Prentice-Hall, Inc.

McEwen, T. J. (1989). *Dedicated computer crime units*. Washington, DC: National Institute of Justice.

Meyer, G., & Thomas, J. (1990). The baudy world of the byte bandit: A postmodernist interpretation of the computer underground . In Schmalleger, F. (Ed.), *Computers in criminal justice*. Bristol, IN: Wyndham Hall.

Michalowski, R. J., & Pfuhl, E. H. (1991). Technology, property, and law - the case of computer crime. *Crime, Law, and Social Change*, *15*(3), 255–275.

Minor, W. W. (1981). Techniques of neutralization: A reconceptualization and empirical examination. *Journal of Research in Crime and Delinquency*, *18*, 295–318. doi:10.1177/002242788101800206

Mitnick, K., & Simon, W. L. (2002). *The art of deception*. Hoboken, NJ: Wiley.

Nelken, D. (1994). *White-collar crime*. Aldershot, MA: Dartmouth.

Parker, D. B. (1989). *Computer crime: Criminal justice resource manual*. (2th ed.). Standfor, CA: Stanford Research Institute (SRI) International.

Piquero, N. L., Tibbetts, S. G., & Blankenship, M. B. (2005). Examining the Role of Differential Association and Techniques of Neutralization in Explaining Corporate Crime. *Deviant Behavior*, *26*, 159–188. doi:10.1080/01639620590881930

Pontell, H. N., & Rosoff, S. M. (2009). White-collar delinquency. *Crime, Law, and Social Change*, *51*(1), 147–162. doi:10.1007/s10611-008-9146-0

Raymond, E. S. (Ed.). (1996). *The new hacker's dictionary*. Cambridge, MA: The MIT Press.

Rosoff, S. M., Pontell, H. N., & Tillman, R. H. (2002). *Profit without honor* (2nd ed.). Englewood-Cliffs, NJ: Prentice-Hall.

Rothman, M., & Gandossy, R. F. (1982). Sad tales: The accounts of white-collar defendants and the decision to sanction. *Pacific Sociological Review*, *4*, 449–473.

Rotter, J. B. (1954). *Social learning and clinical psychology*. Englewood Cliffs, NJ: Prentice-Hall. doi:10.1037/10788-000

Roush, W. (1995). Hackers: Taking a byte out of computer crime. *Technology Review*, *98*, 32–40.

Schell, B. H., & Dodge, J. L. with Moutsatsos, S. (2002). *The hacking of America: Who's doing it, why, and how*. Westport, CT: Quorum Books.

Schoepfer, A., Carmichael, S., & Piquero, N. L. (2007). Do perceptions of punishment vary between white-collar and street crimes? *Journal of Criminal Justice*, *35*(2), 151–163. doi:10.1016/j.jcrimjus.2007.01.003

Scott, M. B., & Lyman, S. M. (1968). Accounts. *American Sociological Review*, *33*, 46–62. doi:10.2307/2092239

Sieber, U. (1986). *The International handbook on computer crime*. Oxford, UK: John Wiley.

Simpson, S. S. (1987). Cycles of illegality: Antitrust violations in corporate America. *Social Forces*, *65*(4), 943–963. doi:10.2307/2579018

Skinner, W. F., & Fream, A. M. (1997). A social learning theory analysis of computer crime among college students. *Journal of Research in Crime and Delinquency*, *34*(4), 495–518. doi:10.1177/0022427897034004005

Steffensmeier, D. (1989). On the causes of "white-collar" crime: An assessment of Hirschi and Gottfredson's claims. *Criminology*, *27*(2), 345–358. doi:10.1111/j.1745-9125.1989.tb01036.x

Sterling, B. (1992). *The hacker crackdown: Law and disorder on the electronic frontier*. London, UK: Viking.

Stewart, J. K. (1990). *Organizing for computer crime: Investigation and prosecution*. Medford, MA: Davis Association.

Sutherland, E. H. (1940). White-collar criminality. *American Sociological Review*, *5*(1), 1–12. doi:10.2307/2083937

Sykes, G. M., & Matza, D. (1957). Techniques of neutralization: A theory of delinquency. *American Sociological Review*, *22*, 664–670. doi:10.2307/2089195

Tappan, P. W. (1947). Who is the criminal? *American Sociological Review*, *12*, 96–102. doi:10.2307/2086496

Tavani, H. (2000). Defining the boundaries of computer crime: Piracy, break-ins, and sabotage in cyberspace. *Computers & Society*, *30*, 3–9. doi:10.1145/572241.572242

Taylor, P. A. (1999). *Hackers: Crime and the digital sublime*. New York: Routledge. doi:10.4324/9780203201503

Turgeman-Goldschmidt, O. (2005). Hackers' accounts: Hacking as a social entertainment. *Social Science Computer Review*, *23*, 8–23. doi:10.1177/0894439304271529

Turgeman-Goldschmidt, O. (2008). The rhetoric of hackers' neutralizations . In Schmalleger, F., & Pittaro, M. (Eds.), *Crimes of the Internet* (pp. 317–335). Englewood-Cliffs, NJ: Prentice-Hall.

Turkle, S. (1984). *The second self: Computers and the human spirit*. New York, NY: Simon and Schuster.

Upitis, R. B. (1998). From hackers to Luddites, game players to game creators: Profiles of adolescent students using technology. *Journal of Curriculum Studies*, *30*(3), 293–318. doi:10.1080/002202798183620

Voiskounsky, A. E., & Smyslova, O. V. (2003). Flow-based model of computer hackers' motivation. *Cyberpsychology & Behavior*, *6*, 171–180. doi:10.1089/109493103321640365

Weisburd, D., & Schlegel, K. (1992). Returning to the mainstream . In Kip, S., & Weisburd, D. (Eds.), *White-collar crime reconsidered*. Boston, MA: Northeastern University Press.

Weisburd, D., Waring, E., & Chayat, E. F. (2001). *White-collar crime and criminal careers*. Cambridge, MA: Cambridge University Press. doi:10.1017/CBO9780511499524

Weisburd, D., Wheeler, S., Waring, E., & Bode, N. (1991). *Crimes of the middle classes*. New Haven, CT: Yale University Press.

Willott, S., Griffin, C., & Torrance, M. (2001). Snakes and ladders: Upper-middle class male offenders talk about economic crime. *Criminology*, *39*(2), 441–466. doi:10.1111/j.1745-9125.2001.tb00929.x

Woo, Hyung-jin, Kim, Yeora & Dominick, Joseph (2004). Hackers: Militants or Merry Pranksters? A content analysis of defaced web pages. *Media Psychology*, *6*(1), 63-82.

Yar, M. (2005). Computer hacking: Just another case of juvenile delinquency? *Howard Journal of Criminal Justice*, *44*, 387–399. doi:10.1111/j.1468-2311.2005.00383.x

Chapter 3
The General Theory of Crime and Computer Hacking:
Low Self-Control Hackers?

Adam M. Bossler
Georgia Southern University, USA

George W. Burruss
University of Missouri-St. Louis, USA

ABSTRACT

Though in recent years, a number of studies have been completed on hackers' personality and communication traits by experts in the fields of psychology and criminology, a number of questions regarding this population remain. Does Gottfredson and Hirschi's concept of low self-control predict the unauthorized access of computer systems? Do computer hackers have low levels of self-control, as has been found for other criminals in mainstream society? If low self-control can predict the commission of computer hacking, this finding would seem to support the generality argument of self-control theory and imply that computer hacking and other forms of cybercrime are substantively similar to terrestrial crime. This chapter focuses on the results of a study where we examined whether Gottfredson and Hirschi's general theory of crime is applicable to computer hacking in a college sample.

INTRODUCTION

The evolution of computer technology and the growth of the Internet have both positively and negatively impacted modern life. Although newer technology makes communication and business transactions more efficient, the same technologies have made it easier for criminals, including mal-inclined computer hackers, to victimize individuals and businesses without ever being in the same physical space. Computer hacking, as defined in this chapter, can be viewed as the unauthorized access and use or manipulation of other people's computer systems (Taylor, Tory, Caeti, Loper, Fritsch, & Liederbach, 2006; Yar, 2005a).

Unfortunately, good data do not exist to indicate the frequency and severity of computer hacking (Richardson, 2008), a problem similar to that encountered by white-collar crime scholars

DOI: 10.4018/978-1-61692-805-6.ch003

(Benson & Simpson, 2009). Anecdotal evidence, however, illustrates that unauthorized access to computer systems is a serious and growing problem. For example, the 2008 CSI Computer Crime and Security Survey (Richardson, 2008) found that 29% of all security professionals indicated that their systems had experienced unauthorized access in 2007. In addition, the examination of any news website will contain stories covering data breaches, critical infrastructure deficiencies, website defacements, and successful computer hacks. Some of these news stories appear alarmist (see Wall, 2008), but they do indicate that hacking occurs frequently enough to say that it causes substantial damage and that it is not rare. These attacks against computer systems are not only increasing in frequency, but are increasing in sophistication as well (Holt & Kilger, 2008; Schell, Dodge, & Moutsatsos, 2002). To make matters worse, hackers have become more involved with organized crime and state-sponsored terrorism (Holt & Kilger, 2008; Taylor et al., 2006).

Many of the issues and policies regarding cyber security are too technical and beyond the skills and knowledge of traditional criminologists trained in sociology. Criminology's progress in studying cybercrime has been much slower than the evolution of technology itself. One of the greatest benefits that criminologists have made to the cyber security field, however, is the application of criminological theories to different varieties of cybercrime to explore whether traditional criminological theories created for the physical world can help explain crime in the virtual world. If only the medium differentiates crime in the physical and virtual worlds (see Grabosky, 2001), then knowledge previously gained from theoretically-based tests examining terrestrial crime would presumably apply to virtual crime as well; thus, scholars would not have to treat cybercrime as being theoretically different. If terrestrial and virtual crimes were substantially different, traditional criminological theories would not be as useful in the cyber world (Wall, 2005; Yar, 2005b).

In general, research has shown that much of our knowledge regarding crime in the physical world applies to cybercrime as well. For example, research has shown that routine activity theory (Cohen & Felson, 1979) can be applied to both on-line harassment (Holt & Bossler, 2009) and malware victimization (Bossler & Holt, 2009). The general theory of crime (Gottfredson & Hirschi, 1990) and aspects of social learning theory (Akers, 1998) have both been extensively applied to digital and software piracy (e.g., Higgins, 2005, 2006; Higgins, Fell, & Wilson, 2006).

Although the studying of hackers is not new (see Landreth, 1985), there have been few criminological examinations of these groups or their behaviors (Taylor et al., 2006; Yar, 2005a). Most examinations have focused on hackers as a subculture and have largely ignored other theoretical approaches (see Skinner & Fream, 1997, for an exception). Considering that traditional criminological theories have been successfully applied to other forms of cybercrime, our knowledge on computer hacking could potentially be improved if these same theories, such as Gottfredson and Hirschi's (1990) general theory of crime, were examined in relationship to hacking.

Michael Gottfredson and Travis Hirschi's (1990) general theory of crime, or self-control theory, argues that individuals commit crime because they have the inability to resist temptation and, therefore, commit acts having long-term consequences greater than the short-term benefits. Self-control has been demonstrated to be one of the most influential correlates of crime in both the traditional (see Pratt & Cullen, 2000) and digital piracy literature (e.g., Higgins, 2005). Gottfredson and Hirschi would argue that most hacking is simplistic and that hackers take advantage of easy opportunities. Thus, they have characteristics similar to criminals in general. Given this view, the cause of computer hacking is the same as for all other crimes—low self-control.

THE PURPOSE OF THIS STUDY AND CHAPTER

Although some of the aforementioned arguments have merit (see Grabosky, 2001), many hackers possess high levels of computer proficiency and a strong commitment to learning (Holt & Kilger, 2008; Jordan & Taylor, 1998), both of which are antithetical to the idea of low self-control. In addition, the literature heavily supports the importance of the socialization process for hackers, including associating with other hackers on- and off-line (Holt, 2009) and having their behavior socially reinforced (e.g., Taylor et al., 2006).

Many questions remain. Does Gottfredson and Hirschi's concept of low self-control predict the unauthorized access of computer systems? Simply stated, "Do hackers have low levels of self-control?" If low self-control can predict the commission of computer hacking, this finding would support the generality argument of self-control theory and imply that computer hacking and other forms of cybercrime are substantively similar to terrestrial crime and that the differences between them are overstated.

In our recent study (and the focus of this chapter), we examined whether Gottfredson and Hirschi's general theory of crime is applicable to computer hacking in a college sample. We utilized Structural Equation Modeling (SEM) to examine the effect of low self-control on computer hacking, while controlling for the social learning process and control variables. In addition, we examined whether the social learning process mediates any possible effect that self-control has on hacking. Thus, we examined whether one of the most popular criminological theories of the past twenty years can explain a crime that will continue to plague our society into the next century—mal-intentioned hacking (or cracking).

COMPUTER HACKING AND HACKING PROFILES DEFINED

Defining what "computer hacking" is and what it entails has proven to be difficult and has led to lengthy exchanges, similar to the debates surrounding "gangs" (see Curry & Decker, 2007) and "terrorism" (see Primoratz, 2004). The term "hacker" encompasses several different types of behaviors and connotations (Beveren, 2001; Chisea, Ducci, & Ciappi, 2008; Denning, 1998; Furnell, 2002; Holt & Kilger, 2008; Schell et al., 2002; Taylor, 1999; Thomas, 2002). The term was originally a positive label referring to outstanding and possibly radical uses of technology to solve existing technological limitations (Taylor et al., 2006; Yar, 2005). These earlier hackers were more closely associated with a hacker's ethic positing the following: (i) the free access and exchange of knowledge; (ii) the belief that technology could better our lives; (iii) a strong distrust of authority; and (iv) a resistance to conventionality (Taylor et al., 2006; Thomas, 2002). Although they did "explore" other people's systems, they purported to do so out of curiosity and because of a strong desire to learn and share this information with others, thereby improving computer technology and security (Chiesa et al., 2008; Taylor et al., 2006). Today, the term "hacker," assuming that there is mal-intent in the hacking "acts," is more closely associated with criminality, maliciousness, and profiteering, much to the disproval of old school hackers (Taylor, 1999).[1]

Hacker Typologies

Scholars have extensively focused on different hacker categories in order to better define and understand the phenomena (Holt & Kilger, 2008; Taylor et al., 2006).[2] The most common categorization scheme is to categorize hackers by their intentions, with the most popular-used terms being White Hat, Black Hat, and Grey Hat (Taylor et al., 2006). White Hats typically work for security corporations and are assigned the task of improving and securing computer services by identifying and fixing security flaws. Black Hats, on the other hand, are those that use their computer skills to cause problems for others. This term can encompass a range of motivations, including those who direct their negative actions at a specific company or group (i.e. angry hackers), those with lower levels of skill but use hacking tools to cause mischief for fun (i.e. script kiddies), and those who are interested in political and economic upheaval and view technology as the means to accomplish this goal (i.e. agenda hackers). Finally, Grey Hats are independent security experts and consultants who are quite often reformed Black Hats.

Other scholars, however, have argued that typologies should be based on skill and the ability to use technology, rather than intentions, because these characteristics are essential to the hacker subculture (Holt & Kilger, 2008). For example, Holt and Kilger (2008) divide hackers into those who produce new materials, called "makecrafters," and those who are consumers of these tools, called "techcrafters."

Although it appears that hackers are not a homogeneous group, scholars argue that hacking can still be viewed as the unauthorized access and use or manipulation of other people's computer systems, and that hackers, in general, are part of a hacker subculture (e.g., Holt & Kilger, 2008; Taylor, 1999; Yar, 2005a), regardless of categorization scheme.

Hacker Subculture

Much of the empirical research on computer hacking has focused on the composition of the hacker subculture (Holt, 2007; Holt & Kilger, 2008; Jordan & Taylor, 1998; Miller & Slater, 2000; Wilson & Atkinson, 2005). Certain characteristics, such as technology, mastery, secrecy/anonymity, and membership fluidity, are consistently discovered. In order for individuals to be truly embraced in the hacker subculture, they must have a strong connection to computer technology and a drive to find new ways to apply this technology. "Mastery" involves the continuous learning of new skills and the mastering of both social and physical environments (see also Furnell, 2002). Hackers can demonstrate technological mastery with their inventive applications of technology, while indicating "their mastery of hacker culture by making references to the history of hacking or use of hacker argot when communicating with others" (Holt & Kilger, 2008, p. 68). The hacker subculture has what can be considered an ambivalent relationship with secrecy – the concealment of a hack – since they do not want to gain the attention of law enforcement, but gaining recognition for a successful hack and sharing information requires the divulgement of what one has done (Jordan & Taylor, 1998). Hackers place a high priority, however, on anonymity (i.e. concealment of one's off-line identity). Finally, similar to gangs, hacker groups are informal, loosely organized, and they have rapid membership changes (Jordan & Taylor, 1998; Taylor et al., 2006).[3] With the rapid changes that have occurred to aspects of the hacker subculture over the last thirty years, especially regarding who is considered a hacker and the types of hacks that are reinforces and encouraged, it should be noted that researchers will need to continue to examine the central characteristics of the hacker subculture in order to understand how certain elements evolve and whether other characteristics take a more primary role in the subculture.

SELF-CONTROL THEORY AND POSSIBLE LINKS TO HACKING

Self-Control Theory: Basic Tenets

Michael Gottfredson and Travis Hirschi's (1990) general theory of crime, commonly referred to as "self-control theory," is a classic control theory arguing that motivation is invariant among individuals, and that what differentiates "criminals" from "non-criminals" is the level of constraint placed upon them. These theorists posit that humans are rational beings who weigh the potential pleasure and pain of their behavior and act accordingly. Crime is an efficient and effective means to obtain immediate gratification, but the benefits are normally short-term and meager, while the long-term consequences are more certain and severe. Most individuals would not rationally choose to commit crime, since the future pain outweighs the immediate pleasure. Individuals with inadequate levels of self-control, however, cannot resist the temptation and immediate pleasures of crime.

Self-control theory has been extensively critiqued (e.g., Akers, 1991; Geis, 2000) and empirically tested over the last twenty years (e.g., Gibson & Wright, 2001; Higgins, 2005; Pratt & Cullen, 2000). Low self-control has consistently been found to be related to multiple forms of crime and deviance, ranging from traditional forms of street crime to school deviance (e.g., Arneklev, Grasmick, Tittle, & Bursik, 1993; Gibbs & Giever, 1995; Grasmick, Tittle, Bursik, & Arneklev, 2003; Piquero & Tibbetts, 1996). Meta-analyses indicate that low self-control is one of the strongest correlates of crime, regardless of how self-control is operationalized (Pratt & Cullen, 2000).

In addition, self-control has been theoretically and empirically connected to the virtual world. Buzzell, Foss, & Middleton (2006) found that low self-control can predict both the downloading of pornographic images and the visiting of sexually-explicit websites. Low self-control has also been extensively connected to digital piracy (Higgins, 2007; Higgins, Fell, & Wilson, 2006; Higgins, Wolfe, & Marcum, 2008), movie piracy (Higgins, Fell, & Wilson, 2007), and software piracy (Higgins, 2005, 2006; Higgins & Makin, 2004; Higgins & Wilson, 2006). Thus, the empirical research to date illustrating that self-control levels are related to a wide range of crimes, including various forms of cybercrime, and Gottfredson and Hirschi's argument that inadequate levels of self-control are the cause of *all* crime, would suggest that the general theory of crime should empirically predict computer hacking as well.

Self-Control Theory: Applicable to Hackers?

Empirical tests on the applicability of self-control theory to computer hacking, however, are scant. With "control" operationalized as the perception of how easy or difficult an activity would be, Gordon and Ma (2003) found that self-control was not related to hacking intentions. Rogers, Smoak, and Liu (2006) discovered that computer deviants, including hacking behaviors, have less social moral choice and were more exploitive and manipulative. Holt and Kilger (2008) found that hackers "in the wild" did not have different levels of self-control than did self-reported hackers in a college sample. Thus, direct empirical studies on the effects of self-control on computer hacking are pretty much absent from the literature.

Although tests on self-control and hacking are rare, comparing the findings of past hacker studies with Gottfredson and Hirschi's views of crime can indirectly assess whether their theory is consistent with known hacking behaviors. Based on their definition of crime as "acts of force or fraud undertaken in the pursuit of self-interest" (Gottfredson & Hirschi, 1990, p. 15), these theorists view crime as encompassing the following: providing easy or simple immediate gratification of desires; being exciting, risky, or thrilling; providing few or meager long-term benefits; requiring little skill or planning; resulting in pain or discomfort for the victim; and relieving momentary irritation. Therefore, individuals committing these acts have the following characteristics in common: impulsiveness; "lack diligence, tenacity, or persistence in a course of action" (Gottfredson & Hirschi, 1990, p. 89); uninterested in long-term goals; not necessarily possessing cognitive or academic skills; self-centered and non-empathetic; and can easily be frustrated.

Comparing the findings of past hacker studies with Gottfredson and Hirschi's characteristics of crime illustrates similarities between hacking and traditional crime, but it also produces some major inconsistencies. One of the clearest similarities between traditional crime and hacking is that it demonstrates insensitivity to other people's pain. Gordon (1994) found that virus writers were often not concerned with the effects of their viruses, even if they knew that they were illegal and harmful. Quite often, hackers use neutralization techniques, arguing that they did not have any malicious intent, or that no harm was actually done (Gordon & Ma, 2004; Turgeman-Goldschmidt, 2005). Finally, hackers often blame the victim for not having enough skill or security to prevent victimization, even stating that they are hacking for the *benefit* of others (Jordan & Taylor, 1998; Taylor et al., 2006).

Hackers have been characterized as engaging in hacking acts because they are exciting, thrilling, and providing a "rush" (Taylor et al., 2006). Hackers' desire to explore what technology can do demonstrates their adventurous side. Interestingly, Gordon (1994) found that ex-virus writers stopped writing viruses because of a lack of time and boredom; they did not find it thrilling or exciting anymore. Although hacking may appear to be thrilling to hackers, at least for some finite period, Gottfredson and Hirschi (1990, p. 89) deduced that criminals would be "adventuresome, active, or physical," while individuals with higher levels of self-control would be "cautious, cognitive, and verbal." Hackers clearly demonstrate their adventurous side, although in a virtual context. Inconsistent with the traditional criminal profile, however, hackers also possess characteristics of individuals with high levels of self-control, such as being cognitive and verbal, as illustrated by their strong commitment to technology and their mastery of technology and the hacker social world.

The evidence is also mixed regarding the other central characteristics of low self-control because it depends on what type of hacker and hacking behavior one is examining and his/her computer skill level. This is inconsistent with Gottfredson and Hirschi's view that criminals do not specialize and that typologies are unnecessary and unwarranted. Hacking that involves lower-skill levels is more consistent with Gottfredson and Hirschi's view of crime. For example, Taylor et al. (2006) state that "script kiddies" can fulfill their instant gratification by simply downloading other people's programs to complete their attacks without being concerned of the technology behind the attack. Easy access to computers and the Internet allows almost anyone to go on-line and download viruses and hacking tools. In addition, there are unsophisticated hacking options such as "shoulder-surfing" (i.e. looking over someone's shoulder to get passwords), brute-force attacks (i.e. guessing passwords until successful), and social engineering (i.e. obtaining the password from someone within an organization) that can allow for easy gratification (Taylor et al., 2006; Wall, 2008). Similarly, recent data show that more than half of all investigated data breaches required no or little skill to commit these offenses and that minimal security tools would have prevented these crimes (Richardson, 2008).

The hacker subculture components of technology and mastery, however, strongly indicate that hackers, in general, and especially those with more computer skills, are not interested in pleasure through simple means but rather are interested in the technical challenge of fixing a problem that has not been solved before, thus illustrating "mastery" (Gordon, 2000; Holt & Kilger, 2008; Jordan & Taylor, 1998). Indeed, many forms of computer hacking take specific technical skills and knowledge of computers and networks. In addition, many hackers are enrolled as students in high school and college while many others are employed, even in the security field (Taylor et al., 2006; Holt & Kilger, 2008). This demonstrates that many hackers are prepared and interested in long-term occupational pursuits. Thus, hackers possessing higher levels of computer skills and associating more closely with the hacker subculture, which emphasizes mastery, are not described accurately by Gottfredson and Hirschi's descriptions of criminals.

Self-Control Theory and White-Collar Crime: Is There a Link to Hackers?

Examining the research on self-control theory and white-collar crime provides further insight because computer hacking can be considered a white-collar offense.[4] The ability of low self-control to explain white-collar crime, however, has not been as successfully defended as other forms of crime (Benson & Moore, 1992; Benson & Simpson, 2009; Reed & Yeager, 1996; Simpson & Piquero, 2002). Gottfredson and Hirschi (1990) have consistently argued that white-collar crime, and therefore presumably computer hacking, is not problematic for self-control theory and that special theories are not necessary (see also Gottfredson & Hirschi, 2000). They have posited that most white-collar crime simply involves lower-level employees stealing from their companies; thus, presumably, one could argue that stealing is similar to computer hacking committed by employees or ex-employees. Low self-control has been found to be empirically related to employee theft in a college sample (Langton, Piquero, & Hollinger, 2006).

In addition, Wall (2008) has argued that most computer hacking is simply conducted through social engineering rather than through complex hacking. Combined with the findings that low self-control is related to software piracy (Higgins, 2005, 2006; Higgins & Makin, 2004; Higgins & Wilson, 2006), it appears that the general theory of crime can explain white-collar crime, including computer hacking, *if it only requires lower levels of skill.*

That said, much of the evidence in the white-collar crime literature, however, does not support self-control theory. Gottfredson and Hirschi (1990) have argued that criminals do not specialize and that white-collar offenders are the same individuals who commit other crimes. Benson and Moore (1992), however, found that individuals who commit even the lowest forms of white-collar crime can be distinguished from street criminals. In addition, Simpson and Piquero (2002) found that self-control was not related to corporate offending in a sample of corporate manages and managers-in-training. They further argued that organizational crime is not necessarily simple, and that many of these cases involve detailed planning and farsightedness. Walters (2002) argued that white-collar criminals can be separated by those with low and high levels of self-control.

Thus, self-control theory does not fare as well when white-collar crime requires advanced management experience or higher levels of skill. These negative findings could imply that: 1) computer hackers are not necessarily the same individuals as street criminals; 2) low self-control is not related to computer hacking involving higher levels of computer skills; and 3) the category "hackers" might contain individuals with both low and high levels of self-control.

SOCIAL LEARNING THEORY AND ITS LINK TO HACKING

Ron Akers' (1998) social learning theory argues that crime is a learned behavior resulting from the interaction of four components: differential association, definitions, differential reinforcement, and imitation. Individuals associating with delinquents will be more likely to imitate delinquent behavior and be exposed to definitions that favor the breaking of the law. An individual will repeat and continue this behavior as long as it is reinforced.

Social learning theory has been extensively tested and has been found to explain a wide range of criminal and deviant behaviors (see Akers & Jensen, 2006, for a thorough review), including software piracy (Higgins & Makin, 2004; Higgins,

2005, 2006; Higgins & Wilson, 2006), movie piracy (Higgins et al., 2007), digital piracy (Higgins et al., 2006), and even computer hacking (Skinner & Fream, 1997). In one of the few direct social learning theory tests involving hacking measures, Skinner and Fream (1997) found that each of the four social learning components was at least related to one hacking behavior. Research has also found that social learning variables significantly predict crime even when controlling for self-control levels, and that the social learning measures improve the ability of the model to predict crime (Pratt & Cullen, 2000; see also Gibson & Wright, 2001). Thus, the exclusion of social learning theory measures from a study creates the possibility of model misspecification.

It is not surprising that Akers' social learning theory appears theoretically congruent with computer hacking, considering that his theory is the individual-level equivalent of subcultural theories. Hackers gain knowledge and training by associating with other hackers, both on- and off-line (Holt, 2009; Jordan & Taylor, 1998; Rogers et al., 2006; Taylor et al., 2006). Many of these associations are not strong or deep, but they still supply helpful information and reinforce the hacker subculture (Holt, 2009; Taylor et al., 2006).

Although hackers differ on their willingness to cause damage to computer systems (Furnell, 2002), the hacker subculture consists of values that differentiate it from the mainstream (Taylor et al., 2006), especially their flexible or lower ethical boundaries regarding computer systems (Gordon, 1994; Gordon & Ma, 2003; Rogers et al., 2006), as well as their use of defense mechanisms to shift the blame from themselves to the victims (Turgeman-Goldschmidt, 2005). In the early stages of their careers, computer hackers might try to imitate others, but praise is rewarded to those who provide information or demonstrate mastery and ingenuity (Gordon, 2000; Holt, 2009; Jordan & Taylor, 1998). Thus, the hacker subculture reinforces and encourages successful hacks by promising more status in the subculture (Holt, 2009; Taylor et al, 2006).

PRESENT STUDY PARAMETERS

scholars have infrequently applied traditional criminological theories beyond subcultural analyses to the growing problem of computer hacking. Gottfredson and Hirschi's (1990) general theory of crime is one of the most extensively tested and supported theories, indicating that levels of self-control are one of the most influential correlates of crime, including both downloading of pornography (Buzzell et al., 2006) and pirating media (e.g., Higgins, 2005, 2007). Gottfredson and Hirschi (1990) would argue that computer hacking is simply another action resulting from low self-control. Many hacking activities, especially those requiring little or no skill, are consistent with Gottfredson and Hirschi's view of crime and could presumably be explained by self-control. However, the literature review has also indicated, as discussed, that hacking activities requiring mastery and dedication to learning computer skills are incongruent with Gottfredson and Hirschi's theory. It would appear that these individuals would need higher levels of self-control to persevere.

In this study, we utilized Structural Equation Modeling (SEM) to empirically test whether low self-control predicts computer hacking. In addition, we explored whether self-control directly affects computer hacking or whether any possible effect is mediated through the social learning process.

Procedure

We examined data collected for a larger project regarding college students' computer activities, perceptions, and beliefs. Students in ten courses, five of which allowed any student to enroll, completed a self-report survey during the fall of 2006 at a large southeastern university. The respondent sample (n= 566) was 58.8% female and 78.3% White, findings consistent with the larger university demographic population (52.5% female; 75% White).

Rationale for Using a College Sample to Assess Hacking

College samples are quite commonly cited in the criminological literature (see Payne & Chappell, 2008) to test hypotheses and have been used successfully for tests of self-control and social learning theories in both cybercrime (e.g., Buzzell et al., 2006; Higgins, 2005; Higgins, Fell, & Wilson 2006, 2007) and the hacking literature (Rogers, Smoak, and Liu, 2006; Skinner & Fream, 1997). Both self-control and social learning theories purport to be general theories that should explain crime in a college sample.

University students have also been viewed as appropriate groups to sample because of their high levels of cybercrime offending (Higgins & Wilson, 2006; Hinduja 2001; Holt & Bossler, 2009), including hacking (Hollinger, 1992; Skinner & Fream, 1997). In fact, the utilization of a college sample might be preferable for a test of self-control theory and hacking, considering that the theoretical discussion section illustrated that self-control theory is more congruent with low-skilled hackers. Holt and Kilger (2008, p. 76) found that their college self-proclaimed hackers "reported lower skill levels and knowledge of programming languages, reinforcing the notion that some hackers engage in relatively unsophisticated or non-technical behaviors." This is not to say that our sample consisted only of low-skilled hackers, but it is safe to assume that our college sample contained a wide variety of hacker types, some of who would more closely fit Gottfredson and Hirschi's characteristics of criminals, as compared to highly-skilled hackers who are part of organized crime or international terrorism. Thus, sampling hackers at the lower end of the skill spectrum could provide a more conservative test of self-control theory.

Measures

Hacking. Hacking, the dependent variable of interest in this study, was modeled as a latent factor consisting of three observed variables measuring the number of times respondents had engaged in hacking behaviors on a five-point scale over the previous twelve months. Respondents indicated how often they had:

1) guessed another person's password to get into his/her computer account or files (Hack 1);
2) accessed another's computer account or files without his/her knowledge or permission to look at information or files (Hack 2);
3) added, deleted, changed, or printed any information in another's files without permission (Hack 3). (See Rogers et al., 2006; Skinner & Fream, 1997)

The five-point scale was: never (0); 1 to 2 times (1); 3 to 5 times (2); 6 to 9 times (3); and 10 or more times (4). The modal category for each of the hacking variables was 'never' at 86%, 86%, and 94%, respectively.[5] See Table 1 for descriptives.

Low Self-Control. As noted, research has shown that self-control is one of the strongest correlates of crime, regardless of how it is measured (Pratt &Cullen, 2000; Tittle, Ward, & Grasmick, 2003). We utilized Grasmick et al.'s (1993) scale of twenty-four items representing the six subcomponents of low self-control: impulsivity, simple tasks, risk-taking, physical activity, volatile temper, and self-centeredness. For each item, respondents chose options ranging from 1 (strongly disagree) to 4 (strongly agree).

Among researchers, there is some disagreement about whether summing the twenty-four items into a single index is the most valid measure of the concept. For instance, scholars using con-

Table 1. Descriptive statistics for observed variables (n=566)

Variable	Min.	Max.	Mean	SD
Hack 1	0	4	0.239	0.669
Hack 2	0	4	0.235	0.670
Hack 3	0	4	0.102	0.476
DA 1	0	4	0.477	0.723
DA 2	0	4	0.362	0.664
DA 3	0	4	0.272	0.592
DEF 1	1	4	1.486	0.819
DEF 2	1	4	1.873	1.040
DEF 3	1	4	2.228	1.089
DEF 4	1	4	1.717	0.851
DEF 5	1	4	1.371	0.635
RE 1	1	5	2.175	1.307
RE 2	1	5	1.118	0.482
RE 3	1	5	1.127	0.478
I 1	1	5	1.463	0.857
I 2	1	5	2.263	1.118
I 3	1	5	1.721	1.095
LSC	24	96	50.788	10.567
Black	0	1	0.104	0.306
Race Other	0	1	0.113	0.317
Skill	0	2	0.668	0.567
Female	0	1	0.588	0.493
Age	0	3	0.841	0.894
Employment	0	2	0.818	0.604

firmatory factor analysis (CFA) found that low self-control did not reflect a single dimension; rather, low self-control was better measured as a correlated five- or six-subcomponent model (Longshore, Chang, Hsieh, & Messina, 2004; Piquero & Rosay, 1998).

We examined three CFA self-control model configurations (see Figure 1). Figure 1a is a single-factor model, where all twenty-four items reflect low self-control. This CFA model has been routinely rejected in the literature (Flora, Finkel, & Foshee, 2003; Higgins, Fell, & Wilson, 2006; Longshore et al., 2004). Figure 1b is the correlated subcomponents model (Longshore et al., 2004). Figure 1c, a second-order factor model, is mathematically equivalent to 1b. The high correlations, however, among the six underlying subcomponents suggest a single higher-order factor for low self-control. For example, Flora et al. (2003) found that their second-order factor model, shown in 1c, was a good fit with their data. Similarly, Higgins et al. (2006) found that low self-control was a second-order factor; however, they summed the observed survey items into the six subscales and then modeled low self-control as a higher-order factor (model is not shown in

Figure 1. Measurement models for low self-control

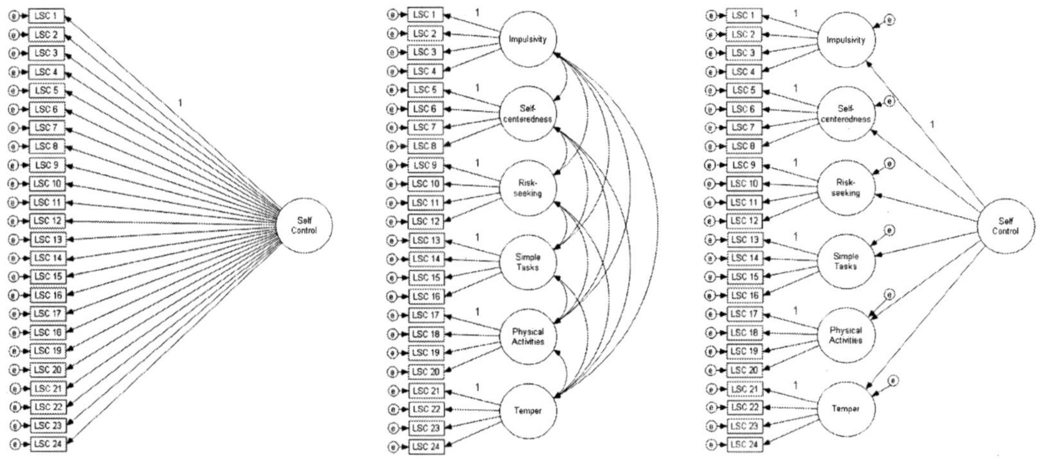

Model 1a: Single factor Model 1b: Correlated factors Model 1c: Second-order factor

figure 1). To summarize, scholars have used different methods to measure low self-control, and there appears to be no consensus as to which model is most valid.

Based upon our analyses that found that self-control was not a second-order factor (i.e. figure 1c) (see results section below), we used the prevalently employed Grasmick et al. (1993) 24-item scale to measure low self-control. Thus, we utilized a formative indicator of self-control strongly supported by the literature rather than measuring self-control as a reflective indicator not supported by our data. A principal components analysis duplicated the dimensionality of the original scale found in the literature. The scree plot and eigenvalues indicated that the twenty-four self-control survey items coalesced into a single dimension (see Grasmick et al., 1993; Piquero et al., 2001; Pratt & Cullen, 2000; Tittle et al., 2003). Furthermore, the scale showed internal consistency in line with other reported studies (Cronbach's alpha = 0.884). The final measure ranged from 24 to 96, with *higher* scores representing lower self-control.

Social Learning Theory. To measure the social learning process, we used a second-order factor model suggested by the literature (Akers & Lee, 1996; Lee, Akers, & Borg, 2004). While it is common to model the social learning process by including differential association and definitions measures, yet excluding differential reinforcement and imitation (e.g., Higgins, 2005, 2006; Higgins & Makin, 2004; Higgins et al., 2007), we tested a model that included all four components of the process. The measurement model for social learning is shown in Figure 2.

The first-order factor *differential association* was assessed using three items based on peer involvement in hacking. These asked how many of their friends had engaged in the following mal-intended hacking (or cracking) acts:

1) added, deleted, changed, or printed any information in another's computer files without the owner's knowledge or permission (*DA 1*);
2) tried to access another's computer account or files without his/her knowledge or permission just to look at the information (*DA 2*);
3) tried to guess another's password to get into his/her computer account or files (*DA 3*).

Figure 2. Social learning measurement model

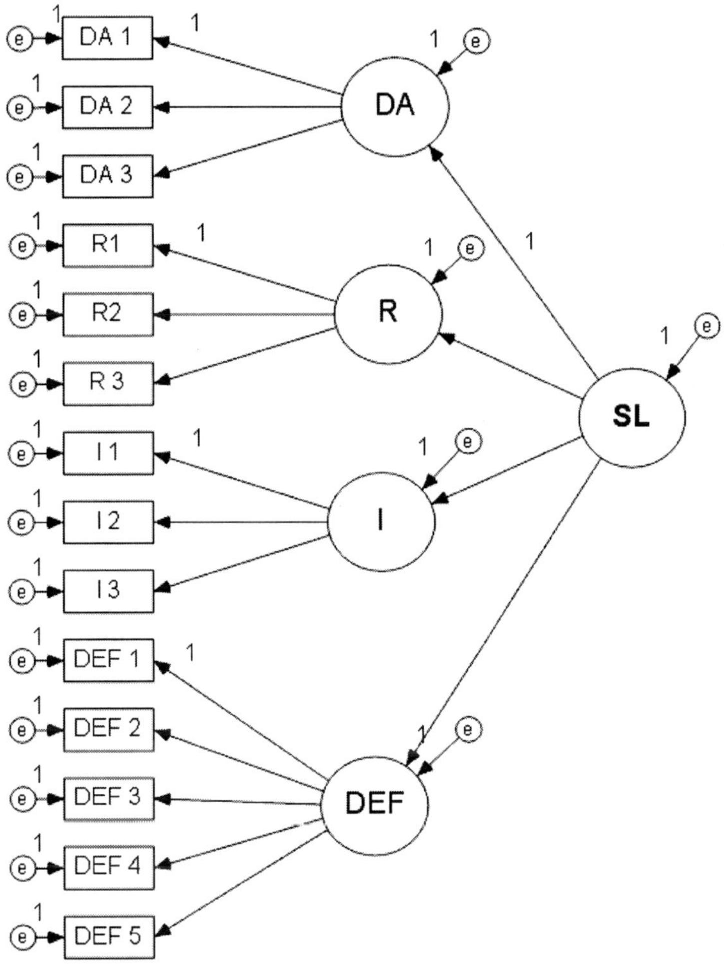

These three items used a five-point scale: none of them = 0; very few of them = 1; about half of them = 2; more than half of them = 3; all of them=4 (Rogers, 2001; Skinner & Fream, 1997).

To assess respondents' *definitions* favoring hacking and its neutralization, the following five items were used:

1) People should be allowed to use computers they don't own in any way they see fit *(DEF 1)*;
2) If people do not want me to get access to their computer or computer systems they should have better computer security *(DEF 2)*;
3) I should be able to look at any information that the government, a school, a business, or an individual, has on me even if they do not give us access *(DEF 3)*;
4) Compared with other illegal acts people do, gaining unauthorized access to a computer system or someone's account is not very serious *(DEF 4)*; and
5) People who break into computer systems are actually helping society *(DEF 5)*. (Rogers, 2001; Skinner & Fream, 1997).

Each item was measured on a four-point Likert scale (1 = strongly agree to 4 = strongly disagree).

To assess respondents' *differential reinforcement,* three items were asked:

1) How many times they witnessed a professor/instructor, boss, or colleague mention that some computer activities are unethical or illegal to perform (R1);
2) How many times they witnessed a professor/instructor, boss, or colleague praise or encourage students to use *campus* computers to engage in unethical or illegal computer activities (R2);
3) How many times they witnessed a professor/instructor, boss, or colleague use computers, in general, to engage in unethical or illegal computer activities (R3).

These items were measured on five-point scales from never (1) to 10 or more (5) (Rogers, 2001; Skinner & Fream, 1997).

Sources of *imitation* were assessed through three items dealing with how much the respondents have learned about hacking by watching family (I1) or friends (I2) engage in these acts or by viewing it in Internet chat rooms, Internet Relay Chat, or Web forums (I3). They were asked to use a scale ranging from 1 = learned nothing to 5 = learned everything (Rogers, 2001; Skinner & Fream, 1997).

Demographic Variables. We used several demographic control variables that are not simply potential confounders but are theoretically relevant, given literature findings: age, sex, employment, race, and computer skill. Research has consistently found that hackers are typically young, white, males (Foster, 2004; Hollinger, 1992; Jordan & Taylor, 1998; Skinner & Fream, 1997; Sterling, 1994; Taylor, 1999; Yar, 2005). Within a college sample, however, earlier research studies found that older students, including graduate students, are more likely to pirate software (Cronan, Foltz, & Jones, 2006; Hollinger, 1993; Skinner & Fream, 1997). In addition, employment can often be a risk factor for youth since it increases their exposure to delinquents (Staff & Uggen, 2003; Wright & Cullen, 2004). Consistent with these findings, we hypothesized that within a college sample, self-professed hackers will tend to be older, employed, white males with computer skills.

Age was measured as a four-point ordinal scale: (0) under 19, (1) 20 to 21, (2) 22 to 25, and (3) 26 and over. *Sex* was coded as follows: female (1), male being (0). Race was measured by two dummy variables: *African-American* and *race-other*, with white as the comparison group. *Employment status* was coded as unemployed (0), part-time/temporary employed (1), and full-time employed (2). Finally, we coded *skill level* with computers as: 0 = "I can surf the 'net, use common software, but not fix my own computer" (normal); 1 = "I can use a variety of software and fix some computer problems I have" (intermediate); and 2 = "I can use Linux, most software, and fix most computer problems I have" (advanced) (see Rogers, 2001).

DATA ANALYSIS

Approach

We employed Structural Equation Modeling (SEM) to consider the influence of latent factors on observed indicators and, simultaneously, the influence of the social learning factor, the low self-control index, and the control variables on hacking. SEM can be thought of as a combination of factor analysis (the measurement models) and multivariate regression (structural models). In this analysis, we used confirmatory factor analysis. We employed weighted least squares mean and variance adjusted estimator (WLSMV) through Mplus version 5 (Muthén & Muthén, 2007).

WLSMV is the appropriate estimation for models with categorical indicators (Bollen, 1989; Muthén & Muthén, 2007). We assessed each model through the following Mplus goodness-of-fit indices: the chi-square test and its *p*-value, the comparative fit index (CFI), the Tucker-Lewis index (TLI), the root mean square error of approximation (RMSEA), and the weighted root mean square residual (WRMR).[6] We also evaluated the models based on the substantive loading of each latent factor on the observed variables. We expected that each of the latent variables would have a reasonably high and statistically significant factor loading on the observed variables; a factor loading is considered reasonable if it is above 0.30 (Kline, 2005). Finally, because the dependant variable, hacking, is a latent factor measured through ordered categorical observed variables, the unstandardized estimates are probit coefficients. Unless otherwise noted, we refer to the standardized regression coefficients (indicated as β). In addition, the model R-square is the variance explained for the continuous latent response variable (y*), rather than the observed ordinal dependent variable (y) (for a detailed explanation, see Bollen, 1989, pp. 439 – 446).

Measurement Models and Findings

Hacking Measurement Model. We first evaluated the hacking measurement model (see Table 2). All three of the observed indicators loaded high on the latent hacking factor ($\beta > 0.900$; $p < 0.000$); thus, we concluded that our measure of hacking was valid. The three measures reflect hacking and their correlations were reproduced by the modeled relationship. This observation was indicated by the fit indices (χ^2=1.692, 2, p<0.429; CFI=1.00; TLI=1.00; RMSEA=0.00; WRMR=0.192).[7]

Low Self-Control Measurement Models. Next, we evaluated three low self-control models through confirmatory factor analysis. A single-factor model where the twenty-four items reflected the underlying self-control latent factor (figure 1a) was not a good fit to the data (χ^2=2598.09, 77, p<0.000; CFI=0.26; TLI=0.71; RMSEA=0.22; WRMR=4.00), supporting past studies (e.g., Flora et al., 2003; Longshore et al., 2004).[8]

The second model, which included a single factor that reflected the six summed indices of the self-control subcomponents, was also a poor fit to the data (χ^2=163.60, 9, p<0.000; CFI=0.83; TLI=0.72; RMSEA=0.16).

Finally, we examined a second-order factor model, where each of the observed measures reflected the six first-order factors (Figure 1c), which in turn were reflective of a single second-order factor (e.g., Flora et al., 2003). This model was also a poor fit to the data (χ^2= 3434.94, 30, p=0.000; CFI=0.81; TLI=0.93; RMSEA=0.11; WRMR=2.01).

Therefore, we used the summed Grasmick et al. (1993) scale since none of the CFA self-control measurement models fit the data. (Note: the results of the principal component analysis and Cronbach's alpha are reported in the measurement section.) While our analysis certainly does not finalize which measure is more appropriate, it would have been imprudent to use any of the CFA models, given the poor fit in our analysis.

The Social Learning Measurement Model. The social learning model proved to be a good fit to the data (χ^2= 92.521, 40, p=0.000; CFI=0.99; TLI=0.99; RMSEA=0.04; WRMR=0.90), supporting the use of all four components (Skinner & Fream, 1997) and the measurement of the social learning process as a second-order latent factor (Akers & Lee, 1996; Lee et al., 2004). The factor loadings for the first and second-order factors are reported in Table 2. All of the factor loadings on the first-order factors from the observed variables are significant and above 0.300, indicating that observed measures reflect the four latent factors of differential association, definitions, reinforcement, and imitation. Furthermore, the factor loadings from the four first-order factors to the second-order social learning factor were significant and above 0.500.

Structural Models. We first tested whether lower levels of self-control were positively related

Table 2. Factor loadings for social learning and hacking measurement models (n=566)

Latent Factor	**Estimate**		**s.e.**	**Standardized Loading**
Computer Hacking				
Hacking 1	1.000	†		0.936
Hacking 2	1.029	***	0.027	0.961
Hacking 3	0.978	***	0.029	0.918
Social Learning Secord-order Factor				
Differential Association	**1.000**	†		**0.801**
DA 1	1.000		0.000	0.917
DA 2	1.090	***	0.029	0.984
DA 3	1.022	***	0.020	0.934
Definitions	**0.2562**	***	**0.071**	**0.622**
DEF 1	1.000	†		0.330
DEF 2	1.355	***	0.392	0.577
DEF 3	1.151	***	0.317	0.445
DEF 4	1.383	***	0.419	0.598
DEF 5	1.802	***	0.471	0.679
Reinforcement	**0.2630**	***	**0.071**	**0.597**
R1	1.000	†		0.352
R2	2.404	***	0.690	0.950
R3	2.255	***	0.549	0.881
Imitation	**0.416**	***	**0.113**	**0.722**
I1	1.000	†		0.457
I2	1.129	***	0.219	0.610
I3	1.146	***	0.304	0.674

†The path coefficient is set to one and the s.e. is not reported.

*** $p < 0.001$

to computer hacking as the general theory of crime and the past literature linking self-control to traditional crime and cybercrime would suggest (see Table 3, Model 1; Figure 3). Next, we examined whether a social learning process favoring computer hacking was positively related to computer hacking as well (see Table 3, Model 2). Furthermore, we examined whether the social learning process mediates the relationship between self-control and computer hacking (see Table 3, Model 2; Figure 4). Gottfredson and Hirschi (1990) suggested that lower levels of self-control can increase the probability of someone associating with delinquents, providing opportunities to foster more crime. Recent research has supported this link (Gibson & Wright, 2001; Higgins et

Table 3. Structural models for computer hacking

Model 1 (n=566)				Model 2 (n=566)		
Low Self-Control only				**Social Learning Added**		
Estimate s.e. β				**Estimate s.e. β**		
Measures						
Predicting Hacking						
Low Self-control	0.067***	0.019	0.268	-0.014*	0.007	-0.155
Social Learning	—	—	—	1.211***	0.113	0.995
Skill	0.785*	0.317	0.168	0.063	0.100	0.037
Female	0.487	0.395	0.090	0.460***	0.133	0.231
Age	-0.001	0.197	-0.000	0.146*	0.067	0.133
Black	0.149	0.571	0.017	0.014	0.211	0.005
Other	-0.364	0.548	-0.043	-0.291	0.205	-0.094
Employment	0.072	0.273	0.017	-0.168	0.089	-0.103
Predicting Social Learning						
Low Self-control				0.032***	0.004	0.452
Skill				0.187*	0.076	0.131
Female				-0.232**	0.086	-0.142
Age				-0.120*	0.050	-0.133
Black				-0.057	0.114	-0.022
Other				0.130	0.115	0.051
Employment				0.160*	0.072	0.120
Indirect Effect of Demographic Variables on Cyber-Deviance through Social Learning						
Low Self-control				.039***	0.006	0.423
Skill				0.226*	0.094	0.131
Female				-0.281**	0.108	-0.141
Age				-0.145*	0.061	-0.132
Black				-0.069	0.138	-0.071
Other				0.157	0.141	0.051
Employment				0.194*	0.087	0.121
Model Fit Indices						
χ^2, (df)			2.857 (10)			201.407 (104)
p-value			0.985			0.000
CFI			1.000			0.979
TLI			1.005			0.983
RMSEA			0.000			0.041
WRMR			0.230			1.101
Hacking R^2			0.101			0.781

Notes: * $p < 0.05$ ** $p < .01$ *** $p < .001$ Estimates are probit coefficients; thus, the R^2 coefficients for hacking are for the latent response variable (y*) al., 2006; Longshore et al., 2004). If the social learning process fully mediates the relationship between low-self control and computer hacking, low self-control will become non-significant when social learning is entered into the model. If social learning partially mediates the relationship, the direct effect will remain significant but attenuated.[9]

The first structural model, shown in Figure 3 and reported in Table 3, examined the direct effect of low self-control on hacking, controlling for skill, sex, age, black, other race, and employment. As predicted by the general theory of crime, low self-control had a significant, positive effect on computer hacking (β=0.268). Computer skill was the only significant control variable (β=0.168), but it had less impact than low self-control. *Thus, individuals with lower levels of self-control and higher levels of skills were more likely to hack computers.* This model was a good fit to the data (χ^2= 2.985, 10, p=0.981; CFI=1.000; TLI=1.005; RMSEA=0.000; WRMR=0.230).

When social learning was entered into the model (see Model 2 in Table 3; Figure 4), however, low self-control showed a significant, *negative* effect on hacking (β=-0.155). Individuals with lower levels of self-control were *less likely* to hack computers compared to those with higher levels of self-control. Thus, self-control flipped direction from positive to negative, indicating a suppression situation (discussed in more detail below). The social learning process favoring computer hacking had a significant, positive effect on hacking (β=0.955), as expected. In fact, it had the strongest influence on computer hacking and should be considered the most theoretically important. Those more likely to hack computers were respondents who (i) associated with computer hackers, (ii) had definitions favoring the illegal use of computers, (iii) had sources for imitation, and (iv) had their hacking behaviors socially reinforced. For the control variables, skill was no longer significant, but female and age became significant (β=0.231 and β=0.133, respectively).

The direct effects on social learning as a dependent variable are reported in Model 2 of Table 3 and shown in Figure 4. *Younger males with more computer skills and lower levels of self-control were more likely to participate in the hacker social learning process.* Low self-control had a stronger influence on who participated in a hacker social

Figure 3. Structural model for self-control on hacking

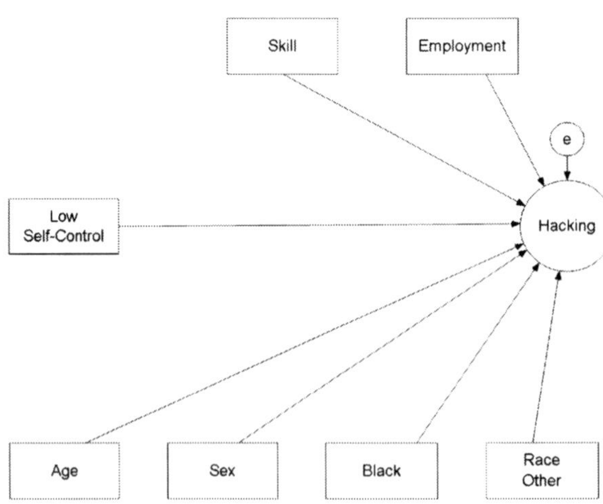

Notes: Direct paths are standardized regression coefficients.
Circles are latent factors; squares are observed variables.
Circles labeled "e" represent measurement error of the exogenous variables.
* p < .05
** p < .001

Figure 4. Structural model for direct effects and indirect effects on hacking and social learning

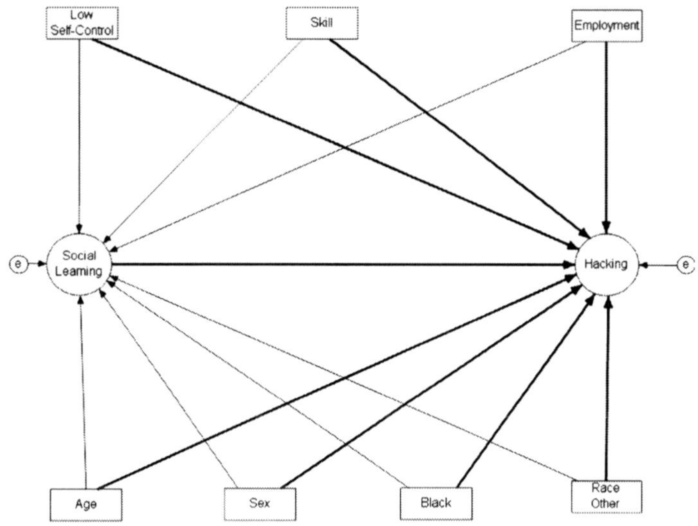

Note: Direct paths for hacking are standardized regression coefficients in bold.
Indirect paths from the variables through social learning to hacking are in parentheses.
Circles labeled "e" represent measurement error of the exogenous variables.
* p < .05 ** p < .001

learning process than did demographics (female, age, and employment) and computer skill.

As for the indirect effects, low self-control had a positive indirect effect on hacking through social learning (β=0.423). It is theoretically important to note that low self-control had a larger influence on hacking indirectly through the social learning process (β=0.423) than its direct effect (β=-.155). This observation is important since the direct effect was negative, indicating that higher levels of self-control predicted hacking, while the indirect effect was positive, illustrating that individuals with lower levels of self-control became involved in the hacker social learning process, increasing the odds of their committing computer hacks. *Thus, one can argue that lower levels of self-control are more related to computer hacking than higher levels.* Female, age, and employment also had significant indirect effects through the social learning process. *Young employed males were more likely to participate in the hacker social learning process and were, therefore, more likely to hack, thus supporting previous studies* (e.g., Jordan & Taylor, 1998).

With regard to mediation, skill was the only variable to be fully mediated by social learning. Low self-control was partially mediated, although the effect was surprising, in that the direction of the effect was reversed when social learning was entered into the model. Also, the direct effect of female and age became significant when social learning was entered into the model as well, showing an indirect effect through social learning opposite of the direct effects. *These findings imply that individuals who are not usually welcome or involved in a hacker social learning process (i.e. hacker subculture), such as females and older individuals, have to commit hacking on their own if they cannot learn techniques and definitions through the process.* Thus, they need higher levels of self-control.

Finally, employment did not show a significant direct effect in either model, but the indirect effect through social learning was significant and positive. Employment is not directly a risk factor. It only increases the odds of computer hacking if it increases their proximity to delinquent others who have definitions favoring computer hacking and who socially reinforce these types of behaviors, consistent with the literature (Staff & Uggen, 2003; Wright & Cullen, 2004).

Suppression Situation. The results from structural model 2 (Table 3) indicated suppression situations had occurred. A suppression situation results when the relationship between an independent variable (x1) and a dependent variable (y) improves when a third variable (x2) is added to the equation. This observation can often result in unexpected effects, such as an increase in explained variance of y even though one of the predictors (x_2) is not related to the dependent variable (i.e., $r\,y\,x_2 = 0.00$), or the initial sign of x_2 changes direction from positive to negative (i.e., βyx_2 is positive, but $\beta yx_2.x_1$ is negative). (For an excellent discussion, see Nickerson, 2008.)

There are several indicators of a suppression situation that have been met in this analysis (Nickerson, 2008). First, in the net suppression situation indicated in CFA Model 2, the suppressor variable self-control reversed direction from Model 1 to Model 2 ($\beta = +0.268 \rightarrow (\beta = -0.155)$ when social learning was entered in to the model. Second, the suppressed variable social learning increased its effect ($\beta = 0.834 \rightarrow \beta = 0.995$).[10] This might seem counter-intuitive because the expected direct effect of low self-control on hacking was positive; however, the suppression situation has removed the variance of those with low levels of self-control and social learning from self-control's relationship with hacking. In other words, people with low self-control are removed from the prediction of hacking by those who learn from peers, enhancing social learning's predictability of hacking. Consequently, the self-control measure flips direction because the variable now only includes those with no peer associations from which to learn hacking. *Therefore, those with lower levels of self-control and no peers to learn from are less likely to hack.*

Third, the zero-order correlations among the three main predictors—hacking, low self-control, and social learning—are all positive. All of these results indicate that a net suppressor situation had occurred (Conger, 1974; Nickerson, 2008; Paulhus, Robins, Trzesniewski, & Tracy, 2004; Tzelgov & Stern, 1978). In addition, the control variable for female also showed signs of a suppression situation (but only low self-control is discussed here). Table 4 summarizes the indicators of a suppression effect between social learning and low self control, namely a reverse in direction of the suppressor variable (low self-control) and an increase in the beta weight for the suppressed variable (social learning).[11]

To further examine this relationship, we dichotomized the low self-control measure into two groups: 0 = levels of self-control above the mean (or low self-control), and 1 = levels of self-control below the mean (i.e., high self-control). When we substituted this dummy variable for the scale measure of low self-control into the regression analysis, *our observations showed that those with high self-control were more likely to engage in*

Table 4. Indications of suppressor situation[1]

Correlations		**Direct Effects**		**Indirect Effects**	
$r_{LSC\ SL}$	$\beta_{HACK\ LSC}$	$\beta_{HACK\ LSC.SL}$	$\beta_{HACK.SL}$	$\beta_{HACK\ SL.LSC}$	$\beta_{LSC \rightarrow SL \rightarrow HACK}$
0.514***	0.173***	-0.233***	0.834***	0.971***	0.475*

Notes: The coefficients reported here exclude the control variables in the model. Thus, the relationships are between two predictors and the dependent variable hacking. A *r* denotes the zero-order correlation between variables hacking (Hack) and low self-control (LSC). β denotes the standardized regression coefficient (or beta weight). A variable following a period indicates that it is included in the regression. For example, hacking $\beta_{HACK\ LSC\ .\ SL}$ indicates the beta weight for the direct effect of low self-control on hacking, controlling for social learning. *** $p < 0.001$

hacking than those with low self-control. This indicates that the variance being removed in this suppression situation is from those with high self-control.

Furthermore, to test whether the suppression situation was simply an artifact of the data, we pulled a random sample from the dataset and re-ran the analysis, The same results were obtained.

DISCUSSION

Gottfredson and Hirschi's General Theory of Crime and Hacking

In this study, we examined whether one of the most empirically tested and supported theories in the traditional and cybercrime literature—Gottfredson and Hirschi's (1990) general theory of crime—could help explain unauthorized access of computer systems, or computer hacking. Gottfredson and Hirschi would argue that computer hacking is similar to all other forms of crime, in that cracking is a simple way to satisfy immediate gratification, caused by inadequate levels of self-control. The hacker literature is not entirely congruent with Gottfredson and Hirschi's assertions about crime, for many instances of computer hacking take skill, preparation, and a focus on long-term benefits. In addition, the hacker subculture heavily emphasizes technological mastery and learning. Thus, it was important to examine in this study whether one of the most important correlates of crime was related to computer hacking to better understand why individuals commit these forms of crime and to assess the uniqueness of computer hacking.

Model 1 (Table 3) found that lower levels of self-control were positively related to computer hacking, strongly supporting Gottfredson and Hirschi's self-control theory. Thus, it would appear that computer hackers actually have inadequate levels of self-control. This observation would be a major coup for self-control theory, considering how different computer hacking appears to be from many important aspects found in traditional crime. Model 1, however, suffered from model misspecification because it did not contain important social learning measures (see Pratt & Cullen, 2000).

When the social learning process was included in the model (see Model 2, Table 3), the findings indicated that low self-control *did not* have a direct positive effect on computer hacking anymore. Individuals with higher levels of self-control were *more* likely to hack when the social learning process is controlled for. If individuals cannot learn techniques and definitions from computer hackers, they will need higher levels of self-control to have the patience and time to spend the effort to gain computer skills and to find flaws in computer systems. Individuals with lower levels of self-control, however, were more likely to participate in the hacker social learning process, the strongest predictor of computer hacking. Thus, low self-control's positive, indirect effect through the social learning process was actually stronger than its negative direct effect.

One could interpret these findings as providing "partial support" for Gottfredson and Hirschi's theory since low levels of self-control predict computer hacking better than higher levels of self-control. This conclusion, however, would overlook many fundamental assumptions and arguments made by the general theory of crime. Gottfredson and Hirschi (1990, p. 18) argued that crime is simple and that anyone can commit the offense if they so choose to. In addition, they wrote, "There is nothing in crime that requires the transmission of values or the support of other people … [or] the transmission of skills, or techniques, or knowledge from other people" (Gottfredson & Hirschi, 1990, p. 151). Our study findings contradict these views. Participating in the hacker social learning process was the strongest predictor of computer hacking. To commit computer hacking acts, most individuals needed to associate with computer hackers, learn hacker values, and be socially reinforced in

Figure 5. Correlation matrix

	Hack 1	Hack 2	Hack 3	DA 1	DA 2	DA 3	DEF 1	DEF 2	DEF 3	DEF 4	DEF 5	RE 1	RE 2	RE 3	I 1	I 2	I 3	LSC	Black	Race Other	Skill	Female	Age
Hack 1	1.000																						
Hack 2	0.799**	1.000																					
Hack 3	0.662**	0.673**	1.000																				
DA 1	0.387**	0.397**	0.321**	1.000																			
DA 2	0.379**	0.425**	0.314**	0.757**	1.000																		
DA 3	0.394**	0.369**	0.378**	0.660**	0.780**	1.000																	
DEF 1	0.047	0.088*	0.017	0.059	0.105*	0.125**	1.000																
DEF 2	0.196**	0.157**	0.169**	0.182**	0.162**	0.177**	0.237**	1.000															
DEF 3	0.108*	0.111**	0.095*	0.136**	0.079	0.101*	0.145**	0.284**	1.000														
DEF 4	0.187**	0.191**	0.137**	0.202**	0.191**	0.188**	0.152**	0.217**	0.156**	1.000													
DEF 5	0.175**	0.157**	0.178**	0.177**	0.180**	0.230**	0.211**	0.281**	0.243**	0.312**	1.000												
RE 1	0.084*	0.064	0.142**	0.138**	0.151**	0.160**	-0.007	-0.002	0.045	-0.030	0.111**	1.000											
RE 2	0.198**	0.199**	0.209**	0.137**	0.165**	0.154**	0.110**	0.136**	0.141**	0.103*	0.163**	0.155**	1.000										
RE 3	0.182**	0.155**	0.153**	0.137**	0.106*	0.153**	0.095*	0.065	0.101*	0.093*	0.153**	0.194**	0.658**	1.000									
I 1	0.171**	0.115**	0.066	00.134**	0.140**	0.132**	0.057	0.174**	0.114**	0.088*	0.149**	0.097*	0.086*	0.115**	1.000								
I 2	0.250**	0.224**	0.175**	0.276**	0.291**	0.234**	-0.065	0.059	0.028	0.127**	0.164**	0.080	0.093*	0.113**	0.475**	1.000							
I 3	0.212**	0.205**	0.214**	0.206**	0.232**	0.237**	-0.006	0.079	0.064	0.206**	0.241**	0.093*	0.123**	0.119**	0.228**	0.323**	1.000						
LSC	0.163**	0.138**	0.163**	0.263**	0.217**	0.212**	0.187**	0.204**	0.129**	0.218**	0.300**	0.069	0.114**	0.058	0.209**	0.277**	0.167**	1.000					
Black	-0.018	-0.025	-0.025	-0.049	-0.047	-0.059	-0.068	-0.092*	-0.040	-0.002	-0.099*	0.034	0.012	0.018	-0.009	-0.086*	0.050	-0.100*	1.000				
Race Other	-0.044	-0.034	-0.030	-0.035	-0.002	-0.004	0.054	0.124**	0.038	-0.052	0.011	0.123**	0.098*	0.092*	0.081	0.041	-0.036	0.009	-0.122**	1.000			
Skill	0.102*	0.141**	0.074	0.076	0.038	0.069	0.047	0.039	0.037	0.069	0.107*	0.074	0.079	0.071	0.040	0.119**	0.244**	0.121**	-0.035	-0.086*	1.000		
Female	-0.024	-0.023	-0.054	-0.069	-0.085*	-0.125**	-0.131**	-0.106*	-0.076	-0.126**	-0.178**	-0.094*	-0.100*	-0.138**	-0.126**	-0.201**	-0.171**	-0.299**	0.074	0.004	-0.250**	1.000	
Age	-0.022	-0.005	-0.028	-0.112**	-0.085*	-0.065	-0.044	-0.071	0.021	-0.082*	-0.064	0.165**	0.023	0.085*	0.018	-0.101*	-0.053	-0.168**	0.080	0.014	0.088*	-0.169**	1.000

this domain. If individuals did not associate with other hackers to learn techniques and Computer Underground values, they actually needed higher levels of self-control to be able to learn how to commit the offense themselves.

The finding that higher levels of self-control are related to computer hacking, after controlling for the social learning process, is antithetical to self-control theory. According to control theories, everyone has the same motivation to commit crime, including hacking. Individuals with low self-control cannot resist the temptation. "[H]igh self-control effectively reduces the possibility of crime; that is, those possessing it will be substantially less likely at all periods of life to engage in criminal acts" (Gottfredson and Hirschi, 1990, p. 89). Although we found that lower self-control levels were more of a risk factor than higher self-control levels regarding hacking acts, the fact remains that higher levels of self-control still had a positive direct effect on computer hacking. Although it logically makes sense why individuals would need higher levels of self-control to commit certain forms of computer hacking (Holt & Kilger, 2008, p. 76), Gottfredson and Hirschi would argue that individuals with high levels of self-control simply do not commit crime.

Study Implications Regarding White-Collar Crime and Hacking

The latter study finding has implications for both hacking and certain forms of white-collar crime. Low self-control is better at explaining simpler forms of white-collar crime (e.g., employee theft) and cybercrime (e.g., software piracy), thus having more similarities with traditional crime (Higgins & Makin, 2004; Langton et al., 2006). However, its ability to explain white-collar crime and cybercrime requiring specific skills and knowledge is much poorer, *supporting arguments that have been made for twenty years that the social learning process and an organization's culture are more important* (Benson & Simpson, 2009).

The suppressor effect may manifest itself in other forms of white-collar crime, especially crimes requiring a degree of difficulty and investment. Thus, our analyses appear to be supportive of Walters' (2002) argument that white-collar criminals can be divided by their levels of self-control.

Study Implications Regarding Hacker Typologies

In addition, our study findings vindicate the focus in the qualitative literature on classifying hackers into specific types (Holt & Kilger, 2008; Taylor et al., 2006). Hackers are not a homogeneous group, as indicated by our findings, for there are hackers with low and high levels of self-control. Though through our analyses, we cannot assess which typologies in the hacking literature are correct, we can suggest that these typologies need to take into consideration a person's level of self-control. Future testing examining whether self-control and social learning predict different categories of hacking would provide some useful insights. In addition, it would be fruitful to know if hackers with higher levels of self-control have more motivation, or possibly different motivations, to hack computers, relative to those with lower levels of self-control. Also, if their motivations do not differ, why do the higher levels of self-control not act as preventative measures?

CONCLUSION

To conclude, our analyses indicate that computer hacking is, in fact, not simply another form of crime or juvenile delinquency. Yar (2005a) posed an important question in the title of his recent article, "Computer hacking: Just another form of juvenile delinquency?" In his research, Yar found that computer hacking was closely associated with teenagers by all groups concerned about on-line security. Although we do not disagree with Yar's study findings examining *perceptions*, our study examining *behavior* does not find that computer hacking is just another form of juvenile delinquency. Although much of computer hacking could be explained in our study by the social learning process and low levels of self-control, there were still individuals who committed computer hacking with higher levels of self-control. This observation is substantively different from the prevalent conclusions published in the juvenile delinquency literature, or even in the criminological literature outside of white-collar crime. In short, our findings suggest that hacking is truly a unique behavior, different from most other crimes, and deserving of specialized attention from scholars. Future research on how hacking is correlated with other forms of computer crime and traditional deviance will provide more insights into the empirical relationship between computer hacking and other forms of crime.

While the suppression situation reported in our study findings has important implications, the results must be replicated in other studies. There is ongoing debate among scholars about the relevance of such findings. Some scholars, for example, dismiss the appearance of suppressor situations as artifacts of the data or study design (see Paulhus et al., 2004). While we are confident that the net suppressor situation is real in our data, replication with another dataset, always important for structural equation models, can only confirm the suppression situation involving self-control, female, age and social learning as generalizable. It would be especially important to include the same measures of the theories on different cybercrime outcomes, such as software piracy or deploying malicious software.

LIMITATIONS OF PRESENT STUDY

Several limitations within our study should be noted. First, we measured self-control only with the Grasmick et al. scale. Gottfredson and Hirschi (1993) argued that behavioral measures are more valid, and that low self-control can influence the survey process (Piquero et al., 2000). Studies, however, have found that self-control is a significant predictor of crime regardless of how it is operationalized (Higgins et al., 2008; Pratt & Cullen, 2000; Tittle et al., 2003). It is possible that this assertion is not true for the prediction of hacking. Therefore, future tests involving multiple measures of self-control, including behavioral measures, are warranted.

Second, the generalizability of our study findings could be questioned since we utilized a cross-sectional college sample at one university. College samples, however, are commonly used in the criminological literature (see Payne & Chappell, 2008), especially within the cybercrime literature (e.g., Buzzell et al., 2006; Higgins et al., 2008). In addition, Gottfredson and Hirschi (1990) argue that cross-sectional studies are appropriate for tests of self-control theory since self-control is stable. However, we only sampled at one university; consequently, future studies using different samples would help support our findings.

Third, we, presumably, studied mostly minor forms of computer hacking. This likelihood does not appear problematic for our study, however, since lower levels of self-control should, theoretically, predict minor forms of hacking requiring fewer computer skills better than more complex computer hacking exploits. Thus, including more skilled hackers within a study sample would probably only decrease the effect of low self-control on computer hacking, but increase the influence of higher levels of self-control.

Finally, most of our measures for reinforcement within the social learning process focused on social aspects and ignored legal and financial ramifications. This reality, however, would probably only increase the power of the social learning process in predicting computer hacking and decrease the influence of self-control.

REFERENCES

Akers, R. L. (1991). Self-control theory as a general theory of crime. *Journal of Quantitative Criminology*, *7*, 201–211. doi:10.1007/BF01268629

Akers, R. L. (1998). *Social learning and social structure: A general theory of crime and deviance*. Boston: Northeastern University Press.

Akers, R. L., & Jensen, G. F. (2006). The empirical status of social learning theory of crime and deviance: The past, present, and future . In Cullen, F. T., Wright, J. P., & Blevins, K. R. (Eds.), *Taking stock: The status of criminological theory*. New Brunswick, NJ: Transaction Publishers.

Akers, R. L., & Lee, G. (1996). A longitudinal test of social learning theory: Adolescent smoking. *Journal of Drug Issues*, *26*, 317–343.

Arneklev, B. J., Grasmick, H. G., Tittle, C. R., & Bursik, R. J. (1993). Low self-control and imprudent behavior. *Journal of Quantitative Criminology*, *9*, 225–247. doi:10.1007/BF01064461

Benson, M. L., & Moore, E. (1992). Are white-collar and common offenders the same? An empirical and theoretical critique of a recently proposed general theory of crime. *Journal of Research in Crime and Delinquency*, *29*, 251–272. doi:10.1177/0022427892029003001

Benson, M. L., & Simpson, S. S. (2009). *White collar crime: An opportunity perspective*. Oxford, UK: Taylor & Francis.

Beveren, J. V. (2001). A conceptual model of hacker development and motivations. *The Journal of Business*, *1*, 1–9.

Bollen, K. A. (1989). *Structural equations with latent variables*. New York: Wiley.

Bollen, K. A., & Lennox, R. (1991). Conventional wisdom on measurement: a structural equation perspective. *Psychological Bulletin*, *110*, 305–314. doi:10.1037/0033-2909.110.2.305

Bollen, K. A., & Ting, T. (2000). A tetrad test for causal indicators. *Psychological Methods*, *15*, 3–22. doi:10.1037/1082-989X.5.1.3

Bossler, A. M., & Holt, T. J. (2009). On-line activities, guardianship, and malware infection: An examination of routine activities theory. *International Journal of Cyber Criminology*, *3*, 400–420.

Buzzell, T., Foss, D., & Middleton, Z. (2006). Explaining use of online pornography: A test of self-control theory and opportunities for deviance. *Journal of Criminal Justice and Popular Culture*, *13*, 96–116.

Chisea, R., Ducci, D., & Ciappi, S. (2008). *Profiling hackers: The science of criminal profiling as applied to the world of hacking*. Boca Raton, FL: Auerbach Publications. doi:10.1201/9781420086942

Cohen, L. E., & Felson, M. (1979). Social change and crime rate trends: A routine activityapproach. *American Sociological Review*, *44*, 588–608. doi:10.2307/2094589

Coleman, E. G., & Golub, A. (2008). Hacker practice: Moral genres and the cultural articulation of liberalism. *Anthropological Theory*, *8*, 255–277. doi:10.1177/1463499608093814

Conger, A. J. (1974). A revised definition for suppressor variables: A guide to their identification and interpretation. *Educational and Psychological Measurement*, *34*, 35–46. doi:10.1177/001316447403400105

Cronan, T. P., Foltz, C. B., & Jones, T. W. (2006). Piracy, computer crime, and IS misuse at the university. *Communications of the ACM*, *49*, 85–90. doi:10.1145/1132469.1132472

Curry, G. D., & Decker, S. H. (2007). *Confronting gangs: Crime and community* (2nd ed.). Oxford, UK: Oxford University Press.

Denning, D. (1998). *Information warfare and security*. Reading, MA: Addison-Wesley.

Finney, S. J., & DiStefano, C. (2006). Nonnormal and categorical data . In Hancock, G. R., & Mueller, R. O. (Eds.), *Structural equation modeling: A second course*. Greenwhich, CT: Information Age Publishing.

Flora, D. B., Finkel, E. J., & Foshee, V. A. (2003). Higher order factor structure of a self-control test: Evidence from confirmatory factor analysis with polychoric correlations. *Educational and Psychological Measurement*, *63*, 112–127. doi:10.1177/0013164402239320

Furnell, S. (2002). *Cybercrime: Vandalizing the information society*. Boston, MA: Addison-Wesley.

Geis, G. (2000). On the absence of self-control as the basis for a general theory of crime: A critique. *Theoretical Criminology*, *4*, 35–53. doi:10.1177/1362480600004001002

Gibbs, J. J., & Giever, D. M. (1995). Self-control and its manifestations among university students: An empirical test of Gottfredson and Hirschi's general theory. *Justice Quarterly*, *12*, 231–255. doi:10.1080/07418829500092661

Gibson, C., & Wright, J. (2001). Low self-control and coworker delinquency: A research note. *Journal of Criminal Justice*, *29*, 483–492. doi:10.1016/S0047-2352(01)00111-8

Gordon, S. (1994). The generic virus writer. In *Proceedings of the International Virus Bulletin Conference*. Jersey, Channel Islands, pp.121-138.

Gordon, S. (2000). *Virus writers: The end of innocence*? Retrieved 2000 from http://www.research.ibm.com/antivirus/SciPapers/VB2000SG.pdf

Gordon, S., & Ma, Q. (2003). *Convergence of virus writers and hackers: Fact or fantasy*. Cupertine, CA: Symantec Security White paper.

Gottfredson, M. R., & Hirschi, T. (1990). *A general theory of crime*. Stanford, CA: Stanford University Press.

Grabosky, P. N. (2001). Virtual criminality: Old wine in new bottles? *Social & Legal Studies*, *10*, 243–249.

Grasmick, H. G., Tittle, C. R., Bursik, R. J., & Arneklev, B. J. (1993). Testing the core empirical implications of Gottfredson and Hirschi's general theory. *Journal of Research in Crime and Delinquency*, *35*, 42–72.

Higgins, G. E. (2005). Can low self-control help with the understanding of the software piracy problem? *Deviant Behavior*, *26*, 1–24. doi:10.1080/01639620490497947

Higgins, G. E. (2006). Gender differences in software piracy: The mediating roles of self-control theory and social learning theory. *Journal of Economic Crime Management*, *4*, 1–30.

Higgins, G. E. (2007). Digital piracy, self-control theory, and rational choice: An examination of the role of value. *International Journal of Cyber Criminology*, *1*, 33–55.

Higgins, G. E., Fell, B. D., & Wilson, A. L. (2006). Digital piracy: Assessing the contributions of an integrated self-control theory and social learning theory using structural equation modeling. *Criminal Justice Studies*, *19*, 3–22. doi:10.1080/14786010600615934

Higgins, G. E., Fell, B. D., & Wilson, A. L. (2007). Low self-control and social learning in understanding students' intentions to pirate movies in the United States. *Social Science Computer Review*, *25*, 339–357. doi:10.1177/0894439307299934

Higgins, G. E., & Makin, D. A. (2004a). Self-control, deviant peers, and software piracy. *Psychological Reports*, *95*, 921–931. doi:10.2466/PR0.95.7.921-931

Higgins, G. E., & Makin, D. A. (2004b). Does social learning theory condition the effects of low self-control on college students' software piracy? *Journal of Economic Crime Management*, *2*, 1–22.

Higgins, G. E., & Wilson, A. L. (2006). Low self-control, moral beliefs, and social learning theory in university students' intentions to pirate software. *Security Journal*, *19*, 75–92. doi:10.1057/palgrave.sj.8350002

Higgins, G. E., Wolfe, S. E., & Marcum, C. (2008). Digital piracy: An examination of three measurements of self-control. *Deviant Behavior*, *29*, 440–460. doi:10.1080/01639620701598023

Hinduja, S. (2001). Correlates of Internet software piracy. *Journal of Contemporary Criminal Justice*, *17*(4), 369–382. doi:10.1177/1043986201017004006

Hirschi, T., & Gottfredson, M. R. (1994). The generality of deviance . In Hirschi, T., & Gottfredson, M. R. (Eds.), *Generality of deviance* (pp. 1–22). New Brunswick, NJ: Transaction.

Hirschi, T., & Gottfredson, M. R. (2000). In defense of self-control. *Theoretical Criminology*, *4*, 55–69. doi:10.1177/1362480600004001003

Hollinger, R. C. (1992). Crime by computer: Correlates of software piracy and unauthorized account access. *Security Journal*, *2*, 2–12.

Holt, T. J. (2007). Subcultural evolution? Examining the influence of on- and off-line experiences on deviant subcultures. *Deviant Behavior*, *28*, 171–198. doi:10.1080/01639620601131065

Holt, T. J. (2009). Lone hacks or group: Examining the social organization of computer hackers . In Schmalleger, F. J., & Pittaro, M. (Eds.), *Crimes of the Internet*. Upper Saddle River, NJ: Prentice Hall.

Holt, T. J., & Bossler, A. M. (2009). Examining the applicability of lifestyle-routine activities theory for cybercrime victimization. *Deviant Behavior*, *30*, 1–25. doi:10.1080/01639620701876577

Holt, T. J., & Kilger, M. (2008). *Techcrafters and makecrafters: A comparison of two populations of hackers*. 2008 WOMBAT Workshop on Information Security Threats Data Collection and Sharing. Pp. 67-78.

Hu, L., & Bentler, P. M. (1999). Cutoff criteria for fit indexes in covariance structure analysis: Conventional criteria versus new alternatives. *Structural Equation Modeling*, *6*, 1–55. doi:10.1080/10705519909540118

Jordan, T., & Taylor, P. (1998). A sociology of hackers. *The Sociological Review*, *46*, 757–780. doi:10.1111/1467-954X.00139

Kline, R. B. (2005). *Principles and practice of structural equation modeling*. New York: The Guilford Press.

Landreth, B. (1985). *Out of the inner circle: A hacker's guide to computer security*. Bellevue, WA: Microsoft Press.

Langton, L., Piquero, N. L., & Hollinger, R. C. (2006). An empirical test of the relationship between employee theft and self-control. *Deviant Behavior*, *27*, 537–565. doi:10.1080/01639620600781548

Lee, G., Akers, R. L., & Borg, M. J. (2004). Social learning and structural factors in adolescent substance use. *Western Criminology Review*, *5*, 17–34.

Longshore, D., Chang, E., Hsieh, S. C., & Messina, N. (2004). Self-control and social bonds: A combined control perspective on deviance. *Crime and Delinquency*, *50*, 542–564. doi:10.1177/0011128703260684

Miller, D., & Slater, D. (2000). *The Internet: An ethnographic approach*. New York, NY: Berg.

Muthén, L. K., & Muthén, B. O. (2007). *Mplus user's guide* (4th ed.). Los Angeles, CA: Muthén & Muthén.

Nickerson, C. (2008). Mutual Suppression: Comment on Paulhus et al. (2004). *Multivariate Behavioral Research, 43*, 556–563. doi:10.1080/00273170802490640

Paulhus, D. L., Robins, R. W., Trzesniewski, K. H., & Tracy, J. L. (2004). Two replicable suppressor situations in personality research. *Multivariate Behavioral Research, 39*, 303–328. doi:10.1207/s15327906mbr3902_7

Payne, B. K., & Chappell, A. T. (2008). Using student samples in criminological. research. *Journal of Criminal Justice Education, 19*, 177–194. doi:10.1080/10511250802137226

Piquero, A., & Tibbetts, S. (1996). Specifying the direct and indirect effects of low self control and situational factors in offenders' decision making: Toward a more complete model of rational offending. *Justice Quarterly, 13*, 481–510. doi:10.1080/07418829600093061

Piquero, A. R., MacIntosh, R., & Hickman, M. (2000). Does self-control affect survey response? Applying exploratory, confirmatory, and item response theory analysis to Grasmick et al.'s self-control scale. *Criminology, 38*, 897–929. doi:10.1111/j.1745-9125.2000.tb00910.x

Piquero, A. R., & Rosay, A. B. (1998). The reliability and validity of Grasmick et al.'s self-control scale. A comment on Longshore et al. *Criminology, 36*, 157–174. doi:10.1111/j.1745-9125.1998.tb01244.x

Pratt, T. C., & Cullen, F. T. (2000). The empirical status of Gottfredson and Hirschi's general theory of crime: A meta-analysis. *Criminology, 38*, 931–964. doi:10.1111/j.1745-9125.2000.tb00911.x

Primoratz, I. (2004). *Terrorism: The philosophical issues*. New York: Palgrave Macmillan.

Reed, G. E., & Yeager, P. C. (1996). Organizational offending and neoclassical criminology: Challenging the reach of A General Theory of Crime . *Criminology, 34*, 357–382. doi:10.1111/j.1745-9125.1996.tb01211.x

Richardson, R. (2008). *CSI computer crime and security survey.* Retrieved December 16, 2009, from http://www.cse.msstate.edu/~cse2v3/readings/CSIsurvey2008.pdf

Rogers, M., Smoak, N. D., & Liu, J. (2006). Self-reported deviant computer behavior: A big-5, moral choice, and manipulative exploitive behavior analysis. *Deviant Behavior, 27*, 245–268. doi:10.1080/01639620600605333

Rogers, M. K. (2001). A social learning theory and moral disengagement analysis of criminal computer behavior: An exploratory study. (PhD dissertation), University of Manitoba, Canada.

Schell, B. H., Dodge, J. L., & Moutsatsos, S. S. (2002). *The hacking of America: Who's doing it, why, and how*. Westport, CT: Quorum Books.

Sijtsma, K. (2009). On the use, misuse, and the very limited usefulness of Cronbach's alpha. *Psychometrika, 1*, 107–120. doi:10.1007/s11336-008-9101-0

Simpson, S. S., & Piquero, N. L. (2002). Low self-control, organizational theory, and corporate crime. *Law & Society Review, 36*, 509–548. doi:10.2307/1512161

Skinner, W. F., & Fream, A. M. (1997). A social learning theory analysis of computer crime among college students. *Journal of Research in Crime and Delinquency, 34*, 495–518. doi:10.1177/0022427897034004005

Staff, J., & Uggen, C. (2003). The fruits of good work: Early work experiences and adolescent deviance. *Journal of Research in Crime and Delinquency, 40*, 263–290. doi:10.1177/0022427803253799

Taylor, P. (1999). *Hackers: Crime in the digital sublime*. London, UK: Routledge. doi:10.4324/9780203201503

Taylor, R. W., Caeti, T. J., Loper, D. K., Fritsch, E. J., & Liederbach, J. (2006). *Digital crime and digital terrorism*. Upper Saddle River, NJ: Pearson.

Thomas, D. (2002). *Hacker culture*. Minneapolis, MN: University of Minnesota Press.

Tittle, C. R., Ward, D. A., & Grasmick, H. G. (2003). Self-control and crime/deviance: Cognitive vs. behavioral measures. *Journal of Quantitative Criminology, 19*, 333–365. doi:10.1023/B:JOQC.0000005439.45614.24

Turgeman-Goldschmidt, O. (2005). Hacker's accounts: Hacking as a social entertainment. *Social Science Computer Review, 23*, 8–23. doi:10.1177/0894439304271529

Tzelgov, J., & Stern, I. (1978). Relationships between variables in three variable linear regression and the concept of suppressor. *Educational and Psychological Measurement, 38*, 325–335. doi:10.1177/001316447803800213

Wall, D. S. (2005). The Internet as a conduit for criminal activity . In Pattavina, A. (Ed.), *Information technology and the criminal justice system* (pp. 78–94). Thousand Oaks, CA: Sage.

Wall, D. S. (2008). Cybercrime, media, and insecurity: The shaping of public perceptions of cybercrime. *International Review of Law Computers & Technology, 22*, 45–63. doi:10.1080/13600860801924907

Walters, G. D. (2002). *Criminal belief systems: An integrated-interactive theory of lifestyles*. Westport, CT: Greenwood Publishing Group.

Wilson, B., & Atkinson, M. (2005). Rave and straightedge, the virtual and the real: Exploring online and offline experiences in Canadian youth subcultures. *Youth & Society, 36*, 276–311. doi:10.1177/0044118X03260498

Wright, J. P., & Cullen, F. T. (2004). Employment, peers, and life-course transitions. *Justice Quarterly, 21*, 183–205. doi:10.1080/07418820400095781

Yar, M. (2005a). Computer hacking: Just another case of juvenile delinquency? *The Howard Journal, 44*, 387–399. doi:10.1111/j.1468-2311.2005.00383.x

Yar, M. (2005b). The novelty of "cybercrime": An assessment in light of routine activity theory. *European Journal of Criminology, 2*, 407–427. doi:10.1177/147737080556056

ENDNOTES

1 Hackers, as defined by the older hacker ethics, do not accept this newer connotation of the term and refer to individuals who abuse computer systems for gain as "crackers" (Taylor, 1999). We used the term "hacker" rather than "cracker" to be consistent with the extant literature. In addition, we agree with Coleman and Golub (2008) that it is inappropriate to represent hackers as simply either visionaries or sinister devils. As the discussion below will illustrate, "hacker" can refer to many different groups. Therefore, it is better to use the same term to refer to similar behaviors, even if intentions and ethics may vary.

2 It is beyond the scope of this paper to detail the extensive discussions regarding hacker categories The examples provided are given in order to illustrate that hacker categorization is an important topic in the literature and that they normally focus on either intent or computer proficiency. However, many other

categorizations exist beyond white/black/grey hats and makecrafters/techcrafters. For example, Hollinger (1988) categorized hackers as pirates, browsers, and crackers. Based on access to resources, enculturation in the hacker subculture, and skill, Taylor et al. (2006) created the categories of old school, bedroom hackers, and internet hackers.

3 We return to discussing membership fluidity, and more importantly the strength of hacker associations, in our discussion of social learning in our methods section.

4 The applicability of self-control theory for white-collar crime is relevant for this paper because computer hacking can be considered a white-collar crime, regardless of whether one uses an offense-based or offender-based definition (see Benson & Simpson, 2009, for further discussion on these definitions). Higgins and Wilson (2006) conclude that software piracy can be considered a form of white-collar crime because its characteristics are congruent with an offense-based definition of white-collar crime. Computer hacking has these same characteristics as well and can therefore be considered a white-collar crime if defined by the offense. Many hacking crimes involve disgruntled employees or ex-employees (i.e. internals) who abuse their privileges and knowledge regarding the employer's computer systems. Thus, a majority of computer hacking can also be considered white-collar crime by an offender-based definition.

5 Certainly these three hacking measures did not exhaust all possible hacking behaviors. The latent factor therefore indicated an underlying propensity to hack someone else's computer. For example, we did not specifically ask about using Trojan horses or other malware to access others' computers. Skinner and Fream (1997), however, could not examine virus writing individually because it was too rare in their sample. When we evaluated the hacking latent factor as a measurement model, it indicated a good fit to the data (see results below).

6 There are general guidelines to evaluate the fit indices. The model chi-square should be nonsignificant, indicating that the hypothesized model is *not* significantly different from a perfectly fitting model. For a good fit in this case, the p-value should be greater than 0.05. The chi-square fit statistic can lead to an erroneous rejection of the model, especially in large samples because the chi-square test will be more sensitive to small model differences (Bollen, 1989; Kline, 2005, p. 135-137). Thus, researchers consider the chi-square statistic in relation to sample size and other fit indices. CFI and TLI values above .90 indicate a reasonably good fit (Bollen, 1989). A RMSEA less than or equal to 0.05 indicates a close fit, between 0.06 and 0.10 indicates a reasonable fit, and greater than 0.10 indicates a poor fit (Hu & Bentler, 1999). The WRMR, specific to weighted least squares analysis, should be below 1.00; however, there is as yet no consensus on what signifies a good fit (Finney & DiStefano, 2006).

7 We correlated computer skill with the latent hacking variable to see whether there was any issue with multi-collinearity. The correlation between skill and hacking was significant, but low ($r = 0.19$).

8 Due to space limitations and because the models were not a good fit to the data, we do not provide the full results of the analysis.

9 The following question might be posed by readers: "Why are they examining whether social learning can mediate the relationship between self-control and computer hacking rather than examining whether it conditions or moderates the relationship?" Although research has indicated that definitions and differential associations condition the effect of self-control on digital piracy (Higgins &

Makin, 2004), software piracy (Higgins & Makin, 2004) and movie piracy (Higgins et al., 2007), z-tests comparing the regression coefficients between subsamples do not support these conclusions. Thus, because self-control has not been empirically linked with computer hacking, unlike the extensive research illustrating that self-control is related to various forms of digital piracy, it seems prudent to first examine the direct effects of self-control and social learning on computer hacking, followed by an examination of the indirect effects, before future research explores what variables can possibly condition these relationships.

[10] We evaluated a structural model with social learning and the control variables and without self-control. This showed that the beta weight for social learning increases when self-control is entered into the model. The results of the social learning model only are omitted due to space limitations.

[11] The results of the models conform to Nickerson's (2008, p. 558) criteria for suppression; namely βyx_2 is positive; $\beta yx_1 > \beta yx_2$ and $rx_1x_2 > \beta yx_2/\beta yx_1$ where x_1 (social learning in this analysis) is the suppressed variable and x_2 (self-control) is the suppressor variable.

Chapter 4
Micro-Frauds:
Virtual Robberies, Stings and Scams in the Information Age

David. S. Wall
University of Durham, UK

ABSTRACT

During the past two decades, network technologies have shaped just about every aspect of our lives, not least the ways by which we are now victimized. From the criminal's point of view, networked technologies are a gift. The technologies act as a force multiplier of grand proportions, providing individual criminals with personal access to an entirely new field of 'distanciated' victims across a global span. So effective is this multiplier effect, there is no longer the compulsion to commit highly visible and risky multi-million-dollar robberies when new technologies enable offenders to commit multi-million-dollar thefts from the comfort of their own home, with a relatively high yield and little risk to themselves. From a Criminological perspective, network technologies have effectively democratized fraud. Once a 'crime of the powerful (Sutherland, 1949; Pearce, 1976; Weisburd, et al., 1991; Tombs and Whyte, 2003) that was committed by offenders who abused their privileged position in society, fraud can now be committed by all with access to the internet. This illustration highlights the way that computers can now be used to commit crimes, and this chapter will specifically focus upon the different ways that offenders can use networked computers to assist them in performing deceptions upon individual or corporate victims in to obtain an informational or pecuniary advantage.

INTRODUCTION

A deliberate distinction is made here between *crimes using computers,* such as frauds, *crimes against computers*, where computers themselves are the focus of attack, and *crimes in computers*, where their content is exploited. These latter two groups of cybercrimes are discussed elsewhere (see, for example, Wall, 2007: 45-47, and chs. 4 & 5).

DOI: 10.4018/978-1-61692-805-6.ch004

The most common use of computers for criminal gain is to fraudulently appropriate informational goods, not just money. For the purposes of this discussion, the term 'micro-fraud' is used intentionally, this is because most of the victimizations are not only informational, but also networked and globalised. They also tend to be individually small in impact, but so numerous that they only become significant in their aggregate (Wall, 2007). Conceptually, micro-frauds are those online frauds that are deemed to be too small to be acted upon and which are either written off by victims (typically banks) or not large enough to be investigated by policing agencies. These qualities distinguish the micro-fraud from the larger frauds that also take place online and which tend to capture a disproportionate amount of media attention – even if it is mainly because of their 'infotainment' value (Levi, 2006: 1037). Yet, these larger frauds are relatively small in number when placed against a backdrop of the sheer volume of online transactions. Micro-frauds are the opposite; they are highly numerous and relatively invisible. As a consequence, their *de minimis* quality stimulates a series of interesting criminal justice debates, not the least because micro-frauds tend to be resolved to satisfy private (business or personal) rather than public interests.

The purpose of this chapter is, therefore, to map out online fraud in terms of its distinctive qualities and to outline any changes that have taken place over time. Part one explores the *virtual bank robbery*, in which offenders exploit financial management systems online, mainly banking and billing. Part two looks at the *virtual sting* and the way that offenders use the Internet to exploit system deficiencies to defraud businesses. Part three focuses on the *virtual scam,* defined as the techniques by which individuals are 'socially engineered' into parting with their money. The final part discusses the prevalence of micro-fraud and some of the issues arising for criminal justice systems and agencies.

PART ONE: THE VIRTUAL BANK ROBBERY

As the Internet has become a popular means by which individuals and organizations manage their financial affairs, financial and billing systems have increasingly become exploited as targets for criminal opportunity. Fraudsters have for some time used the Internet to defraud banks, build up false identities, open accounts, and then run them to build up credit ratings to obtain personal loans that are subsequently defaulted upon. Electronic banking is also used to launder money and to turn 'dirty money' into clean money by obscuring its origins through quick transfer from one bank to another and across jurisdictions. Although easy in principal, it is nevertheless quite hard in practice to deceive banking security checks, so offenders will weigh-up the risks of being caught (or prevented) against opportunities. However, "criminals will go to wherever the easiest target is" (Cards International, 2003), so fraudsters will seek out system weaknesses, which tend to lie at the input and output stages. Although not always easy to separate in practice, *input fraud*, or identity theft, is where fraudsters obtain personal or financial information that can give them illegal access to finance [Note: input frauds are discussed elsewhere; see, for example, Wall, 2007; Finch, 2002; Finch & Fafinski, 2010)]. *Output frauds* are where access to credit, usually credit cards, is used to fraudulently obtain goods, services or money.

From the earliest days of e-commerce, online retailers have fallen victim to fraudsters who have obtained their goods by deception, either by supplying false payment details or by using a false address to have goods sent to. During the early days of e-commerce, personal cheques and bank drafts were the focus of online frauds, simply because they were the preferred methods of payment at the time; but they were quickly surpassed by credit cards when online credit card payment facilities became more popular and practical. Although third-party escrowed Internet payment systems, such as PayPal and Mondex, have emerged as intermediaries, most payments are still made by Credit or Debit Cards, with the former being favoured because of the issuing bank's guarantee.

The Internet's virtual shop window offers many opportunities for payment (or output) fraud. Goods and services can be obtained deceptively by using genuine credit cards that have been obtained legitimately with fraudulent information; for example, via identity theft or account take-over. Alternatively, they can be obtained by using counterfeit cards created from stolen information bought off the Internet, or usually, by just using the information directly in less secure jurisdictions. Counterfeit card details can be generated by software programmes like CreditMaster 4.0, which used to be readily available via the Internet. For a number of years, CreditMaster and other similar programmes were used to generate strings of valid credit card numbers for use in transactions, mainly for the purchase of mobile phone airtime (Kravetz, 2002). Important to note here is that while the counterfeit numbers were generated by downloaded programmes obtained online, the Internet was not usually the means by which the transaction took place. The counterfeit card transactions tended to take place using mobile phone systems requiring only the card number. The introduction of additional card validation codes, such as the CVC2 (the 3 digit number on the back of credit cards), dramatically reduced the value of card number generators and has rendered them fairly worthless today. The illegal 'carding websites' that once existed to provide cloned credit cards along with their validation codes, such as 'carderplanet' and 'shadowcrew' (BBC, 2005a), are no longer in existence.

If a credit card cannot be counterfeited, then it can likely be cloned. The information needed to clone a credit card can be obtained either by 'skimming' the card (using an illicit card reader) during a legitimate transaction, or from discarded credit card receipts. Fraudsters have in the past bought discarded receipts from accomplices working in petrol stations or restaurants (Wall, 2002). The effectiveness of counterfeit or cloned credit cards has been greatly reduced by changes in transactional procedures, such as introducing the CVC2 codes mentioned earlier. However, while this addition has reduced the incidence of minor card frauds, it has nevertheless increased the market value of cloned credit card information when supplied with the card validation code, and these are still traded on the Internet.

While the actual process of putting the card details into the web site is something that anybody could do when placing an order online, the key to the payment fraud is to supply an address that is not the billing address to where goods can be sent and be signed for. What demarcates Internet-related fraud from other credit card-not-present frauds is the 'distanciation' of the offender from the victim. Fraudsters do not engage directly with their victims and experience spatial and emotional distancing, in that they have no mental picture of their victims as victims. Furthermore, they see their own offending as victimless, believing that nobody is deceived, and that the financial loss will likely be borne by the banks or insurance companies.

Unfortunately, this psychological neutralisation-strategy-cum-urban-myth tends to be reinforced and perpetuated by the actions of banks that appear to write off losses. In practice, they 'charge back' some of the losses to the merchants and retailers. These increased operational risks to the merchants are offset either by passing costs onto customers or by offsetting them against the savings made from the costs of terrestrial retail operations, in terms of rental costs, and also to losses to merchandise through store-theft and in-store damage. Moreover, card-not-present frauds themselves originate outside the technology of the banking systems--in changes made to the banking rules set up to allow retailers (initially in phone transactions) to take credit card details without the credit card being present. These changes in policy arguably took the credit card beyond its original purpose and opened the door to new types of fraud (Wall, 2002).

Card-not-present transactions have become the mainstay of e-commerce based retail operations. Not surprisingly, there has been a considerable increase in all losses incurred from card-not-present frauds (CNPFs). Levi's (2000) statistics indicate that during the five years between 1995 and 1999, there was a six-fold increase in UK CNPFs from £4.5m to £29.5. Most resulted from a spate of prepayment mobile phone (airtime) frauds during the late 1990s, whereby false credit card details were used to purchase mobile phone credits. Some of this loss, however, was also due to Internet- based CNPFs (Levi, 2000). Early concerns about the rise in losses due to Internet activities have since been substantiated. In 2001, the UK's APACS (now called UK Payments) card fraud loss statistics indicated that £7m (2%) of the £292m losses in 2000 due to credit card fraud were Internet-related (APACS, 2005a; 2005b). APACS later calculated that in 2004, all of the different forms of Internet fraud were responsible for 23 per cent (£117m) of all losses through credit card fraud (APACS, 2005c; 2006). Since then, the introduction of chip and pin in transactions has reduced losses in face-to-face frauds dramatically. However, where chip and pin protections are not used, such as in Internet or telephone transactions, card-not-present losses have risen. In 2004, CNPFs constituted £150.8m, a figure that more than doubled (to £328.4m) in 2008. Similarly, online banking losses increased four-fold during this period from £12.2m to £52.5m (APACS, 2009). These increases must, however, be viewed against the background of an unprecedented expansion in global Internet-based transactions during the early twenty first century. It was an expansion that included the hitherto office-based administration of local, national, and international services ranging from insurance purchase to the purchase of travel documents. To put this all into perspective, APACS found that although UK card-not-present fraud losses had increased by 350 per cent between 2000 and 2008, the total value of online shopping alone increased by 1077 per cent (up from £3.5 billion in 2000 to £41.2 billion in 2008) (APACS, 2009a).

On the subject of virtual banks and thefts, the first truly virtual bank robbery allegedly took place in mid-2009 when the virtual bank of the space trading game 'Eve Online' (which deals in virtual currency specific to that game) was raided by one of its controllers. News of the theft subsequently caused a run on the bank which mirrored the pattern of the real-time credit crunch (BBC, 2009b) – life imitates art!

PART TWO: VIRTUAL STINGS

Hand-in-hand with new opportunities for e-commerce comes the potential for them to be exploited, with virtual stings clinging tightly onto the coat-tail of technological innovation. Virtual stings are the range of online techniques used by offenders to exploit legal and financial system deficiencies to defraud businesses. However, although the technological media through which offenders engage with business victims have changed, and are still likely to change, history reminds us that the principles and practices of deception remain similar.

Arbitrage and Grey Markets

The global reach of the Internet enables the exploitation of 'grey markets,' created by price differentials between jurisdictions (see Granovsky, 2002). The Internet is a tool which allows pricing differences to be identified from afar and enables the goods to be traded in such a manner as to circumvent the pricing control mechanisms imposed by manufacturers, producers, or government-authorised channels for the distribution of goods. In this way, any price differentials caused by local differences in the costs of producing basic commodities, or in currency exchange rates, or taxation (VAT or import tax) can be exploited.

Needless to say, arbitrage results in illicit cross-border trade in portable items such as cigarettes, alcohol, consumer durables, pharmaceuticals, fuel, and exotic rare animals, their skins and furs (BBC, 2005b; IFAW, 2005). In addition to price differentials is legal arbitrage, legal differentials where goods that are illicit or restricted in one jurisdiction are purchased from jurisdictions where they are legal; such is the case with prescription medicines, sexual services, rare stones, antiquities, rare animal skins and even human body parts.

More recently, legal arbitrage has been found in the rapidly growing online gambling industry, which is gaining popularity in jurisdictions that have negative legal and moral attitudes towards gambling. The size of the online gambling industry is illustrated by statistics released by GamCare, a UK-based charity addressing the social impact of gambling. GamCare estimates that there are approximately 1,700 gambling websites on the Internet (GamCare.co.uk). Further, Merrill Lynch found that the online gambling market had a turnover of $6.3bn in 2003, estimated to increase to $86bn in 2005 (Leyden, 2004). The debate over online gambling has, predictably, focused upon its legality and morality, particularly in the US--"which has both a puritanical streak running right through the national psyche and a thriving, and powerful, home-grown gaming sector" (Fay, 2005). So the main thrust of this debate has, understandably, been about increasing US jurisdictional control over the inter-jurisdictional aspects of running illegal gambling operations in and from other countries (Goss, 2001).

What is certain about online gambling is its popularity; the latter arises from the desire of punters to "beat the system" either within its own rules (topic not dealt with here), or outside them by defrauding gambling operations. With regard to the latter, in 2002, Europay, MasterCard's partner in mainland Europe, claimed that one fifth of losses due to online fraud were related to gambling (Leyden, 2002). The revision of acceptable use policies by electronic payment providers, such as PayPal, to no longer allow customers to subscribe to online gambling sites, combined with new security technology, will likely lessen incidents of online gambling fraud.

Internet Advertising Frauds

New commercial opportunities online quickly become the focus of fraud. One such example is 'pay-per-click' advertising, whereby Internet sites that display adverts receive a small fee from the advertiser each time the advertisement is viewed. Individually, these are minute payments, but they aggregate within a high volume environment. As a consequence, they have given rise to 'Click fraud', or 'bogus click syndrome' (Liedtke, 2005; Modine, 2009), which defrauds the Internet advertising billing systems. Unscrupulous website owners employ individuals to bulk click advertisements, sometimes outsourcing to third-world countries where labour is cheap. Here, 'factories' of low-wage workers will click manually on web ads, often in circumstances where the boundary between wage-labour and coercion is vague. More common, however, is the use of bespoke software, such as 'Google Clique' which effects computer scripted clicking to perform the same task (USDOJ, 2004). Another related example is 'Link spamming' which also exploits the burgeoning Internet advertising industry. The aim of 'link spamming' is to link a keyword, such as 'pornography', with a particular WWW site. Although it is not necessarily illegal (depending upon jurisdiction), it does often flout fair trade practice rules. Link spammers, or search engine optimisers as they often describe themselves, regularly spam websites and personal web-blogs with blocks of text that contain key words to inflate the search engine rankings of web sites that offer "PPC--pills, porn and casinos" (Arthur, 2005). A recent development on link spamming is the blog spam (or spamdexing), a series of comments or phrases whose purpose is to entice people to go to another site, thus boosting its rankings (Johansson, 2008).

Premium Line Switching Frauds

Before broadband replaced the dial-in modem, a fairly common form of telephone billing fraud was premium line switching. Here, visitors to unscrupulous WWW sites, usually pornography related, would, during the course of their browsing, unknowingly become the victim of a 'drive-by download.' They would find themselves infected with a virus, a 'rogue dialler,' that would automatically and discretely transfer their existing telephone service from the normal domestic rate to a premium line service and defraud them (Richardson, 2005). New variations of the premium line switching frauds are beginning to exploit mobile phone services rather than landlines.

Short-Firm Frauds

Short-firm frauds exploit online auction reputation management systems (See Wall, 2007: 85). Brought in to protect users of auction houses, such as e-bay, reputation management systems enable purchasers to rate vendors on their conduct during previous sales prior to doing business with them. Vendors, subsequently, build up profiles based upon customer feedback and past sales performance, enabling potential purchasers to vet them before making bids. Good reputations are highly valued, and maintaining them discourages dishonest behaviour by vendors and bidders. An interesting knock-on effect of these reputation management systems is the emergence of 'the short-firm fraud', the virtual equivalent of the long-firm fraud, where trust is artificially built up, at a cost, by selling some quality articles below their true market value. Once a good vendor rating is acquired, then a very expensive item is sold, often off-line, to a runner-up in the bidding war, and then the vendor disappears once the money has been received.

PART THREE: VIRTUAL SCAMS

Whereas virtual stings are primarily aimed at the business community, the virtual scam is aimed at victimizing individual users. Virtual scams bait victims with attractive hooks such as cut-price goods or services far below the market value, 'better than normal' returns on investments, or some other advantage, such as alternative cures to serious illness or rare drugs not available in the jurisdiction (Hall, 2005). From an analytical point of view, it is often hard to discern between enthusiastic, even aggressive marketing, bad business, and wilfully criminal deceptions. What we can do, however, is outline the spectrum of deceptive behaviours related to e-commerce that are causing concern, noting that they are mainly spam driven. Particularly prevalent on the margins of e-commerce are the scams that sit on the border between aggressive entrapment marketing and deception, such as get-rich quick schemes which tempt Internet users to invest in financial products that they think will yield a substantial return. The potential for scamming is often fairly clear, if not obvious; the US IC3 (Internet Crime Complaints Center), the UK Department for Business Innovation and Skills, and many other sources of victimization statistics clearly show that even normally risk-averse Internet users can fall victim to virtual scams.

Pyramid Selling Scams Online

Pyramid selling schemes and their variants have been successful scamming tactics for many hundreds of years and have, like other lucrative scams, found their way on to the Internet in many ingenious disguises. They are also sometimes known as Ponzi scams (after Charles Ponzi, an Italian immigrant who ran such schemes in the United States in the 1920s). Pyramid selling is an elaborate confidence trick recruiting victims with the promise of a good return on investment. The secret of the schemes' success is that early investors are paid from money invested by later investors, and confidence builds quickly to encourage further investors. New recruits are encouraged by, often genuine, claims of early investors so that they can recoup their initial investment by introducing new recruits to the scheme. Pyramid selling is a numbers game, and because returns are based upon new recruitment numbers rather than profit from product sales, as is the case with legitimate multi-level marketing practices, the pyramid selling schemes are mathematically doomed to fail. They merely redistribute income toward the initiators, and the many losers pay for the few winners. The Internet versions of pyramid schemes, usually (though not exclusively) communicated by email, reflect the terrestrial versions, although the Internet gives the scammer access to a larger number of potential recruits, and the stakes are, therefore, higher.

There are many variations of the pyramid scheme. Some may use chain letters, others use more imaginative devices--such as the purchase of Ostrich eggs, specific numbers of investments, works of art, or, in fact, anything that generates multiple investors. All devices have the same distinctive recruitment features and exploit characteristics of the pyramid algorithm. The hook is usually greed and exploits those looking for a high return on investment, but with limited means and a limited knowledge of business. However, there are also examples of the exploitation of specific trust characteristics. The 'Women Empowering Women' scam operates through a chain letter distributed by email across women's friendship networks. It purports to be a 'gifting' scheme, appealing to women to donate gifts to other women and receive a return on investment for doing so (Levene, 2003). To be allowed to participate, new recruits first have to sign statements declaring their payments to be unconditional gifts to other women, which, frustratingly for law enforcement, makes the scheme legal despite considerable losses to participants.

Direct Investment Scams

Direct investment scams on the Internet are legendary. Some focus on businesses, whilst others focus upon individuals. Some may be genuine – though misguided--attempts to stimulate business by providing recipients with a genuine investment service. Others are less genuine, seeking to persuade interested recipients to part with money without receiving any service in return. Alternatively, they offer investors the opportunity to earn large incomes whilst working at home. In the latter case, victims are encouraged to send off a fee for a package of information that explains the scheme. If, indeed, they do receive anything at all, usually what subscribers receive is worthless, impractical, or may even involve them participating in a nefarious activity. Particularly vulnerable to these scams are the less-mobile, the unemployed, or those housebound (such as single-parents or care-givers).

Beyond the work-at home schemes are the more harmful scams perpetrated by those purporting to be legitimate investment brokers who, upon sign-up (and sometimes also requiring a fee to join) produce free investment reports to customers, subsequently tricking them into investing their funds in dubious stocks and shares. Another direct investment scam is the 'Pump and Dump' scam, whereby investors playing the stock market are deceived by misinformation circulating on the Internet about real stock. This information artificially drives up the price of the stock (the pump), which is then sold off at inflated prices (the dump). Research by Frieder and Zittrain in 2006 found that respondents to "pump and dump" emails can lose up to 8 per cent of their investment within two days, whereas "the spammers who buy low-priced stock before sending the e-mails, typically see a return of between 4.9% and 6% when they sell" (Frieder & Zittrain, 2006).

Loans, Credit Options, or the Repair of Credit Ratings

A particularly insidious group of financial scams committed via the Internet are those which prey upon the poor and financially excluded sections of society with promises to repair their credit ratings, provide credit options or credit facilities, credit cards with zero or very low interest, or instant and unlimited loans without credit checks or security. Such offers, if followed up, tend to come at a considerable cost to victims in terms of high interest rates or entrapping them into a nexus from which it is hard to escape. Even worse, the entrapment may lead to the victim becoming embroiled in a wider range of criminal activity to pay off the original debt.

Deceptive Advertisements for Products and Services

Deceptive advertisements purport to sell goods at greatly reduced prices to hook victims. Some simply fail to deliver, whereas others sell substandard goods (e.g., reconditioned), and others exploit grey markets. The traditional (offline) deceptive advertising has tended to focus on the sale of desirable consumer durables. However, a majority of deceptive online advertisements appear to be targeted at businesses and, particularly, business managers responsible for purchasing office, medical or other supplies who might be attracted by the prospects of low costs or a perk. Typically, office supply advertisements offer specially-priced print cartridges or greatly discounted computing and, in some cases, expensive equipment.

Other deceptive advertisements are aimed at the individual, offering a range of consumer durables or other branded goods or services at greatly discounted prices; bogus educational qualifications; appeals for money, usually to (fake) charities linked to obscure religious based activities or organisations; or soliciting donations to help victims of disasters. In the case of the latter, the events of September 11, 2001, the 2004 Boxing Day Tsunami, the 2005 London bombings, Hurricane Katrina, the Pakistan Earthquake and Asian bird-flu remedies all inspired attempts to exploit public sympathy and extort money by deception or by deceiving recipients into opening infected attachments. The purpose of these scam emails is not always to directly elicit money; sometimes the purpose is to cause a drive-by download and infect the recipient's computer, thus rendering it receptive to remote administration as a Zombie. Robot networks (Botnets) of Zombie computers are themselves very valuable commodities. In 2006, during Slobodan Milosevic's trial for war crimes at The Hague, for example, spam emails circulated claiming that he had been murdered. The emails listed various websites and their addresses where early news footage and photographs of the alleged murder were posted. Once the web addresses were accessed, the computers of the curious were infected by a malicious Trojan (Dropper-FB) which rendered them susceptible to remote administration (Leyden, 2006).

Entrapment Marketing Scams

Entrapment is the stage beyond deception, because it locks the victim into a situation from which they cannot easily extricate themselves, with the consequences that they may become repeat victims and their losses will become even greater. Entrapment can occur upon being deceived into participating in some of the activities mentioned earlier, or by falling victim to one of the many entrapment marketing scams, of which there are many. The classic, often legal, entrapment marketing scam is that whereby individuals are enticed to subscribe to a service by the offer of a free product, usually a mobile phone, pager, satellite TV decoder, etc. Alternatively, the subscriber may be seduced by the offer of a free trial, for example, of access to sites containing sexually-explicit materials, or to sites where they will be given free lines of credit in trial gambling WWW sites. The key to the scam, assuming that the content is legal, is to place the onus of responsibility to notify the vendor of the cancellation upon the applicant, thus keeping many scams on the "right side" of the law. To withdraw from the service, free trial subscribers often have to give a prescribed period of advance notice and usually in writing; these are facts that may be obscured in rather lengthy terms and conditions. Because of this reality, subscribers can end up paying an additional monthly subscription fee.

Scareware Scams

An interesting twist on entrapment marketing scams experienced in recent years has been the increase in Scareware scams (BBC, 2009a). Scareware is an aggressive sales technique through which the scare (soft)ware inundates computer users with misleading messages that emulate Windows security messages. Usually (though not always) delivered by Windows messenger, these messages are designed to distress recipients through scare or shock tactics that their personal computer has been infected by malicious software and, therefore, requires fixing. Of course, the recommended solution is the 'scare-mongers' own brand of software (see entrapment marketing). Scareware signifies a move toward true cybercrime, because the software conducts both the scam and sends the fraudulent gains to the offender. More recent versions are deliberately stealthy with the 'look and feel' and authority of common operation systems. Consequently, victims do not always know that they have been scammed (see Wall, 2010a).

Auction Frauds

The popularity of online auction sites attracts fraudsters. Although auction sites advertise rigorous security procedures to build consumer trust, fraudsters still manage to exploit them. The US Internet Crime Complaint Center report for 2009 shows that, next to non-delivery of items, auction fraud was the single largest category of reported fraud during 2008. It constituted 26 percent of all complaints received (IC3, 2009). The fraudsters' key objective is to lure the bidder outside the well protected online auction environment. In October 2005, three people were jailed for 'second chance' online frauds amounting to £300,000. They placed advertisements for items ranging from concert tickets to cars, some of which were genuine, others not. After the auction concluded, the fraudsters would get in touch with unsuccessful bidders to give them a second chance to buy the goods which they would be encouraged to pay for using money transfers – though the bidders did not subsequently receive the goods (BBC, 2005c). Other examples of online auction-related frauds include the overpayment scam, whereby the scammer (the bidder this time) intentionally pays more than the agreed sum. The payment check clears the banking system after a few days, and the seller sends off the goods and refunds the overpayment. The fact that the check is counterfeit is usually not discovered until a few weeks later, leaving the victim liable for both losses. In a variant of this scam, the buyer agrees to collect goods bought over the internet, such as a car, and overpays the seller using a counterfeit cheque. The overpayment is then refunded by the seller before the cheque clears, but the goods are not collected; thus, the seller retains the goods but loses the value of the overpayment (Rupnow, 2003).

Advanced Fee Frauds

At the hard end of entrapment scams are the advanced fee frauds, sometimes called 419 frauds, because they originated in Nigeria and contravene Code 419 of the Nigerian Penal Code. Advanced fee fraudsters have bilked money from individuals and companies for many years, but concerns have intensified because of the increasing use of emails to contact potential victims. Prior to the popularization of email as a key means of communication, advanced fee frauds were mainly conducted by official-looking letters purporting to be from the relative of a former senior government official, who, prior to their death, accrued a large amount of money currently being held in an overseas bank account. The sender invites the recipient to assist with the removal of the money by channelling it through his or her own bank account. In return for collaborating, the recipient is offered a percentage of the money (say, $12m, 20 per cent of the $60m money; see Wall, 2007) to be transferred. When the recipient responds to the sender, an advanced fee is sought from them to pay for banking fees and currency exchange, etc. But the experience drawn from many cases shows that as the victim becomes more embroiled in the advanced fee fraud and pays out their money, it becomes harder for them to withdraw. Needless to say, the majority, if not all, of these invitations are bogus and are designed to defraud the respondents, sometimes for considerable amounts of money.

The link between the massive increases in emailed advanced fee 'invitations" and the numbers of actual victimizations resulting from them is inconclusive –that is as opposed to those from the more persuasive hardcopy invitations. Research conducted by the UK National Crime Intelligence Service (NCIS) in 2001 found no direct link between the number of emailed requests and the increase in victimizations (Wall, 2007), with the main reason being that individuals tend to be fairly risk averse to most of the email invitations because of their lack of plausibility or poorly written English and bad narrative. The hard copy invitations tended to have been more thoroughly researched and personal. However, there are a number of conflicting forces at play here. On the one hand, it must also be recognized that there are also reporting disincentives in play here, because many victims will usually destroy the letter or email that drew them into the fraud so that they are not, subsequently, accused of being involved in a conspiracy. On the other hand, having said this, the incentives to report do, nevertheless, tend to increase as the loss escalates, or even worse, if victims feel a threat to their well-being. Furthermore, an increase of only one victimization per hundred million emails (an arbitrarily chosen figure) can be catastrophic in one of two ways because of the consequences of falling victim to an advanced fee fraud.

The first consequence is financial. The NCIS calculated in 2001 that 72 victims reported falling for 419 advanced fee fraud, with a total loss of £10.5m and an average loss per victim of £146k. Eight of the victims had lost £300,000 or more (5 X £300k, 1 X £1m, 1 X £2.7m, 1 X £3.6m). When the larger losses were removed from the statistics, the average loss fell to £32,000. While this gives the reader an idea of the extent of losses, it does not give a clear demarcation of the break down between physical- and Internet- initiated victimizations. The more recent US statistics compiled using a different methodology and on a different time frame shed some light on this divide by suggesting high aggregate sums, but lower personal losses, than the earlier UK study. The US National Internet Fraud Information Center's Internet fraud report of 2005 shows that 8 per cent, or 985 out of 12,315 fraud complaints, were about 'Nigerian' Money Offers, with an average loss of about $7,000. By 2008, the Internet Crime Complaint Center (IC3) found that advanced fee complaints were 3 per cent (or 8,256 out of 275,284 complaints), with a lower average loss of $1,650 (based upon a lower number of cases subsequently referred to the authorities).

The second consequence is the increase in personal risk. Not only do the funds never materialize, but personal risk also increases dramatically, especially if the victims attempt to recover their lost funds (Reuters, 2005). A few individuals who have travelled abroad in an attempt to recover their money have subsequently been kidnapped, and a few have reportedly been murdered (BBC, 2001).

The jury is still out on the actual impact of 419 fraud victimization by email, but a number of interesting variations of the advanced fee theme have been found in emailed letters requesting loans rather than fees. In other examples of advanced fee frauds, of which there are many, relationships may be deliberately struck up on online dating services and then flight costs and other expenses are requested in advance by the correspondee to visit the person advertising on the dating services, leaving love-struck victims waiting for beaus who never arrive. Alternatively, users may receive an email telling them that they have won a lottery prize, or that they have been entered into a prize pot in a promotions exercise. They are directed by the email to a website which supposedly will provide the information that will release their prize. At this site, they will be asked for their personal information and also, because the money comes from overseas, a small administration fee to pay for bank or administration charges. All variants of advanced fee frauds are designed to elicit money in advance of any action.

Drug Sales/ Health Cures/ Snake Oil Remedies

The sale of prescription drugs through Internet sites provokes widespread concern because of the potential dangers that can arise from the circulation of unregulated or even fake drugs (Hall, 2005). Promises of quality goods, value for money, availability, and convenience of access would appear to be quickly shattered by broken promises and fraud. A poignant example is the booming international trade in Viagra and the anti-impotence drug Cialis (Satchwell, 2004; Humble, 2005). Aside from the many Viagra emails that are so often thinly veiled attempts either to link-spam or to infect computers with Trojans, the more plausible invitations to treat, which usually provide a trading address and some other credible business credential, will (often legally) transport drugs across borders to circumnavigate local prescription restrictions; or they are exploiting pricing differentials caused by taxes. Similar markets are also found trading steroids and other body- enhancing drugs, such as slimming pills (Satchwell, 2004). The growing use of the Internet to sell counterfeit drugs is worrying for drug regulators, as it makes global an already booming business (Satchwell, 2004). The World Health Organisation (WHO) has estimated that about eight to 10 per cent of all medicines available globally are counterfeit. Of particular concern are stories that indicate, for example, over 60 per cent of drugs sold in Nigeria were found to be counterfeit, some sold via the Internet. Such examples provoke demands for international regulation to verify the quality and legality of manufacture and also to authorise their purchase (WHO, 2004). The two primary concerns about Internet drug sales relate to mass sales, which is what the WHO addresses, and to private selling to individuals—which is much harder to regulate.

Alongside the sales of pharmaceuticals is a robust market for alternative health cures and snake oil remedies attempting to persuade buyer/victims that the product or service is to be trusted. Unlike the entrapment scams, which hook potential victims through their greed-driven gullibility, the snake oil scams play upon personal insecurities, or even the individual's ill-health. It is, of course, no surprise that individuals should seek longevity, and the classical literature is full of tales about the quest to restore youth and to achieve immortality. Indeed, these tales go back 4,000 years to the Epic of Gilgamesh set in ancient Mesopotamia (Sandars, 1972). Miracle cures became popular on the stalls of the Mediaeval English fairs, and in the Nineteenth-Century, they became the basis for the American medicine show (Anderson, 2000). It is, therefore, also of no surprise that the Internet has become the site of the twenty-first century virtual medicine show feeding the same old personal insecurities and peddling miracle cures and snake oil, but on a global scale. Commonly found in email inboxes are offers to maintain and enhance vitality, youthfulness, health and longevity; miracle diets and potions; body enhancement lotions or operations to reduce body fat; and lotions and creams to enlarge breasts and penises. At the very bottom of the (moral) barrel are the bold claims of cures for cancer and other serious illnesses.

PART FOUR: THE PREVALENCE OF MICRO-FRAUD AND THE CHALLENGE FOR CRIMINAL JUSTICE

Before moving on to the challenges that micro-frauds pose for criminal justice systems, it is important to get some feel for the risks of scams to individuals. The problem with estimates of fraud levels, as with all forms of cybercrime, is in obtaining reliable and impartial statistics of crime in a medium (the Internet) that is, by its very nature, informational, global, and networked (Wall, 2007). It is also a medium in which a strong security industry has in past years had a vested interest in presenting gloomy predictions of, and, therefore, overestimating the prevalence of, fraud. We see in the UK, for example, APACS (now UK Payments), an independent trade organisation set up by the banking industry to provide authoritative statistics, criticising CPP, the credit card protection organisation, for using "misleading information and spurious statistics to support their claim that over 12 million people nationwide were victims of card fraud last year" [in 2007], noting that not all of these were Internet- related]. APACS counter-argued that there were about 1 million cases of card fraud in the UK in 2007, rather than the 12 million claimed by CPP (APACS, 2009b). Hopefully the UK statistics will be improved with the introduction of the Action Fraud national fraud reporting centre (See later and Wall, 2010b). By any standard, 1 million cases per year is still high, and the average card fraud loss works out to be approximately $750 -$1000, a ballpark figure that is not dissimilar to the Internet fraud losses experienced in the USA.

Specifically related to Internet fraud, the US Internet Crime Complaint Centre (IC3) - formed as a partnership between the Federal Bureau of Investigation, the National White Collar Crime Center, and the Bureau of Justice Assistance - received a total of 275,284 (self-reported) complaints in 2008. Most of these were from US citizens. The Internet Crime Complaint Centre subsequently passed on 26 per cent (72,490) of these complaints to federal, state, and local law enforcement agencies around the USA for further consideration (IC3, 2009). These statistics, as with all Internet statistics, carry a health warning, because they mainly indicate victims' concerns rather than give an accurate picture of crime; plus, it is possibly the case that reports of some categories (such as credit card fraud) may be lower than actual, because they tend to be dealt with by the issuing banks. But, the statistics are independently collated and drawn from over a quarter of a million cases and have some interpretive value, especially showing change over time.

Table 1, gives a detailed breakdown of reported complaints and shows that some of the numerically larger categories of complaints reflected lower individual losses than some of the smaller ones. While they do not map directly onto the categories of fraudulent behaviour described earlier in this chapter, they do give ball park estimates of prevalence from 2008 and show how victimization patterns shift from year to year.

Another very important point to make here with regard to the central argument of this chapter is that although the individual losses appear relatively large, they do, in fact, still qualify as micro-frauds, those frauds that are too small to be investigated and which tend to be written-off. Anecdotal evidence from earlier research found that police were reluctant to commit investigative resources with losses below $5-7,500 (and, in some cases, even more, depending upon the force), and that banks appeared willing to write off losses below $1,500 (Wall, 2002, 2007). [Note: these are ball park figures, because write-offs can vary across organizations, sectors, and jurisdiction].

Table 1. Top 10 complaints made to the Internet Crime Complaint Centre in 2008

	% complaints	Referred cases	
	Received	% of all losses	Average loss
Non-delivered merchandise and/ or payment	33%	29%	$800
Internet auction fraud	26%	16%	$610
Credit/debit card fraud made	9%	5%	$223
Confidence fraud	8%	14%	$2,000
Computer fraud	6%	4%	$1,000
Check fraud	5%	8%	$3,000
Nigerian letter fraud	3%	5%	$1,650
Identity theft	3%	4%	$1,000
Financial institutions fraud	2%	No figure available	
Threat	2%	No figure available	

Based on 275284 received complaints (Col 1) and 72,490 referrals (Columns 2 & 3) (Source: IC3, 2009).

Micro-frauds are significant, because they are conspicuous by their absence in the criminal justice system; this omission introduces a number of challenges for the criminal justice system to overcome, resolve, or, in some circumstances, accept. For the following reasons they tend to get missed by the Criminal Justice radar.

First, there is the problem of under-reporting by victims. Although media reporting seems to over-exaggerate the Internet fraud problem (see Wall, 2008), there is also the curious phenomenon of the simultaneous under-reporting of fraud. Incidents may, for example, be reported straight to the bank; thus, they may not ever appear as an official police statistic. Even when there is a clear Internet link, individuals may be too embarrassed to report their victimization, or the loss may not be immediately evident, or it may be regarded as being too small to warrant action. Alternatively, as with credit card fraud, police may refer reportees back to their banks who are viewed as the real victims; this has certainly been the experience in some UK police areas (Wall, 2007). Where the victims are corporate entities, reporting losses may expose a particular commercial weakness and threaten their business model, which raises clear conflicts between the private vs. public justice interest with regard to cybercrimes. Even though the UK APACS model (see earlier) does provide the banking sector with a means by which to anonymously submit loss data, banks are still reluctant to freely admit publicly that they have fallen victim to fraudsters.

Second, offender profiles are low, because so few micro-frauds are reported, especially those who commit the small-impact, bulk-impact victimizations. Third, there are jurisdictional disparities in fraud, and computer misuse law across jurisdictions can frustrate law enforcement efforts, despite attempts by the likes of the Council of Europe Cybercrime Convention to harmonize laws. Pan-jurisdictional idiosyncrasies in legal process can also interfere with levels of inter-jurisdictional police cooperation. Even where there may be a common legal understanding of what constitutes fraud across jurisdictions; there may still be a lack of common operational definitions due to differential police experience in dealing with fraud. Fourth, is a generally low overall level of public knowledge about associated risks. Because of the lack of public knowledge about the real risks of online fraud, those who are not discouraged from going online are often unable to make informed choices about the risks that they may face, especially where the threat is new.

Even if micro-frauds were deemed serious enough to get reported to the police, their distinct informational and globalised qualities would arguably conspire to impede the traditional investigative processes. Most significant is that they fall outside the traditional localized, even national, operational purview of police. They are clearly different from the regular police crime diet, which is one reason that they can evade the criminal justice gaze. On the few occasions where online frauds become known to the police, it is often the case that the computing misuse component of the offending gets dropped in favour the fraud charge for the offence for which the computer was used. For the most part, however, cybercrimes tend to be too individually small in impact (*de minimis*) to warrant the expenditure of finite police resources in the public interest. Also, by falling outside routine police activities, the police accrue little general experience in dealing with them as a mainstream crime. This becomes additionally problematic when disparities in legal coding across jurisdictions conspire to frustrate law enforcement initiatives.

The big question here is: how might these challenges be addressed? In the US, the National Internet Crime Complaint Center (IC3) has been in operation for a number of years. It receives complaints, decides upon an appropriate course of action (e.g., advice to victim, refer to law enforcement agency, etc), and collates data for broader analysis.

The UK has also sought to address online frauds by developing a national fraud reporting, analysis and response capacity as part of its *Cyber Security Policy* (Cabinet Office, 2009). Intended to be fully operational from 2010, Action Fraud, the national fraud reporting centre, will receive reports from fraud victims. These reports will then be triaged by a National Fraud Intelligence Bureau, based in the City of London Police force who will decide upon appropriate responses (Wall, 2010b; NFSA, 2009). The central collation of intelligence helps to overcome the longstanding problem of locality and contributes toward developing a national, or even international, picture of a 'distributed' fraud problem. The NFRC will also work alongside the National Police Central e-Crime Unit (PCeU), based in the Metropolitan Police, which works in close collaboration with the Metropolitan Police's own Dedicated Cheque and Plastic Card Unit (DCPCU). Much of the DCPCU's work is focused upon the physical corruption of technological devices used in the banking system. The more serious frauds and those relating to organised crime could also involve the Serious Fraud Office or SOCA (the Serious Organised Crime Agency) (Wall, 2010b).

CONCLUSION

This chapter has illustrated how inventive, reflexive, and responsive fraudsters can be when using networked technologies. It also looked at how closely online fraud sits to legitimate business opportunities. The organization of online fraud is increasingly reflecting popular contemporary Internet based e-retailing 'Affiliate Marketing' practices, whereby 'affiliates' use networked technologies to broker relationships between merchants (read "offender") and consumers (read "victim") (Wall, 2010a).

Furthermore, since the software is now showing capability to independently conduct the whole criminal process, it is entirely possible that we are entering an era characterized by "the long tail" of crime (mimicking Chris Anderson's 2006 analysis of business in the information age). The future holds not just multiple victimizations from one scam, but multiple victimizations will circulate from multiple scams as in the scareware example. One criminal (or many) can now carry out many different automated crimes at the same time. Also evident is the increased feasibility for the offender to operate inside the business being attacked or operate from it. Micro-frauds are significant in that they shift the focus of the criminological debate away from white collar crime and the crimes of the powerful to a debate over crimes of the knowledgeable. Indeed, there is a strong argument that they are illustrative of the way that mass access to cheap information technologies has rather perversely begun to democratize crime.

More specifically, this chapter has shown how the *virtual bank robbery* (of financial management systems online), *the virtual sting* (exploiting system deficiencies to defraud individual and commercial victims), and *the virtual scam* (socially engineering individuals into parting from their money) are each areas of deceptive criminal behaviour that are rapidly evolving along with technological developments. While it is clear that new global opportunities have arisen for traditional fraudulent behaviours to be committed online, it is also the case that new forms of fraud are emerging. The online fraud profile will gradually broaden as new opportunities for offending are created by the convergence of networked technologies of home, work, and leisure with technologies that manage identity and location. Importantly, this new world of convergence will be characterised even more by the brokering of information with an exchange value (Bates, 2001; O'Harrow, 2001), and that this information and its value (information capital) will become a prime target for criminals.

The future holds many uncertainties, not least the acceptance of new technologies for managing finance by an increasingly suspicious public (after the 2009 credit crunch). One thing that we can be certain of is that fraud will not go away. No matter how security develops, new types or configurations of fraud will emerge to create new challenges for law enforcement, such as continually having to overcome disparities in legal definitions as to what constitutes a particular type of fraud across jurisdictions, getting local criminal justice agencies (including the police) to respond to fraud on a global scale, being able to deal with *de minimis* crimes, and being able to deal with crimes that fall outside the regular police workload and experience.

These issues are not new, and many jurisdictions have already developed, or are currently developing strategies to address them. But the question remains as to the role of the victim in this form of small-impact multiple offending. There is also the question of how individual victims' financial and moral reputations are to be restored if they are compromised. Moreover, there is the question of how individuals will be protected against sleeper fraud (defined as data which is stored and acted upon later). All of the these parameters beg the awkward question as to whether law is the most effective local solution to what has become a global problem. Is there an alternative, say, of using technology to enforce law, requiring significant further debate because of its implications for liberty? Should public or private organizations in any given jurisdiction deal with global micro-fraudsters? There is clearly a need for much future discussion about the public interest with regard to crimes involving informational content.

REFERENCES

Anderson, A. (2000). *Snake Oil, Hustlers and Hambones: The American Medicine Show*. Jefferson, NC: McFarland.

Anderson, C. (2006). *The Long Tail: Why the Future of Business is Selling Less of More*. New York: Hyperion.

APACS. (2005a) *The UK Payments Industry: A Review of 2004*, London: APACS at www.apacs.org.uk/downloads/Annual Review 2004.pdf(now archived)

APACS. (2005b) 'UK card fraud losses reach £504.8m: criminals increase their efforts as chip and PIN starts to make its mark', *APACS press release*, 8 March, London: APACS, at www.apacs.org.uk/downloads/cardfraudfigures%20national&regional%20-%208mar05.pdf (now archived)

APACS. (2005c) *Card Fraud: The Facts 2005*, APACS, at http://www.cardwatch.org.uk/publications.asp?sectionid=all&pid=76&gid=&Title=Publications

APACS. (2006) *Fraud: The Facts 2006*, APACS, at http://www.cardwatch.org.uk/publications.asp?sectionid=all&pid=76&gid=&Title=Publications.

APACS. (2009a) *Fraud: The Facts 2009*, APACS, at http://www.cardwatch.org.uk/publications.asp?sectionid=all&pid=221&gid=&Title=Publications

APACS. (2009b) 'APACS responds to latest CPP release', *APACS press release*, 30 January, at http://www.ukpayments.org.uk/media_centre/press_releases/-/page/684/

Arthur, C. (2005) 'Interview with a link spammer', *The Register*, 31 January, at www.theregister.co.uk/2005/01/31/link_spamer_interview/.

Bates, M. (2001). Emerging trends in information brokering . *Competitive Intelligence Review*, *8*(4), 48–53. doi:10.1002/(SICI)1520-6386(199724)8:4<48::AID-CIR8>3.0.CO;2-K

BBC (2001) 'Warning over Nigerian mail scam', *BBC News Online*, 10 July, at news.bbc.co.uk/hi/english/uk/newsid_1431000/1431761.stm

BBC (2005a) 'Phishing pair jailed for ID fraud', *BBC News Online*, 29 June, at news.bbc.co.uk/1/hi/uk/4628213.stm

BBC (2005b) 'Web trade threat to rare species', *BBC News Online*, 15 August, at news.bbc.co.uk/1/hi/sci/tech/4153726.stm.

BBC (2005c) 'How eBay fraudsters stole £300k', *BBC News Online*, 28 October, at news.bbc.co.uk/1/hi/uk/4386952.stm.

BBC (2009a) 'Scareware' scams trick searchers: Peddlers of bogus anti-virus try to scare people into buying', *BBC News Online*, 23 March, news.bbc.co.uk/1/hi/technology/7955358.stm

BBC (2009b) 'Billions stolen in online robbery', *BBC News Online*, 3 July, at news.bbc.co.uk/1/hi/technology/8132547.stm

Cabinet Office. (2009) *Cyber Security Strategy of the United Kingdom: safety, security and resilience in cyber space*, http://www.cabinetoffice.gov.uk/media/216620/css0906.pdf

Cards International. (2003) 'Europe "needs mag-stripe until US adopts chip"', *epaynews.com*, 28 July, at www.epaynews.com/ index.cgi?survey_&ref_browse&f_view&id_105939 2963622215212&block_.(no longer available online)

Fay, J. (2005) 'WTO rules in online gambling dispute', *The Register*, 8 April, at www.theregister.co.uk/2005/04/08/wto_online_gambling/.

Finch, E. (2002) 'What a tangled web we weave: identify theft and the internet', in Y. Jewkes (ed.), *dot.cons: Crime, Deviance and Identity on the Internet*, Cullompton: Willan, 86–104.

Finch, E. and Fafinski, S. (2010) *Identity Theft*, Cullompton: Willan

Frieder, L., & Zittrain, J. (2006) 'Spam works: evidence from stock touts and corresponding market activity', *Working Paper, Krannert School of Management and Oxford Internet Institute*, 25 July, at www.ssrn.com/abstract_920553.

Goss, A. (2001) 'Jay Cohen's brave new world: the liability of offshore operators of licensed internet casinos for breach of United States' anti-gambling laws', *Richmond Journal of Law & Technology*, 7 (4): 32, at http://jolt.richmond.edu/v7i4/article2.html.

Granovsky, Y. (2002) 'Yevroset tainted by gray imports', *The Moscow Times*, 9 July: 8, at www.themoscowtimes.com/stories/2002/07/09/045.html.

Hall, C. (2005) 'Internet fuels boom in counterfeit drugs', *Sunday Telegraph*, 16 August, at http://www.telegraph.co.uk/news/uknews/3322447/Internet-fuels-boom-in-counterfeit-drugs.html.

Humble, C. (2005) 'Inside the fake Viagra factory', *Sunday Telegraph*, 21 August, at http://www.telegraph.co.uk/news/uknews/3322770/Inside-the-fake-Viagra-factory.html.

IC3. (2009) 2008 *Internet Crime Report*, Internet Crime Complaint Center, at www.ic3.gov/media/annualreport/2008_IC3Report.pdf

IFAW. (2005) *Born to be Wild: Primates are Not Pets*, London: International Fund for Animal Welfare, at http://www.ifaw.org/Publications/Program_Publications/Wildlife_Trade/Campaign_Scientific_Publications/asset_upload_file812_49478.pdf.

Johansson, J. (2008) 'Anatomy of a malware scam: The evil genius of XP Antivirus 2008', *The Register*, 22 August, at www.theregister.co.uk/2008/08/22/anatomy_of_a_hack/print.html

Kravetz, A. (2002) 'Qatari national taken into federal custody in wake of terrorist attacks allegedly committed credit card fraud', *Peoria Journal Star*, 29 January.

Levene, T. (2003) 'The artful dodgers', Guardian, 29 November, at *money.guardian.co.uk/*scamsandfraud/story/0,13802,1095616,00.html.

Levi, M. (2000). *The Prevention of Plastic and Cheque Fraud: A Briefing Paper*. London: Home Office Research, Development, and Statistics Directorate.

Levi, M. (2006). The Media Construction of Financial White-Collar Crimes. *The British Journal of Criminology*, *46*(6), 1037–1057. doi:10.1093/bjc/azl079

Leyden, J. (2002) 'Online gambling tops Internet card fraud league', *The Register*, 28 March, at www.theregister.co.uk/content/23/24633.html.

Leyden, J. (2004) 'WTO rules against US gambling laws', *The Register*, 11 November., at www.theregister.co.uk/2004/11/11/us_gambling_wto_rumble/.

Leyden, J. (2006) 'Slobodan Trojan poses as murder pics', *The Register*, 15 March, at www.theregister.co.uk/2006/03/15/slobodan_trojan/.

Liedtke, M. (2005) 'Click fraud' threatens online advertising boom, *Legal Technology*, 14 February.

Modine, A. (2009) 'Sports site sues Facebook for click fraud: RootZoo files class-action complaint', *The Register*, 14 July, at www.theregister.co.uk/2009/07/14/rootzoo_sues_facebook_for_click_fraud/

NFSA. (2009) *The National Fraud Strategy A new approach to combating fraud*, The National Fraud Strategic Authority, at http://www.attorney-general.gov.uk/NewsCentre/News/Documents/NFSA_STRATEGY_AW_Web%5B1%5D.pdf

O'Harrow, R. (2001) 'Identity thieves thrive in information age: rise of online data brokers makes criminal impersonation easier', *Washington Post*, 31 May, at http://www.encyclopedia.com/doc/1P2-438258.html.

Pearce, F. (1976). *Crimes of the Powerful – Marxism, Crime and Deviance*. London: Pluto Press.

Reuters (2005) 'Microsoft, Nigeria fight e-mail scammers', *e-week.com*, 14 October, at www.eweek.com/article2/0,1895,1871565,00.asp.

Richardson, T. (2005) 'BT cracks down on rogue diallers', *The Register*, 27 May, at www.theregister.co.uk/2005/05/27/rogue_bt_diallers/.

Rupnow, C. (2003) 'Not "made of money" ', *Wisconsin Leader-Telegram*, 23 April, at www.xpressmart.com/thebikernetwork/scam.html.

Sandars, N. K. (1972). *The Epic of Gilgamesh: An English Version with an Introduction*. Harmondsworth: Penguin Classics.

Satchwell, G. (2004). *A Sick Business: Counterfeit medicines and organised crime*. Lyon: Interpol.

Sutherland, E. (1949). *White Collar Crime*. New York: Dryden.

Tombs, S., & Whyte, D. (2003). Unmasking the Crimes of the Powerful . *Critical Criminology*, *11*(3), 217–236. doi:10.1023/B:CRIT.0000005811.87302.17

USDOJ. (2004) 'Computer programmer arrested for extortion and mail fraud scheme targeting Google, Inc.', *US Department of Justice press release*, 18 March, at http://www.justice.gov/criminal/cybercrime/bradleyArrest.htm.

Wall, D. S. (2002) DOT.CONS: *Internet Related Frauds and Deceptions upon Individuals within the UK*, Final Report to the Home Office, March (unpublished).

Wall, D. S. (2007). *Cybercrime: The transformation of crime in the information age*. Cambridge: Polity.

Wall, D.S. (2010a) 'Micro-Frauds and Scareware: The birth of a new generation of cybercrime?', *Jane's Intelligence Review*, January.

Wall, D. S. (2010b) 'The UK tackles crimes against the machine', *Jane's Intelligence Weekly*, 2(15) 28 April, 13.

Weisburd, D., Wheeler, S., Waring, E., & Bode, N. (1991). *Crimes of the Middle Classes: White-Collar Offenders in the Federal Courts*. New Haven, CT: Yale University Press.

WHO. (2004) *Report of Pre-eleventh ICDRA Satellite Workshop on Counterfeit Drugs*, Madrid, Spain, 13–14 February, at http://www.who.int/medicines/services/counterfeit/Pre_ICDRA_Conf_Madrid_Feb2004.pdf

Section 2

Frameworks and Models

Chapter 5
Policing of Movie and Music Piracy:
The Utility of a Nodal Governance Security Framework

Johnny Nhan
Texas Christian University, USA

Alesandra Garbagnati
University of California Hastings College of Law, USA

ABSTRACT

Ongoing skirmishes between mainstream Hollywood entertainment conglomerates and Peer-to-Peer (P2P) file-sharing networks recently reached a crescendo when a Swedish court convicted members of the world's largest BitTorrent, The Pirate Bay, and handed out the stiffest sentence to date.[1] Four operators of The Pirate Bay received one year imprisonments and fines totaling $30 million, including confiscation of equipment. While this verdict sent shockwaves amongst P2P networks, piracy remains rampant, and this incident further exacerbated relations between file sharers and Hollywood. In retaliation, supporters of P2P file-sharing attacked websites of the law firms representing the Hollywood studios (Johnson, 2009). This victory by Hollywood studios may be a Pyrrhic defeat in the long run if the studios do not soften their antagonistic relations with the public. This chapter explores structural and cultural conflicts amongst security actors that make fighting piracy extremely difficult. In addition, it considers the role of law enforcement, government, industries, and the general public in creating long-term security models.

INTRODUCTION

The Problem

The rapid digitization of film and music and their distribution via the Internet is reflective of a changing business model. Hollywood's delay in adapting to and securing this new medium has resulted in unauthorized alternative sources supplying digital music and movies. Advanced covert illegal distribution networks known as "Darknets" have emerged (Biddle, England, Peinado & Bryan, 2002; Lasica, 2003). Darknets mask malefactors' identities and counter enforcement efforts by employing sophisticated technical measures within

DOI: 10.4018/978-1-61692-805-6.ch005

a closed hierarchical social structure resembling that of organized crime. In some instances, the lucrative operation of illegal file-sharing has drawn in traditional organized crime groups (Treverton, Matthies, Cunningham, Goulka, Ridgeway, & Wong, 2009).

The Motion Picture Association (MPA) estimated worldwide film industry losses from Internet piracy five years ago to be at $2.3 billion, with 80% of downloads originating from overseas (Siwek, 2006). On an annual basis, the recording industry estimates losses to be at $3.7 billion annually (Siwek, 2007). Rampant Peer-to-Peer (P2P)[2] file-sharing has been blamed for the decline of the music industry (Rupp & Smith, 2004). While these figures are debatable (Cheng, 2009), they do suggest that illegal file-sharing is a large and expensive problem. Large losses are, in part, indicative of a security deficit from industry's inadequacy to self-police.

To close the security gap, industry has collaborated with law enforcement in recent years. The Pirate Bay's recent conviction in Sweden may be attributed, in part, to the creation of an FB- and MPAA-trained elite "P2P hit squad" consisting of Swedish police.[3] Despite this recent success, law enforcement, in general, has been a reluctant partner in policing corporate victimization matters. This reluctance may result from a number of cultural and structural factors that prioritize street crimes. Historically, law enforcement has lacked the legal and jurisdictional flexibility to enforce complex crimes requiring inter-organizational relationships (Schlegel, 2000). Instead, it is a "slow-moving institution," rooted in social norms (Rowland, 2004) and fortified by a strong subculture resistant to change (Skolnick & Fyfe, 1993). Nevertheless, high-tech crimes in the past few decades have forced police to change their orientation from strictly crime control to embracing new policing models based on information and risk management (Ericson & Haggerty, 1997).

The Nodal Governance Model

Security in the new policing model is co-produced by both police and non-state institutions (Bayley & Shearing, 1996). Maintaining security in this "plural" model is achieved by a decentralized network of public, private, and "hybrid" security actors (Dupont, 2006). In this new "Nodal Governance" model, institutional actors, or "nodes," actively participate in security by sharing capital in various forms, such as technology, resources, and expertise (Johnston & Shearing, 2003; Shearing & Wood, 2004; Burris, Drahos, & Shearing, 2005). Bayley and Shearing (1996) draw a distinction between *police* and *policing*, stressing the latter is performed by other non-state security stakeholders, such as private security and corporations.

We employ the nodal governance conceptual framework to analyze policing piracy efforts in cyberspace. We examine four aggregate nodal sets determined to be relevant to cyber security: (i) state law enforcement/government, (ii) the motion picture industry, (iii) the recording industry, and (iv) the general public. We draw distinctions between the enforcement of music and film piracy by empirically "mapping" the security network in California. This "mapping exercise" identifies formal and informal key actors, their security assets, and their relationships to each other in the security field (Wood & Font, 2004; Wood, 2006). An examination of relationship "gaps" will draw out conflicting cultural and structural variables among nodes and the overall capacity of the security network (Burris, 2004). We use these variables to explore policing effectiveness of Internet piracy.

In our chapter, we first discuss the study completed, starting with the methods of inquiry. Next, we review literature on nodal governance in greater depth. We also examine the Internet geography in situating nodal governance networks. In addition, we map each security actor: Law enforcement/government, the film industry, the music industry, and the general public. An analysis of inter-nodal "gaps" extracts variables affecting security. Finally, we consider study limitations, initial findings, some policy implications, and suggested future research.

STUDY

Methods of Inquiry

Research data were derived from three sources: (i) interviews, (ii) observations of steering committee meetings, and (iii) published public opinion polls. This method of inquiry was deemed appropriate for the exploratory nature of this research study. Interview data were collected from several groups determined to be significant stakeholders in Internet piracy and security: law enforcement, the film industry, recording industry, and government. Their importance was identified through a review of the cyber-security literature and initial informal interviews with computer security practitioners and law enforcement. A significant group, the general public, was not interviewed due to the practical limitations of the study but accounted for from existing published literature and surveys.

The Study Sample

Fifty eight subjects were interviewed (n=58) from 2005 to 2007 in California, Arizona, and Washington. Each nodal set was identified and defined functionally from their involvement with cyber security and piracy work in California. California was chosen for convenience and for its high concentration of illegal Internet piracy activity, considered to be the highest in the U.S.[4] It is also headquarters to the music and film industry and their respective security trade groups, the Recording Industry Association of America (RIAA), and the Motion Picture Association (MPA).[5] The mapping of California's cyber security network, while not generalizable to or reflective of all security networks, reveals insight into general issues of police and corporate culture, as well as national and international issues associated with policing cyberspace.

Sixteen (n=16) security practitioners and policymakers from the film (n=8) and music industry (n=8) were interviewed. In addition, eighteen (n=18) Internet security practitioners from the tech sector were interviewed in California, Arizona, and Washington to incorporate elements of software piracy and draw some comparisons in enforcement. Moreover, the tech sector owns and operates the majority of the Internet infrastructure and is heavily involved in monitoring Internet activity (Dewan, Friemer & Gundepudi, 1999; Lewis & Anthony, 2005).

Procedure

Interviews were conducted in-person (n=50) and over the telephone (n=8). Interviews typically lasted between one and two hours and consisted of semi-structured thematic questions. Some subjects were interviewed multiple times to ensure validity. Questions were tailored to each group and altered as important issues emerged for depth of answers. For example, law enforcement subjects were asked about investigative processes and attitudes, while film and music industry representatives were asked about the impact of Internet music distribution and current policing strategies and laws. Subjects were allowed to elaborate on answers and dictate the flow of questioning. This approach is consistent with the exploratory nature of qualitative studies with an "open-ended and emergent process" (Lofland & Lofland, 1995, p. 5).

The authors interviewed eighteen (n=18) subjects from law enforcement, consisting of members from five regional high-tech crime task forces in California. Task force members included federal, state, county, and local law enforcement investigators as well as special state and county prosecutors. In addition, two (n=2) members of the California Governor's Office of Emergency

Services (OES) with oversight of task force budgets and policy were observed.

In addition to interviews, the authors observed interactions between law enforcement, government, and industries during quarterly steering committee meetings. The OES-led steering committee has members from each regional task force and different industries. These public meetings serve as an open forum to exchange ideas, settle disputes, and discuss current issues. These observations gave insight into power dynamics and communications between security actors.

Nodal Governance Theoretical Framework

The nodal governance theoretical framework emerged from the 1970s information and communications revolution that redefined social relations between producer, consumer, and governments through networked relations (Castells, 1996). The degree to which social order is produced and maintained in the information age relies upon the capacity to manage societal dangers, conceptualized by *risk* (Ericson & Haggerty, 1997). Therefore, risk institutions, such as police, define and classify perceived levels of risk of members of the modern society. Information gathering and analysis becomes the primary institutional function to manage risk.

The crime control policing model has been increasingly expensive and insufficient for dealing with crime in the information age. Police power in the crime control model is derived from exclusive state-sanctioned coercive authority acquired through professionalization. This model achieves increasing security capacity by allocating more resources to police. Hiring more police officers, however, has yielded mixed results on its effects on crime rates (Muhlhausen & Little, 2007; Bennett & Bennett, 1983; Klick & Tabarrok, 2005; Craig, 1984). Police technologies, such as closed-circuit television, have also yielded mixed results (Welsh & Farrington, 2002, 2006). Overall, linear police-centric strategies have shown marginal effects on crime, suggesting diminishing returns on security.

Diffusion of police powers to non-state institutions is used to close the security deficit in the information age. A network of institutional actors, or nodes, co-produces security in the risk society (Burris, Drahos, & Shearing, 2005). Police power shifts away from a centralized "monopolistic" model of crime control to "pluralized" forms of security commodified and shared with private and hybrid security stakeholders (Bayley & Shearing, 1996; Loader, 1999; Dupont, 2006; Bayley, 2006). Nodes share security resources, mentalities, and technologies (Johnston & Shearing, 2003). Security participants actively contribute as "denizens," a conceptual term used to illustrate co-producers of security in a democratic process of security governance (Shearing & Wood, 2003).

Security capacity of a nodal network is a function of the collective strength of relationships--indicated by the number and nature of inter-nodal relationships within a given network. Relational strength can be conceptualized by the "density" or ratio of possible connections amongst nodal stakeholders, and "centrality" is a measurement of an organization's position in the network--the number and pattern of connecting stakeholders (Wasserman & Faust, 1994; Dupont, 2006). High-capacity networks have more interconnected nodes and denser connections, giving them greater access to security resources. Nodes with centralized positions, such as police departments, have higher levels of influence and power to leverage resources (Dupont, 2006).

Security capacity can be expanded to larger macro-level networks. Local- and state- level security networks can be nested within larger national and global networks. The scalability and flexibility of this theoretical model is ideal for analyzing security in the Internet geography.

STUDY FINDINGS: ANALYZING SECURITY IN THE INTERNET GEOGRAPHY

Cyberspace and Borders

The Internet has shifted definitions of territory from the physical to the conceptual (Gould, 1991; Loader, 1997). This shift does not suggest that the online world is entirely borderless and disconnected from geographic boundaries but only that borders are not strictly politically- and legally-defined. Wilson and Corey (2000) classified the Internet into three distinct geographies: (1) the physical infrastructure, (2) virtual disparities, or separation between the "haves" and the "have nots," and (3) spaces defined by demarcation and interaction of places, or online communities. Security actors can create boundaries and exercise social control online through conceptual borders based on limits to information (Marx, 1997).

The global nature of cyberspace has made its prosecution and enforcement difficult (Herbert, 1999; Grabosky, 2004; Brenner & Schwerha, 2004). Jurisdictional and legal complexities of cybercrime often result in prosecutorial minimum loss thresholds and frequent use of plea bargaining (Smith, Grabosky & Urbas 2004; Nhan, 2008). This set of outcomes gives law enforcement further disincentive to pursue cybercrimes such as piracy. Police are rooted in institutional *habitus* tied to the enforcement of geographic territory, creating difficulties in understanding cyberspace (Huey, 2002).

Security Actor: Law Enforcement

Police professionalization during the Reform Era created several fundamental changes in policing that explain resistance to change. First, modern policing has evolved from a Peelian model based on institutional authority (Uchida, 1997). To eradicate police corruption, O.W. Wilson's bureaucratic model brought a quasi-military structure minimizing external relationships. Second, a strong subculture emerged characterized by deep group loyalties and cynicism toward the public (Skolnick & Fyfe, 1993). Third, traditional measures of success shifted away from enforcement of community norms during the Political Era to statistics-based measures categorized by crime type and geographic region, such as the FBI's Uniform Crime Report (UCR). Traditional measures of success involve crime rates frequently used in comparative studies between countries (Bayley, 1991; Barclay, Tavares, Kenny, Siddique, & Wilby, 2003).

While security discourse often centers on public order, safety, and amenity, these measures of success are ultimately proxies for crime control processes such as arrest rates and response times (Wilson, 1993). These measures of success are consistent with the primary role of the police as exclusive state-sanctioned institutions for making arrests and serving as gatekeepers of the criminal justice and legal system. According to one task force supervisor, "Everything must channel into the criminal justice system and this is exactly how and the only way it can be done for the foreseeable future."

Emergent social issues and crimes have been handled consistently in a manner that fits this professional model of policing. Police have traditionally responded by increasing personnel, additional training, and acquiring more equipment. This reality has two ramifications: First, it expands police powers. Second, it reinforces the police mandate for crime control in predefined geographic spaces. Internet crimes, despite conflicting with this geographic-based function of police, have been addressed with strategies similar to street crimes.

The police mandate dictates its strategies and attitudes towards cybercrime. Police function to apprehend suspects for the purpose of legal processing. Law enforcement employs computer forensics to carry out this directive. Several law enforcement interviewees stressed the importance of preserving the chain of evidence derived from expert knowledge and investigatory experience. One task force prosecutor explains:

While it is possible to trace IP addresses back to the origin, it is difficult to prove who was actually on the keyboard at the time of the incident. This part takes a lot of traditional police work. . .The huge amounts of data can more effectively be searched by a seasoned investigator who knows what he's looking for.

This model has fit well with street crimes (such as child exploitation) that have shifted to the online medium. However, its use by corporate nodes depends upon security goals.

Computer forensics can be a valuable security asset to certain industries concerned with incapacitating attackers and gaining insight into the nature of attacks. However, very few private companies conduct costly digital forensics investigations. One network security expert explains, "To do a full forensic work for eventual litigation can cost [our company] $50,000 to $100,000." Another computer network security engineer described the value of law enforcement as "the biggest area of need," adding, "Law enforcement will become more critical because information is becoming more digitized."

Law enforcement's strong subculture also influences its security capital. It takes approximately four years to fully train an investigator to conduct cyber investigations. Rather than outsourcing technical work or recruiting computer security experts or college graduates with computer backgrounds, police forces often only consider sworn personnel with patrol and general detective experience for task force membership. Consistent with the police worldview, one supervisor explains, "The ideal candidate for the task force is someone with a lot of patrol experience plus a little computer base knowledge and experience and investigative experience." Law enforcement officers gain esoteric knowledge through years of experience and recognition of their unique central nodal position, allowing them to wield greater power and access to capital.

Police familiarity with criminal justice and legal processes further reinforces the police subculture. According to one prosecutor, "It is better to train officers and detectives to be cyber investigators than [computer science] students because they are actually *faster*." Police experience and ability to mobilize security capital available as central nodes translates into expertise useful for digital forensics. According to one task force investigator, "What makes a good police investigator is the ability to think like a crook and [the] ability to develop skills and learn resources available to cops."

Group exclusivity is reflective of police cultural norms and an embedded value system taking pride in "real police work" associated with arresting criminals (Chan, 1997). Successful outcomes are associated with good detective work leading to "big busts" associated with a high degree of positive reputation. Since the nature of corporate victimization does not trigger public outrage or prosecutorial interest, only substantial cases meeting minimum loss thresholds can launch computer piracy investigations. "Undercover officers frequent swap meets and investigate vendors from tips called in," explains one investigator, adding, "The threshold is approximately 500 CDs and 100 DVDs to make it worthwhile." The degree to which external security actors can align outcomes with law enforcement nodes determines the level of utility of law enforcement security capital and the density of inter-nodal relations.

A comparison of desirable security outcomes by the recording industry and film industry will provide insight into inter-nodal compatibilities with law enforcement and the capacity of security networks.

Security Actor: Recording Industry

The recording industry was the first to experience the adverse impact of large-scale P2P file- sharing during the 1990s Napster MP3 era. This industry failed to recognize and act quickly on the potential impact of the Internet and digital distribution. One music studio representative explains, "[The industry] was late to respond to it, I think as a whole. I think they are trying to stop an avalanche from coming by putting up a small wall." Another representative points out the consequences of illegal downloading, stating, "Thousands of record label employees have been laid off, numerous record stores are closing throughout the country, and due to declining sales, record companies are finding their ability to invest in new artists at risk." This perception of harm and victimization has influenced reactive security strategies based largely on civil litigation against individual end-users (Nhan, 2008).

This industry's perception of Internet crime as equivalent to street crime can explain its worldview and subsequent security strategies. One industry representative likens Internet file- sharing to simple theft, expressing, "If a store owner catches someone shoplifting merchandise, you can bet that owner takes action, just as he or she should." This viewpoint justifies the controversial use of civil litigation as a security strategy.

He further explains:

Suing individuals was by no means our first choice. Unfortunately, without the threat of consequences, far too many people were just not changing their behavior...it is critical that we simultaneously send a message to individuals that engaging in the theft of music is illegal.

This industry also actively attempts to change public discourse from terms such as "unauthorized" and "file-sharing" to more impactful terms reflective of street crime such as, "illegal" and "theft." One RIAA representative explains:

While the term is commonly used, "piracy" doesn't even begin to describe what is taking place. When you go online and download songs without permission, you are stealing. The illegal downloading of music is just as wrong as shoplifting from a local convenience store--and the impact on those who create music and bring it to fans is equally devastating.

Self perceptions of victimization and inadequacy of legal and enforcement support have resulted in more aggressive security strategies using litigation as coercive instruments for desired outcomes. One studio representative frankly stated, "I think that the RIAA has found that the laws are not adequate to achieve the desired effects. It's why they use those suits...they've turned to extralegal bullying instead of the law."

To a lesser degree, the music industry also employs covert and disruptive technologies. The lack of integrated security features and the small file sizes of compact discs have made it relatively easy to digitally copy and distribute content. Criminals have circumvented *ad hoc* technological solutions, however. For example, in 1992, a simple felt tip marker defeated Sony-BMG's CD "hi-tech" copy protection technology. Later in 2005, Sony-BMG discretely installed copy protection software on Microsoft Windows-based personal computers, creating vulnerabilities to hack attacks, resulting in public backlash and class-action lawsuits (Halderman & Felton, 2006).

Security Actor: Film Industry

The film industry faces a similar problem with piracy but operates under a different security philosophy. Larger file sizes have given the industry more time to implement security technologies and policies. However, increased broadband penetration in the U.S. and internationally has placed this industry in the middle of a "piracy war" (Ahrens, 2006). Incapacitating illegal piracy distribution networks using a combination of technology and covert infiltration of top distribution "release groups" is the primary security strategy of the film industry. Successful security outcomes involve criminal apprehension and prosecution of elite release group members.

This nodal set perceives the Internet as a new avenue for traditional crime, described by one industry Internet security expert as "the next-generation of organized crime." Highly organized and sophisticated "Darknets" allow membership only to a select group of trusted individuals (Biddle, England, Peinado, & Willman, 2002; Lasica, 2005). Membership to these elite "Top-sites" or release groups often requires members to contribute valuable digital media content, such as unreleased movies. Members receive access to high-speed servers containing exclusive digital content and can profit by charging membership fees for smaller networks. This content is soon distributed globally to end-users via P2P indexing services with an exponential momentum described by the MPAA as a "global avalanche of Internet piracy."[6] Successful security outcomes, therefore, target the source of the supply chain.

A sophisticated organizational hierarchy insulates elite film piracy release group members from apprehension and prosecution. A recent RAND report has linked lucrative film piracy to organized crime and terrorism (Treverton et al., 2009). Low-level associates facing the highest risk of apprehension, explains one security expert, are "supplying organized crime with the masters, [who are in turn] leveraging talent." Identifying top-release group members requires employing security capital in the form of covert operations. Being too aggressive in infiltrating release groups can raise suspicion, resulting in "the account [being] banned which includes an IP block, making it difficult to infiltrate top members." Such efforts can destroy years of work in building insider trust.

The film industry also utilizes security capital in the form of technologies used to identify Intellectual Property (IP) and disrupt file-sharing. In addition, the industry can use identification technology as a utility that aligns security outcomes with law enforcement, potentially creating stronger security partnerships and gaining public support.

One of the new technologies being worked on is Video DNA, which means a fingerprint on videos used for content recognition. This might be huge for child pornography. This might be the angle that the public and studios and law enforcement can use to get a foot in the door to P2P sites, since protection of children is universally prioritized [and] child pornography is universally reprehensible.

However, technology-based forms of security capital continue to be circumvented. One security expert claims, "It's a battle between us and P2P networks. They keep coming up with more robust technologies."

Perceptions of victimization and the criminal dictate the nature of security strategies for each industry. While both the recording and film industry share common sentiments that the Internet is a medium for traditional crime, the film industry perceives its worst offenders not as delinquent thieves but as malicious organized criminals. One film industry Internet security expert explains, "The reality is there are *true bad guys* who run these operations on a large scale," adding, "This is a billion-dollar market for these pirated goods, and similar to drugs, it can get violent and territorial."

Consequently, the recording and film industries have divergent security strategies, with one based on targeting front-end release groups, while the other targets end-users. However, both strategies have failed to deter file-sharing and to garner public support.

Governments and their Publics

The founding principles of the Internet, which continue to influence the public mindset, can explain, in part, the proliferation of piracy. The Internet was conceived under a "community code" of open research, shared ideas and works, decentralized control, and mutual trust (Kleinrock, 2004).

Security was not a foreseen necessity and, therefore, was not integrated into its architecture. Consequently, as the Internet was released for public and commercial use, it became an insecure environment susceptible to criminal activity. Despite a patchwork of *ad hoc* security measures, these principles of Internet freedom continued to manifest in the public conscience. The public tend to perceive antipiracy activities as violations of this code, while seeing any attempts to block security as justified.

Many regard the Internet as a disembodied free domain where the legal rules and constraints of the physical world do not apply. One public survey conducted in Singapore shows that 94% of respondents felt that it is morally wrong to steal a CD from a shop, compared to the 43% who felt the same for illegally downloading a song.[7] The same study finds illegal file- sharers seeing themselves as community members sharing digital content for the benefit of everyone. Another survey of eight countries [8] found that 38% of the respondents felt it was acceptable to download a movie before its theatrical release, while 72% felt it was acceptable after a theatrical and DVD release (Morphy, 2004). These inconsistencies in public attitudes may be explained by behavioral neutralizations outlined by Sykes and Matza (1957), who categorized these as denial of responsibility, injury, victimization, condemnation of condemners, and appealing to higher moral authority.

Public viewpoints often manifest in governmental attitudes toward security. Countries with more developed economies, higher incomes, and a greater culture of individualism tend to have higher levels of enforcement (Marron & Steel, 2000). Less developed nations with no legitimate distribution channels tend to have minimal enforcement and legislation. One film studio Internet security expert explains, "Over [in some less developed countries], piracy is the only way to watch certain movies, so piracy is at 100%." Without greater public support and clear victimization, governments often do not perceive piracy as worthy of much political attention and funding.

Piracy enforcement often competes and loses to street crimes for government funding. For example, California's task force network is insufficiently staffed and funded, resulting in regions without coverage. "There are blank spots" without coverage, explains one OES supervisor. This may be putting things lightly; the entire area of Central California is the blank spot. Unlike high-priority well-funded crimes (such as drug enforcement), high-tech crime in California is a line-item budget. This reality means that the OES must request the continuation of funding annually. An annual report stressing the importance of high-tech crimes is submitted to The Office of the Governor for consideration.

The government node uses its central position, having greater access to social and political capital as a communications hub connecting nodes within the network. The OES supervisor describes its nodal function as a communications and "resource broker." He explains, "One of the services we provide is a bridge linking task forces [and other agencies]." This is a critical role in securing cyberspace, according to industry experts who have criticized the U.S. government in the past for lack of leadership and understanding (Blitstein, 2007). The government can also resolve inter-nodal conflicts. One OES coordinator explains her conflict resolution role, stating, "There's a whole thing about control. I know counties don't like other counties messing with their business but it's a growing problem."

The State can curtail political and jurisdictional obstacles by establishing and maintaining inter-nodal participation and addressing structural frictions. The same OES coordinator underscores the difficulty and frustration of connecting nodes and amending structural discords, stating:

We as the state have a responsibility. We really do. To bring people together. [Former California State] Senator Poochigian had some great ideas and very much a friend of high-tech and ID theft. Are we doing the best we can do on a statewide process?...Are we getting the most out of the money? Are we lobbying enough in Washington? Are we doing enough? I would say not. We have all child porn, et cetera. We have the banking industry. They write it off. Don't they have an obligation?

However, inter-nodal dis-junctures may be difficult to overcome with strong cultural differences between nodal sets.

THE NATURE OF INTER-NODAL RELATIONSHIPS, OR GAPS

Establishing Normative Social Control in Cyberspace

Having theoretically mapped each nodal set using Wood's (2006) exploratory guidelines, we now turn our attention to the nature of inter-nodal relationships, or "gaps." First, we explore the formation of security alliances. Second, we examine the compatibility of security outcomes. Third, we examine the lack of public participation as security stakeholders. Finally, we analyze the effects of public attitudes and political friction between countries on security stakeholder participation.

Formation of Nodal Partnerships and Security Alliances

The outbreak of Internet piracy has exceeded the capacity of the recording and film industries to self-police. In California, a conglomerate of private industries began lobbying the state to address special policing needs. One California state OES coordinator explains, "[Industries] came to the legislature saying we have a problem; this is a growing trend." Historically, "law enforcement wants to lock 'em up, throw away the keys. They weren't addressing business' needs." To address these needs, the state formed regional task forces.

These regional task forces sought to minimize bureaucratic and jurisdictional issues associated with high-tech and cyber cases. Regional task forces were created to meet the unique and growing demands of industries impacted by high-tech and computer crimes outlined in California Penal Code §13848-13848.8.[9] Special prosecutors embedded within each task force ensured adherence to evidentiary guidelines, resulting in very successful legal outcomes. One prosecutor explains, "[The defense] won't go to trial. Essentially they're going to lose. We have high conviction rates; eighty to ninety percent." Industry participation was essential in the nodal model to expand the security capacity of the network.

Expanding the security network involves personal referrals over structured arrangements. Industry steering committee members have long-standing task force contacts. Industry representatives often contact investigators through colleague referrals. One investigator explains, "They'll just get all my information, and before you know it, another company will call asking for me, being referred by so and so; they come looking for me." One prosecutor explains why structured relations are not widely utilized in law enforcement, stating, "The old time personal communication vouching for somebody is what cops work on. Having an official network where you can go online and talk to somebody is not necessarily going to foster that." Despite the scalability of nodal connections, international cases have been problematic.

Compatibility of Desirable Security Outcomes

The utility of nodal security capital and density of network connections is influenced by the convergence of security outcomes between nodes. The utility of law enforcement by industries is dependent on the degree to which security outcomes are compatible. The film industry's strategy of incapacitating release group members has yielded greater utility for law enforcement's security capital and has led to more sustained inter-nodal relations. One task force supervisor explained:

The RIAA hasn't brought us end-user cases. They know for us that's not a big target. We get more MPAA cases because those are more of the type of cases; we work those. The RIAA likes to take off the street vendors with street people. We get newsletters of what they do. With the MPAA, they try to choke off the sources.

The music industry's focus on civil litigation against individual file-sharers has required less utility for law enforcement's apprehension-based security capital, resulting in weaker inter-nodal relations. Accordingly, most RIAA investigations are conducted internally for the purpose of civil litigation.

Regardless of security strategies, both industries must compete with traditional street crimes in the law enforcement and public mindset. Crimes directly impacting individual victims draw greater support over corporate victimization. One task force representative poignantly justified focusing on street crimes during a heated debate at a steering committee meeting, stating, "My community is concerned about child exploitation!" The MPAA representative's reaction was indicative of the marginalization of corporate victimization. He stated, "On behalf of people with lesser crimes, we don't at the end of the day [want to] feel we're going to lose out." Developing a security network will require overcoming this dichotomous relationship and incorporate the general public.

Lack of Public Buy-in as Security Stakeholders

The general public represents the largest and most unrealized security resource for curtailing piracy and, potentially, the most influential stakeholder. Instead of perceiving the public as prospective security partners, industry maintains a producer-consumer relationship. An antagonistic relationship has developed into a dichotomy between security nodes and non-security nodes (the public). This contentious "us versus them" mentality undermines public participation as key security stakeholders.

The RIAA's civil suits have created inter-nodal friction between the general public and security nodes. The hundreds of lawsuits filed against users identified only by Internet Protocol (IP) addresses by the RIAA have caused a rift between not only the RIAA and the public but with other industries. For example, Internet Service Providers (ISPs) were subpoenaed to release customer information, leading to a series of lawsuits between the RIAA and Verizon in 2003 (Tavani & Grodzinsky, 2005). The fallout of these lawsuits adversely affected relations between the film industry and ISPs. One studio security expert explains, "ISPs worked with us. We were never asking for [customer] info. When that lawsuit happened, we were shut out." Moreover, these lawsuits, perceived by the public as "bullying" tactics, have damaged public relations. Consequently, many consider piracy as a justifiable form of "just desserts."

Illegal activities such as hacking and file-sharing are largely regarded as virtuous retribution against large corporations. Moreover, some individuals are motivated by a sense of excitement and pleasure with subverting formal authority, consistent with Katz's (1988) Moral Seduction Theory. One studio Internet security expert expresses the attitudes of file-sharers, stating, "I can beat *The Man* and it's fun to beat *The Man*." In addition, the nature of corporate victimization does not elicit public empathy. One task force investigator explains:

Banks don't make good victims; technology doesn't make good victims. They're already rich. Pirating isn't such a crime. It's costly to investigate, it's going to take forever to train and very expensive.

The Problem is public perception. It will never be prioritized.

While reversing public mentality will be a difficult task for industry and law enforcement, it is especially difficult to persuade governments to participate as security partners.

Government Buy-in as Security Stakeholders: Effects of Political Friction

Governmental indifference towards piracy often reflects public sentiments and often justifies inaction. Developing countries have been notorious for ignoring U.S. and international IP laws (Globerman, 1988). For example, piracy rates in Russia are estimated to be at 70% (Sewik, 2006). According to U.S. trade negotiator Victoria Espinel, law enforcement efforts "have not resulted in the kind of robust prosecution and meaningful penalties that would deter the significant increase in piracy that our industry has observed in Russia" (Thomas, 2005).

Piracy can serve political and economic ends. One tech industry security expert explains the tacit motivations for allowing piracy of foreign nations, stating, "[Y]ou're draining the money from your enemies." This drain disproportionately impacts innovation-based economies, such as the U.S. and Japan. One film studio security expert further explains, "When you go to countries that don't give a shit, it's already taking a big chunk out of the U.S; talking about the lack of production in the U.S. economy."

The degree to which governments participate as stakeholders depends largely on the utility of piracy. China, for example, has the highest rate of film piracy, estimated to be at 90% (Siwek, 2006). One expert in Chinese foreign relations explains, "Piracy benefits China's economy by providing jobs and a cheap way to quickly catch up with modern technology" (McKenzie, 2007). This statement was supported by one film industry security expert interviewed who stressed, "China will not significantly shift to protect our IP until they have IP to protect." Inconsistencies in enforcement and laws have led to industry frustration.

The music industry, in particular, has relied heavily on the governments to police and protect its IP internationally. One studio representative expresses his frustration in dealing with organizations operating in countries with lax laws:

I don't know if you've heard of Pirate Bay, but it is located in Sweden. They can do what they want. Their purpose is to steal music. The RIAA can't be effective if laws are not there to support the efforts. I don't think it's the place of a trade group for policing anyway. Law and government should be doing that.[10]

Foreign laws and policies have also adversely affected law enforcement efforts internationally. One prosecutor explains the why many cases are not pursued internationally:

When law enforcement goes out of the country, you have to deal with the state department and protocols that no one knows of that can run afoul. Those complications, to say nothing of the practical matters of financial wherewithal to go places and to secure evidence that's submissible when it gets back here.

Individuals and organizations exploit jurisdictional and legal inconsistencies by constantly shifting operations. One film industry Internet security expert expresses this frustration, stating:

The problem with this system is that laws aren't universal. You can't win this.... Pirates will move their operations to Europe, and if that's clogged up, they'll move it to Asia, then Africa, until there's a rogue nation with the bandwidth willing to host everything for a fee.

Without strong international support, political, legal and jurisdictional bottlenecks limit enforcement and prosecution efforts locally and reduce the overall security capacity.

CONCLUSION

It has been shown that policing Internet piracy remains a difficult task. Structural, cultural, and political issues amongst security actors continue to be impediments to creating a more effective policing model. The degree to which security can be established is by the strength of network connections and capital possessed by each node.

Exploring each security actor and inter-nodal relations using the nodal governance model has given insight into structural and cultural dynamics of relations amongst actors. Particularly, the differences between the recording and film industries have highlighted the divergence in the utility of law enforcement and legal apparatuses. Understanding these points of cooperation and conflicts can give better insight into dealing with Internet piracy.

This research undertaking has several limitations. First, this chapter is exploratory in nature and limits its findings to California's cyber security network. While the findings are not generalizable much beyond California, its findings are consistent with national and international enforcement issues. The high-tech task forces in California law enforcement have participated in international cases. In addition, both the recording and film industries are headquartered in the state. Future research should consider comparisons with security networks in other states and other countries using larger sample sizes. It must be noted that while the sample size in this study is relatively small, this reality is reflective of the limited number of high-tech investigators in the state. As we obtain a better understanding of how the Internet is policed, larger sample sizes can be drawn from different populations, and quantitative studies can be considered.

The value of this study, however, lends empirical insight into the power dynamics and conflicts in policing online space. The intersection between geographically-based laws and control mechanisms with the online environment challenges current paradigms of policing, government, and security. In addition, this study contributes to the growing body of nodal governance research, where researchers are mapping security networks, ranging from airports (Dupont & Mulone, 2007) to anti-terrorism security in Olympic events (Manning, 2006). The flexibility of this theoretical framework lends nicely to the decentralized Internet environment, where the traditional geographic mapping of crime is problematic. This framework serves as a good theoretical tool in analyzing Internet piracy.

One future endeavor is to explore the establishment of a normative security infrastructure with more permanent and integrated partnerships. Specifically, the general public and foreign governments must play a more active role in security. Policing efforts in cyberspace remain based around *ad hoc* collaborations hindered by structural, cultural, and political frictions amongst nodes. These enforcement strategies can be undermined by having an antagonistic relationship with the public.

Developing online community spaces requires extending security responsibilities to the general public to participate as "Netizens," or members with common interests capable of policing online social spaces (Hauben & Hauben, 1997). The result of this effort can be likened to the online equivalence of Newman's (1973) "defensible spaces"--which stresses crime prevention through community self-efficacy, or "digital defensible spaces" (Nhan & Huey, 2008). Until that time, the Internet will continue to be a dynamic environment challenging our notions of territory, governance, crime, and social control.

REFERENCES

Ahrens, F. (2006, June 15). U.S. joins industry in piracy war: Nations pressed on copyrights. *The Washington Post*, A01.

Barclay, G., Tavares C., Kenny, S., Siddique, A. & Wilby, E. (2003). International Comparisons of Criminal Justice Statistics 2001. *Home Office Statistics Bulletin, May 6, 2001.*

Bayley, D. H. (1991). *Forces of order: Modern policing in Japan*. Berkeley, CA: University of California Press.

Bayley, D. H. (2006). *Changing the guard: Developing democratic police abroad.* New York: Oxford University Press.

Bayley, D. H., & Shearing, C. D. (1996). The future of policing. *Law & Society Review*, *30*(3), 585–606. doi:10.2307/3054129

Bennett, R. R., & Bennett, S. B. (1983). Police personnel levels and the incidence of crime: A cross-national investigation. *Criminal Justice Review*, *8*(31), 32–40. doi:10.1177/073401688300800206

Biddle, P., England, P., Peinado, M., & Willman, B. (2002). The darknet and the future of content distribution. *ACM Workshop on Digital Rights Management 2002.*

Blitstein, R. (2007). *Experts fail government on cybersecurity*. Retrieved January 2, 2007, from http://www.ohio.com/business/12844007.html

Brenner, S. J., & Schwerha, J. J. (2004). Introduction-cybercrime: A note on international issues. *Information Systems Frontiers*, *6*(2), 111–114. doi:10.1023/B:ISFI.0000025779.42497.30

Burris, S. C. (2004). Governance, micro-governance and health. *Temple Law Review*, *77*, 335–361.

Burris, S. C., Drahos, P., & Shearing, C. (2005). Nodal governance. *Australian Journal of Legal Philosophy*, *30*, 30–58.

Castells, M. (1996). The rise of the network society.: *Vol. 1. The information age: Economy, society and culture*. Cambridge, MA: Blackwell Publishers.

Chan, J. B. L. (1997). *Changing police culture: Policing in a multicultural society*. New York: Cambridge University Press. doi:10.1017/CBO9780511518195

Cheng, J. (2009). *Judge: 17,000 illegal downloads don't equal 17,000 lost sales. Retrieved onFebruary13, 2009*, from http://arstechnica.com/tech-policy/news/2009/01/judge-17000-illegal-downloads-dont-equal-17000-lost-sales.ars

Craig, S. G. (1984). The deterrent impact of police: An examination of a locally provided public service. *Journal of Urban Economics*, *21*(3), 298–311. doi:10.1016/0094-1190(87)90004-0

Dewan, R., Friemer, M., & Gundepudi, P. (1999). Evolution of the internet infrastructure in the twenty-first century: The role of private interconnection agreements. In *Proceedings of the 20th International Conference on Information System*s, Charlotte, North Carolina, (pp.144-154).

Dupont, B. (2006). Power struggles in the field of security: Implications for democratic transformation . In Wood, J., & Dupont, B. (Eds.), *Democracy, Society and the Governance of Security* (pp. 86–110). New York: Cambridge University Press. doi:10.1017/CBO9780511489358.006

Dupont, B., & Mulone, M. (2007). *Airport security: A different kind of alliance*. Paper presented at the American Society of Criminology Annual Meeting on November 14-17, 2007, in Atlanta, GA.

Ericson, R. V., & Haggerty, K. D. (1997). *Policing the risk society*. Toronto, ON: University of Toronto Press.

Globerman, S. (1988). Addressing international product piracy. *Journal of International Business Studies*, *19*(3), 497–504. doi:10.1057/palgrave.jibs.8490384

Gould, P. (1991). Dynamic structures of geographic space. In S.D. Brunn, S. D. & T.R. Leinbach (Ed.) *Collapsing space and time: Geographic aspects of communication and information* (pp. 3-30). London, UK: Harper Collins Academic.

Grabosky, P. (2004). The global dimension of cybercrime. *Global Crime*, *6*(1), 146–157. doi:10.1080/1744057042000297034

Halderman, J. A., & Felton, E. W. (2006). Lessons from the Sony CD DRM episode. *Proceedings from the 15th USENIX Security Symposium*, July 31-August 4, 2006, Vancouver, B.C.

Hauben, M., & Hauben, R. (1997). *Netizens: On the history and impact of usenet and the internet.* Los Alamitos, CA: IEEE Computer Society Press.

Herbert, S. (1999). The end of the territorial sovereign state? The Case of Criminal Control in the United States. *Political Geography*, *18*, 149–172. doi:10.1016/S0962-6298(98)00080-8

Huey, L. (2002). Policing the abstract: Some observations on policing cyberspace. *Canadian Journal of Criminology*, *44*(3), 248–254.

Johnson, B. (2009, April 27). *Pirate bay: Industry lawyers' websites attacked.* Retrieved April 28, 2009, from http://www.guardian.co.uk/technology/2009/apr/27/pirate-bay-law-firms-attack

Johnston, L., & Sharing, C. (2003). *Governing security: Explorations in policing and justice.* New York: Routeledge.

Katz, J. (1988). *Seductions of crime: Moral and sensual attractions in doing evil.* New York: Basic.

Kleinrock, L. (2004). The internet rules of engagement: Then and now. *Technology and Society*, *24*, 193–207. doi:10.1016/j.techsoc.2004.01.015

Klick, J., & Tabarrok, A. (2005). Using terror alert levels to estimate the effect of police on crime. *The Journal of Law & Economics*, *48*, 267–279. doi:10.1086/426877

Lasica, J. D. (2005). *Darknet: Hollywood's war against the digital generation.* Hoboken, NJ: John Wiley & Sons.

Lewis, E., & Anthony, D. (2005, August 12). Social Networks and Organizational Learning During a Crisis: A Simulated Attack on the Internet Infrastructure. Paper presented at the annual meeting of the American Sociological Association, Marriott Hotel, Loews Philadelphia Hotel, Philadelphia, PA

Loader, B. D. (1997). The governance of cyberspace: Politics, technology, and global restructuring . In Loaderv, B. D. (Ed.), *The governance of cyberspace: Politics, technology and global Restructuring* (pp. 1–19). New York, NY: Routledge. doi:10.4324/9780203360408_chapter_1

Loader, I. (1999). Consumer culture and the commodification of policing and security. *Sociology*, *33*(2), 373–392.

Lofland, J., & Lofland, L. H. (1995). *Analyzing social settings: A guide to qualitative observation and analysis* (3rd ed.). Belmont, CA: Wadsworth Publishing.

Manning, P. K. (2006). Two cases of American anti-terrorism . In Wood, J., & Dupont, B. (Eds.), *Democracy, society and the governance of security* (pp. 52–85). New York: Cambridge University Press. doi:10.1017/CBO9780511489358.005

Marron, D. B., & Steel, D. G. (2000). Which countries protect intellectual property? The case of software piracy. *Economic Inquiry*, *38*(2), 159–174.

Marx, G. T. (1997). Some conceptual issues in the study of borders and surveillance. In E. Zureik, E. & M.B. Salter (Ed.), *Global surveillance and policing: Borders, security, identity* (pp. 11-35). Portland, OR: Willan Publishing.

McKenzie, H. (2007, July 31). *Faking it: Piracy poses headache for Olympics.* Retrieved October 26, 2007, from http://www.cnn.com/2007/WORLD/asiapcf/07/24/olympics.piracy/index.html

Morphy, E. (2004). *MPAA steps up fight against piracy*. Retrieved October 24, 2007, from http://www.newsfactor.com/story.xhtml?story_title=MPAA-Steps-Up-Fight-Against-Piracy&story_id=25800

Muhlhausen, D. B., & Little, E. (2007). *Federal law enforcement grants and crime rates: No connection except for waste and abuse*. Retrieved October 10, 2007, from http://www.heritage.org/Research/Crime/upload/bg_2015.pdf

Newman, O. (1973). *Defensible space: Crime prevention through urban design*. New York: Macmillan Publishing.

Nhan, J. (2008). Criminal justice firewalls: Prosecutorial decision-making in cyber and high-tech crime cases . In Jaishankar, K. (Ed.), *International perspectives on crime and justice*. Oxford, UK: Cambridge Scholars Publishing.

Nhan, J., & Huey, L. (2008). Policing through nodes, clusters and bandwidth: The role of network relations in the prevention of and response to cyber-crimes . In Leman-Langlois, S. (Ed.), *Techo-crime: Technology, crime, and social control*. Portland, OR: Willan Press.

Rowland, G. (2004). Fast-moving and slow-moving institutions. *Studies in Comparative International Development, 38*, 109–131. doi:10.1007/BF02686330

Rupp, W. T., & Smith, A. D. (2004). Exploring the impacts of P2P networks on the entertainment industry. *Information Management & Computer Security, 12*(1), 102–116. doi:10.1108/09685220410518865

Schlegel, K. (2000). Transnational crime: Implications for local law enforcement. *Journal of Contemporary Criminal Justice, 16*(4), 365–385. doi:10.1177/1043986200016004002

Shearing, C. D., & Wood, J. (2003). Nodal governance, democracy, and the new 'denizens.' . *Journal of Law and Society, 30*(3), 400–419. doi:10.1111/1467-6478.00263

Siwek, S. E. (2006). *The true cost of motion picture piracy to the U.S. economy*. Retrieved September 20, 2007, from http://www.ipi.org/ipi%5CIPIPublications.nsf/PublicationLookupFullText/E274F77ADF58BD08862571F8001BA6BF

Siwek, S. E. (2007). *The true cost of sound recording piracy to the U.S. economy*. Retrieved September 20, 2007, from http://www.ipi.org/ipi%5CIPIPublications.nsf/PublicationLookupMain/D95DCB90F513F7D78625733E005246FA

Skolnick, J. H., & Fyfe, J. J. (1993). *Above the law: Police and the excessive use of force*. New York: The Free Press.

Smith, R. G., Grabosky, P., & Urbas, G. (2004). *Cyber criminals on trial*. New York: Cambridge University Press. doi:10.1017/CBO9780511481604

Sykes, G. M., & Matza, D. (1957). Techniques of neutralizations: A theory of delinquency. *American Sociological Review, 22*(6), 664–670. doi:10.2307/2089195

Tavani, H. T., & Grodzinsky, F. S. (2005). Threat to democratic ideals in cyberspace. *Technology and Society Magazine, IEEE, 24*(3), 40–44. doi:10.1109/MTAS.2005.1507539

Thomas, J. (2005). *Intellectual property theft in Russia increasing dramatically: U.S. officials warns of "rampant piracy and counterfeiting"*. Retrieved October 24, 2007, from http://usinfo.state.gov/ei/Archive/2005/May/19-415943.html

Treverton, G. F., Matthies, C., Cunningham, K. J., Goulka, J., Ridgeway, G., & Wong, A. (2009). *Film piracy, organized crime, and terrorism*. Retrieved April 20, 2009, from http://www.rand.org/pubs/monographs/2009/RAND_MG742.pdf

Uchida, C. D. (1997). The development of the American police: An historical overview. In R.D. Dunham, R. D., & G.P. Alpert (Ed.) *Critical issues in policing: Contemporary readings 3rd ed.* (pp. 13-35). Prospect Heights, IL: Waveland Press.

Wasserman, S., & Faust, K. (1994). *Social network analysis: Methods and applications*. New York: Cambridge University Press.

Welsh, B. C., & Farrington, D. P. (2002). Crime prevention effects of closed circuit television: A systematic review. Retrieved October 10, 2007, from http://www.homeoffice.gov.uk/rds/pdfs2/hors252.pdf

Welsh, B. C., & Farrington, D. P. (2006). Closed-circuit television surveillance. In B.C. Welsh & D.P. Farrington (Ed.) *Preventing crime: What works for children, offenders, victims, and places* (pp. 193-208). Dordrecht, NL: Springer.

Wilson, J. Q. (1993). *Performance measures for the criminal justice system. Article prepared for the U* (pp. 153–167). Washington, DC: S. Department of Justice, Bureau of Justice Assistance. Bureau of Justice Statistics.

Wilson, M. I., & Corey, K. (2000). *Information tectonics: Space, place, and technology in an electronic age*. West Sussex, UK: John Wiley and Sons Ltd.

Wood, J. (2006). Research and innovation in the field of security: A nodal governance view . In Wood, J., & Dupont, B. (Eds.), *Democracy, society and the governance of security* (pp. 217–240). New York: Cambridge University Press. doi:10.1017/CBO9780511489358.011

Wood, J., & Font, E. (2004, July 12-13). *Is "community policing" a desirable export? On crafting the global constabulary ethic*. Paper presented at the workshop on Constabulary Ethics and the Spirit of Transnational Policing. Oñati, Spain.

ENDNOTES

1 Stockholm district court case 13301-06. Defendants were in violation of §§ 1, 2, 46, 53, and 57 of the Copyright Act and Chapter 23§ 4 of the Swedish Penal code. *See*http://www.ifpi.org/content/library/Pirate-Bay-verdict-English-translation.pdf

2 Peer-to-Peer (P2P) file-sharing is a distributed network resource sharing model based on decentralized client to client (nodes) such that information transfer does not require central servers to store and distribute data (client-server model). This model can allow for collectively higher network throughput (bandwidth), storage capacity, and computing power.

3 *See*http://www.zeropaid.com/news/8428/us_trains_new_elite_swedish_antipiracy_police_force/

4 California's piracy concentration can be explained by its proximity to the Asia-Pacific region, which accounts for 67% of pirated optical discs seized worldwide by the MPA. *See*http://www.mpaa.org/inter_asia.asp

5 The Motion Picture Association of America (MPAA) handles U.S. domestic piracy and is a subset of the Motion Picture Association (MPA), handling international copyright infringement.

6 See http://www.mpaa.org/piracy_internet.asp

7 IP Academy Executive Summary: Illegal Downloading and Pirated Media in Singapore: Consumer Awareness, Motivations and Attitudes, 2006. *See*http://www.ipacademy.com.sg/site/ipa_cws/resource/executive%20summaries/Exec_Sum_Illegal.pdf

8 Survey included the U.S., United Kingdom, Germany, Italy, France, South Korea, Australia and Japan.

9 *See*http://lawyers.wizards.pro/california/codes/pen/13848-13848.8.php

10 Please note that this interview was conducted prior to Sweden's action against The Pirate Bay.

Section 3
Empirical Assessments

Chapter 6
Deciphering the Hacker Underground:
First Quantitative Insights

Michael Bachmann
Texas Christian University, USA

ABSTRACT

The increasing dependence of modern societies, industries, and individuals on information technology and computer networks renders them ever more vulnerable to attacks on critical IT infrastructures. While the societal threat posed by malicious hackers and other types of cyber criminals has been growing significantly in the last decade, mainstream criminology has only recently begun to realize the significance of this threat. Cyber criminology is slowly emerging as a subfield of criminological study and has yet to overcome many of the problems other areas of criminological research have already mastered. Aside from substantial methodological and theoretical problems, cyber criminology currently also suffers from the scarcity of available data. As a result, scientific answers to crucial questions remain. Questions like: Who exactly are these network attackers? Why do they engage in malicious hacking activities? This chapter begins to fill this gap in the literature by examining survey data about malicious hackers, their involvement in hacking, their motivations to hack, and their hacking careers. The data for this study was collected during a large hacking convention in Washington, D.C, in February 2008. The study findings suggest that a significant motivational shift takes place over the trajectory of hackers' careers, and that the creation of more effective countermeasures requires adjustments to our current understanding of who hackers are and why they hack.

DOI: 10.4018/978-1-61692-805-6.ch006

INTRODUCTION

Deciphering the Hacker Underground: First Quantitative Insights

The recent attacks on Estonia's computer and network infrastructures were an event of such unprecedented magnitude that it sent shockwaves throughout the world. In April, 2007, pro-Russian hackers launched a month-long retaliation campaign for the removal of a World War II statue—a campaign that has become known as the first war in cyberspace. Using a technique known as Distributed Denial-of-Service (DDoS) attacks on a hitherto-unprecedented scale, the attackers managed to effectively shut down vital parts of Estonia's digital infrastructures. In a coordinated effort, an estimated one million remote-controlled computers from 178 countries were used to bombard with requests the Web sites of the president, the prime minister, Parliament and other government agencies, Estonia's biggest bank, and several national newspapers (Landler & Markoff, 2007). Members of the Kremlin-backed youth movement 'Nashe' later claimed responsibility for the attacks, which they described as an 'adequate response' intended to 'teach the Estonian regime a lesson' (Clover, 2009). The group of young Russians also emphasized that they acted on their own initiative, not on government orders.

While the description as the first cyber war remains controversial because nobody died or was wounded, the events in Estonia, nevertheless, demonstrate the devastating consequences of Internet-borne attacks. In reference to the events in Estonia, Suleyman Anil, the head of NATO's incident response center, later warned attendees of the 2008 E-Crime Congress in London that "cyber defense is now mentioned at the highest level along with missile defense and energy security." According to Anil, "we have seen more of these attacks and we don't think this problem will disappear soon. Unless globally supported measures are taken, it can become a global problem" (Johnson, 2008, p. 1).

Today, the Internet has developed into a mission-critical entity for almost all parts of modern societies. Although warnings of the societal threat posed by cyber attacks on critical network infrastructures have been heralded since the 1980s, it is only in recent years that the problem has made it onto the radar of governments. Partly due to the experiences of Estonia and later in the conflict between Russia and Georgia, countries around the globe are now reassessing the security situation of their key information systems. They are enacting new security measures to better protect their critical network infrastructures, and they are increasing their readiness to respond to large-scale computer incidents (NCIRC, 2008). In the United States, security experts went as far as to warn against an 'electronic Pearl Harbor,' a 'digital September 11,' or a 'cybergeddon' (Stohl, 2006).

The implementation of effective countermeasures against hacking attacks is facilitated by the vast amount of knowledge already accumulated in numerous computer science research projects (cf. Chirillo, 2001; Curran, Morrisey, Fagan, Murphy, O'Donnell, & Firzpatrick, 2005; Erickson, 2008). Several studies conducted by computer scientists and computer engineers have closely examined the technical details of the various attack methods and have produced a significant body of information that can now be applied to help protect network infrastructures (Casey, 2004). Unfortunately, the guidance provided by these studies is limited to only the technical aspects of hacking attacks and, sharply contrasting from the substantial amount of knowledge already gathered about how the attacks are performed, answers to the questions of who the attackers are and why they engage in malicious hacking activities continue to remain largely speculative. Today, the persons committing the attacks remain mysterious, for the most part, and scientific information about them continues to be only fragmentary.

The present lack of information concerning the socio-demographic characteristics and the motives of cybercrime offenders can be attributed to a number of causes. One of the main reasons can be traced back to the unfortunate circumstance that, until recently, mainstream criminology has underestimated the potentially devastating societal impacts of cybercrimes and has diverted only limited attention to this relatively new type of criminal behavior (Jaishankar, 2007; Jewkes, 2006; Mann & Sutton, 1998). Cyber criminology is only now beginning to evolve as a distinct field of criminological research, and it has yet to overcome many methodological and theoretical problems that other areas of criminological research have already solved (Nhan & Bachmann, 2009; Yar, 2005, 2006).

A particular challenge for researchers in this young field of study arises from the various methodological obstacles entailed in the sampling of cyber criminals. As a result of these difficulties, available data sources are scarce, and quantitative studies are limited to surveys of cybercrime victims. At this point, only a few studies (Holt, 2007; Holt & Kilger, 2008; Mitnick & Simon, 2005; Schell, Dodge, with Moutsatsos, 2002; Taylor, 1999, 2000) and biographies (e.g. Mitnick, Simon, & Wozniak, 2002; Nuwere & Chanoff, 2003) exist that mostly examine individuals or smaller groups of hackers, their motivations, their preferences, and their hacking careers. While such studies are well suited to provide in-depth insights into the lives of a few individuals, many of them are less fit for generating generalizable information about the population of hackers, at large. Yet, just "like in traditional crimes, it's important to try to understand what motivates these people to get involved in computer crimes in the first place, how they choose their targets and what keeps them in this deviant behavior after the first initial thrill" (Bednarz, 2004, p. 1). This comment, stated by Marcus Rogers, an associate professor at Purdue University and head of the cyber forensics research in the department of computer technology, accurately describes the task cyber criminologists have to accomplish.

The aim of the study presented in this chapter was to undertake this task and to begin filling the remaining gap in the criminological literature on hackers and the hacking community by providing quantifiable insights into the hacking underground. Such insights are needed to create a more profound understanding of the nature of the threat and a more complete assessment of the problem and its solutions. The identification of the reasons and motives for an attack helps to better identify the actors' behaviors, to develop better countermeasures, and to foster investigative efforts to identify the individuals responsible for the attacks.

The Problem: Gathering Quantitative Data on Cyber Offenders

Obtaining an accurate assessment of cyber offenders is a difficult undertaking. Unfortunately, this is true for many of the types of offenders studied by criminologists. The same problems that plague the examinations of other types of offenders, however, are exacerbated in the case of cyber offenders. Official crime data, oftentimes used for criminological offender studies, contain hardly any measures of cybercrime, in general, and the few existing measures suffer from serious problems. To begin, the two most important official crime data sources, the Uniform Crime Report (UCR) and the National Incident Based Reporting System (NIBRS) contain hardly any useful information for the study of cyber offenders. The UCR records no cybercrime and the NIBRS contains only one, highly ambiguous computer crime variable that merely indicates whether a computer was used in the commission of the criminal act. It is also important to bear in mind that all official crime statistics are plagued by underreporting problems, because they do not measure incident trends and distributions objectively but are instead essentially socially constructed. Official datasets include only crimes that have been reported, and there are several reasons why crime victims are oftentimes reluctant to report offenses. The most common of these factors is the perception of the offense as private or trivial, fears of retaliation, unawareness of the victimization, or a lack of faith in an effective response. Especially corporate actors oftentimes also fear the potential damage the reporting of their victimization can have for their public reputation.

While the aforementioned problems are faced by all quantitative criminological studies, they are magnified with respect to hacking attacks and, to varying degrees, to all other forms of cybercrimes. As was stated previously, the intangibility of evidence and the lack of traditional forensic artifacts make online offenses more difficult to detect than terrestrial crimes. Even in cases where traces of the attack are recovered as evidence, cybercrime victims are hardly ever able to report offender information beyond what can be inferred from the attack itself.

Cybercrime offenders enjoy a significantly higher level of anonymity than, for example, offenders who attack their victims physically. Complicating matters further is the remaining lack of knowledge as to what exactly constitutes a cybercrime, and, consequently, whether reporting of a particular incident is appropriate (Howell, 2007). Moreover, the global nature of cyber attacks and the high level of offender anonymity in the online environment are two aspects that discourage both victims and law enforcement from reporting such crimes, because they drastically decrease the perceived chance of apprehending the offender. As a result, many police stations prioritize reporting of local problems. Taken together, the above factors justify the conclusion that cybercrimes are greatly underreported in official statistics, thus rendering official data sources of limited utility for cyber offender studies.

Crime and victimization surveys offer an alternate assessment of crime levels. Victimization surveys are often used by criminologists because of their ability to encompass offenses that are typically underreported in official statistics. Despite their advantages, crime and victimization surveys cannot completely eliminate all of the difficulties faced by official measurements. To begin with, it is self-evident that an undetected crime cannot be reported. Of higher importance for the quality of survey data, however, are systematic errors and the bias they introduce. Systematic errors can result from many different sources, such as incongruities in the definition of what constitutes a crime between interviewer and interviewee, various other interviewer effects, the presence of third persons, sponsorship-biases, or the so-called response set of the participant, to name but a few. Survey researchers have long recognized that even the highest possible optimization of survey instruments will never completely eliminate survey errors (cf. Groves, Fowler, Couper, Lepkowski, Singer, & Torangeau, 2004).

Despite their shortcomings, victimization surveys are especially relevant for cybercrime studies, because official data on computer offenders remains scarce. Unfortunately, survey-related problems are exacerbated when measuring cybercrimes. Cybercrime victimization surveys typically have selective populations and study samples. The majority of surveys, including the annual CSI/FBI Computer Crime and Security Survey, measure only corporate or organizational victimization and exclude private computer users. More importantly, the vast majority of surveys focus exclusively on the victims of cybercrimes, not on the offenders. At this point, hardly any surveys of cybercrime offenders exist.

All of the above difficulties suggest that more studies and more direct measurement techniques are needed, particularly for the study of cyber offenders. These difficulties should lead cybercrime researchers to be cautious about the validity of their data. However, researchers should refrain from using all available data, for more current data are needed for a greater understanding of the limitations of the various data sources and for the refining of methodological techniques to better address them.

Eventually, meta-studies of official data and victimization surveys will be able to provide a reasonably adequate picture of Internet threats. When pursuing this approach, however, one has to be cautious about drawing conclusions about the offenders, because the high degree of anonymity and inaccessibility granted by the Internet environment conceals many relevant offender characteristics to the victims, and the low apprehension rate prevents accurate estimates of systematic differences between offenders who get caught and those who do not.

THIS STUDY'S APPROACH

The goal of this chapter is to examine the socio-demographic characteristics of malicious hackers and to unveil their motives for hacking. To achieve these goals, the research project was designed to produce quantifiable results more representative and generalizable to a wider target population than previous qualitative case studies completed on hackers (Jordan & Taylor, 1998; Taylor, 1999). A survey was designed for the investigation of malicious hackers and used to collect data (Boudreau, Gefen, & Straub, 2001), because surveys are the one data-collection method particularly suited to produce quantitative results generalizable to other members of the population of interest and oftentimes even to other similar populations (Newsted, Chin, Ngwenyama, & Lee, 1996).

Pretest

To minimize unanticipated encounters during the fielding of the survey, a pretest of the initial draft of the questionnaire was conducted with an availability sample comprised of six self-proclaimed hackers known to the researcher. The pretest panel members were asked to provide detailed written feedback after their completion of the survey and to return their comments via email. The feedback received from this pretest focused primarily on revisions of the wording and was aimed at eliminating potential ambiguities in some of the hacking-related questions. It also included some suggestions for minor changes in the standard answer categories provided. Overall, there was general agreement among the reviewers on the suitability and appropriateness of the items in the survey and on the exhaustiveness of the standard answer categories.

In a subsequent step, the revised version of the survey was reviewed by two experienced survey researchers on the sociology faculty at the University of Central Florida. Aside from providing a second scrutiny of the appropriateness of the survey tool and the unambiguousness of the individual items, this expert assessment was to ensure the appropriateness of the survey as a scientific measurement instrument and to examine the content validity of the items, many developed for the present study and not yet validated.

Based on the recommendations of these experts, some modifications and refinements were implemented in the final version of the questionnaire; for example, the wording of a few individual items was revised and some items were rearranged. There was agreement among the reviewers on the importance of all main sections of the questionnaire, on the appropriate length of the measurement tool, and on the suitability of the included items to address the intended dimensions of the underlying concepts. Following the pretest of the questionnaire, the research proposal was approved by the University of Central Florida Institutional Review Board.

Procedure

The questionnaire was fielded during the 2008 ShmooCon convention in Washington, D.C. Since its first convening in 2004, ShmooCon has developed into one of the largest annual conventions worldwide. Today, it ranks among the most popular conventions, and it is attended by both U.S. and international hackers and security experts. In addition, it has one of the most diverse programs, attractive to a wide variety of hackers (Grecs, 2008). The convention is commonly announced as "an annual East Coast hacker convention hell-bent on offering an interesting and new atmosphere for demonstrating technology exploitation, inventive software and hardware solutions, and open discussion of critical information security issues."

During the convention, attendees were approached by the researcher and invited to participate in the study. They were told that the survey referred to hacking (defined as the unauthorized intrusion into computer systems, networks, or website servers), and they were asked to participate--*only if they had ever committed such an intrusion* and had not gotten permission from the owner of the system or the network.

Attendees who indicated that they worked as penetration testers were asked to participate only if they had ever invaded a computer system outside of a contractual agreement; if they agreed to these terms and conditions, they were instructed to refer only to these intrusions in their answers. Penetration testers and other attendees who reported to have never committed such an unauthorized hack were told that the survey did not pertain to them and were excluded from the analysis.

In all, 164 questionnaires were distributed among qualified attendees. Most of the persons who agreed to participate filled out the questionnaire on site. Some, however, asked to take it with them and fill it out at a more convenient situation. Of the 164 distributed surveys, 129 were returned to the researcher, 124 of which were filled out completely and included in the analysis of the study. Thus, the response rate of completed and returned surveys was an impressive 75 percent.

The Survey Instrument

The measurement instrument consisted of a total of 72 items in three main sections. The questionnaire gathered detailed information about the various phases of the respondents' hacking careers. It embodied items pertaining to the initiation of the hacking activity, its habituation, and the eventual desistance from hacking. It further assessed several other details of the respondent's hacking activity, including a variety of involved decisions and motivations. Given the exploratory nature of this research project, many items in the first section offered open-ended "other answer" categories, in addition to the answer options provided. The answers recorded in the latter were included as string variables in the dataset.

The Socio-Demographic Composition of the Sample

The socio-demographic characteristics displayed in Table 1 show a vastly skewed gender distribution among the hacker respondents. Only seven of the 124 participants (5.6%) were females. The wide gender gap revealed in this study confirms other reports that describe hacker communities as being predominantly male (Adam, 2004; Taylor, 1999).

The underrepresentation of women in all areas related to computing and Information Technology—except in office or administrative positions—has already received considerable scrutiny in the literature (Webster, 1996). Against this background, the domination of males in the hacking community is not surprising. However, the gender difference in this study exceeded even the discrepancies found in other areas of computing and IT, in which women are estimated to account for 10 to 30 percent of participants (Zarrett & Malanchuk, 2005).

Taylor traces the absence of women in the hacking community (which he finds to be an "unexplained statistic") to what he sees as the fundamentally masculine nature of hacking. He describes the hacking culture as young, male, technology-oriented, and laden with factors that discourage women from joining. Among the factors listed by Taylor are social stereotyping,

Table 1. Sociodemographic characteristics of sample respondents

Variable	N[1]	%[2]
Sex		
Male	117	94.4
Female	7	5.6
Age[3]	120	30.6/(6.7)
Education		
None, or grades 1-8	0	0.0
High school incomplete	4	3.2
High school graduate	7	5.6
Vocational school	2	1.6
Some college	30	24.2
College graduate	47	37.9
Post-graduate Master's or Ph.D.	34	27.4
Race		
Hispanic descent	3	2.4
White	116	93.5
Black	2	1.6
Asian	5	4.0
Other	1	0.8
Marriage status[4]		
Never married	63	50.8
Living as married	17	13.7
Married	43	34.7
Divorced	1	0.8
Employment		
Full-time	92	74.2
Part-time	22	17.7
Unemployed	10	8.1
Student status		
Yes, full-time	14	11.3
Yes, part-time	31	25.0
Not a student	79	63.7
Actively hacking		
Yes	97	78.2
No	27	21.8
[1] The total sample size is n=124.		
[2] Percentages may not add up due to rounding.		
[3] Measured in years, means reported (std. dev. in parentheses).		

a masculine "locker room" environment, and a gender-biased computing language (Taylor, 1999, pp. 32, 36).

Adam goes one step further by describing the hacker culture as one that, despite the explicit egalitarianism expressed in the Hacker Ethic, is, nevertheless, characterized by a "frontier masculinity," a "Wild West brand of masculinity," and a deeply rooted misogyny displayed by men who hide behind the anonymity of the Internet and associate "technology with desire, eroticism and artificial creation" (Adam, 2004, p. 6).

The data collected in the present study confirmed the existence of a substantial gender gap, but it did not include any additional attitude measurements with regard to gender. Hence, it is not possible to confirm or reject any of the above-mentioned explanations.

Aside from the large gender gap, the data also display a skewed race distribution. Over 93 percent of the hackers in the sample were White, a percentage vastly exceeding that in the U.S. population. Another noteworthy finding in the race distribution is that Asians were the largest minority in the sample. While the low cell count of all minorities in the present study did not permit accurate generalizations of this finding, this result reflects the racial distributions in most IT professions (Zarrett & Malanchuk, 2005). A common explanation for this finding is the prevalence of positive attitudes toward math, science, and computer-related occupations among Whites and Asian cultures (Bement, Ward, Carlson, Frase, & Fecso, 2004).

The age distribution of the convention attendees shows a much higher mean value than the one suggested by the common notion of the prototypical hacker as a juvenile delinquent teenager (Yar, 2005). It is reasonable to assume that the higher average age in this study of ShmooCon convention attendees was caused by the sampling frame of this project. The profile of the ShmooCon convention is geared more toward security experts and computer professionals than to teenagers pursuing their hacking interests merely as a leisure-time hobby. Thus, while the distribution in this particular sample is certainly not enough to falsify any claims that the majority of hackers are teenagers, it indicates that the hacking community is by no means limited to only teenagers. To the contrary, it involves many mature security experts and many seasoned hackers pursuing their hacking activity in a professional manner. The data clearly show that hacking is not just a 'young man's game.' The oldest active hacker in the sample was 52 years of age and reported to have been hacking for close to three decades.

The professionalism of most respondents was also reflected in their educational attainments. Ninety percent of the hackers in the study sample had at least some college education, and about one-fourth of them obtained a Master's or Ph.D. degree. Moreover, about one-third of all respondents were enrolled either as full-time or part-time students. An examination of the four cases with an incomplete high school education revealed that most of them were young participants (between 18 and 19 years old) who also reported to be full-time students. These four cases were most likely high school students who had not yet graduated.

The high fraction of students in the survey sample is particularly surprising when considering that over 90 percent of all respondents were employed. About three-fourths reported being employed full-time and an additional 18 percent reported being employed part-time.

The high employment rate was probably part of the reason why more than double as many respondents indicated that they were part-time students than full-time students. When asked about their marital status, about half of all respondents said that they were never married. A significantly smaller fraction--about one-third of all participants--reported being married.

In short, the socio-demographic characteristics sampled in this study paint the picture of a hacking community that is predominantly male, White, and comprised of highly-educated members. Most of these hacker conference attendees also work regular jobs and are oftentimes studying; however, they appear to be hesitant about engaging in serious relationship commitments.

KEY STUDY FINDINGS: DIFFERENT PHASES AND SHIFTING MOTIVATIONS

Initiation Phase

Some of the most interesting questions asked in the survey related to the initiation phase of hacking, including: (1) what sparked the initial interest in hacking? (2) what led hackers to commit their first actual hacking attempt? (3) at what age did they attempt such? The results show that many hackers became interested in hacking even before their early teenage years. One person reported that he was only nine years of age when he first became interested in hacking. While this respondent was the youngest in the sample, he was no exception.

Table 2 shows the age respondents became interested in hacking and the motivations for doing so. The first peak in the initial interest distribution was 12 years of age with about twenty percent of respondents reporting being interested by that age. The median was 15 years, and the mean was 16 years.

The self-reported motives for the initial interest in hacking show that the majority of participants became interested because of "intellectual curiosity" (95%), "experimentation" (85%), and "excitement, thrill, or fun" (66%). A second set of motives revolving around self-expression and peer-recognition turned out to be of significantly lesser importance. Among these motives were "feeling of power" (21%), "peer recognition" (19%), "self-concept boost" (18%), "status and prestige" (15%), and "personal revenge" (10%).

Some of the motives oftentimes associated with hackers in media reports (Alexander, 2005) as well as in scientific (Grabosky & Smith, 1998; Kilger, Arkin, & Stutzman, 2004) and governmental publications (Krone, 2005) played only a marginal role as initial interests. Among these motives were the following: "political ideology" (5%), "protest against corporations" (3%), "financial gain" (2%), and "media attention" (2%).

These study results clearly demonstrate that motives associated with youth, boredom, frivolity, mischief, or curiosity are the main reasons for young persons to become initially interested in hacking. In contrast, only a few respondents became interested in hacking because of political or financial considerations, or other motives with a stronger criminal intent.

A similar pattern emerged from the question about the single most important motive for the initial interest. Here, roughly four times more respondents (60%) answered because of "intellectual curiosity" than with the next popular answer option: "experimentation" (17%). "Media attention," "financial gain," "protest against corporations," and "status and prestige," were not mentioned at all and were, therefore, excluded from Table 2.

Only five "other" reasons were specified. Of those, the desire to spy on a girlfriend--who the respondent believed to be cheating--was named twice. The other reasons were independence, learning of security, and playing pranks on friends. Overall, the few reasons given in addition to the list of standard answer options suggest that the list was comprehensive. One item that should be considered for inclusion in the theoretical model and future measurements is "spying."

The separate measure of the motives for the first actual hack produced roughly the same results as the item measuring the motives for the initial interest. The main difference between the two items was that the reason for the first actual hack was more specific than that for the initial interest. Accordingly, most respondents marked fewer motives, resulting in lower percentages for all motives. The patterns between the different motives were very similar to the ones emerging from the question about initial interests. Two noteworthy

Table 2. Motivations for interest in hacking and first hack

Variable	N[1]	%[2]
Age interested in hacking[3]	124	16.0/(4.3)
Motive for initial interest[4]		
Intellectual curiosity	118	95.2
Experimentation	105	84.7
Excitement, thrill, fun	82	66.1
Feeling of power	26	21.0
Peer recognition	23	18.5
Self-concept boost	22	17.7
Status and prestige	19	15.3
Personal revenge	12	9.7
Other	7	5.6
Political ideology	6	4.8
Protest against corporations	4	3.2
Financial gain	3	2.4
Media attention	2	1.6
Primary motive for interest[4]		
Intellectual curiosity	74	59.7
Experimentation	21	16.9
Excitement, thrill, fun	15	12.1
Feeling of power	4	3.2
Other	4	3.2
Self-concept boost	2	1.6
Political ideology	2	1.6
Peer recognition	1	0.8
Personal revenge	1	0.8
Motive for first hack[4]		
Intellectual curiosity	91	73.4
Experimentation	84	67.7
Excitement, thrill, fun	56	45.2
Feeling of power	13	10.5
Peer recognition	10	8.1
Self-concept boost	10	8.1
Status and prestige	4	3.2
Personal revenge	6	4.8
Other	3	2.4
Protest against corporations	2	1.6
Financial gain	2	1.6

continued on following page

Table 2. continued

Variable	N[1]	%[2]
[1] The total sample size is n=124.		
[2] Percentages may not add up due to rounding.		
[3] Measured in years, means reported (std. dev. in parentheses).		
[4] For better readability, the motives are rank ordered by importance.		

findings in the distribution of motives for the first hack were that "political ideology" was not mentioned by any respondent, and that "financial gain" was a motive for only two respondents.

Aside from the motivations for the initial interest and the first actual hack, the survey also measured the length of the time span between these two events. The time measure was recorded in days in the dataset but is presented in more meaningful categories in Table 3. Interestingly, about one-third of all respondents committed their first hacking attempt within the first week of becoming interested in hacking. An additional 20 percent committed their first hack within the first month of becoming interested. These findings suggest that the initial interest of many hackers is not an abstract, intellectual enterprise, but rather a preparation for their first actual hack. It further indicates that the initial interest is guided by the intent to actually launch attacks. Less than 50 percent of respondents were interested in hacking longer than a month before they actually attempted a hack. The longest reported time span was clearly an outlier--10 years. Table 3 displays the recorded time spans between initial interests and first hacks.

Table 3 further shows that the most popular targets of the first hack were single, private computer hosts (40%) and private networks (23%). Corporate computers and networks were the second-most popular targets (4% and 6%, respectively). With regard to corporate targets, the relationship between single hosts and networks was reversed. More corporate networks were attacked than single computers. This difference is probably due to accessibility reasons. While many single private hosts can be located in unprotected wireless networks or public networks, an attack on corporate computers typically requires a preceding attack on the network in which the computer is located. Only one hacker selected a government host and network as the target for his first attack. For all others, these targets were probably too risky and too high profile to be considered as a reasonable first target.

Most hackers selected their first target based on practical considerations. The majority of participants (57%) reported that the ease of gaining access was their primary selection criteria. About half as many chose a particular target because it offered interesting information (29%). Revenge or antipathy with the host played only a minor role as selection criteria. Only seven respondents attacked their targets because of personal dislike (6%). Some specifications of answers in the "other category" (9%) revealed that some respondents counted attempts to hack their own computer system or network as their first hacking attempt. Future survey designs will need to be more explicit to rule out this interpretation of the question.

The answers to the selection criteria question confirmed the irrelevance of commonly assumed motives in the initiation phase. None of the respondents attacked their targets in search of profitable information or because they were particularly suited for gaining a reputation as a hacker. The finding that financial interests played hardly any role during the onset of hacking activity was

Table 3. Details of the first hacking attempt

Variable	N[1]	%[2]
Time span between interest and hack[3]		
Up to 1 week	45	36.3
Up to 1 month	23	18.5
Up to 1 year	31	25.0
2 to 10 years	25	20.2

1st target owner / type	N	(%)	N	(%)	N	(%)
	Single host		Network		Website	
Private	50	(40.3)	29	(23.4)	4	(3.2)
Corporate	5	(4.0)	7	(5.6)	3	(2.4)
Non-profit	0	0	4	(3.2)	1	(0.8)
Government	1	(0.8)	1	(0.8)	0	0

1st target selection criteria		
Easy access	70	56.5
Interesting information	36	29.0
Profitable information	0	
Reputation gain	0	
Antipathy	7	5.6
Other	11	8.9
Employed when 1st hacked		
Yes, full-time	28	22.6
Yes, part-time	28	22.6
No	68	54.8
Economic profit a motive at all		
Yes, an important one	0	
Yes, but not very important	5	4.0
No	119	96.0

[1] The total sample size is n=124.

[2] Percentages may not add up due to rounding.

[3] Categories are not cumulative.

confirmed by the answers to the explicit question asking whether economic profits were a motive. While only five respondents (4%) said it played a minor role, the majority (94%) indicated that economic considerations or potential financial gains had nothing to do with their decision to start hacking.

The finding that a majority of respondents (55%) were unemployed when they first hacked is not surprising, given the young age of most respondents when they started to hack. During their first hacks, most of them were still dependent teenagers with little or no income of their own. Despite little or no income, it is important to note

Table 4. Developments during hacking career

Variable	N[1]	%[2]
Time hacking (in years)		
Up to 1	8	6.5
2-5	30	24.2
6-10	47	37.9
10-15	20	16.1
16-20	10	8.1
20-28	9	7.3
Change friends (more hackers)		
Yes, very much	28	22.6
Yes, somewhat	66	53.2
No	30	24.2
Improved skills		
Yes, very much	89	71.8
Yes, somewhat	34	27.4
No	1	0.8
Hacking more frequent		
Yes, very much	37	29.8
Yes, somewhat	39	31.5
No, it's the same	18	14.5
No, it's less frequent	30	24.2
Motives changed		
Yes, very much	38	30.6
Yes, somewhat	37	29.8
No	49	39.5
Current primary motive (initial interest)		
Intellectual curiosity	37/(74)	29.8/(59.7)
Financial gain	28/(0)	22.6
Experimentation	22/(21)	17.7/(16.9)
Other	21/(4)	16.9/(3.2)
Excitement, thrill, fun	14/(15)	11.3/(12.1)
Self-concept boost	2/(2)	1.6/(1.6)
Feeling of power	0/(4)	(3.2)
Political ideology	0/(2)	(1.6)

continued on following page

Table 4. continued

Variable	N[1]	%[2]
Peer recognition	0/(1)	(0.8)
Personal revenge	0/(1)	(0.8)
[1] The total sample size is n=124.		
[2] Percentages may not add up due to rounding.		

that economic interests hardly played any role in the decision to engage in hacking activities.

Habituation and Desistance

The length of hacking careers (as shown in Table 4) reaffirmed the considerable experience of most hackers in the present sample. The normal-shaped distribution of hacking experiences ranged from "less than a year" to" 28 years," averaging 10 years. The length of most hacking careers in the present sample was a clear indication that the majority of respondents were not beginners but had already habitualized their hacking activities.

Most respondents befriended other hackers during their time as active hackers. Seventy-five percent of all respondents said they had changed their social networks to include other hackers, and 23 percent did so "very much." Besides the changes in their networks, most hackers also reported changes in their motives, their engagement in hacking, and their skills. Only one respondent said that he had not improved his hacking skills since he began hacking. This particular hacker was one of the least experienced in the sample. He had less than one year of hacking experience and had committed only one hack. All other respondents claimed to have improved their skills over the course of their careers, and 72 percent said they did so "very much."

A majority of respondents reported that their hacking activities had intensified over the course of their careers. Of all hackers in the sample, 30 percent said they are hacking much more frequently now than when they started, and 32 percent reported that their hacking activities have somewhat increased. Only 30 respondents (24%) said their hacking activities had become less frequent. Of those, 27 respondents also said that they are no longer actively hacking. Thus, only 3 active hackers had decreased their hacking frequency, while 60 percent of the active hackers had increased it. The data in Table 4 show an apparent trend toward an intensification of hacking activities over time.

Sixty percent of respondents further indicated that their motives had changed since their initial interest in hacking. Indeed, the comparison of initial motives with current ones revealed three dramatic changes had occurred between the two measures. First, the importance of intellectual curiosity as the primary motive decreased by 50 percent over time (from 60% to 30%).

Second, financial gain, a motive of no importance for the initial interest, had become the second-most important motive for hacking. Twenty-three percent of all subjects said that their main motives for continuing to hack were financial gains. The sharp increase of financial gains as motives for hacking is an intriguing finding. It means that while most hackers set out to become hackers because they were curious about the technology and keen to experiment with it, along the way some of them realized the financial possibilities achievable through their engagement in hacking.

Table 5. Target preferences

<table>
<tr><th colspan="3">Variable</th><th colspan="2">N[1]</th><th colspan="2">%[2]</th></tr>
<tr><td colspan="7"></td></tr>
<tr><td colspan="7">Targets changed since 1st hack</td></tr>
<tr><td colspan="3">Yes, very much</td><td colspan="2">52</td><td colspan="2">41.9</td></tr>
<tr><td colspan="3">Yes, somewhat</td><td colspan="2">36</td><td colspan="2">29.0</td></tr>
<tr><td colspan="3">No</td><td colspan="2">36</td><td colspan="2">29.0</td></tr>
<tr><td colspan="7"></td></tr>
<tr><td colspan="7">Higher profile targets</td></tr>
<tr><td colspan="3">Yes, very much</td><td colspan="2">29</td><td colspan="2">23.4</td></tr>
<tr><td colspan="3">Yes, somewhat</td><td colspan="2">34</td><td colspan="2">27.4</td></tr>
<tr><td colspan="3">No</td><td colspan="2">61</td><td colspan="2">49.2</td></tr>
<tr><td colspan="7"></td></tr>
<tr><td>Current target owner / type</td><td>N</td><td>(%)[3]</td><td>N</td><td>(%)[3]</td><td>N</td><td>(%)[3]</td></tr>
<tr><td colspan="7"></td></tr>
<tr><td></td><td colspan="2">Single host</td><td colspan="2">Network</td><td colspan="2">Website</td></tr>
<tr><td>Private</td><td>49</td><td>(39.5)</td><td>56</td><td>(45.2)</td><td>23</td><td>(18.5)</td></tr>
<tr><td>Corporate</td><td>21</td><td>(16.9)</td><td>49</td><td>(39.5)</td><td>35</td><td>(28.2)</td></tr>
<tr><td>Non-profit</td><td>4</td><td>(3.2)</td><td>4</td><td>(3.2)</td><td>7</td><td>(5.6)</td></tr>
<tr><td>Government</td><td>18</td><td>(14.5)</td><td>31</td><td>(25.0)</td><td>25</td><td>(20.2)</td></tr>
<tr><td colspan="7"></td></tr>
<tr><td colspan="7">Current target selection criteria (initial criteria)</td></tr>
<tr><td colspan="3">Easy access</td><td colspan="2">58/(70)</td><td colspan="2">46.8/(56.5)</td></tr>
<tr><td colspan="3">Interesting information</td><td colspan="2">87/(36)</td><td colspan="2">70.2/(29.0)</td></tr>
<tr><td colspan="3">Profitable information</td><td colspan="2">31/(0)</td><td colspan="2">25.0</td></tr>
<tr><td colspan="3">Reputation gain</td><td colspan="2">2/(0)</td><td colspan="2">1.6</td></tr>
<tr><td colspan="3">Antipathy</td><td colspan="2">2/(7)</td><td colspan="2">1.6/(5.6)</td></tr>
<tr><td colspan="3">Other</td><td colspan="2">11/(11)</td><td colspan="2">8.9/(8.9)</td></tr>
<tr><td colspan="7"></td></tr>
<tr><td colspan="7">Rejection reasons</td></tr>
<tr><td colspan="3">No interesting information</td><td colspan="2">60</td><td colspan="2">48.4</td></tr>
<tr><td colspan="3">Unfamiliarity with architecture</td><td colspan="2">48</td><td colspan="2">38.7</td></tr>
<tr><td colspan="3">Sympathy with host</td><td colspan="2">23</td><td colspan="2">18.5</td></tr>
<tr><td colspan="3">No profitable information</td><td colspan="2">19</td><td colspan="2">15.3</td></tr>
<tr><td colspan="3">Other</td><td colspan="2">9</td><td colspan="2">7.3</td></tr>
<tr><td colspan="3">None of the above</td><td colspan="2">30</td><td colspan="2">24.2</td></tr>
<tr><td colspan="7"></td></tr>
<tr><td colspan="7">Change in methods and tactics</td></tr>
<tr><td colspan="3">Yes, very much</td><td colspan="2">51</td><td colspan="2">50.0</td></tr>
<tr><td colspan="3">Yes, somewhat</td><td colspan="2">37</td><td colspan="2">36.3</td></tr>
<tr><td colspan="3">No</td><td colspan="2">14</td><td colspan="2">13.7</td></tr>
</table>

continued on following page

Table 5. continued

Variable	N[1]	%[2]
Variability of methods (scale 1-7)	123	4.7/(1.7)
Variability of tools (scale 1-7)	123	3.9/(1.7)
[1] The total sample size is n=124.		
[2] Percentages may not add up due to rounding.		
[3] Multiple answers were possible. % values refer to complete sample.		

The third main difference between the two measures is the reduction of motives. While the list of initial motives included ten motives, this list was reduced to six persistent motives. Feelings of power, political ideology, peer recognition, and personal revenge no longer played a role for the continued engagement in hacking. The changes in motives demonstrate that for many respondents, hacking efforts evolved into a professional business. This trend was also reflected in the "other" category. Most entries in this category pertained to the gathering of sensitive and security-related information.

The changes in motives were mirrored in the changes that occurred in the preferences for certain targets. As Table 5 illustrates, 71 percent of all respondents reported having changed their targets over the course of their careers. Also, 50 percent said they are now attacking higher profile targets, and 86 percent reported having changed their methods and tools to attack the different kinds of targets.

The increased preference of many hackers for higher-profile targets was visibly reflected in their preferred types of targets. Both corporate and governmental targets were attacked much more frequently. The preference for corporate computers quadrupled (from 4% to 17%), the preference for corporate networks septupled (from 6% to 40%), and the preference for corporate websites increased twelve-fold (from 2.4% to 28%). Similarly, governmental targets, virtually not targeted during the onset of the hacking activity, were much more popular among experienced hackers. Fifteen percent reported having attacked governmental hosts, 25 percent attacked governmental networks, and 20 percent targeted governmental websites.

The selection criteria for targets changed in accordance with the motives and the targets. The prospect of obtaining profitable information, initially irrelevant during the onset of hacking activities, had become the third-most important criterion. Twenty-five percent of all respondents said this criterion was relevant for their selection of targets. The significantly increased importance of profitable information confirmed the trend toward a professionalization of illegal activities.

Easy access remained the most important criterion, but its significance was notably reduced (from 57% to 47%). Following an opposite trend, the prospect of interesting information had vastly gained importance. More than double as many hackers listed "interesting information" as one of their selection criteria (from 29% to 70%).

Among rejection criteria, "the absence of interesting information" was the most frequent one cited. Almost half of all participants (48%) listed it as a reason to refrain from an attack. "Unfamiliarity with the architecture of a computer system or network" was the second-most common reason for a rejection (39%), followed by "sympathy with the host of that system or network" (19%). Analogous to its importance as a selection criterion, 15 percent of all hackers in the sample marked "the absence of profitable information" as a reason for rejecting a particular target. This result underlines the profound change many hackers undergo over the course of their hacking careers. Hackers apparently become more professional, and many of them begin to see hacking not only as an intellectual challenge but as a potential source of income.

DISCUSSION

The present study showed that the common hacker stereotype as a clever, lonesome, deviant male adolescent whose computer proficiency compensates social shortcomings barely tells the whole story of who hackers are. That is not to say that this stereotypical portrayal of hackers is completely mistaken. Several aspects of this characterization were confirmed by the study results as well as by the researcher's personal observations during the conference. First, the participants in this study were highly educated, intelligent persons who had their inquiring minds set on technological developments. Many of these technophiles also seemed to be equally inventive, creative, and determined.

Second, the convention attendees were predominantly males, and minority hackers were rare exceptions. The near-uniformity with regard to the sex and race distributions, however, stood in sharp contrast to the strong emphasis of many attendees on an individualistic appearance. Many hackers conveyed their individualistic nature in conversations with the researcher as well as through their physical appearance. The physical expressions of individualism ranged from extravagant haircuts and hair colors, to unusual clothing styles, to large tattoos on various body parts, sometimes even on faces.

The two most important inadequacies of the hacker stereotype seem to be the notions that hackers are invariably young, and that they are socially inept. The study found that hacking is by no means only a young man's game, as Yar suggested (Yar, 2005). It remains to be seen what fraction of hackers is actually comprised of teenagers, but the findings of this study clearly showed that persons of various age groups engage in hacking activities. More importantly, the data also revealed that hackers undergo a maturation process over the course of their hacking careers, and that the more experienced and seasoned hackers tend to be the most dangerous ones. They are more likely to attack higher-profile targets, and some of them even engage in their illegal hacking activities with the stronger criminal intent of making financial profits.

Young and inexperienced hackers can certainly cause damage with their mischief, but the study showed that these hackers attack primarily private targets out of intellectual curiosity, love for knowledge, experimentation, boredom, or youthful "tomfoolery." Many hackers first became interested in hacking very early in their lives, and, they tended not to be driven by a pronounced initial criminal intent. As their hacking activities continued to become habitualized, many of them developed into more professional and ambitious hackers. Over the course of their hacking careers, many intensified their hacking activities and began to attack higher-profile targets,such as governmental and corporate information systems. Some hackers even reported having turned their once merely deviant juvenile behavior into a criminal business activity.

About 15 percent of all respondents said that hacking had become their main source of income, and that they would reject a target unless it were profitable. Undoubtedly, these experienced veteran hackers are the ones causing the most concern and to whom attention should be directed.

Although the comparatively high fraction of unmarried hackers showed that many of them are hesitant to engage in serious relationships and commitments, the vast popularity of social hacking methods and their high success rates also indicated that the commonly presumed social incompetence of hackers is wrong and misleading. The falseness of this assumption was further reaffirmed by some of the observations the researcher made during the convention.

Most attendees appeared to be outgoing and sociable. Many attended the convention with their friends, and most of the attendees seemed to share a distinct sense of humor, mingling quickly. Certainly, the informal observations during the convention and the findings that hackers are skilled in manipulating and "programming" other persons (commonly referred to as "social engineering"). Oftentimes, they manage to exploit the trust or carelessness of other computer users for their hacking purposes. While there was not enough evidence in this study for a strong rebuttal of the notion that hackers are social hermits, it might be the case that the sociability of hackers is limited to interactions with other like-minded technophiles. Although many appear to be skilled manipulators, genuine and affectionate social relations with others seem to be of lesser importance to them.

Additional examinations of the social networks of hackers, their amount, frequency, and quality of interactions with close contacts, the types of contacts they engage in (face-to-face or online), and the importance they attribute to these social contacts are needed before a firmer conclusion about the appropriateness of the assumption that hackers are recluses can be reached.

CONCLUSION

Study Limitations

Even though this study produced valuable insights into the socio-demographic composition of the hacking underground and the various developments hackers undergo over the course of their hacking careers, it was limited in certain ways. One set of potential shortcomings relates to the sampling frame and the sample size of the study. The study analyzed only data from one particular convention, a circumstance that constricts the confidence with which the present findings can be generalized to larger populations. Although the ShmooCon convention attracted a diverse clientele, it remains unclear how general the profile of this particular convention really is.

It also remains uncertain whether there are significant differences between the attendees of different conventions. More datasets from different conventions are needed to enable researchers to draw comparisons between them and to assess the reliability and validity of the present data. Once multiple studies from different conventions exist, meta-studies will eventually be able to compare the results of these studies and extract highly reliable and valid findings.

Although repeated studies from different conventions will eventually be able to generate valid and generalizable results, they will be only to the subset of hackers attending hacker conventions or, more narrowly, have already attended them. It remains to be seen whether there are systematic and consistent differences between hackers potentially attending conventions and those who do not.

The average age of respondents in this study was considerably higher than the typical age of hackers other authors have suggested (Yar, 2005). This finding indicates that studies operating with conventions as their sampling frames are suffering from some systematic selection biases. An assessment of the exact areas in which such systematic differences exist and the degree to they render the results of convention studies distinctively different from other studies with different sampling frames can only be achieved by comparative studies. Until other sampling frames, such as message boards, have been utilized and until their results have been compared with the ones produced by convention studies, researchers have to remain cautious when generalizing convention-based study findings to all hackers.

Second, studies with larger sample sizes are needed to confirm some of the findings in the present study. The relatively small sample size of this survey reduced the case numbers in some subgroups below commonly-accepted margins of statistical generalizability. The regression results with regard to female hackers, minority hackers, and unemployed hackers, for example, have to be interpreted with caution, and their validity should be reassessed with larger samples to verify accuracy.

One important sample-size aspect that has to be considered in this context is that, while larger sample sizes are certainly desirable, their creation bears practical problems. Despite the fact that the ShmooCon conference is one of the largest international hacker conventions, it was attended by "only" about 800 persons, many of who were not eligible for participation in the study. Accordingly, even though this study approached achieved a relatively high response rate among eligible attendees, it yielded less than 130 cases. Two possible solutions for this problem come to mind.

First, researchers could solve this problem by collecting data from the world's largest hacking convention: DefCon. The latter, an annual event in Las Vegas, is attended by over 7,000 persons and has a reputation of attracting many Black Hat (mal-intentioned) hackers. The large size of this convention makes it the ideal candidate for studies seeking to obtain larger sample sizes. Researchers attempting to utilize the DefCon convention for their research purposes, however, are most likely facing a different kind of challenge, for DefCon has a reputation of being a less professional convention and one attended by hackers wanting to enjoy a fun weekend in Las Vegas with like-minded people. Compensating for this shortcoming, however, is the fact that many of the professional hackers attending the preceding Black Hat hacker convention in Las Vegas also attend the DefCon convention, for their Black Hat badges also get them free entry into the Defcon convention.

Another solution for the sample-size problem would be to combine the datasets from different hacking conventions in different locations. The results from different studies of various conventions could be merged into one larger dataset. Although this approach promises to provide larger case numbers and will likely yield generalizable results regarding the study population, it is not without disadvantages. The individual surveys would have to repeatedly ask the same item in order for the subsets to be comparable, thus hindering and delaying the assessment of different hacking-related aspects and the development of more advanced survey instruments.

Aside from potential biases resulting from the sampling frame and the problems associated with the small sample sizes, it is reasonable to assume that the present research project was also confronted with the problem of social-desirability biases introduced through the propensity of respondents to give socially-desirable responses. This is a common problem in studies relying on indirect, subjective information provided by respondents rather than on objective or direct measures, or a combination of the two (Fisher, 1993).

In the case of cyber criminals, social-desirability biases are extremely difficult to overcome, because objective measures of cybercriminal activities are difficult to obtain. One possible assessment of social-desirability biases could be achieved by conducting a research study combineing a survey section with a direct measurement of hacking skills and expertise. For example, a Honeypot could be used as one possibility to assess criterion validity by obtaining a more direct measurement of the skill levels respondents claim to have. The inclusion of such a direct measurement, however, complicates the study. It would be more difficult to receive research ethics board approvals, and it significantly increases the effort for respondents. For this reason, conducting the suggested combined study during a convention is highly unfeasible.

Suggestions for Future Study Approaches

The present study was a first attempt to generate quantifiable information about the hacking underground, and, as such, it was limited with regard to how many aspects of this community were assessable. While the current study provided some answers, it also raised many more questions. Future studies need to include other measurements of attitudes, social networks, and personal background information to refine and extend our understanding of hackers. Such studies could specify and detail many additional characteristics in a more precise way.

The large fraction of college-educated hackers in this study, for example, rendered the educational achievement variable close to a constant. To better assess the impact of varying educational backgrounds, future studies could ask respondents what their study subject is or what type of college they attend. The same is true for the measures of employment; it would be interesting to know the exact profession of respondents and how their occupations are related to their hacking activities.

Parallel to analyzing the various personality traits influencing the behavior of hackers, cybercrime researchers should begin to construct typologies of hacker profiles. The multitude of motives and skills confirmed by this study suggest that a variety of different types of hackers exist in the Computer Underground. Researchers should attempt to isolate prototypical types of hackers, collect empirical evidence to ensure the included "types" of hackers are exhaustive and mutually exclusive, and examine how the various "types" of hackers differ from and relate to each other.

The bottom-line is that cyber criminology is just beginning to develop, and our knowledge about cybercrime offenders remains fragmentary, at best. The present study yielded some important insights into the composition of the hacking underground, and it shed some light on the motivations and maturation processes of hackers. Nevertheless, it was but one step toward the establishment of cyber criminology as a distinct subfield of criminological research. A long and difficult road is still ahead for this young field of criminological research.

REFERENCES

Bednarz, A. (2004). *Profiling cybercriminals: A promising but immature science*. Retrieved May 03, 2008, from http://www.networkworld.com/supp/2004/cybercrime/112904profile.html

Boudreau, M. C., Gefen, D., & Straub, D. W. (2001). Validation in information systems research: A state-of-the-art assessment. *Management Information Systems Quarterly*, *11*(1), 1–16. doi:10.2307/3250956

Casey, E. (2004). *Digital evidence and computer crime: Forensic science, computers and the internet* (2 ed.). San Diego, CA and London, UK: Academic Press.

Chirillo, J. (2001). *Hack attacks revealed: A complete reference with custom security hacking toolkit*. New York: John Wiley & Sons.

Clover, C. (2009). *Kremlin-backed group behind Estonia cyber blitz*. Retrieved March 16, 2009, from http://www.ft.com/cms/s/0/57536d5a-0ddc-11de-8ea3-0000779fd2ac.html

Curran, K., Morrissey, C., Fagan, C., Murphy, C., O'Donnell, B., & Firzpatrick, G. (2005). Monitoring hacker activity with a honeynet. *International Journal of Network Management*, *15*(2), 123–134. doi:10.1002/nem.549

D'Arcy, J. P. (2007). *The misuse of information systems: The impact of security countermeasures*. New York: Lfb Scholarly Pub.

Erickson, J. (2008). *Hacking: The art of exploitation* (2 ed.). San Francisco, CA: No Starch Press.

Gordon, L. A., Loeb, M. P., Lucyshyn, W., & Richardson, R. (2005). *Computer crime and security survey*: Retrieved December 22, 2009, from http://www.cpppe.umd.edu/Bookstore/Documents/2005CSISurvey.pdf

Grecs. (2008). *ShmooCon 2008 infosec conference event*. Retrieved April 25, 2008, from http://www.novainfosecportal.com/2008/02/18/shmoocon-2008-infosec-conference-event-saturday/

Groves, R. M., Fowler, F. J., Couper, M. P., & Lepkowski, J. M., Singer, E., & Tourangeau, R. (2004). *Survey methodology*. Hoboken, NJ: Wiley.

Holt, T. J. (2007). Subcultural evolution? Examining the influence of on- and off-line experiences on deviant subcultures. *Deviant Behavior, 28*, 171–198. doi:10.1080/01639620601131065

Holt, T. J., & Kilger, M. (2008). Techcrafters and makecrafters: A comparison of two populations of hackers. *WOMBAT Workshop on Information Security Threats Data Collection and Sharing, 2008*, 67-78.

Howell, B. A. (2007). Real-world problems of virtual crime . In Balkin, J. M., Grimmelmann, J., Katz, E., Kozlovski, N., Wagman, S., & Zarsky, T. (Eds.), *Cybercrime: Digital cops in a networked environment*. New York: New York University Press.

Jaishankar, K. (2007). Cyber criminology: Evolving a novel discipline with a new journal. *International Journal of Cyber Criminology, 1*(1), 1–6.

Jewkes, Y. (2006). *Comment on the book 'cyber crime and society by Majid Yar*. Retrieved September 09, 2007, from http://www.sagepub.co.uk/booksProdDesc.nav?prodId=Book227351

Johnson, B. (2008). *Nato says cyber warfare poses as great a threat as a missile attack*. Retrieved May 02, 2008, from http://www.guardian.co.uk/technology/2008/mar/06/hitechcrime.uksecurity

Jordan, T., & Taylor, P. A. (1998). A sociology of hackers. *The Sociological Review, 46*(4), 757–780. doi:10.1111/1467-954X.00139

Lakhani, K. R., & Wolf, R. G. (2003). *Why hackers do what they do: Understanding motivation and effort in free/open source software projects*. SSRN.

Landler, M., & Markoff, J. (2007, May 29). *Digital fears emerge after data siege in Estonia*. Retrieved August 25, 2007, from http://www.nytimes.com/2007/05/29/technology/29estonia.html?pagewanted=1&ei=5070&en=15ee9940d96714da&ex=1188187200

Mann, D., & Sutton, M. (1998). NetCrime. More change in the organisation of thieving. *The British Journal of Criminology, 38*(2), 210–229.

Mitnick, K. D., & Simon, W. L. (2005). *The art of intrusion: The real stories behind the exploits of hackers, intruders & deceivers*. New York: John Wiley and Sons.

Mitnick, K. D., Simon, W. L., & Wozniak, S. (2002). *The art of deception: Controlling the human element of security*. New York: John Wiley and Sons.

NCIRC. (2008). *NATO opens new centre of excellence on cyber defense*. Retrieved May 03, 2008, from http://www.nato.int/docu/update/2008/05-may/e0514a.html

Newsted, P. R., Chin, W., Ngwenyama, O., & Lee, A. (1996, December 16-18). *Resolved: surveys have outlived their usefulness in IS research*. Paper presented at the Seventeenth International Conference on Information Systems, Cleveland, OH.

Nhan, J., & Bachmann, M. (2009). The challenges of cybercriminological research . In Maguire, M., & Okada, D. (Eds.), *Critical Issues of Crime and Criminal Justice*. Washington D.C., London: Sage.

Nuwere, E., & Chanoff, D. (2003). *Hacker cracker: A journey from the mean streets of Brooklyn to the frontiers of cyberspace*. New York: HarperCollins Publishers.

Schell, B. H., & Dodge, J. L. with Moutsatsos, S. (2002). *The hacking of America: Who's doing it, why, and how*. Westport, CT: Quorum.

Stohl, M. (2006). Cyber terrorism: a clear and present danger, the sum of all fears, breaking point or patriot games? *Crime, Law, and Social Change*, *46*, 223–238. doi:10.1007/s10611-007-9061-9

Taylor, P. A. (1999). *Hackers: Crime in the digital sublime*. London, UK and New York, NY: Routledge. doi:10.4324/9780203201503

Taylor, P. A. (2000). Hackers - cyberpunks or microserfs . In Thomas, D., & Loader, B. (Eds.), *Cybercrime: law enforcement, security and surveillance in the information age*. London, UK: Routledge.

Yar, M. (2005). The novelty of 'cybercrime': An assessment in light of routine activity theory. *European Journal of Criminology*, *2*(4), 407–427. doi:10.1177/147737080556056

Yar, M. (2006). *Cybercrime and society*. London: Sage.

Chapter 7
Examining the Language of Carders

Thomas J. Holt
Michigan State University, USA

ABSTRACT

The threat posed by a new form of cybercrime called carding—or the illegal acquisition, sale, and exchange of sensitive information—has increased in recent years. Few researchers, however, have considered the social dynamics driving this behavior. This chapter explores the argot, or language, used by carders through a qualitative analysis of 300 threads from six web forums run by and for data thieves. The terms used to convey knowledge about the information and services sold are explored in this chapter. In addition, the hierarchy and status of actors within carding communities are examined to understand how language shapes the social dynamics of the market. The findings provide insight into this emerging form of cybercrime, and the values driving carders' behavior. Policy implications for law enforcement intervention are also discussed.

INTRODUCTION

A great deal of research has explored the impact of technology on human behavior (Bryant, 1984; Forsyth, 1986; Holt, 2007; Melbin, 1978; Ogburn, 1932; Quinn & Forsyth, 2005). Individuals adapt their norms and behaviors in response to scientific and technological innovations. Eventually, new forms of behavior may supplant old practices, resulting in behavioral shifts referred to as "technicways" (Odum, 1937; Parker, 1943; Vance, 1972). Understanding technicways has significant value for criminologists, as offenders change their patterns of behavior due to evolving technologies (Quinn & Forsyth, 2005). For example, pagers, cellular telephones, and the Internet are increasingly used by prostitutes to attract and solicit customers (Holt & Blevins, 2007; Lucas, 2005). Embossing, scanning, and printing technologies have also been employed to improve the quality and volume of counterfeit credit cards (Mativat

DOI: 10.4018/978-1-61692-805-6.ch007

&Tremblay, 1997) and to develop counterfeit currency (Morris, Copes, & Perry-Mullis, 2009).

The Internet and computer-mediated communications, such as newsgroups and web forums, have also been adapted by criminals to exchange all sorts of information—almost instantaneously (Taylor, Caeti, Loper, Fritsch, & Liederbach, 2006). Computer hackers (Holt, 2007; Taylor, 1999), digital pirates (Cooper & Harrison, 2001; Ingram & Hinduja, 2008) and pedophiles (Quayle & Taylor, 2003) all utilize technology to communicate on-line across great distances, facilitating the global transmission of knowledge and resources without the need for physical contact.

Technology can also lead to the direct creation of new forms of crime and deviance (see Quinn & Forsyth, 2005). In fact, the ubiquity of computers and the Internet in modern society have led to the growth of criminal subcultures centered on technology (see Furnell, 2002; Taylor, et al. 2006). Few researchers have considered the development and structure of technologically-focused criminal subcultures, and what insights they provide on the nature of technology and crime. This study and this chapter attempt to address this gap in the literature by examining a new form of fraud called "carding" (see Holt & Lampke, 2010; Honeynet Research Alliance, 2003; Franklin, Paxson, Perrig, & Savage, 2007; Thomas & Martin, 2006).

The practice of carding involves obtaining sensitive personal information through computer hacks and attacks against networked systems, phishing, and other types of fraud and then selling this information to others (Holt & Lampke, 2010; Honeynet Research Alliance, 2003; Franklin et al., 2007; Thomas & Martin, 2006). Carding is a significant and emerging problem, as demonstrated by the recent arrest of members of an international group called the Shadowcrew, who sold at least 1.7 million stolen credit card accounts, passports, and other information obtained fraudulently (Parizo, 2005). Also in 2007, the TJX corporation reported that hackers compromised an internal database and stole at least 94 million customer credit card accounts (Goodin, 2007). The hackers responsible for this attack used the information obtained for their own profit and then sold some of the stolen information to others for their use (Vamosi, 2008).

Despite the significant scope and magnitude of the problem of carding, few researchers have considered the social dynamics driving this problem. To better understand this phenomenon, this chapter will examine the argot of carders.

Argot Defined

By definition, an argot is a specialized and secret language within a subculture (see Clark, 1986; Mauruer, 1981; Johnson, Bardhi, Sifaneck, & Dunlap, 2006). Argots are comprised of a variety of phrases, acronyms, and language, including commonplace words that develop special meanings--called "neosemanticisms," or completely new words—called "neologisms" (Kaplan, C.D., Kampe, H., & Farfan, J.A.F., 1990; Maurer, 1981). An argot is unique to a group and serves to communicate information to others, as well as highlight the boundaries of the subculture (Clark 1986; Einat & Einat, 2000; Hamm, 1993; Hensley, Wright, Tewksbury, & Castle, 2003; Johnson et al., 2006; Kaplan et al., 1990; Lerman, 1967; Maurer, 1981). Those who correctly use the argot when speaking to others may indicate their membership and status within the subculture (see Dumond, 1992; Halliday, 1977; Hensley et al., 2003; Maurer, 1981). This specialized language also functions to conceal deviant or criminal activities and communications from outsiders (Johnson et al., 2006; Maurer, 1981). Argots are traditionally spoken, yet few have considered the role and function of argot in deviant subcultures on-line.

Purpose of Chapter

This exploratory chapter examines the argot used by carders through a qualitative analysis of 300 threads from six web forums used by these individuals. The language used to convey knowledge about the information and services sold is explored. In addition, the hierarchy and status of actors within carding communities is examined to understand how language shapes the social dynamics of the market. The findings provide insight into this emerging form of cybercrime, and the subcultural norms that drive their behavior. Policy implications for law enforcement intervention are also discussed at the chapter's end.

BACKGROUND

Before discussing the problem of carding, it is necessary to consider how this form of crime developed as a consequence of the Internet and computer technology. The opportunities to engage in electronic theft have increased significantly with the development and penetration of computer technology and the Internet (see Holt & Graves, 2007; Newman & Clarke, 2003; Taylor et al., 2006; Wall, 2001, 2007). Computerized data, such as bank records, personal information, and other electronic files have significant value for criminals, as they can be used to access or create new financial service accounts, illegally obtain funds, and steal individuals' identities (see Allison, Schuck, & Learsch, 2005; Furnell, 2002; Mativat & Tremblay, 1997; Newman & Clarke, 2003; Wall, 2001, 2007).

Businesses and financial institutions store sensitive customer information in massive electronic databases that can be accessed and compromised by hackers (Newman & Clarke, 2003; Wall, 2007). In fact, in 2007, businesses in the U.S. lost over $5 million dollars due to the theft of confidential electronic data by computer attackers (Computer Security Institute, 2007).

The increased use of on-line banking and shopping sites also allows consumers to transmit sensitive personal and financial information over the Internet (James, 2005; Newman & Clarke, 2003). This information can, however, be surreptitiously obtained by criminals through different methods, with one common means being phishing (James, 2005; Wall, 2007). In a phishing attack, consumers are tricked into transmitting financial information into fraudulent websites where the information is housed for later fraud (see James, 2005; Wall, 2007). These crimes are particularly costly for both the individual victim and the financial institutions, alike; the Gartner Group estimates that phishing victims in the U.S. lost $3 billion dollars in 2007, alone (Rogers, 2007).

In light of the growing prominence of data theft and carding, an emerging body of research has begun to examine this problem through the identification of carding markets on-line, where computer criminals sell and buy information (Holt & Lampke, 2010; Honeynet Research Alliance, 2003; Franklin, Paxson, Perrig, & Savage, 2007; Thomas & Martin, 2006). These studies have found that Internet Relay Chat, or IRC channels and web forums provide an environment where hackers sell significant volumes of data obtained through phishing, database compromises, and other means (Holt & Lampke, 2010; Honeynet Research Alliance, 2003; Franklin et al., 2007; Thomas & Martin, 2006).

The most common forms of information sold in these markets in bulk lots include credit card and bank accounts, PIN numbers, and supporting customer information from around the world. Some mal-inclined hackers have also sold their services and knowledge, and have offered "cash out services" to obtain physical money from electronic accounts (Holt & Lampke, 2010; Franklin et al., 2007; Thomas & Martin, 2006). As a consequence, criminals who frequent carding markets can quickly and efficiently engage in credit card fraud and identity theft without any technical knowledge or skill (Holt & Lampke, 2010; Thomas & Martin, 2006). In addition, these markets can lead individuals to become victimized multiple times without their knowing it (Honeynet Research Alliance, 2003; Franklin et al., 2007; Thomas & Martin, 2006).

Taken as a whole, previous research has considered the products and resources available by carders. These studies, however, have given little insight into the social structure and relationships that undergird the practice of carders. Exploring the function and nature of the argot of carders can provide a more thorough examination of their practices and the overall market for stolen data. In turn, this can inform our understanding of the social dynamics driving cybercrime and Black Hat hacking.

STUDY METHOD

To examine the argot of carders and its role in stolen data markets, this study utilizes a set of 300 threads from six web forums devoted to the sale and exchange of identity information. Web forums, by definition, are a form of computer-mediated communication allowing individuals to connect and discuss their resources and needs. Forums are comprised of threads, which begin when an individual creates a post describing a product or service, asking a question, giving an opinion, or simply sharing past experiences. Others respond online to the initial post with posts of their own, creating a thread running conversations or dialogue. Thus, threads are comprised of posts centering on a specific topic under a forum's general heading. Since posters respond to other users, the exchanges present in the threads of a forum may "resemble a kind of marathon focused discussion group" (Mann & Sutton, 1998, p. 210).

As a result, web forums demonstrate relationships between individuals and provide information on the quality and strength of ties between hackers and data thieves. They also include a variety of users with different skill levels and knowledge of market processes, providing insight into the ways that argot is used among newcomers and experienced members of these markets.

The forums identified for this data set were selected on several criteria--including size, traffic, and public accessibility. Forums with both large and small user populations were identified to represent the range of forums currently operating on-line. Additionally, high traffic forums with a large number of existing posts were selected, as frequent posts suggest high activity. Finally, public forums were selected because they do not require individuals to register with the website to examine previous posts. As a consequence, anyone can access the forum without the need to interact with posters, reducing the potential for researcher contamination or bias (Silverman, 2001).

A sort of snowball sampling procedure was used to develop the sample of six forums used in this analysis. Three publicly accessible forums were identified through the search engine www.google.com using search threads based on terms used by carders, including "carding dump purchase sale cvv." Three additional websites were identified within the posts provided by the forum users. The six forums that comprise this data set provide a copious amount of data to analyze, as the threads span three years, from 2004 to 2007. (See Table 1 for forum information breakdowns.) Moreover, they represent a range of user populations--from 34 to 244 users.

To create the data sets, the threads from each forum were copied, pasted, and saved to a word file for analysis. The files were then printed and analyzed by hand, using grounded theory methodology to identify specific terms applied to resources and tools sold in stolen data markets and the forces shapeing this subculture (Corbin & Strauss, 1990).

Terms and their meanings were inductively derived from the repeated appearance of a specific phrase or idea in the data. The value of each term is derived from positive or negative comments of the respondents. In turn, theoretical links between these concepts are derived from the data to highlight its' role within stolen data markets. In this way, concepts become relevant via repeated appearances or absences in the data, ensuring they

Table 1. Descriptive data on forums used

Forum	Total Number of Threads	User Population	Timeframe Covered
1	50	34	6 months
2	50	63	3 months
3	50	46	1 months
4	50	56	15 months
5	50	68	11 months
6	50	244	21 months

are derived and grounded in the "reality of data" (Corbin & Strauss, 1990, p. 7).

STUDY FINDINGS

This analysis considers the terms used to describe the tools and social dynamics shaping stolen data markets and defining the boundaries of this subculture. The data also considers the ways argot structures identity and status within these markets, utilizing passages from the data sets as appropriate.

Terms for Stolen Data

Carders utilize a number of unique terms to refer to the variety of information and resources that they steal, buy, and sell on a day-to-day basis. In fact, carders in this sample operate within a marketplace environment in web forums where they can create unique threads advertising their products or services. Sellers provided as thorough a description of their products or tools as possible, including pricing information, payment methods, and contact information. The most prevalent item sold in stolen data markets was *dumps*, or stolen credit card or bank accounts and associated personal customer data (see also Holt & Lampke, 2010; Honeynet Research Alliance, 2003; Franklin et al., 2007; Thomas & Martin, 2006). The word *dump* is used to reflect the variety of information related to a financial account and its owner obtainable through different means. In fact, there were 480 instances of dumps sold by 61 individuals at different prices, depending on the customer data associated with each account (see Table 2).

Carders advertised dumps by describing the country or region of origin and the associated information contained on Track 1 and Track 2 of the magnetic stripe on each card. Track 1 stores the cardholder's name as well as account number and other discretionary data (see also Newman & Clarke, 2003). Track 2 data is the most commonly used track, and contains the account information and encrypted PIN, as well as other discretionary data (see also Newman & Clarke, 2003). It is important to note that the amount of information contained in a dump affected its price, as demonstrated in a post from the carder Blacktie:

!! Hello Everyone. I want to offer great things for your needs from Me - Official Dump Seller !!!
1) Dumps from all over the world Original Track 1/Track 2
1.1) EUROPE Dumps Track 1/Track 2
Europe and the rest of world (Following countries are not included: Swiss, Spain, France, Italy, Turkey, Germany, Australia)
Visa Classic, MasterCard Standart - $60 per 1 dump
Visa Classic, MasterCard Standart(Swiss, Spain, France, Italy, Turkey, Germany, Australia) - $70 per 1 dump
Visa Gold | Platinum | Business, MasterCard Gold | Platinum - $100 per 1 dump Visa Gold | Platinum | Business, MasterCard Gold | Platinum (Swiss,

Table 2. Data available in carding markets

Product	Minimum Price	Maximum Price	Average Price	Count with price	Count with no price	Number of Sellers
Cashout Services	NA	NA	NA	0	16	10
Checking Services	$15.00	$55.00	$35.00	2	0	2
COBS	$35.00	$140.00	$85.00	7	12	7
CVV2	$1.00	$14.00	$3.14	55	77	28
Dumps	$1.30	$500.00	$56.08	456	480	61
Fullz	$5.00	$260.00	$46.34	29	40	21
Logins: Bank Accounts	$20.00	$300.00	$143.70	23	35	5
Logins: PayPal Accounts	$4.00	$50.00	$12.82	11	13	6
Logins: Ebay Accounts	$1.00	$3.00	$2.00	2	5	5
Lookup Services	$10.00	$100.00	$75.00	3	0	2
Malware	$10.00	$3000.00	$275.00	8	9	5
Plastics	$40.00	$110.00	$71.43	7	8	2
Skimmers	$300.00	$5000.00	$2262.50	4	7	6

Spain, France, Italy, Turkey, Germany, Australia) - $120 per 1 dump
1.2) USA Dumps Original Track 1/Track 2
Dumps with Name,Address,City,State,Zip,Phone - $100 per 1 dump
Dumps with Name,Address,City,State,Zip,Phone,SSN and DOB - $120 per 1 dump
Dumps with Name,Address,City,State,Zip,Phone - $80 per 1 dump
Dumps with Name,Address,City,State,Zip,Phone,SSN and DOB - $90 per 1 dump

Individuals also sold credit card accounts with their Card Verification Value, or *cvv* (see Table 2). This type of data was referred to as *CVV* or *CVV2* (actually part of the larger jargon of the financial service industry). Jargon consists of technical terminology and specialized words often found in textbooks, manuals, and scientific articles available to the general public (see Andersson & Trudgill, 1990). CVVs are an excellent example of the use of jargon in the carder community, as the term refers to the three-to-four-digit number imprinted on the signature line of credit cards, enabling the cardholder to make purchases without being physically present at the time of the transaction (see also Newman & Clarke, 2003). Thus, selling CVV information enables individuals to immediately access and purchase goods electronically with these accounts.

The quantity of information sold within a CVV2 was indicated by the carder Houzer who wrote:

My CC/Cvv2 comes with these infos:
Name:
Address:
City:
State:
Zip:
Phone:
Email:
CC number:
Exp day:
CVN: (come with Cvv2, not with CC)

The average cost of CVV2s was $3.14, much less expensive than dumps. This bargain rate may be a reflection of the limited application of CVV2s, relative to dumps containing more data.

Sellers also offered *fullz*, or dumps containing all of the information associated with the account and account holder (see Table 2). Thus, this term signifies the volume and depth of information available to a potential carder, as demonstrated in a post by the fullz seller Farnsworth, who described his products in some detail:

```
Full info first name: last name:
address: city: state: zip:
phone:  name on card: CCnum-
ber: Exp month: Exp year: cvv:
ATM PIN code: (optinal) [SIC]:
Social security Number: Mother
Maiden Name: Date Of Birth: Is-
suing Bank: Account Type: (opti-
nal)
Routing Number: (optinal): Ac-
count Number:(optinal):  pins
main price is $20 for each full
info with/without pin code
if u need the full info include
routing number & account number
price will be $50 each
if u need full info for spicial
[SIC] state add $10 to the main
pricc
if u need full info for spicial
gender add $10 to the main price
also availabe full infos for
this countries: UK Canada France
Australia Japan
```

The cost of fullz ranged between $5 and $260, a significantly higher price than that of a standard dump or CVV2. This difference in price is a reflection of the amount of information attached to the account, as the volume of data allows an individual greater access to the account and its owner. Fullz, however, can share the same pricing structure as dumps, based on country and account type.

Seven individuals also sold *Change of Billing* address information, or *COBs*. This term is indicative of the way that the information can be used to hijack credit accounts and have all correspondence directed to a new address. The price of COBs ranged between $35 and $140, though the average price was $85 dollars (see Table 2). The generally higher price reflects the fact that the seller provided a full battery of information associated with the account and the customer, as well as on-line login and password information, when possible.

For example, Foldinmon3 described the amount of information available in the PayPal COBS he sold:

```
PayPal username: PayPal pass-
word: Firstname: Middlename:
Lastname: Address1: Address2:
City: State: Zip: Phone: SSN:
MMN: DOB: CC Number: CC Exp
Month: CC Exp Year: CVV/CVC:
PIN: Bank account:Routing: Pre-
vious Address (1st): Previous
Address (2nd):
```

Carding markets also offered electronic access to all manner of financial accounts that had been compromised in some way. These resources were referred to as *logins*, as they would enable individuals to log into a customer's account electronically and remove funds. Five individuals sold access to bank accounts and stock market portfolios at prices ranging from $20 to $300, depending on the value of the account.

For example, the seller Backd00r offered logins at a high cost, because they included the following information:

Personal and Corporative USA Bank accounts with online access starting from 5% from available balance. All bank accounts comes with link to bank, login and password, Account Holder Information (Name,Addresst,State,Zip,City, SSN, DOB,Phone), Account Information(Account Number). All bank accounts have BillPay function.

Comparatively, the seller Drax charged much less for his login services, as they only contained" LOGIN: PASS: SECURITY ANSWER 1: SECURITY ANSWER 2." Sellers also offered access to EBay and PayPal accounts, though they were far less valuable. The average price of PayPal accounts was $12.82, though prices ranged between $4 and $50 dollars, depending on the value of the account and the amount of personal information attached to the account.

Carders also offered the hardware, software, and materials needed to steal or use financial data in the real world. For example, individuals sold *skimmers,* devices designed to capture and store the magnetic stripe data from debit and credit cards. This term encompasses the way that information is stolen from a consumer, as the readers skim or capture the data from a credit or debit card as it is passed through an ATM or credit card reader (see also Mativat & Tremblay, 1997).

Skimming devices were sold by a small number of individuals, such as Slimm, who described his skimming devices, stating:

Model: s1 & b2 Bank Series (specs are the same for the both of them)

- Bezel is plastic
- Reads track 1 and 2 [magnetic strip information]
- Stores up to 2000 swipes
- Contains a rechargeable internal battery which lasts for approximately 2 days before it dies (53 to 54 hours none stop)
- Battery takes about 4 hours to fully charge, charges by plugging skimmer in.
- All data read is time stamped by time, seconds, day, month and year.
- Reads both bi-directional swipes (this means this skimmer will read cards when they go in and also when they are pulled out.
- The button to power on and off skimmer is at the backside.
- Contains a green and red LED to show when it reads and gives errors on the back of bezel.
- Skimmer is password protected, this means you cannot collected the dumps from it without a password. This works good for people who work with partners they may not trust.
- Comes with full manual and software included in the package.
- Backside of bezel that sticks to the machine is completely flush (flat).
- Backside of the slot in the bezel is open more so a card can slide right back inside the bezel without problems
- Bezel is filled with special hard epoxy to protect the electronics from breaking and to insure no wires ever come lose.
- Skimmer is jitter proof.

Individuals also sold *plastics*, consisting of blank credit cards with unwritten magnetic stripes that can be developed into fraudulent cards through the use of holograms, embossing equipment, and dumps (see also Morselli &Tremblay, 1997). For example, Trackmaster sold materials to produce cards, stating:

VISA, MASTER, DISCO AND AMEX cards look really good they will pass any place as I use them my self. they have a fake halo and you will need a sharpie to sign the back, cards are embossed with a Data card 150I, they have fake micro print and UV and all embossed with security symbols. orders ship more or less within 2 days

In fact, the symbols, embossing, and appearance of plastics were critical to ensure that they are not detected by individuals in stores or in the real world. Thus, plastics sellers noted the quality of their designs and the care that they took in creating fraudulent cards, as evidenced in this post:

We guarantee a correct bank microfont, with an excellent strip of the signature. . . The design of a card is identical to the bank original. Holograms on cards are IDENTICAL to the presents.

A limited number of carders advertised access to *cashout services* allowing online thieves to access, remove, and drain funds from bank accounts both on- and off-line. For example, a seller named d0llaBi1l advertised that he was "a good drop for cashing online bank access (bank Logins information) and WesternUnion (WU) in UK." d0llaBi1l would electronically withdraw funds from bank accounts and convert them into hard currency via wire transfers. There were 16 instances of sellers offering cashout services, though no consistent prices were provided (see Table 2).

As is commonplace, sellers took a percentage of the funds that they obtained as a form of payment. This sales transaction was demonstrated in the listing by a cash-out seller named ATMandingo:

```
For amount under 50:  50/50 ratio
For amounts over 50:  adjusted % welcome
Always First batch is 50/50 no matter what. I'm looking for long time respectable partners. We can wire funds by e-gold but will take 24hrs also remember time differences. We can do western union daily too. We'll also save log of error codes shown if problems arise. We go for quality, if your dumps + pins have a bad conversion to ratio like say only 4 out of 10 work we'll need to end our partnership.
```

A small number of carders provided *checking services* to verify the validity and activity within a given dump. This type of service enables carders to maximize the resources that they purchase by efficiently ensuring the value and utility of dumps. This point was demonstrated in a post by the carder Spanks, who described his diverse checking services:

1) Balance checking:
   - by using this feature you will be able to know how much money you can spend using your card/dump before you go in store or even online all you need is the ccnumber/exp[iration] date/the amount you need to check
2) billing address checking:
   - this is so useful for the cobs players since most online banks do not change the billing address instantly and you never know when your new billing address will be actually changed which may kill your card when you go shopping online since the billing address you provide on the online store did not match the billing address listed on the bank server but this is no more, by using this future you will be able to know if the card billing address really changed or not. you need ccnumber/expdate/billing street address/zip code.
3) Multiple card checking:
   - you have many dumps/ccs and need to check them all by one click this is the best solution for you all you

need is the card number/expdate you can choose between 2 formats dump format: ccnumber=yyMM (ie. 4111111111111111=0612) cc formate: ccnumber=MMyy (ie. 4111111111111111=1206)just one card per line and click check all at once and all done

4) Single card checking:
   - just the ccnumber and the expdate needed to check its validity

5) BIN seach:
   - the bin seach features is free to all my clients you can check up to 50 bins by one click

Individuals also offered *look-up services*, identifying and obtaining sensitive personal and financial information about individuals. Look-up services could include credit records, passport information, or drivers license information, court paperwork, bankruptcy information, and other pertinent personal data. Such information could enable individuals to engage in more serious forms of cybercrime like identity theft, particularly when it was used in conjunction with dumps or other information sold. The quantity and quality of information available in look-up services was demonstrated in a post by the seller z00m who offered:

Background History - $24.99
Credit Reports
1.1.1 Experian Credit Report without credit score - $39.99
1.1.2 Experian, Equifax, Trans Union Report with credit score - $49.99
1.1.3 Specific report by Score, Age, Race and etc starting from - $99.99
You should give me First Name, Last Name, Address and SSN of a person you want to make credit report on. If you dont have ssn no problem I will find it.
Credit Report includes these things:
1) Personal Information: SSN, FULL DOB, Addresses, Current Phone
2) Accounts, Installment Accounts, Credit Summary, Balances, Limits, Public Records, Inquiries
3) Employment History
4) Fraud Alerts
1.2 Criminal History
You should give me First Name, Last Name, Address, SSN and DOB of a person you want to make criminal history on.
If you dont have ssn and dob no problem I will find it.
1.3 SSN and DOB Lookup
SSN and DOB (some times) lookup by Name and Address
For peoples who will buy lot of SSN Lookups i will give login to Website where you could find SSN automatically
1.4. I am looking for peoples who will buy a lot of credit reports and ssn lookups. I will give good and excellent discounts for them
1.7.1 Drive Licenses (15 states covered updated monthly) - $14.99 per 1 search

Finally, a small number of carders offered tools to facilitate Black Hat hacking and carding activity. In this case, the terms used are commonly found in the computer security and Information Technology fields (see Schell & Martin with Moutsatsos, 2006; Taylor, 1999). These complimentary fields, developed in tandem with Black Hat hacking, cause a great deal of specialized terms to be used across these groups, despite their somewhat conflicting outlooks (see Furnell, 2002; Taylor, 1999).

For example, a small number of individuals sold malicious software, known as malware, that could be used to steal information from virus- and worm- infected computer systems. The lead coder for this group described the services offered, stating:

We'd like to offer a perfect way to increase your income without problems and loosing much time Our team is specialised in spyware development.

We are coding all types of spyware, from remote administration tools with GUI to simple keyloggers. Our main direction is to create effective and powerful spyware. Coding is not just hobby for us, its out job and style of life. As for my package it's easy to configure it. All you have to do is run 3 programs included in package: 2 of then is to configure urls there your logs will be kept(you'll hate to enter one url in each program), one for pack exe [executable] file. And off course you'll have to upload php scripts to your server. Done. You can spread it now It is not detectible by AV software. It has polymorthic algorythm which makes trojan hard to detect. But from time to time it becomes detectible. This happening then AV companies learn polymorthic engine and makes all possible definitions for it. It's takes about one day to make it undetecteble again

In sum, the argot of carders reflects the range of products sold and their utility to engage in Black Hat hacking, fraud, and theft, both on- and off-line.

Terms for Actors and Relationships

The argot of carders also utilizes a range of terms for actors within carding markets. Carders depend on one another for assistance in the course of buying and selling information, and their argot indicates the role, status, and reputation of actors in these markets. Specifically, the labels are used to communicate the integrity of an individual and the level of trust they have generated among fellow carders. Those with the greatest respect and power in carding markets are *moderators*, responsible for managing the content and activity within their forum. Moderators assess the quality of sellers within these markets and assign rankings to individuals based on their performance. For example, one of the forum moderators would regularly warn users to take care when purchasing, writing: "All SERVICES that I marked as NOT VERIFIED potencially [SIC} WILL be RIPPING [you off]."

The group below moderators include the *testers*, who play an important role within carding markets. Three of the forums in this sample required sellers to provide a sample of their products for review by the forum administration. Specifically, a carder would have to provide a series of dumps, access to a service, or a copy of malicious software to a moderator, which would then be provided to a *tester* appointed by the forum. *Testers* would then write and post a review and a recommendation for purchase. The review process acts as a sort of vetting process for the seller, and it gives potential buyers some knowledge of the person and their products. Reviewers would describe the quality of the information or service sold, as well as any problems or difficulties in utilizing the product. This process was exemplified in the review of a seller named Drax, who offered login information:

Drax asked for review, and I asked him for 10 samples of his login information. They came in this format:

```
LOGIN:
PASS:
SECURITY ANSWER 1:
SECURITY ANSWER 2:
```

I bunkered up with some au proxies (non-standard port of course) and got to work. I logged in and checked balances and whether they were enabled for international wires.

These are the results:

```
Account #1: Balance: 90K, Inter-
national: No
Account #2: Balance: Small, In-
ternational: No
Account #3: Balance: 90K, Inter-
national: Yes
Account #4: FROZEN (after trying
to logon twice with apparently
wrong password)
```

```
Account #5: Balance: 1,3K, In-
ternational: Yes
Account #6: Balance: 16K, In-
ternational: Yes, BUT SECURITY
ANSWERS WRONG
Account #7: "Currently unable
to logon. For more information
contact..."
Account #8: Balance: Small, In-
ternational: No
Account #9: Balance: 4K, Inter-
national: Yes
Account #10: Balance: 100K+, In-
ternational: Yes
```

As can be seen I was able to logon to all but two and one had the security answers wrong. All in all I think this was a good result. Be sure to ask vendor for specific accounts that has the qualities you need and you should be satisfied. Vendor is recommended for status as verified vendor.

This sort of positive review would allow an individual to gain status as a seller within these markets. In the other three forums, however, no such vetting process was present. Rather, sellers would directly post their services in a thread and wait for buyers to provide feedback. In these websites, individual buyers faced much greater risk, because they were not able to have independent assessments of the products being sold.

Regardless of the presence of testers in forums, customer feedback played a significant role on the status of a carder. The presence of positive comments verified that a seller was reputable, reliable, and trustworthy. Customer feedback was a critical component of the stolen data market, as it provided a way for individuals to directly inform their counterparts about the service and reliability of sellers. Buyers regularly gave feedback on their experience, and positive or negative comments affected the reputation of sellers.

For example, a carder named b1gb0ss sold large lots of credit cards and bank account login information. One of his customers, Fortunada, posted a very favourable review of his products, stating: "thanks for the good ccs [credit cards] boss they all worked and the logins too thank you and im looking to do more heavy business with you."

There is also a demonstrable hierarchy of sellers, beginning with *unverified sellers*. First- time sellers, or individuals new to a carding market were labeled as *unverified sellers*, as little is known about them or their trustworthiness. For example, a new seller described his business carefully, stating:

```
Hi everyone,
I'm just a newcommer [SIC] here
and I offer you a great ser-
vice with cheapest prices. I
sell mainly CC/Cvv2 US and UK. I
also sell International Cvv2 if
you want. Before I get Verified
here, I sold Cvv2 in many fo-
rums. Some members in this forum
know me. Hope I can serve you
all long time.
```

Once he received a positive review from the forum moderator and tester, he was able to gain greater status and become a *verified seller* or gain *verified status*. In fact, carders receiving verified status used this as a signature for their posts, as demonstrated by the signature of Frank which read: "Verified Vendor for USA Credit Reports and MG Answering Service," and raxx who was the "Verified Vendor for Full Infos & COBs." By indicating their status, buyers could easily identify trustworthy individuals and, therefore, make purchases with confidence.

Customer complaints about a carder's products could also lead to a lack of confidence in his/her ability to provide goods and services. Multiple negative comments could even lead a carder to lose their verified status. Comments about dead or inactive dumps, missing information, delayed deliveries, and slow product turnover negatively impacted a carder's reputation. For instance, an individual attempted to purchase data from a carder, but had a bad experience and described it in the forum:

I bought 50 cvv2's the last time I bought from him. 40% have been bad. Some in the list where expired, wrong address, and not correct info ect.. Having that many bad really fucks up my business, and wastes alot of my time. I have tried contacting him the past the days for replacements. He states that he replaces his bad ones. I have got no reply from him and today when He was signed on the same time I was, I asked him nicely to replace and he just signed off when I did.

The repeated appearance of such comments would often force a seller to quickly deal with customer complaints, or lose his/her status and be penalized. In such instances, moderators would replace a seller's verified status with the label *unresolved problems status*, *donkey*, or a similar negative term. The exact meaning of these terms was demonstrated in a comment from a forum moderator who wrote: "Unresolved Problems means all orders to him is stopped untill he show up and clean things up." Changes in user status signified that the individual was difficult to deal with and untrustworthy. The carder must then deal with all of their customers to regain their status.

If a seller made no effort to correct problems, forum users would further downgrade the individual to *ripper* status. The term ripper refers to "rip-offs," or thieves stealing money from other carders. Being labeled "a ripper" had significant negative ramifications for the seller, as others would not trust or buy from a ripper. This point was demonstrated in a post by the user sm0k3 who described how he was "ripped" in some detail:

I was ripped by those guys. . .i asked him to buy 5 dumps.. . then he replyed me as he has those dumps, i send him money he asked me to wait 12 hours after he got the money. one day later, i meet him on icq and he said many things only not send the dumps to me.

THIS IS AN UNHONEST VENDOR,MAYBE HE HAS SOME DUMPS TO RESELL,BUT BECARE-FUL THIS RIPPER,COS IT'S YOUR MONEY BEFORE YOU TRANSFER TO THIS RIPPER! AFTER TRANSFER, ALL YOU HAVE JUST NOTHING FROM HIM.

A similar example of the importance of the "ripper" label came from a post by Donniebaker, who was dissatisfied with the experience he had with a carder and posted this message:

THIS GUY IS A RIPPER HE RIP ME FOR A LOT OF MONEY AND SENT ME ALL BOGUS DUMPS. . . WE HAVE TO HAVE HONOR WITH EACH OTHER IN ORDER TO KEEP THIS BUSI-NESS FLOWING YOU HAVE TOOK MONEY FROM A FEWLLOW CARDER KNOWING YOUR DUMPS ARE BOGUS YOU WILL NOT SUC-CEED. YOU'RE A MARK IN THE DARK AND A PUNK IN THE TRUNK FUCK YOU!

The use of the term "ripper" could also lead a carder to lose all customers and be permanently banned from the forum. In fact, placing someone on "ripper status" is one of the few methods available to manage conflict in stolen data markets. Since the data and services sold in carding markets are illegally acquired, buyers could not pursue civil or criminal claims in court against a less-than-reputable seller. Thus, the use of the "ripper" label was the most serious action an individual could take against a seller, as it can force that person out of the market. As a consequence, rippers appear to operate on the periphery of the carder community and are actively removed from forums to ensure the safety of all participants.

CONCLUSION

This study sought to explore the argot of carders to understand this phenomenon and the relationships between actors in carding markets. The findings suggest that the argot of carders reflects the technical nature of cybercrime, helping to ensure the secrecy of participants (Clark, 1986; Einat & Einat, 2000; Hamm, 1993; Hensley et al., 2003; Johnson et al., 2006; Kaplan et al., 1990; Lerman, 1967; Maurer, 1981).

Specifically, carders used their secretive language to confer about all facets of data theft, including the types of information available and various methods used to engage in fraud. Their unique vocabulary was comprised of both neosemanticisms and neologisms, borrowing from both the financial and computer security industries (see Johnson et al., 2006). The open nature of the forums, coupled with the sale of stolen information and tools to engage in fraud, led carders to carefully manage and disguise their discussions. The use of a distinct argot served to disguise many aspects of their activities from outsiders, much like the argot of marijuana users (Johnson et al., 2006) and prisoners (Einat & Einat, 2000; Hensley et al., 2003).

In addition, the terms used for data and products clearly reflected their intended use, which is somewhat different from other argots, such as that of marijuana sellers (see Johnson et al., 2006). Taken as a whole, the argot of carders may help them avoid legal sanctions and reduce penetration by outsiders, particularly law enforcement.

A clear hierarchy was also evident in the carder argot, helping to delineate the status and practices of this community. Specifically, moderators and testers managed carding markets and established the operating parameters of sellers within the forums. Sellers were judged on the quality of their products and the trust they could foster among buyers. Rippers, however, had the lowest status among carders, as they prey upon other buyers. In fact, the application of the term "ripper" is critical, as participants cannot contact law enforcement if they are mistreated due to their purchase of stolen data. The use of this term allows actors to recognize and separate risky individuals from the market, thereby enabling internal policing and regulation of the carding market. Thus, the argot of carders serves to structure social relationships and define the boundaries of this market (see also Einat & Einat, 2000; Hensley et al., 2003; Johnson et al., 2006).

The findings of this study also suggest that a wide range of stolen information is sold in mass quantities at variable prices, particularly credit card and bank account information, as well as sensitive personal information (see also Holt & Lampke, forthcoming; Honeynet Research Alliance, 2003; Franklin et al., 2007; Thomas & Martin, 2006). Some carders also sold specialized equipment to utilize this data through ATMs and businesses in the real world. Thus, carding markets appear to simplify and engender identity theft and computer-based financial crimes (see also Holt & Lampke, forthcoming; Honeynet Research Alliance, 2003; Franklin et al., 2007; Thomas &Martin, 2006).

In addition, this study has key policy implications for law enforcement and computer security. Specifically, law enforcement must begin to examine and monitor the activities of stolen data markets to identify the source of these forums and further our understanding of the problem of stolen data generally. By successfully applying the argot of carders, agents can better mimic participants and further penetrate these underground economy communities.

Collaborative initiatives are also needed between law enforcement agencies and financial institutions to track the relationships between large-scale data compromises and initial reports of victimization. Such information can improve our knowledge of the role of data markets in the prevalence of identity theft and cybercrime. There is also a need for increased collaborative relationships between federal law enforcement agencies around the world. Individuals in disparate countries may be victimized as a consequence of information sold in stolen data market. Without question, expanding connections and investigative resources are needed to improve the prosecution and arrest of those behind these crimes.

Criminologists must also begin to address the lack of attention given to more serious forms of computer crimes, particularly the interplay between large-scale data theft, malicious software, and identity crimes. Such information is critical to develop effective prevention and enforcement strategies. For example, if research can be focused on the practices and beliefs of malicious computer hackers and malicious software programmers (see Holt, 2007), this information can be systematically applied to reduce the presence and utility of stolen data markets. Such research is critical to improving our understanding of the ways the Internet acts as a conduit for crime, as well as the ways that cybercrimes parallel real-world offending.

REFERENCES

Allison, S. F. H., Schuck, A. M., & Learsch, K. M. (2005). Exploring the crime of identity theft: prevalence, clearance rates, and victim/offender characteristics. *Journal of Criminal Justice*, *33*, 19–29. doi:.doi:10.1016/j.jcrimjus.2004.10.007

Andersson, L., & Trudgill, P. (1990). *Bad language*. Oxford, UK: Blackwell.

Bryant, C. D. (1984). Odum's concept of the technicways: Some reflections on an underdeveloped sociological notion. *Sociological Spectrum*, *4*, 115–142. doi:.doi:10.1080/02732173.1984.9981714

Clark, T. L. (1986). Cheating terms in cards and dice. *American Speech*, *61*, 3–32. doi:.doi:10.2307/454707

Computer Security Institute (CSI). (2007). *Computer Crime and Security Survey*. Retrieved March 2007 from http://www.cybercrime.gov/FBI2006.pdf

Cooper, J., & Harrison, D. M. (2001). The social organization of audio piracy on the internet. *Media Culture & Society*, *23*, 71–89. doi:.doi:10.1177/016344301023001004

Corbin, J., & Strauss, A. (1990). Grounded theory research: Procedures, canons, and evaluative criteria. *Qualitative Sociology*, *13*, 3–21. doi:.doi:10.1007/BF00988593

Dumond, R. W. (1992). The sexual assault of male inmates in incarcerated settings. *International Journal of the Sociology of Law*, *2*, 135–157.

Einat, T., & Einat, H. (2000). Inmate argot as an expression of prison subculture: The Israeli case. *The Prison Journal*, *80*, 309–325. doi:.doi:10.1177/0032885500080003005

Forsyth, C. (1986). Sea daddy: An excursus into an endangered social species. *Maritime Policy and Management: The International Journal of Shipping and Port Research*, *13*(1), 53–60.

Franklin, J., Paxson, V., Perrig, A., & Savage, S. (2007). An inquiry into the nature and cause of the wealth of internet miscreants. Paper presented at CCS07, October 29-November 2, 2007 in Alexandria, VA.

Furnell, S. (2002). *Cybercrime: Vandalizing the information society*. Reading, MA: Addison-Wesley.

Goodin, D. (2007). *TJX breach was twice as big as admitted, banks say*. Retrieved March 27, 2008, from http://www.theregister.co.uk/2007/10/24/tjx_breach_estimate_grows/

Halliday, M. A. K. (1977). Language structure and language function . In Lyons, J. (Ed.), *New Horizons in Linguistic Structure* (pp. 140–165). Harmondsworth, UK: Penguin.

Hamm, M. S. (1993). *American skinheads: The criminology and control of hate crime*. Westport, CT: Praeger.

Hensley, C., Wright, J., Tewksbury, R., & Castle, T. (2003). The evolving nature of prison argot and sexual hierarchies. *The Prison Journal*, *83*, 289–300. doi:.doi:10.1177/0032885503256330

Holt, T. J. (2007). Subcultural evolution? Examining the influence of on- and off-line experiences on deviant subcultures. *Deviant Behavior*, *28*, 171–198. doi:.doi:10.1080/01639620601131065

Holt, T. J., & Blevins, K. R. (2007). Examining sex work from the client's perspective: Assessing johns using online data. *Deviant Behavior*, *28*(3), 333–354. doi:.doi:10.1080/01639620701233282

Holt, T. J., & Graves, D. C. (2007). A Qualitative Analysis of Advanced Fee Fraud Schemes. *The International Journal of Cyber-Criminology*, *1*(1), 137–154.

Holt, T. J., & Lampke, E. (2010). Exploring stolen data markets on-line: Products and market forces. *Forthcoming in Criminal Justice Studies*, *33*(2), 33–50. doi:.doi:10.1080/14786011003634415

Honeynet Research Alliance. (2003). Profile: Automated Credit Card Fraud, *Know Your Enemy Paper* series. Retrieved June 21, 2005, from http://www.honeynet.org/papers/profiles/cc-fraud.pdf

Ingram, J., & Hinduja, S. (2008). Neutralizing music piracy: An empirical examination. *Deviant Behavior*, *29*, 334–366. doi:.doi:10.1080/01639620701588131

James, L. (2005). *Phishing Exposed*. Rockland, MA: Syngress.

Johnson, B. D., Bardhi, F., Sifaneck, S. J., & Dunlap, E. (2006). Marijuana argot as subculture threads: Social constructions by users in New York City. *The British Journal of Criminology*, *46*, 46–77. doi:.doi:10.1093/bjc/azi053

Kaplan, C. D., Kampe, H., & Farfan, J. A. F. (1990). Argots as a code-switching process: A case study of sociolinguistic aspects of drug subcultures . In Jacobson, R. (Ed.), *Codeswitching as a Worldwide Phenomenon* (pp. 141–157). New York: Peter Lang.

Lerman, P. (1967). Argot, symbolic deviance, and subcultural delinquency. *American Sociological Review*, *32*, 209–224. doi:.doi:10.2307/2091812

Lucas, A. M. (2005). The work of sex work: Elite prostitutes' vocational orientations and experiences. *Deviant Behavior*, *26*, 513–546. doi:.doi:10.1080/01639620500218252

Mann, D., & Sutton, M. (1998). Netcrime: More change in the organization of thieving. *The British Journal of Criminology*, *38*, 201–229.

Mativat, F., & Tremblay, P. (1997). Counterfeiting credit cards: Displacement effects, suitable offenders, and crime wave patterns. *The British Journal of Criminology*, *37*(2), 165–183.

Maurer, D. W. (1981). *Language of the underworld*. Louisville, KY: University of Kentucky Press.

Melbin, M. (1978). Night as frontier. *American Sociological Review*, *43*, 3–22. doi:.doi:10.2307/2094758

Miller, D., & Slater, D. (2000). *The internet: An ethnographic approach*. New York: Berg.

Morris, R. G., Copes, J., & Perry-Mullis, K. (2009). (in press). Correlates of currency counterfeiting. *Journal of Criminal Justice*. doi:.doi:10.1016/j.jcrimjus.2009.07.007

Newman, G., & Clarke, R. (2003). *Superhighway robbery: Preventing e-commerce crime*. Cullompton, UK: Willan Press.

Odum, H. (1937). Notes on technicways in contemporary society. *American Sociological Review*, *2*, 336–346. doi:.doi:10.2307/2084865

Ogburn, W. (1932). *Social change*. New York: Viking Press.

Parizo, E. B. (2005). *Busted: The inside story of "Operation Firewall."* Retrieved January 18, 2006, from http://searchsecurity.techtarget.com/news/article/0,289142,sid14_gci1146949,00.html

Parker, F. B. (1972). Social control and the technicways. *Social Forces*, *22*(2), 163–168. doi:. doi:10.2307/2572684

Quayle, E., & Taylor, M. (2002). Child pornography and the internet: Perpetuating a cycle of abuse. *Deviant Behavior*, *23*, 331–361. doi:. doi:10.1080/01639620290086413

Quinn, J. F., & Forsyth, C. J. (2005). Describing sexual behavior in the era of the Internet: A typology for empirical research. *Deviant Behavior*, *26*, 191–207. doi:.doi:10.1080/01639620590888285

Rogers, J. (2007). *Gartner: victims of online phishing up nearly 40 percent in 2007*. Retrieved January 2, 2008, from http://www.scmagazineus.com/Gartner-Victims-of-online-phishing-up-nearly-40-percent-in-2007/article/99768/

Schell, B. H., & Martin, C. (2006). *Webster's New World Hacker Dictionary*. Indianapolis, IN: Wiley.

Schneider, J. L. (2005). Stolen-goods markets: Methods of disposal. *The British Journal of Criminology*, *45*, 129–140. doi:.doi:10.1093/bjc/azh100

Silverman, D. (2001). *Interpreting qualitative data: Methods for analyzing talk, text, and interaction* (2nd ed.). Thousand Oaks, CA: SAGE Publications.

Taylor, P. A. (1999). *Hackers: Crime in the digital sublime*. New York: Routledge. doi:10.4324/9780203201503

Taylor, R. W., Caeti, T. J., Loper, D. K., Fritsch, E. J., & Liederbach, J. (2006). *Digital crime and digital terrorism*. Upper Saddle River, NJ: Pearson Prentice Hall.

Thomas, R., & Martin, J. (2006). The underground economy: Priceless. *:login, 31*(6), 7-16.

Vamosi, R. (2008). *Second of 11 alleged TJX hackers pleads guilty*. Retrieved October 1, 2008, from http://news.cnet.com/8301-1009_3-10048507-83.html?tag=mncol

Vance, R. B. (1972). Howard Odum's technicways: A neglected lead in American sociology. *Social Forces*, *50*, 456–461. doi:.doi:10.2307/2576788

Wall, D. S. (2001). Cybercrimes and the internet. In Wall, D. S. (Ed.), *Crime and the internet* (pp. 1–17). New York: Routledge.

Wall, D. S. (2007). *Cybercrime: The transformation of crime in the information age*. Cambridge, UK: Polity Press.

Chapter 8
Female and Male Hacker Conferences Attendees:
Their Autism-Spectrum Quotient (AQ) Scores and Self-Reported Adulthood Experiences

Bernadette H. Schell
Laurentian University, Canada

June Melnychuk
University of Ontario Institute of Technology, Canada

ABSTRACT

To date, studies on those in the Computer Underground have tended to focus not on aspects of hackers' life experiences but on the skills needed to hack, the differences and similarities between insider and outsider crackers, and the differences in motivation for hacking. Little is known about the personality traits of the White Hat hackers, as compared to the Black Hat hackers. This chapter focuses on hacker conference attendees' self-reported Autism-spectrum Quotient (AQ) predispositions. It also focuses on their self-reports about whether they believe their somewhat odd thinking and behaving patterns—at least as others in the mainstream society view them—help them to be successful in their chosen field of endeavor.

INTRODUCTION

On April 27, 2007, when a spree of Distributed Denial of Service (DDoS) attacks started and soon thereafter crippled the financial and academic websites in Estonia (Kirk, 2007), large businesses and government agencies around the globe became increasingly concerned about the dangers of hack attacks and botnets on vulnerable networks. There has also been a renewed interest in what causes mal-inclined hackers to act the way that they do—counter to mainstream society's norms and values.

As new cases surface in the media—such as the December, 2007, case of a New Zealand teen named Owen Walker, accused of being the creator of a botnet gang and discovered by the police under Operation Bot Roast—industry and government

DOI: 10.4018/978-1-61692-805-6.ch008

officials, as well as the public have been pondering about whether such mal-inclined hackers are cognitively and/or behaviorally "different" from adults functioning in mainstream society.

This chapter looks more closely at this notion. The chapter begins with a brief discussion on botnets to clarify why the growing concern, reviews the literature on what is known about hackers—their thinking and behaving predispositions—and closes by presenting new empirical findings on hacker conference attendees regarding their self-reported Asperger syndrome predispositions. The latter are thought to provide a constellation of rather odd traits attributed by the media and mainstream society to males and females inhabiting the Computer Underground (CU).

CONCERNS OVER BOTNETS AND VIRUSES AND THEIR DEVELOPERS

A "bot," short form for robot, is a remote-controlled software program acting as an agent for a user (Schell & Martin, 2006). The reason that botnets are anxiety-producing to organizations and governments is that mal-inclined bots can download malicious binary code intended to compromise the host machine by turning it into a "zombie." A collection of zombies is called a "botnet.'

Since 2002, botnets have become a growing problem. While they have been used for phishing and spam, the present-day threat is that if several botnets form a gang, they could threaten—if not cripple--the networked critical infrastructures of most countries with a series of coordinated Distributed Denial of Service (DDoS) attacks (Sockel & Falk, 2009).

The Case of Bot Writer Owen Walker

It is understandable, then, why there has been considerable media interest in Owen Walker, who, according to his mother, suffers from a mild form of autism known as Asperger syndrome—often indicated in individuals by social isolation and high intelligence. Because of a lack of understanding about the somewhat peculiar behaviors exhibited by high-functioning Asperger individuals, Walker's peers allegedly taunted him during the formative and adolescent years, causing him to drop out of high school in grade 9. Unbeknownst to Walker's mother, after his departure from high school, Owen apparently became involved in an international hacking group known as "the A-Team" (Farrell, 2007).

In a hearing held on July 15, 2008, Justice Judith Potter discharged Owen Walker without conviction on some of the most sophisticated botnet cybercrime seen in New Zealand, even though he pleaded guilty to six charges, including: (i) accessing a computer for dishonest purposes, (ii) damaging or interfering with a computer system, (iii) possessing software for committing crime, and (iv) accessing a computer system without authorization. Part of a ring of 21 mal-inclined hackers, Walkers' exploits apparently cost the local economy around $20.4 million in US dollars. If convicted, the teen could have spent up to seven years in prison.

In his defense, Owen Walker said that he was motivated not by maliciousness but by his intense interest in computers and his need to stretch their capabilities. In her decision, Justice Potter referred to an affidavit from Walker in which he told her that he had received approaches about employment from large overseas companies and the New Zealand police because of his "special" hacker knowledge and talents. The national manager of New Zealand's police e-crime laboratory was quoted in the media as admitting that Walker had some unique ability, given that he appeared to be at the "elite" level of hacking (Gleeson, 2008).

The judge ordered Walker to pay $11,000 in costs and damages (even though he reportedly earned $32,000 during his crime spree). He was also ordered to assist the local police to combat online criminal activities. Apparently the primary reason for his lack of a conviction is that Owen was paid to only write the software that illegally earned others in the botnet gang their money. Walker claims that he did not receive any of the "stolen" money himself. (Humphries, 2008)

The Case of Virus Writer Kimberley Vanvaeck

Male hackers with special talents like Walker's are not the only ones who have made headlines and caused anxieties for industry and government over the past five years. A 19-year-old female hacker from Belgium named Gigabyte got considerable media attention in February, 2004. Kimberley (Kim) Vanvaeck created the Coconut-A, the Sahay-A, and the Sharp-A computer viruses while studying for an undergraduate degree in applied computer science. She was arrested and charged by police with computer data sabotage, a charge which could have placed her behind prison bars for three years and forced her to pay fines as high as €100,000, if convicted. In the Sahay-A worm, Gigabyte claimed to belong to the "Metaphase VX Team." When questioned by the media upon her arrest, Gigabyte portrayed herself as a Lara Croft in a very male-dominated hacker field and a definite female minority in the elite virus-writing specialty (Sophos, 2004).

Gigabyte had a reputation in the Computer Underground for waging a protracted virtual war against an antivirus expert known as Graham Cluley. Oddly enough, Kim's viruses could all be identified by their antipathy toward Cluley. For example, one virus launched a game on infected computers challenging readers to answer questions about Cluley, whom Kim nicknamed "Clueless." Another virus launched a game requiring users to "knock-off" Cluley's head. Apparently, Kim's anger at Cluley started years ago when he maintained that most virus writers are male—an act that put her on a mission to prove that females can wreak as much havoc in the virtual world as men.

Outside of the computer underground, Kim allegedly had few friends (Sturgeon, 2004). Her updated homepage indicates that she now has a Master's degree in engineering, and while in university, she says that she was active as a student leader and Information Technology (IT) advisor.

In an online post on March 26, 2009, Cluley noted that Kim was released by the legal system with just a "slap on the wrist" and a promise to not cause trouble again. (Cluley, 2009)

Are Mal-inclined Bot Writers and Virus Writers Wired Differently?

The interesting cases of Owen Walker and Gigabyte raise a question about whether hackers—male and female—are likely to be neurologically wired differently from many in mainstream society. Could they, for example, be Asperger syndrome individuals who, like Owen Walker, had childhoods tainted by peer rejection? To date, studies have tended to focus not on these aspects of hackers' life experiences but on the skills needed to hack and the trait differences between insider and outsider hackers. Whether males and females in the hacking community self-report elevated scores on the Autism-spectrum Quotient(AQ)—and whether they believe that their somewhat odd thinking and behaving patterns (as least as others view them) help them to be successful in their chosen field of endeavor is the focus of the balance of this chapter.

LITERATURE REVIEW ON HACKERS' PREDISPOSITIONS

Hacker Defined and the Skills Needed to Hack

The word *hacker* has taken on many different meanings in the past 25 years, ranging from computer-savvy individuals professing to enjoy manipulating computer systems to stretch their capabilities—typically called the White Hats—to the malicious manipulators bent on breaking into computer systems, often by utilizing deceptive or illegal means and with an intent to cause harm—typically called the Black Hats (Steele, Woods, Finkel, Crispin, Stallman, & Goodfellow, 1983).

In earlier times, the word *hacker* in Yiddish had nothing to do with savvy technology types but described an inept furniture maker. Nowadays, the "elite" hackers are recognized within their ranks as the gifted segment, noted for their exceptional hacking talents. An "elite" hacker must be highly skilled to experiment with command structures and explore the many files available to understand and effectively "use" the system (Schell, Dodge, with Moutsatsos, 2002).

Most hack attacks on computer systems involve various degrees of technological knowledge and skill, ranging from little or no skill through to elite status. The least savvy hackers—the script kiddies--use automated software readily available through the Internet to do bothersome things like deface websites. Those wanting to launch more sophisticated attacks require a toolbox of social engineering skills—a deceptive process whereby individuals "engineer" a social situation, thus allowing them to obtain access to an otherwise closed network. Other technical skills needed by the more talented hackers include knowledge of computer languages like C or C++, general UNIX and systems administration theory, theory on Local Area Networks (LAN) and Wide Area Networks (WAN), and access and common security protocol information.

Exploit methods used by the more skilled hackers—continually evolving and becoming more sophisticated—include the following (Schell & Martin, 2004):

- flooding (cyberspace vandalism resulting in Denial of Service (DoS) to authorized users of a website or computer system),
- virus and worm production and release (cyberspace vandalism causing corruption of and possible erasing of data);
- spoofing (the virtual appropriation of an authentic user's identity by non-authentic users, causing fraud or attempted fraud, and commonly known as "identity theft");
- phreaking (theft or fraud consisting of using technology to make free telephone calls); and
- Intellectual Property Right (IPR) infringement (theft involving copying a target's information or software without paying for it and without getting appropriate authorization or consent from the owner to do so).

Sophisticated exploits commonly involve methods of bypassing the entire security system by exploiting gaps in the system programs (i.e., the operating systems, the drivers, or the communications protocols) running the system. Hackers capitalize on vulnerabilities in commands and protocols, such as FTP (file transfer protocol used to transfer files between systems over a network), TFTP (trivial file transfer protocol allowing the unauthenticated transfer of files), Telnet and SSH (two commands used to remotely log into a UNIX computer), and Finger (a UNIX command providing information about users that can be used to retrieve the .plan and .project files from a user's home directory). (Schell & Martin, 2004)

The Cost of Hack Attacks and Countermeasure Readiness by Industry

Considering the significant amount of valuable data stored in business, government, and financial system computers globally, experts have in recent times contemplated the risks and prevalence of attacks against computer networks. During the period from 2000 through 2006, for example, IBM researchers said that by that point, the cost to targeted and damaged systems had exceeded the $10 billion mark (IBM Research, 2006).

The just released 2009 e-crime survey, conducted by the 7th Annual e-Crime Congress in partnership with KPMG, reported that many of the 500 Congress attendees felt that with the recession engulfing North America and the world in 2009, likely out-of-work IT professionals with advanced technical skills would be recruited to join the Black Hat underground economy by developing Internet-related crimeware—and being compensated generously for doing so. This feared trend would result in a serious shifting of the odds of success in the "electronic arms race" from the White Hats to the Black Hats (Hawes, 2009).

Other key points raised by the Congress attendees and noted in the 2009 e-crime Congress report include the following (Hawes, 2009):

- Some organizations may be more vulnerable to cyber attacks than they realize, with 44% of the survey respondents reporting that cyber attacks are growing in sophistication and may be stealth in nature,
- The majority--62% of respondents—did not believe that their enterprise dedicates enough resources to locating vulnerabilities in the networks,
- A significant 79% of the respondents said that signature-based network intrusion detection methods currently in use do not provide enough protection against evolving cyber exploits, and
- About half of the respondents said that their enterprises are not sufficiently protected against the harms caused by malware.

Who Hacks: Known Traits of Insiders and Outsiders

Given the concern about increasingly sophisticated cyber exploits, what is known about those who hack? Since 2000, there has been a relatively consistent negative perception held by the media and those in industry and government agencies about hacker insiders (those who hack systems from inside corporations and government agencies) and hacker outsiders (those who hack systems from the outside).

Despite the media's fascination with and frequent reports about outsiders and the havoc that they cause on enterprise systems, a 1998 survey conducted jointly by the Computer Security Institute (CSI) and the FBI (Federal Bureau of Investigation) indicated that the average cost of successful computer attacks by outsiders was $56,000, while the average cost of malicious acts by insiders was $2.7 million (Schell et al., 2000)—a finding that places more adverse impact on insider hack attacks.

Prior to 2000, much of what was known about outsiders was developed by mental health professionals' assessments of typically young adult males under age 30 caught and charged of hacking-related offenses. The outsider was often described in the literature as being a young man either in high school or just about to attend college or university with no desire to be labeled "a criminal" (Mulhall, 1997). Rather, outsiders, when caught by authorities, often professed to being motivated by stretching the capabilities of computers and to capitalize on their power (Caminada, Van de Riet, Van Zanten, & Van Doorn, 1998).

As for insiders and their claim to fame, one of the most heavily written about insider hacker exploits occurred in 1996 when Timothy Lloyd, an employee at Omega Engineering, placed a logic bomb in the network after he discovered that he was going to be fired. Lloyd's act of sabotage reportedly cost the company an estimated $12 million in damage, and company officials said that extensive damage caused by the incident triggered the layoff of 80 employees and cost the firm its lead in the marketplace (Schell et al., 2000).

After the Timothy Lloyd incident, the U.S. Department of Defense commissioned a team of experts—clinical psychologist Eric Shaw, psychiatrist Jerrold Post, and research analyst Kevin Ruby—to construct the behavioral profiles of insiders, based on 100 cases occurring during the period 1997-1999. Following their investigation,

Shaw, Post, and Ruby (1999) said that insiders tended to have eight traits; they:

1. are introverted, being more comfortable in their own mental world than they are in the more emotional and unpredictable social world, and having fewer sophisticated social skills than their more extraverted counterparts;
2. have a history of significant family problems in early childhood, leaving them with negative attitudes toward authority— carrying over into adulthood and the workplace;
3. have an online computer dependency significantly interfering with or replacing direct social and professional interactions in adulthood;
4. have an ethical flexibility helping them to justify their exploits—a trait not typically found in more ethically-conventional types who, when similarly provoked, would not commit such acts;
5. have a stronger loyalty to their computer comrades than to their employers;
6. hold a sense of entitlement, seeing themselves as "special" and, thus, owed the recognition, privilege, or exception to the normative rules governing other employees.
7. have a lack of empathy, tending to disregard or minimize the impact of their actions on others; and
8. are less likely to deal with high degrees of distress in a constructive manner and do not frequently seek assistance from corporate wellness programs.

What Motivates Hackers

In the mid-1990s, with the release of Blake's (1994) work *Hackers in the Mist*, an anthropological study of those in the Computer Underground, the notion of a grey zone was introduced. Simply put, the grey zone is an experimental phase of the under-age 30 hackers who later in adulthood (usually by age 30) become motivationally either White Hat in nature or Black Hat in nature. Many in the grey zone are driven by the need to be recognized as one of the "elite" in the hacker world. To this end, these highly intelligent, risk-taking young hackers continually work toward acquiring knowledge and trading information with their peers in the hopes that they will be recognized for their hacking prowess. Many in the grey zone apparently seek this recognition because they feel abused and/or are misunderstood by their parents, mainstream peers, or teachers. Their strength, as they see it, lies in their lack of fear about technology and in their collective ability to detect and capitalize on the opportunities technology affords.

The power of "the collective" to overcome adversity is reflected in "The Hacker Manifesto: The Conscience of a Hacker," written by Mentor (Blankenship, 1986) and widely distributed in the Computer Underground. Below is an excerpt from the manifesto, giving insights into the minds and motivations of those in the grey zone:

You bet your ass we're all alike. . .we've been spoon-fed baby food at school when we hungered for steak. . .the bits of meat that you did let slip through were pre-chewed and tasteless. We've been dominated by sadists, or ignored by the apathetic. The few that had something to teach us found us willing pupils, but those few are like drops of water in the desert. This is our world now. . .the world of the electron and the switch, the beauty of the baud. We make use of a service already existing without paying for what could be dirt-cheap if it wasn't run by profiteering gluttons, and you call us criminals. We explore. . .and you call us criminals. We seek after knowledge. . .and you call us criminals. We exist without skin color, without nationality, without religious bias. . .and you call us criminals. You build atomic bombs, you wage wars, you murder, cheat, and lie to us and try to make us believe it's for our own good, yet we're the criminals. Yes, I am a criminal. My crime is that of curiosity. My crime is that of judg-

ing people by what they say and think, not what they look like. My crime is that of outsmarting you, something you will never forgive me for. I am a hacker, and this is my manifesto. You may stop this individual, but you can't stop us all. After all, we're all alike.

Nowadays, the capability, motivation, and predisposition to hack have moved from the underground and into the mainstream. In May, 2009, for example, survey results released by Panda Security showed that with the variety of hacking tools readily available on the Internet, mainstream adolescents with online access are motivated to hack as a means of fulfilling their personal needs. Unfortunately, these latent needs are often negatively-driven. After surveying 4,100 teenage online users, the study team found that over half of the respondents polled spent, on average, 19 hours a week online, with about 68% of their time spent in leisure activities like gaming, video viewing, music listening, and chatting. What was concerning to the researchers is that about 67% of the respondents said that they tried at least once to hack into their friends' instant messaging or social network accounts by acquiring free tools and content through the Internet. Some respondents admitted to using Trojans to spy on friends, to crack the servers at their schools to peek at exam questions, or to steal the identities of acquaintances in social networks (Masters, 2009).

How Hackers Think and Behave

Prior to 2000, the literature on insider and outsider hackers painted a rather bleak picture of the behaviors and thinking patterns of those in the Computer Underground. Taken as a composite, the studies suggested that hackers under age 30 report and/or exhibit many short-term stress symptoms like anxiety, anger, and depression—caused by a number of factors, including the following: (i) childhood-inducing psychological pain rooted in peer teasing and harassment; (ii) introverted behaving and thinking tendencies maintaining a strong inward cognitive focus; (iii) anger about the generalized perception that parents and others in mainstream society misunderstand or denounce an inquisitive and exploratory nature; (iv) educational environments doing little to sate high-cognitive and creative potentials—resulting in high degrees of boredom and joy-ride-seeking; and (v) a fear of being caught, charged, and convicted of hacking-related exploits (Shaw et al., 1990; Caminada et al., 1998; Blake, 1994).

Given this less-than-positive composite tended to include primarily those charged of computer crimes, White Hat hackers complained in the early 1990s that such a biased profile did not hold for the majority of hackers (Caldwell, 1990, 1993).

The Schell, Dodge, with Moutsatsos Study Findings

To address this assertion made by the White Hats, in 2002, Schell, Dodge, with Moutsatsos released their research study findings following a comprehensive survey investigation of the behaviors, motivations, psychological predispositions, creative potential, and decision-making styles of over 200 hackers (male and female) attending the 2000 Hackers on Planet Earth (HOPE) conference in New York City and the DefCon 8 hacker conference in Las Vegas. These researchers found that some previously reported findings and perceptions held about those in the Computer Underground—labeled" myths"—were founded for the hacker conference participants, while others were not.

For example, contrary to the literature suggesting that only males are active in the Computer Underground, females (like Gigabyte) are also active, though only about 9% of the hacker study participants were female. Contrary to the myth that those in the Computer Underground are typically students in their teens, the study findings revealed a broader hacker conference participant range, with the youngest respondent being 14 years of age and with the eldest being 61 years of age. The mean age for respondents was 25.

Contrary to the belief that hackers tend not to be gainfully employed, the study findings revealed that beyond student status, those approaching age 30 or older tended to be gainfully employed. The largest reported annual income of respondents was $700,000, the mean salary reported for male conference attendees was about $57,000 ($n$ = 190), and that for females was about $50,000 ($n$ = 18). A t-test analysis revealed no evidence of gender discrimination based on annual income, but preference for employment facility size was a significant differentiator for the male and female hacker conference attendees, with male respondents tending to work in large companies with an average of 5,673 employees, and with female respondents tending to work in smaller companies with an average of 1,400 employees.

Other key study findings included the following:

1. Though a definite trend existed along the troubled childhood hacker composite—with almost a third of the hacker respondents saying that they had experienced childhood trauma or significant personal losses (28%, $n = 59$), the majority of hacker respondents did not make such claims. Of those reporting troubled childhoods, 61% said they knew these events had a long-term adverse impact on their thoughts and behaviors. A t-test analysis revealed that female hackers (n = 18) were more likely to admit experiencing childhood trauma or significant personal losses than males ($n = 191$).
2. The stress symptom checklist developed by Derogatis and colleagues (1974) was embedded in the study survey to assess the short-term stress symptoms of the hacker conference participants. Considering a possible range for each stress cluster from 0-3 (where 0 represented no symptoms reported, and where 3 represented strong and frequent symptoms reported), the obtained mean cluster scores for the hacker conference respondents were all below 1, indicating mild, not pronounced stress presentations---a finding running counter to common beliefs. The obtained cluster mean scores were as follows: anger/hostility (0.83, *SD*: 0.75, N = 211); interpersonal sensitivity (0.70, *SD*: 0.62, $N = 211$); obsessive-compulsiveness (0.57, *SD*: 0.50, $N = 208$); depression (0.54, *SD*: 0.50, $N = 208$); somatization presentations (such as asthma and arthritis flare-ups) during times of distress (0.44, *SD*: 0.39, N = 203); and anxiety (0.33, *SD*: 0.35, N = 206). Consistent with reports suggesting that hackers' anger may be rooted in interpersonal misunderstandings, the strongest correlation coefficient was with hostility and interpersonal sensitivity ($r = 0.85$, $p < .01$). No significant difference in stress cluster mean scores was found for hackers charged of criminal offenses and those not charged.
3. Accepting Dr. Kimberly Young's (1996) measure for "computer addicted" individuals as spending, on average, 38 hours a week online (compared to the "non-addicted" types who spend, on average, 5 hours a week online), contrary to popular myths, the hacker conference participants would generally rate as "heavy users" rather than as "addicts." The respondents said that they spent, on average, 24.45 hours (*SD*: 22.33, $N = 207$) in hacking-related activity.
4. Because of well-developed cognitive capabilities among those in the hacker world, as Meyer's earlier (1998) work suggested, the findings indicated a fair degree of multitasking capability among hackers attending conferences. The respondents said that during the average work week, they were engaged in about 3-4 hacking projects.
5. The 70-item Grossarth-Maticek and Eysenck (1990) inventory was also embedded in the

survey to assess the longer-term thinking and behaving patterns of the hacker conference respondents. "Type" scores of the respondents, based on mainstream population norms, were placed on a continuum from the "self-healing and task-and-emotion-balanced" end to the "noise-filled and disease-prone" end. The "Type B" label described the self-healing types of thinking and behaving patterns, whereas the disease-prone types included the Type A (noise-out and cardiovascular disease-prone at earlier ages), the Type C (noise-in and cancer-prone at earlier ages), and the violent-prone Psychopathic and "Unibomber" types. Contrary to prevailing myths about hackers having a strong Type A and computer-addicted predisposition, the study found that the two highest mean Type scores for hacker conference attendees—both male and female--were in the self-healing Type B category (*M*: 7.20, *SD*: 1.55, $N = 200$), followed by the overly-rational, "noise-in" Type C category (*M*: 5.37, *SD*: 2.45, $N = 204$).

6. The 20-item Creative Personality Test of Dubrin (1995) was embedded in the survey to assess the creative potential of the hacker conference attendees, relative to norms established for the general population. Considering a possible score range of 0-20, with higher scores indicating more creative potential (and with a cutoff score for the "creative" labeling being 15 or higher), the mean score for the hacker conference respondents was 15.30 (*SD*: 2.71, $N = 207$)—deserving the "creative" label. A *t*-test analysis revealed no significant differences in the mean creativity scores for the males and the females, for those charged and not charged, and for those under age 30 and over age 30.
7. In terms of possibly self- and other-destructive traits in the hacker conference attendees, the study findings found that, compared to their over-age-30 counterparts ($n = 56$), some hackers in the under-age 30 segment ($n = 118$) had a combination of reported higher risk traits: elevated narcissism, frequent bouts of depression and anxiety, and clearly computer addictive behavior patterns. The researchers concluded that about 5% of the younger, psychologically noise-filled hacker conference attendees were of concern. The respondents seemed to recognize this predisposition, noting in their surveys that they were conscious of their anger and were motivated to "act out" against targets—corporations and/or individuals. The researchers posited that the root of this anger was likely attachment loss and abandonment by significant others in childhood.

BACKGROUND ON THE CURRENT STUDY ON HACKER CONFERENCE ATTENDEES

As the Schell et al. (2002) study findings seem to indicate, when larger numbers and a broader cross-section of hackers are studied, relative to a more narrowly-defined hacker criminal segment, a very different picture—and a much more positive one—is drawn about the motivations, behaviors, and thinking patterns of hacker conference attendees.. In fact, rather than viewing the profile of hackers as being introverted and poorly-adjusted individuals, as earlier reports on exploit-charged insiders and outsiders suggested, there seems to be increasingly more evidence that individuals engaged in hacking-related activities are not only cognitively advanced and creative individuals by early adulthood but task-and-emotion-balanced, as well. Accepting this more positive profile of computer hackers, the study authors questioned, Besides loss and abandonment by significant others in childhood, might there be some other explanation for the hostility and interpersonal sensitivity link found in hackers, as earlier reported in the literature?

A Closer Look at the Traits of Hackers Mitnick and Mafiaboy

One place to start answering this question is to look more closely at some common traits exhibited by two other famous hackers who caught the media's attention in recent times because of their costly cracking exploits: American Kevin Mitnick and Canadian Mafiaboy. While both of them had some noted Black Hat thinking and behavioral tendencies in their adolescence--with Mitnick finding himself behind prison bars a number of times because of his costly exploits to industry and government networks—after age 30, like many of the hacker conference participants studied by Schell et al. (2002), Mitnick and Mafiaboy became productive White Hat adults gainfully employed in the Information Technology Security sector.

Kevin Mitnick, born in the United States in 1963, went by the online handle "Condor." He made it to the FBI's "Ten Most Wanted" fugitives list when he was hunted down for repeatedly hacking into networks, stealing corporate secrets from high-tech companies like Sun Microsystems and Nokia, scrambling telephone networks, and cracking the U.S. national defense warning system—causing an estimated $300 million in damages. These costly exploits to industry and government landed Condor in federal prison a number of times. In media reports, Mitnick described himself as a "James Bond behind the computer" and as an explorer who had no real end. After being released from prison in 2000, Mitnick's overt behaviors seemed to change. He turned his creative energy to writing security books (including *The Art of Deception: Controlling the Human Element of Security*), becoming a regular speaker at hacker conferences—advocating a White Hat rather than a Black Hat stance, and having an IT Security firm carrying his name. When writing of his exploits as Mitnick found his way in and out of prison, the media often focused on the fact that Mitnick had a troubled childhood--with his parents divorcing while he was very young. Post his prison release, the media focused more on Mitnick's talents as a gifted hacker—noting that those skills are now sought by the FBI to help solve difficult network intrusion cases. (Schell, 2007)

Mafiaboy, born in Canada in 1985, was only 15 years of age when in February 2000, he cracked servers and used them to launch costly Denial of Service attacks on several high-profile e-commerce websites—including Amazon, eBay, and Yahoo. After pleading guilty in 2001 to these exploits, Mafiaboy was sentenced to eight months in a youth detention center and fined $250 (Schell, 2007). Subsequent to his arrest, Mafiaboy dropped out of high school and worked as a steakhouse busboy. His lawyer said that Mafiaboy did not intend to cause damage to the targeted networks, but he had difficulty believing that companies such as Yahoo had not put in place adequate security measures to stop him from successfully completing his exploits. Today, Mafiaboy—whose real name is Michael Calce--speaks at Information Technology Security forums on social engineering and other interesting hacking topics, has written an award-winning book about his exploits, and has started his own network penetration testing consulting firm (Kavur, 2009). During his arrest, as with Mitnick, media reports focused on Michael's troubled childhood and the marital separation of his parents (Schell, 2002).

Besides being tech-savvy, creative, angry, and possibly suffering from loss and abandonment issues, could there be other "wiring" commonalities—or unique gifts—in hackers Mitnick, Calce, Walker, and Vanvaeck that drew them into hacking in adolescence—and kept them there throughout adulthood, albeit it in an overtly changed state? Might all four of these hackers, as well as many in the hacker community, be Asperger syndrome individuals, possessing the same kind of special gifts that other professionals in mathematics and science have? This was the question that motivated a follow-up investigation to the Schell et al. (2002) study and whose findings serve as the focus for the rest of this chapter.

Asperger Syndrome: The Catalyst Driving the Current Study

Asperger's syndrome was not added to the *Diagnostic and Statistical Manual of Mental Disorders*, relied upon by mental health professionals when diagnosing clients, until 1994—50 years after the Austrian physician Hans Asperger identified the syndrome in children with impaired communication and social skills. Then, it took about six more years for the media to inform mainstream society about the syndrome. In fact, it wasn't until around the year 2000 that the *New York Times Magazine* called Asperger syndrome "the little professor syndrome," and a year later, *Wired* magazine called it "the geek syndrome," though only case observation was given in the article, with no empirical validation of its presence in the hacker population (Hughes, 2003).

Over the past decade, mental health practitioners have espoused the view that Asperger syndrome appears to have a genetic base. In 2002, Dr. Fred Volkmar, a child psychiatrist at Yale University, said that Asperger syndrome appears to be even more strongly genetic than the more severe forms of classic autism, for about a third of the fathers or brothers of children with Asperger syndrome show signs of the disorder. But, noted Volkmar, the genetic contributor is not all paternal, for there appears to be maternal contributions as well. A prevailing thought shared at the start of the decade was that "assortative mating" was at play. By this was meant that in university towns and Research and Development (R & D) environments, smart but not necessarily well socialized men met and married women much like themselves—leading to "loaded genes" that would predispose their offspring to autism, Asperger syndrome, and related "wiring" or neurological conditions (Nash, 2002).

"Might this same logic pertain to those in the hacker community?" In 2001, psychiatrists John Ratey (Harvard Medical School) and Simon Baron-Cohen (Cambridge University) said that there is very likely some connection between Asperger syndrome and hackers' perceived "geeky" behaviors, but, to date, there has been no actual study to validate this possibility. What does exist, for the most part, are lay observations about hackers' thinking and behaving patterns--and much speculation.

For example, in 2001, Dr. Temple Grandin, a professor of animal science at Colorado State University and an internationally respected authority on the meat industry, was diagnosed with Asperger syndrome. After Kevin Mitnick's most recent release from prison, Dr. Grandin saw him being interviewed on the television show *60 Minutes*. It was during the interview that she noticed some mannerisms in Mitnick that she herself had—a twitchy lack of poise, an inability to look people in the eye, stunted formality in speaking, and a rather obsessive interest in technology—observations about Mitnick which Dr. Grandin later shared with the media. (Zuckerman, 2001)

As the media began to write about Asperger syndrome, more people in mainstream society became interested in its characteristics and causes. Scholars, too, began to explore other causes besides a genetic basis. Experts posited, for example, that the syndrome could have other precursors—such as prenatal positioning in the womb, trauma during the birthing process, a lack of vitamin D intake by pregnant women, and random variation in the process of brain development. Furthermore, there had been a suggestion that males seem to manifest Asperger syndrome much more frequently than females. (Mittelstaedt, 2007; Nash, 2002)

The rest of this chapter defines what is meant by Asperger syndrome, reviews its relevance on the autism continuum, and discusses the findings of a survey of 136 male and female hacker conference attendees regarding their adult life experiences and their scores on the Autism-Spectrum Quotient (AQ) self-report assessment tool.

ASPERGER SYNDROME AND AUTISM DEFINED

Asperger syndrome is a neurological condition thought to be on the autistic spectrum. "Autism" is defined as an individual's presenting with severe abnormalities in social and communication development, marked repetitive behaviors, and limited imagination. "Asperger syndrome" is characterized by milder dysfunctional forms of social skill under-development, repetitive behaviors, communication difficulties, and obsessive interests—as well as with some positively functional traits like high intelligence, exceptional focus, and unique talents in one or more areas, including creative pursuits. (Baron-Cohen, Wheelwright, Skinner, Martin, & Clubley, 2001; Hughes, 2003)

To put Asperger syndrome in an everyday-living perspective, many of those eventually diagnosed with Asperger syndrome tend to learn social skills with the same difficulty that most people learn math, but they tend to learn math with the same ease that most people learn social skills (Hughes, 2003).

Asperger syndrome differs from autism in that afflicted individuals have normal language development and intellectual ability, whereas those afflicted with autism do not (Woodbury-Smith, Robinson, Wheelwright, & Baron-Cohen, 2005). "Pronounced degree" of Asperger syndrome is defined in terms of the assessed individual's meeting the same general criteria for autism, but not meeting the criteria for Pervasive Development Disorder, or PDD. Language delay, associated with autism but not with Asperger syndrome, is defined as "a child's not using single words by 2 years of age, and/or of not using phrase speech by 3 years of age" (Baron-Cohen, 2001).

Genetic Origins of Asperger Syndrome and Autism

Recently, there has been much discussion among mental health experts and scientists about whether Asperger syndrome and autism have genetic origins because of obvious family pedigrees. There has also been debate over whether both conditions lie on a continuum of social-communication disability, with Asperger syndrome being viewed as the bridge between autism and normality (Baron-Cohen, 1995).

In 2007, an international team of researchers, part of the Autism Genome Project involving more than 130 scientists in 50 institutions and 19 countries (at a project cost of about $20 million), began reporting their findings on the genetic underpinnings of autism and Asperger syndrome. Though prior studies had suggested that between 8 and 20 different genes were linked to autism or one of the variants (such as Asperger syndrome), new findings suggest that there are many more genes involved in their presentation, possibly even 100 different genes (Ogilvie, 2007).

In 2009, findings were reported suggesting that changes in brain connections between neurons (called synapses) early in development could underlie some cases of autism. This discovery emerged after the international team studied over 12,000 subjects—some from families having multiple autism cases; for example, one study cohort had 780 families with 3,101 autistic children, while another cohort had 1,204 autistic children. The controls were families with no evidence of autism (Fox, 2009).

One phase of this international study focused on a gene region accounting for as many as 15% of autism cases, while another study phase identified missing or duplicated stretches of DNA along two key gene pathways. Both of these phases detected genes involved in the development of brain circuitry in early childhood. Because earlier study findings suggested that autism arises from abnormal connections among brain cells during early development, it was helpful to find more empirical evidence indicating that mutations in genes involved in brain interconnections increase a young child's risk of developing autism. In short, the international study team found that children with autism spectrum disorders are more likely than controls to have gene variants on a particular region of chromosome 5, located between two genes: cadherin 9 (CDH9) and cadherin 10 (CDH10).

The latter genes carry codes producing neuronal cell-adhesion molecules, important because they affect how nerve cells communicate with each other. As earlier noted, problems in communication are believed to be an underlying cause of autism spectrum disorders. (MTB Europe, 2009; Glessner, Wang, Cai, Korvatska, Kim, et al., 2009; Wang, Zhang, Ma, Bucan, Glessner, et al., 2009)

These recent discoveries appear to be consistent with what has been shown previously from the brain scans of affected children; namely, that individuals with autism seem to show different or reduced connectivity between various parts of the brain. However, affirm researchers, these genetic mutations are not just found in autistic individuals but in the "unaffected" general population, as well. Clearly, much more research investigation is needed to shed more light on these findings (Fox, 2009).

Prevalence of Autism or One of the Variants

Autism or one of its variants is now reported to affect about 1 in 165 children. With Asperger syndrome, in particular, one epidemiological study estimates a population prevalence of 0.7% (Ehlers & Gillberg, 1993). In this study, all school children in a Swedish borough were screened in stage one. Final case selection for Asperger syndrome was based on a second-stage clinical work-up. Results indicated a minimum prevalence in the general population of about 3.6 per 1,000 children (from 7 through 16 years of age), and a male to female ratio of 4:1. When suspected and possible Asperger syndrome cases are included, the prevalence rate rises to 7 per 1,000 children, and the male to female ratio drops to 2:1 (Ehlers & Gillberg, 1993).

Diagnosing and Measuring Asperger Syndrome

Diagnosing Asperger syndrome is often difficult, because it often has a delayed presentation—and is not diagnosed until in late childhood or early adulthood (Barnard, Harvey, Prior, & Potter, 2001; Powell, 2002). Although several diagnostic instruments exist for measuring autistic spectrum conditions, the most widely-used tool by mental health professionals is the Autism Diagnostic Interview—Revised. The latter takes about three hours and is rather costly, since it utilizes a face-to-face interview with highly trained professionals (Lord, Rutter, & Le Couteur, 1994).

To make assessments less expensive and more readily available, Woodbury-Smith and colleagues (2005) developed the Autism Spectrum Quotient (AQ), a 50-item forced-choice self-report instrument, for measuring the degree to which an adult with normal intelligence seems to have some autistic traits. To date, the empirical study results indicate that the AQ has good discriminative validity and good screening properties.

Selective Theory of Mind Deficits in Asperger Syndrome Individuals

Individuals with the more severe presentations of autism are said to have a selective Theory of Mind (ToM) deficit, note the experts, meaning that they have difficulty inferring the mental states of others, a likely contributing factor to their interpersonal sensitivities. People with Asperger syndrome apparently also have this deficit, but in a milder form.

Experts point out that adults with Asperger syndrome may actually pass traditional ToM tests designed for young children, though they do not have normal adult ToM functioning, for they may be able to solve the test tasks using mental processes other than ToM processing. It is also believed that by developing compensatory processing techniques throughout their childhoods,

Asperger syndrome adults can learn to communicate with others quite effectively. Past research studies have shown that children and adolescents with autism traits have deficits in perceiving mood or emotion based on vocal dues. Besides being poor readers of body language and vocal cues in real-life social situations, when tested, these affected individuals show deficits when asked to match vocal segments to videos of faces, vocal segments to photographs of faces, and nonverbal vocalizations to line drawings of body postures or to line drawings of facial expressions (Rutherford, Baron-Cohen, & Wheelwright, 2002).

Intense World Theory in Asperger Syndrome Individuals

As a rule, individuals with Asperger syndrome are often stereotyped by those in mainstream society as being "distant loners" or" unfeeling geeks." However, new research findings suggest that what may look like cold or non-emotionally-responsive individuals to onlookers may actually be individuals having *excesses* of empathy.

This new view would seem to not only resonate with families having Asperger syndrome children (McGinn, 2009) but also coincide with the "intense world" theory. This theory sees the fundamental issue in autism-spectrum disorders as being not a social-deficiency one as previously thought—but a hypersensitivity-to-affective-experience one, including a heightened fear of rejection by peers. Perhaps affected individuals, note researchers, are actually *better* readers of body language in real life than those typically characterized as "controls." Asperger syndrome individuals may actually feel "too much"; consequently, the behaviors of focusing on local details and attention-switching—traits commonly seen in those with the syndrome--may actually be a means of reducing their social anxiety. Perhaps when Asperger syndrome individuals walk into a room, they can "feel" what everyone else is feeling—and all of this emotive information comes in faster than it can be comfortably processed. This pull-back on empathy expression, therefore, makes sense if one considers that individuals with autism spectrum disorders may be experiencing empathetic feelings so intensely that they withdraw in a way that appears to others to be callous and disengaged. (Szalavitz, 2009)

Adults Screened for Asperger Syndrome with the AQ Inventory

In 2001, Baron-Cohen and colleagues used the Autism-Spectrum Quotient (AQ) inventory for assessing the degree to which certain individuals with normal or high intelligence have the characteristics associated with the autistic spectrum. Scores on the AQ range from 0 to 50, with higher scores indicating a stronger autism-spectrum predisposition.

Four groups of adult subjects were assessed by the Baron-Cohen (2001) team: 45 male and 13 female adults with expert-diagnosed Asperger syndrome, 174 randomly selected controls, 840 students attending Cambridge University, and 16 winners of the U.K. Mathematics Olympiad.

Their study findings indicated that adults with Asperger syndrome had a mean AQ score of 35.8 (*SD*: 6.5), significantly higher than the control group's mean AQ score of 16.4 (*SD*: 6.3). Moreover, the majority of Asperger syndrome male and female scorers—80% —had scores on the AQ of 32 or higher, compared to only 2% of the controls (Baron-Cohen et al., 2001).

On the five subscales quantifying traits associated with autistic continuum disorders—(i) poor communication, (ii) poor social and interpersonal skills, (iii) poor imagination, (iv) exceptional attention to detail, and (v) poor attention-switching or a strong focus of attention, the Asperger syndrome subjects (both male and female) had their highest subscale score on poor attention-switching or a strong focus of attention, followed by poor social skills, followed by poor communication skills (Baron-Cohen et al., 2001).

Among the controls, males scored higher on the AQ than the females, and no females scored extremely highly--defined as having AQ scores meeting or exceeding 34. In contrast, 4% of the males had scores in this high range. The AQ scores for the social science students at Cambridge University did not differ from those of the control group (*M*: 16.4, *SD*: 5.8), but science students—including mathematicians—scored significantly higher (*M*: 18.5, *SD*: 6.8) than the controls. The researchers noted that these study findings support the belief that autistic spectrum traits seem to be associated with individuals having highly developed scientific skill sets. (Baron-Cohen et al., 2001)

Mean AQ scores below 16.4 placed the test subjects in the control group, mean scores from 17 through 33 placed the test subjects in the intermediate range, and mean scores 34 and higher placed test subjects in the higher-spectrum range for autism. The researchers concluded that the AQ is a valuable tool for quickly quantifying where any individual is situated on a continuum from autism to normality. The AQ inventory seemed to identify in a non-invasive manner the degree to which an adult of normal or higher IQ may have autistic traits, or what has been called "the broader phenotype." (Bailey, LeCouteur, Gorresman, Bolton, Simonoff, Yuzda, & Rutter, 1995; Baron-Cohen et al., 2001)

THE NEW HACKER CONFERENCE STUDY HYPOTHESES, QUESTIONNAIRE INSTRUMENT, AND PROCEDURE

This new hacker conference study was designed to assess male and female hacker conference attendees for Asperger syndrome traits using the AQ inventory. As well, self-reports on childhood and early adulthood experiences from hackers were sought to ascertain if there were links between AQ scores and negative life experiences.

Study Hypotheses

Consistent with the findings of the Baron-Cohen, et al., 2001, study on Cambridge University students in mathematics and the sciences, and with the findings of Schell et al., 2002, indicating few or minor thinking and behavioral differences for male and female hacker conference attendees--who, as a group, appear to be creative individuals and good stress handlers:

H 1: *The mean AQ scores for male and female hacker conference attendees would place in the intermediate range of Asperger syndrome (with AQ scores from 17 through 33, inclusive)—rather than in the low range like the controls and university students in the humanities and social sciences (with AQ scores equal to or below 16.4) or in the high range (with AQ scores of 34 or higher) like those diagnosed as having debilitating Asperger syndrome traits.*

Consistent with the findings of Schell et al., 2002, and with those of the Baron-Cohen, et al., 2001, study on Cambridge University students in mathematics and sciences:

H2: *The majority of hacker conference respondents would tend to "definitely agree" or "slightly agree" that their thinking and behaving styles helped them to cope with certain personal and professional stressors existing in the IT security/hacking world, due, in part, to their exceptional attention to local details, followed by their poor attention switching/strong focus of attention.*

Questionnaire Instrument

The hacker conference study self-report instrument was 8 pages long and included 68 items. Part I included the nine demographic items used in the Schell et al., 2002, study, primarily for comparison purposes to assess how the 2000 demographic profile of hacker conference attendees compares with a more recent study sample. These items related to respondents' gender, age, country of residency, highest educational degree obtained, employment status, job title, percentage of time spent per week on various hacking activities, and motives for hacking.

Part II was an open-ended, short-answer section with 8 personal history items related to the respondents' interest in technology and IT security as well as online hostility experiences. Items included (i) the age at which respondents became interested in technology and IT security, (ii) their primary reasons for getting interested in technology and IT security, (iii) their views about whether there is equal opportunity for females and other visible minorities in the hacker community, and (iv) if they were victims of cyber-stalking incidents (defined as repeatedly facing online attention from someone you did not want to get attention from or having your safety or life threatened online) or cyber-harassment incidents (defined as being berated online with disgusting language or having your reputation tarnished).

Part III included the Autism-Spectrum Quotient (AQ) inventory of 50 items, with respondents using a "definitely agree, slightly agree, slightly disagree, and definitely disagree" scale. A new item (using the same scale) was added to this section to assess support for the "intense world" theory; namely, "I believe that my routine thinking and behaving styles have helped me cope well with certain personal and professional stressors existing in the IT security/hacking field."

The instrument cover letter stated the objectives of the study; namely, to better understand how women and men in the IT security and hacker community feel about being there. It also informed respondents that this study was a follow-up to the one completed in July 2000 by Schell and colleagues, focusing on myths surrounding hackers. This new survey was designed to discover the reasons why women and men in the IT security and hacker communities remained involved with computer technology beyond high school. Respondents were guaranteed anonymity and confidentiality of responses and were told that forthcoming reports of the findings would cite group data, not individual responses.

Procedure

Because there are so few women actively involved in hacking conferences (i.e., below 10%), the initial phase of survey distribution was aimed at women, in particular, and was distributed to female attendees at: (i) the Black Hat hacker conferences in Las Vegas in 2005 and 2006, (ii) the DefCon hacker conferences in Las Vegas in 2005, 2006, and 2007, (iii) the 2006 Hackers on Planet Earth (HOPE) conference in New York City, (iv) the 2005 Executive Women's Forum for IT Security in Phoenix, Arizona, and (v) the 2006 IBM CASCON conference in Markham, Ontario, Canada.

In the second phase of survey distribution, where the aim was to have about equal numbers of female and male hacker conference respondents, both male and female hacker respondents were solicited for survey completion at the 2007 Black Hat and DefCon conferences in Las Vegas. At all the conferences, the researchers had one prescreening question: "Are you actively involved in the activities of this hacker conference?" Only those answering affirmatively were given the survey instrument to complete. Individuals accompanying the self-identified hackers were not given a survey unless they, too, said that they were active participants.

STUDY FINDINGS

Respondent Demographic Characteristics and Comparisons with the Schell et al., 2002, Study Sample

In the current study, 66 male (49.5%) and 70 female hacker conference attendees (51.5%) completed the 8-page survey, bringing the total sample size for analysis to 136.

A broad age range was found in the respondent sample, with the youngest male being 18 years of age and with the eldest being 56. The youngest female was 19 years of age, and the eldest was 54. For males, the mean age was 33.74 (*SD*: 9.08) and for females, the mean age was 34.50 (*SD*: 10.27). For the overall group, the mean age was 34.13 (*SD*: 9.69), the median was 32.00, and the mode was 28—indicating a more mature set of hacker conference respondents than that obtained in the Schell, et al, 2002, study, where the mean age of respondents was 25.

In the Schell et al, 2002 study, the researchers noted that hacker conference attendees tended to be gainfully employed by the time they approach age 30. Similar findings were obtained in this new study. The mean salary for the respondent group (N = 111) was $87,805 (*SD*: 6,458). For males (n = 56), the mean salary was $86,419 (*SD*: 41,585), and for females (n =55), the mean salary was $89,215 (*SD*: 89,790). The reported job titles contained "student status" as well as professional status, with both female and male respondents citing the following as their workplace titles: Chief Information Security Officer, Director of Security, Company President, CEO, Security Engineer, Network Engineer, System and Network Administrator, and Professor.

These job titles reflect sound economic footing for the respondents and a well- educated study sample. Compared to the Schell et al., 2002, study sample, where the bulk of respondents tended to have 1-3 years of college/business/or trade school, the present study sample had a large percentage graduated from university programs. For example, 82% of the respondents had a university or post-graduate degree. The breakdown was as follows: 57% had an undergraduate degree, 18% had a Masters degree, and 7% had a Ph.D. Of those not university educated, 12% of the respondents had completed high school, and 5% of the respondents had college diplomas.

As with the Schell et al., 2002, study sample, there was international representation, but most of the 136 respondents were from the United States (82%). Of the remainder, 7.5% were from Canada and smaller percentages (ranging from <4% to <1%) were from Mexico, the United Kingdom, Australia, Denmark, Columbia, France, and Japan.

As in the Schell et al., 2002, study, where the respondents said that they hacked for primarily White Hat reasons—with the top two reasons being (i) to advance network, software and computer capabilities (36%) or (ii) to solve interesting puzzles and challenges (34%), the present study respondents said that they hack to (i) solve interesting puzzles and challenges (31%), or (ii) to advance network, software, and computer capabilities (22%).

Compared to the 2002 study respondents who said they were motivated to hack to expose weaknesses in a company's network or in their products (8%), the current older, better-educated sample cited this motive more often (15%). Also, compared to the 2002 study sample—where 1% of the respondents admitted to wanting to cause harm to persons or property (i.e., clearly Black Hat motives), no one in the current study sample said they were motivated to hack to take revenge on a company or on an individual. Finally, about 2.2% (n = 3) of the current respondents said they had hacking-related offences, including cracking passwords/pin numbers, making false allegations online, and changing grades. Penalties included a fine or community service but no jail time.

Respondents' Reported Earlier Life Experiences

In the present study, the mean age that males ($n = 66$) became interested in technology was 11 years, whereas for females ($n = 68$), the mean age was 15.5 years. Furthermore, the mean age that males ($n = 61$) became interested in hacking/IT security was 18 years, whereas for females, the mean age ($n = 57$) was 23. [The difference in n between these two variables is indicative of the respondents' comments specifying they were *not* currently interested in or involved in 'hacking' activities.]

The t-test results indicate a statistically significant difference between males' and females' mean age of interest in technology ($t = -3.339$, $df = 132$, $\alpha = 0.01$) and mean age of interest in hacking/IT security ($t = -3.765$, $df = 116$, $\alpha = 0.01$). These study findings are consistent with those reported in the literature and in the Schell, et al. (2002) study; namely, that females tend to become interested in technology and in hacking at a later age than males, and often after females are introduced to these domains by peers, boyfriends, parents, or mentors.

Regarding respondents' views on whether there is equal opportunity for women and other visible minorities in the Computer Underground and in the IT security field, there were marked differences in views held by males and females. While 79% of the males ($n = 64$) said that "yes" there is equal opportunity, only 38% of the females ($n = 63$) agreed. Moreover, t-test results indicate a statistically significant difference between the males' and females' responses ($t = 5.255$, $df = 125$, $\alpha = 0.01$).

When asked if they had ever been victims of cyber-stalking, the responses of the males ($n = 66$) and those of the females ($n = 64$) were similar; 24% of the male hacker conference participants said that they were victims of cyber-stalking, and 23% of the female conference participants said that they were. When asked if they had ever been victims of cyber-harassment, again the responses of the males and females were similar; while 21% of the males ($n = 67$) said that they were victims of cyber-harassment, 19% of the females ($n = 64$) said that they were victims.

Although in the literature, females report being cyber-stalked and cyber-harassed more than men, as these study results indicate—and as corroborated by recent Cyber911 Emergency statistics (2009)—males are increasingly declaring themselves to be victims of such personal harm acts—and at about the same degree as that reported by females active in virtual worlds. The incident rates for cyber-stalking and cyber-harassment in the hacker community are also consistent with recent statistics reported for mainstream students in middle schools, where about 25% of those surveyed said that they have been victimized by cyber-bullying, cyber-stalking, or cyber-harassment while engaging in online activities (Roher, 2006).

Findings Regarding Autism-Spectrum Quotient (AQ) Scores of Hacker Conference Attendees

In support of **H1**, the current study findings indicate that the majority (66.9%, $N = 133$) of the hacker conference attendees had AQ scores in the intermediate range (scores ranging from 17 through 32, inclusive). See Table I below.

Following t-test analysis, there was a statistically significant difference found between males' and females' mean scores for each of the three sub-levels of AQ scores—low, intermediate, and high ($t = 2.049$, $df = 131$, $\alpha = 0.05$). Of note, there were more males than females scoring in the '*high*' category of the AQ, and there were more females than males who scored in the '*low*' category.

As in earlier reported studies in the literature (see Baron-Cohen et al., 2001) there were more males than females in the '*high*' AQ category (11.1% and 1.5%, respectively), whereas there were more females than males in the '*low*' AQ

Table 1. Mean & total AQ scores, gender and AQ sublevel

			n	% total (by gender)	Total AQ Score
Female	*Total*	Mean	70		19.24
		SD			5.82
	High	Mean	1	1.5%	32.00
		SD			.
	Intermed	Mean	47	67.1%	22.10
		SD			3.90
	Low	Mean	22	31.4%	12.64
		SD			2.59
Male	*Total*	Mean	63		20.12
		SD			7.63
	High	Mean	7	11.1%	33.43
		SD			1.99
	Intermed	Mean	42	66.7%	21.60
		SD			3.53
	Low	Mean	14	22.2%	13.36
		SD			2.17

category (31.4% and 22.2%, respectively). The intermediate category was represented by approximately 2/3 of the respondents within each gendered category.

The mean AQ score (see Table 2) for the overall group ($N = 133$) was 19.67 (*SD*: 6.75), with a minimum of 8 and a maximum of 37. The mean AQ score for females ($n = 70$) was 19.24 (*SD*: 5.82), with a minimum of 11 and a maximum of 32. The mean AQ score for males ($n = 63$) was 20.12 (*SD*: 7.63), with a minimum of 8 and a maximum of 37.

Findings Regarding AQ Subscale Scores of Respondents

The AQ inventory was comprised of 50 questions, as noted, with 10 questions assessing the five domains of the autism spectrum—(i) social skill, (ii) attention switching, (iii) attention to detail, (iv) communication, and (v) imagination. In support of **H2**, the domains that the hacker conference attendees most agreed with placed in (i) exceptional attention to local details, followed by (ii) attention switching/strong focus of attention. Also in support of **H2**, the AQ inventory areas representing the lowest overall scores for the hacker conference attendees were the (i)

Table 2. Mean AQ and subscale scores differentiated by gender

			n	Social Skill	Attention Switching	Attention to Detail	Communication	Imagination	Total AQ Score
Female	*Total*	Mean	70	3.2	4.4	6.1	2.7	2.8	19.24
		SD		2.6	1.7	2.0	1.8	1.6	5.82
	High	Mean	1	9.0	6.0	9.0	5.0	3.0	32.00
		SD		.	.	.	.	.	.
	Intermed	Mean	47	4.0	4.8	6.6	3.5	3.3	22.10
		SD		2.6	1.6	1.7	1.5	1.6	3.90
	Low	Mean	22	1.4	3.5	5.1	1.1	1.7	12.64
		SD		1.1	1.6	2.0	0.9	1.0	2.59
Male	*Total*	Mean	63	3.5	4.4	6.2	3.3	2.8	20.12
		SD		2.6	2.2	2.2	2.7	1.8	7.63
	High	Mean	7	7.4	6.9	7.9	6.6	4.7	33.43
		SD		2.1	1.3	1.5	0.8	1.0	1.99
	Intermed	Mean	42	3.9	4.8	6.3	3.5	3.0	21.60
		SD		1.9	1.9	1.7	1.7	1.7	3.53
	Low	Mean	14	1.1	2.8	6.3	1.6	1.5	13.36
		SD		1.4	1.3	1.7	1.1	1.2	2.17
Group	*Total*	Mean	133	3.4	4.4	6.2	3.0	2.8	19.67
		SD		2.6	2.0	2.0	1.9	1.7	6.75
	High	Mean	8	7.6	6.8	8.0	6.4	4.5	33.25
		SD		2.0	1.3	1.4	0.9	1.1	1.91
	Intermed	Mean	89	3.9	4.8	6.5	3.5	3.2	21.84
		SD		2.3	1.7	1.7	1.6	1.7	3.72
	Low	Mean	36	1.3	3.2	5.5	1.3	1.6	12.92
		SD		1.2	1.5	2.0	1.0	1.1	2.43

social, (ii) communication, and (iii) imagination domains. See Table 2.

Internal Consistency of AQ Inventory Domain Responses

The internal consistency for the 10 items within each of the five domains of the AQ inventory was calculated using the Cronbach alpha coefficient. This analysis revealed a pattern of moderate-to-high coefficients for all five domains assessed: Social Skill = .756; Attention Switching = .470; Attention to Detail = .393; Communication = .486; and Imagination = .406, similar to the Cronbach alpha coefficient findings of the Baron-Cohen et al., 2001, study for the five domains.

Analysis of Self-Reported Ability to Cope with Stressors in Chosen Field

In support of **H2**, both the male and female hacker conference attendees believed that their routine thinking and behaving styles helped them to cope well with certain personal and professional stressors existing in the IT security/hacking field. Of the males ($n = 57$) who responded to this item, 50 of them, or 88%, either "definitely agreed" or "slightly agreed" that this was the case. Of the 66 females who responded to this item, 91% either "definitely agreed" or "slightly agreed" with the item.

Notably, there was a statistically significant moderate linear correlation between the respondents' age and the belief that their routine thinking and behaving patterns helps them to cope well with stressors in their field ($r_s = 0.23$, $\alpha = 0.01$), a finding that lends credence to the earlier study findings of Schell et al., 2002, that by age 30, the hacker conference attendees, as a group, seemed to be good stress managers and positive contributors to society.

The seven items that the overall group of hacker conference attendees ($N = 133$) *agreed with most* (i.e., 70% or more of the sample) and indicative of their thinking and behaving patterns were as follows: "I tend to notice details that others do not" (attention to local details, 92% of respondents); "I notice patterns in things all the time" (attention to local details, 88% of respondents); "I frequently get so strongly absorbed in one thing that I lose sight of other things (attention-switching/strong focus of attention, 78% of respondents); "I usually notice car number plates or similar strings of information" (attention to local details, 74% of respondents); "I often notice small sounds when others do not" (attention to local details, 73% of respondents); and "I am fascinated by numbers" (attention to local details, 70% of respondents).

It is interesting to note that of all 50 items on the AQ, the two items that the hacker conference attendees *disagreed* with most was the one item dealing with a perceived communication liability—"I know how to tell if someone listening to me is getting bored" (65% of respondents), and the one item dealing with the attention to local details trait—"I am not very good at remembering phone numbers" (55%). These findings are consistent with others reported in the literature, indicating that individuals on the autistic continuum may never learn to understand subtle signs or signals, such as body language or paralinguistic cues, but over time, they learn to compensate for their social anxieties by attending to details—lending some support to the "intense world" theory.

Study Limitation

Finally, it should be noted that, as with any self-report study, there is a possibility of bias in response and a lack of insight by respondents regarding the traits being assessed by the AQ inventory. Future assessments of hackers' autism spectrum traits might include third-party expert assessments to be evaluated against self-report scores on the AQ inventory for greater accuracy of category placement for respondents.

CONCLUSION

The findings of this study on male and females participants in hacker conferences suggest, as the Schell et al., 2002, study earlier concluded, that hackers tend to lead socially-productive lives as they approach and move beyond age 30. It is likely that, having recognized that they are particularly good at dealing with attention to detail, relative to many in the general population, these hacker conference participants search for careers capitalizing on these traits and compatible with a need to explore the capabilities of hardware and software. These careers would likely include Chief Information Security Officer, Director of Security, Security Engineer, Network Engineer, System and Network Administrator, and IT Security Professor.

Considering that the hacker conference attendees' overall group mean AQ score placed in the intermediate area of the autism spectrum, it seems reasonable to conclude that the bulk of the hacker respondents' thinking and behaving patterns are seemingly not very different from those choosing careers in computer science, mathematics, and the physical sciences. In the samples investigated in the Baron-Cohen, 2001, study, students choosing university curricula in science and in mathematics had mean AQ scores in a similar range. The current study findings on hacker conference attendees are also similar to those reported in the Baron-Cohen et al., 1998, study, suggesting a link between highly-functioning autism spectrum conditions and a unique skill potential to excel in disciplines such as math, physics, and engineering.

Further, the findings from this study on 136 hacker conference attendees earning good incomes is consistent with the assertion espoused by Blake regarding those in the grey zone: As some potential Black Hats gain greater insights into their special skills and exercise compensatory thinking and behaving patterns to offset their social anxiety, even those charged of hacking-related offenses in their rebellious adolescent years can convert to White Hat tendencies and interests by age 30.

Finally, with regard to questions raised by Schell and her colleagues in the 2002 study about whether Human Resource Managers would be well advised to hire hackers for businesses and government agencies to secure enterprise networks, from a thinking-and-behaving perspective, there does not appear to be compelling evidence from this new study that would suggest otherwise, particularly if the applicant's profile suggests active participation in reputable hacker conferences. In short, the dark myth perpetuated in the media that the majority of hackers attending hacker conventions are motivated by revenge, reputation enhancement, and personal financial gain at the expense of others was simply not supported by the data collected. Instead, apart from tending not to read others' body language cues very easily, the majority of hackers attending conferences seem to feel that this personal liability can be compensated by their keen ability to focus on details in creative ways not commonly found in the general population.

REFERENCES

Bailey, T., Le Couteur, A., Gorresman, I., Bolton, P., Simonoff, E., Yuzda, E., & Rutter, M. (1995). Autism as a strongly genetic disorder: Evidence from a British twin study. *Psychological Medicine*, *25*, 63–77. doi:10.1017/S0033291700028099

Barnard, J., Harvey, V., Prior, A., & Potter, D. (2001). *Ignored or ineligible? The reality for adults with autistic spectrum disorders*. London: National Autistic Society.

Baron-Cohen, S., Bolton, P., Wheelwright, S., Short, L., Mead, G., Smith, A., & Scahill, V. (1998). Autism occurs more often in families of physicists, engineers, and mathematicians. *Autism*, *2*, 296–301. doi:10.1177/1362361398023008

Baron-Cohen, S., Wheelwright, S., Skinner, R., Martin, J., & Clubley, E. (2001). The Autism-spectrum quotient (AQ): Evidence from Asperger syndrome/high-functioning autism, males and females, scientists and mathematicians. *Journal of Autism and Developmental Disorders, 31*, 5–17. doi:10.1023/A:1005653411471

Blake, R. (1994). *Hackers in the mist*. Chicago, IL: Northwestern University.

Blenkenship, L. (1986). *The hacker manifesto: The conscience of a hacker*. Retrieved May 4, 2009, from http://www.mithral.com/~beberg/manifesto.html

Caldwell, R. (1990). Some social parameters of computer crime. *Australian Computer Journal, 22*, 43–46.

Caldwell, R. (1993). University students' attitudes toward computer crime: A research note. *Computers & Society, 23*, 11–14. doi:10.1145/174256.174258

Caminada, M., Van de Riet, R., Van Zanten, A., & Van Doorn, L. (1998). Internet security incidents, a survey within Dutch organizations. *Computers & Security, 17*(5), 417–433. doi:10.1016/S0167-4048(98)80066-7

Cluley, G. (2009). *Regarding Gigabyte*. Retrieved March 25, 2009, fromhttp://www.theregister.co.uk/2009/03/26/melissa_virus_anniversary/comments/

Cyber911 Emergency. (2009). *What is the profile of a typical cyberstalking/harassment victim?* Retrieved May 8, 2009, from http://www.wiredsafety.org/cyberstalking_harassment/csh7.html

Denning, D. E. (1990). Concerning hackers who break into computer systems. In *Proceedings of the 13th National Computer Security Conference*. Washington, DC, October, pp. 653-664.

Derogatis, L., Lipman, R., Covi, L., Rickels, K., & Uhlenhuth, E. H. (1974). The Hopkins Symptom Checklist (HSCL): A self-report symptom inventory. *Behavioral Science*, (19): 1–15. doi:10.1002/bs.3830190102

Dubrin, A. J. (1995). *Leadership: Research Findings, Practice, and Skills*. Boston, MA: Houghton Mifflin Co.

Ehlers, S., & Gillberg, C. (1993). The epidemiology of Asperger syndrome: A total population study. *Journal of Child Psychology and Psychiatry, and Allied Disciplines, 34*, 1327–1350. doi:10.1111/j.1469-7610.1993.tb02094.x

Europe, M. T. B. (2009). *Autism genes discovery suggests biological reasons for alteredneural development*. Retrieved May 8, 2009, from http://www.mtbeurope.info/news/2009/905020.htm

Farrell, N. (2007). *Hacker mastermind has Asperger syndrome*. Retrieved December 3, 2007, from http://www.theinquirer.net/inquirer/news/1038901/hacker-mastermind-asperger

Fox, M. (2009). Autism: Brain development: Gene could be link to 15 per cent of cases. *The Globe and Mail*, April 30, p. L6.

Gleeson, S. (2008). *Freed hacker could work for police*. Retrieved July 16, 2008, from http://www.nzherald.co.nz/nz/news/article.cfm?c_id=1&objectid=10521796

Glessner, J. T., Wang, K., Cai, G., Korvatska, O., Kim, C. E., Wood, S., et al. (2009). *Autism genome-wide copy number variation reveals ubiquitin and neuronal genes*. Retrieved on April 28, 2009, from http://dx.doi.org/10.1038/nature07953

Hawes, J. (2009). *E-crime survey 2009*. Retrieved May 3, 2009, from http://www.securingourecity.org/resources/pdf/E-CrimeSurvey2009.pdf

Hughes, B. G. R. (2003). *Understanding our gifted and complex minds: Intelligence, Asperger's Syndrome, and learning disabilities at MIT*. Retrieved July 5, 2007, from http://alum.mit.edu/news/WhatMatters/Archive/200308/

Humphries, M. (2008). *Teen hacker Owen Walker won't be convicted*. Retrieved July 17, 2008, from http://www.geek.com/articles/news/teen-hacker-owen-walker-wont-be-convicted-20080717/

Kavur, J. (2009). *Mafiaboy speech a standing room only affair*. Retrieved April 9, 2009, from http://www.itworldcanada.com/Pages/Docbase/ViewArticle.aspx?title=&ID=idgml-88fa73eb-2d00-4622-986d-e06abe0916fc&lid

Kirk, J. (2007). Estonia recovers from massive denial-of-service attack. *InfoWorld, IDG News Service*. Retrieved May 17, 2007, from http://www.infoworld.com/article/07/05/17/estonia-denial-of-service-attack_1.html

Lord, C., Rutter, M., & Le Couteur, A. (1994). Autism diagnostic interview—Revised. *Journal of Autism and Developmental Disorders, 24*, 659–686. doi:10.1007/BF02172145

Masters, G. (n.d.). *Majority of adolescents online have tried hacking*. Retrieved May 18, from http://www.securecomputing.net.au/News/145298,majority-of-adolescents-online-have-tried-hacking.aspx

McGinn, D. (2009). Asperger's parents resist name change. *The Globe and Mail*, November 4, pp. L1, L5.

Meyer, G. R. (1989). *The social organization of the computer underground*. Master of Arts Thesis. Dekalb, IL: Northern Illinois University.

Mittelstaedt, M. (2007). Researcher sees link between vitamin D and autism. *The Globe and Mail*, July 6, p. L4.

Mulhall, R. (1997). Where have all the hackers gone? A study in motivation, deterrence, and crime displacement. Part I—Introduction and methodology. *Computers & Security, 16*(4), 277–284. doi:10.1016/S0167-4048(97)80190-3

Nash, J. M. (2002). *The geek syndrome*. Retrieved May 6, 2002, from http://www.time.com/time/covers/1101020506/scaspergers.html

Ogilvie, M. (2007). New genetic link to autism. *Toronto Star*, February 19, pp. A1, A12.

Powell, A. (2002). *Taking responsibility: Good practice guidelines for services: Adultswith Asperger syndrome*. London, UK: National Autistic Society.

Research, I. B. M. (2006). *Global security analysis lab: Factsheet. IBM Research*. Retrieved January 16, 2006, from http://domino.research.ibm.com/comm/pr.nsf.pages/rsc.gsal.html

Roher, E. (2006). Cyber bullying: A growing epidemic in schools. *OPC Register, 8*, 12–15.

Rutherford, M.D., Baron-Cohen, S., & Wheelwright, S. (2002). Reading the mind in the voice: A study with normal adults and adults with Asperger syndrome and high functioning autism. *Journal of Autism and Developmental Disorders, 3)*, 189-194.

Schell, B. H. (2007). *Contemporary world issues: The internet and society*. Santa Barbara, CA: ABC-CLIO.

Schell, B. H., Dodge, J. L., & Moutsatsos, S. S. (2002). *The hacking of America: Who'sdoing it, why, and how*. Westport, CT: Quorum Books.

Schell, B. H., & Martin, C. (2004). *Contemporary world issues: Cybercrime*. Santa Barbara, CA: ABC-CLIO.

Schell, B. H., & Martin, C. (2006). *Webster's new world hacker dictionary*. Indianapolis, IN: Wiley Publishing, Inc.

Shaw, E. D., Post, J. M., & Ruby, K. G. (1999). *Inside the mind of the insider*. www.securitymanagement.com, December, pp. 1-11.

Sockel, H., & Falk, L. K. (2009). Online privacy, vulnerabilities, and threats: A manager's perspective . In Chen, K., & Fadlalla, A. (Eds.), *Online consumer protection: Theories of human relativism*. Hershey, PA: Information Science Reference. doi:10.4018/978-1-60566-012-7.ch003

Sophos. (2004). Female virus-writer Gigabyte, arrested in Belgium, Sophos comments. Retrieved February 16, 2004, from http://www.sophos.com/pressoffice/news/articles/2004/02/va_gigabyte.html

Steele, G. Jr, Woods, D. R., Finkel, R. A., Crispin, M. R., Stallman, R. M., & Goodfellow, G. S. (1983). *The hacker's dictionary*. New York: Harper and Row.

Sturgeon, W. (2004). Alleged Belgian virus writer arrested. Retrieved February 17, from http://news.cnet.com/Alleged-Belgian-virus-writer-arrested/2100-7355_3-5160493.html

Szalavitz, M. (2009). Asperger's theory does about-face. *Toronto Star*, May 14, 2009, pp. L1, L3.

Van Doorn, L. (1992). Computer break-ins: A case study. Vrige Universiteit, Amsterdam, *NLUUG Proceedings*, October.

Wang, K., Zhang, H., Ma, D., Bucan, M., Glessner, J. T., Abrahams, B. S., et al. (2009). *Common genetic variants on 5p14.1 associate with autism spectrum disorders*. Retrieved on April 28, 2009, from http://dx.doi.org/10.1038/nature07999

Woodbury-Smith, M. R., Robinson, J., Wheelwright, S., & Baron-Cohen, S. (2005). *Journal of Autism and Developmental Disorders*, *35*, 331–335. doi:10.1007/s10803-005-3300-7

Young, K. S. (1996). Psychology of computer use: XL. Addictive use of the Internet: A case that breaks the stereotype. *Psychological Reports*, *79*, 899–902.

Zuckerman, M. J. (2001). *Kevin Mitnick & Asperger syndrome?* Retrieved March 29, 2001, from http://www.infosecnews.org/hypermail/0103/3818.html

Section 4

Marco–System Issues Regarding Corporate and Government Hacking and Network Intrusions

Chapter 9
Cyber Conflict as an Emergent Social Phenomenon

Dorothy E. Denning
Naval Postgraduate School, USA

ABSTRACT

This chapter examines the emergence of social networks of non-state warriors launching cyber attacks for social and political reasons. It examines the origin and nature of these networks; their objectives, targets, tactics, and use of online forums; and their relationship, if any, to their governments. General concepts are illustrated with case studies drawn from operations by Strano Net, the Electronic Disturbance Theater, the Electrohippies, and other networks of cyber activists; electronic jihad as practiced by those affiliated with al-Qa'ida and the global jihadist movement associated with it; and operations by patriotic hackers from China, Russia, and elsewhere.

INTRODUCTION

Warfare is inherently social. Soldiers train and operate in units, fighting and dying for each other as much as for their countries. Cyber conflict is also social, but whereas traditional warriors work and socialize in physical settings, cyber warriors operate and relate primarily in virtual space. They communicate electronically and meet in online forums, where they coordinate operations and distribute the software tools and knowledge needed to launch attacks. Their targets are electronic networks, computers, and data.

DOI: 10.4018/978-1-61692-805-6.ch009

The Emergence of Cyber Conflict, or Hacking for Political and Social Objectives

Although conflict appears throughout human history, its manifestation in cyberspace is a relatively recent phenomenon. After all, digital computers did not appear until the 1940s, and computer networks until the 1960s. Attacks against computers and the data they held emerged in the late 1950s and early 1960s, but they were perpetrated more for money and revenge than as an instrument of national and international conflict. Typical crimes included bank fraud, embezzlement, information theft, unauthorized use, and vandalism (Parker, 1976). Teenage hacking arrived on the scene in the 1970s, and then grew in the 1980s, as young computer users pursued their desire to explore networks, have fun, and earn bragging rights. By the end of the decade, the single biggest attack on the Internet was a computer worm launched by a college student simply as an experiment. Within this mix of playful hacking and serious computer crime, cyber conflict, or hacking for political and social objectives, emerged, taking root in the 1990s and then blossoming in the 2000s. Now, it accounts for a substantial share of all cyber attacks, as well as some of the highest profile attacks on the Internet, such as the ones perpetrated by patriotic Russian hackers against Estonia in 2007 and Georgia in 2008.

The Hacker Group Phenomenon

From the outset, hackers and cyber criminals have operated in groups. In his examination of early computer-related crime, Donn Parker found that about half of the cases involved collusion, sometimes in groups of six or more (Parker, 1976, p. 51). Youthful hackers met on hacker bulletin boards and formed clubs, one of the earliest and most prestigious being the Legion of Doom (Denning, 1999, p. 49), while serious criminals formed networks to traffic in cyber crime tools and booty, such as stolen credit cards. Today, there are perhaps tens or hundreds of thousands of social networks engaging in cyber attacks. While many of these networks were formed for fun or financial gain, others arose for the purpose of engaging in cyber conflict. Individuals, often already connected through hacker groups or other social networks, came together to hack for a cause.

The Purpose of This Chapter

This chapter examines the emergence of social networks of non-state warriors launching cyber attacks for social and political reasons. These networks support a variety of causes in such areas as human and animal rights, globalization, state politics, and international affairs. This chapter examines the origin and nature of these networks; their objectives, targets, tactics, and use of online forums. It also describes the relationship, if any, to their governments.

THE NATURE OF NON-STATE NETWORKS

Unlike states, non-state networks of cyber soldiers typically operate without the constraints imposed by rigid hierarchies of command and control, formal doctrine, or official rules and procedures. Instead, they operate in loosely-connected networks encouraging and facilitating independent action in support of common objectives--what is sometimes characterized as "leaderless resistance."

However, while the networks are decentralized, they are not actually leaderless. A few individuals, often already connected outside cyberspace or from previous operations, effectively take charge, or at least get things started. They articulate goals and strategy, plan and announce cyber attacks, encourage people to participate, and provide instructions and tools for participating. They manage the online forums--websites, web forums and groups, discussion boards, chat rooms/channels, email lists, and so forth--supporting network activities. They also develop or acquire the automated software tools used by the group. Often, the tools themselves give the leaders some control over the conduct of cyber attacks (e.g., selection of targets and rate of attack), compensating for the lack of a hierarchical command structure over the network players.

The net effect is that non-state cyber warriors are able to mobilize and conduct attacks on relatively short notice, unconstrained by the need to follow time-consuming protocols or wait for an approval process to move through a chain of command. Further, the networks can grow to include thousands of participants, as resources are not needed to pay, train, or relocate individual warriors. Assuming adequate bandwidth, an online forum that supports a small cyber army can just as easily support a large one.

Online forums play a vital social role in the formation, growth, and operation of cyber conflict networks. Participants use the forums to acquire information, discuss issues, and get to know each other. The forums foster a sense of group identity and community, while rhetoric on the forums stirs up emotions, inspires action, and promotes a sense of "us vs. them." Newcomers see that others are engaged in, or planning to engage in, cyber attacks—leading to the overarching perception that such activity is normative for the group. By observing this collective behavior, they are more easily influenced to set aside any personal reservations and go along with the group, especially if they can do so with little risk and exposure, hiding in the cyber crowd behind a veil of relative anonymity. The forums also serve as a support base for operations, providing a means for distributing cyber attack tools and information about how to use the tools and what targets to attack, as well as coordinating the attacks. Participants may be encouraged to compete for recognition or prizes, based on who conducts the most attacks.

THIS CHAPTER'S FOCUS: HACKTIVISM, ELECTRONIC JIHAD, AND PATRIOTIC HACKING

With this background in place, the chapter now examines three areas of cyber conflict: (1) hacktivism, (ii) electronic jihad, and (iii) patriotic hacking. Hacktivism, combining hacking with social and political activism, is the broadest area; it can involve small groups of local activists or large groups crossing international boundaries and coming together over the Internet. Targets are typically government institutions, including both national and international bodies, but they also include businesses and other non-state groups. Electronic jihad refers to cyber attacks conducted in support of the terrorist group al-Qa'ida and the global jihadist movement associated with it. Targets include both government and non-government entities across the globe, but especially in the United States and other Western countries. Patriotic hacking covers state-on-state conflict, but the perpetrators of the cyber attacks are citizens and expatriates rather than governments. Targets are both government and non-government entities in the opposing state.

Although these three areas of conflict are discussed separately, they are not disjoint. Indeed, hacktivism is often used to cover all non-state social and political hacking, and hence could be considered as encompassing the other two areas.

There are some areas of conflict not addressed in this chapter, most notably conflicts involving racists and extremists engaging in hate crimes and terrorism. However, electronic jihad exemplifies this general area of conflict and how it plays out on a large scale across the Internet. Another area not covered is conflict at an individual level. Instead, the chapter focuses on conflicts relating to broader societal issues.

The following sections discuss each area of these three key areas in greater depth. For each type, motives, social networks, and activities are described, and case studies are used to illustrate general principles and historical developments. The final section concludes and discusses implications for the future.

HACKTIVISM

Defined

Hacktivism is the convergence of hacking with activism. It arose when social activists with computer skills began hacking for a cause, usually within networks of other activists.

Cases of Hacktivism

In one of the earliest reported cases of hacktivism, protestors unleashed a computer worm into the National Aeronautic and Space Administration's computer network as a means of protesting nuclear weapons. In addition to spreading, the worm displayed the message "Worms Against Nuclear Killers. Your System Has Been Officially WANKed. You talk of times of peace for all, and then prepare for war." The attack took place in late 1989, while anti-nuclear activists protested NASA's launch of the space shuttle carrying the Galileo probe on its initial leg to Jupiter, as Galileo's booster system was fueled with radioactive plutonium. The protestors failed to stop the launch, but the worm took a month to eradicate from NASA's computers, costing the space agency an estimated half million dollars in wasted time and resources (Denning, 1999, p. 281).

Cyber conflict took off with the introduction of the Web in the 1990's. Websites were not only handy targets to attack, but also visible to the public, making the attacks themselves more visible. In addition, activists could use websites to publicize forthcoming operations, distribute the tools and information needed to participate, and coordinate the actual attacks. Two general types of attack emerged and became commonplace: (i) defacements of websites with political and social messages, and (ii) Denial-of-Service (DoS) attacks--disrupting access to target websites, usually by flooding them with traffic.

One of the first web defacements was performed in 1996 to protest The Communications Decency Act (CDA), a controversial law later ruled unconstitutional by the US Supreme Court. Hackers replaced the US Department of Justice home page with a page that read "Department of Injustice" and included pornographic content censored by the act (Attrition, 1996). Another early defacement was performed by an international group of hackers opposed to nuclear weapons. Called MilwOrm, the group hacked the web site of India's Bhabha Atomic Research Center shortly after India's nuclear weapons tests in 1998, replacing the content with anti-nuclear messages and a picture of a mushroom cloud. The group of six hackers, whose ages ranged from 15 to 19, hailed from four countries: the United States, England, the Netherlands, and New Zealand (Denning, 2001).

Since then, web defacements have become common, and while most are performed for fun and bragging rights, many are motivated by social and political issues. Zone-h, which records and archives web defacements, reported that of the roughly 480,000 defacements recorded in 2007, approximately 31,000 (6.5%) were performed for political reasons and another 28,000 (5.8%) were performed as expressions of patriotism (Zone-h, 2008).

Hacktivists have also "defaced" media other than the Web. In 2007, for example, an art group called Ztohoven tampered with a TV broadcast in the Czech Republic, inserting a mushroom cloud in a landscape scene. A video clip of the transmission was posted to YouTube (Mutina, 2007).

Tactics Used by Hacktivists

The tactic of protesting an organization by flooding its website with traffic was pioneered by an international group of activists called Strano Network. On December 21, 1995, Strano Network organized a one-hour cyber attack against selected websites associated with the French government. At the appointed hour, participants from all over the world were instructed to access the target websites and rapidly hit the "reload" key over and over to clog the sites with traffic. The objective of the DoS attack was to protest French government policies on nuclear and social issues by disrupting access to key government sites. Following the strike, a posting on the Internet proclaimed it had been effective in shutting off access to some of the sites and drawing media attention. The message also asserted that the strike showed "the existence of a world-wide movement able to counteract world-wide injustice; [and] the capacity to develop [such a] movement in a short time" (Denning, 1989, p.237; Schwartau, 1996, pp.406-408).

A few years later, a New York group called the Electronic Disturbance Theater (EDT) automated Strano Network's innovative method of cyber attack so that participants would not have to continually hit the reload key to generate traffic. Instead, they could visit EDT's website and click on a button signaling their desire to join the protest. Upon doing so, a software program named FloodNet would run on their computer and send a rapid and steady stream of packets with web page requests to the target site. This is sometimes called "HTTP flooding," as the page requests are issued with the web's HTTP protocol. Other Internet protocols have also been used to flood websites, including ICMP through "ping" requests ("ping flooding") and TCP through SYN requests ("SYN flooding").

EDT began using their tools in 1998 to support the Zapatistas in their struggle against the Mexican government. Their first attack, conducted on April 10, targeted Mexican President Zedillo's website, while their second hit US President Clinton's site (because of US support to Mexico). Their third strike was more ambitious, simultaneously targeting the websites of President Zedillo, the Pentagon (because the US military helped train Mexican soldiers carrying out human rights abuses), and the Frankfurt Stock Exchange (because it represented globalization--which EDT claimed was at the root of the problem). EDT estimated that 10,000 people participated in the attacks (Denning, 1999; Denning, 2001). Since then, EDT has sponsored numerous other attacks, which they refer to as "virtual sit-ins," to support a range of issues, including the war in Iraq, health care, and immigration. An attack conducted in collaboration with the borderlands Hacklab in March 2008 struck nanotech and biotech firms, because "their science is driven by the war (in Iraq) and drives the war" (EDT, 2008).

By 1999, the virtual sit-in had become a popular means of protest. That year, over 800 animal rights protestors used EDT's FloodNet software against websites in Sweden, while a British group calling itself the Electrohippies Collective developed its own tools and sponsored a massive sit-in against the website of the World Trade Organization during their meeting in Seattle (which also generated street demonstrations). The Electrohippies estimated that over 452,000 people worldwide joined their three-day strike (Cassel, 2000).

EDT's innovation, which took the form of a website with attack software, allowed thousands of people to join a strike with very little effort. All they needed to do was visit EDT's website and click a button. Mobilizing warriors had never been easier. But a later innovation, the "botnet," would give cyber warriors an even more powerful weapon. Instead of rounding up thousands of volunteers, a single warrior could compromise and take over thousands of computers on the Internet. This botnet, defined as a network of machines running robot-like malicious software (bots), would then be instructed to attack the target website in a robot-like fashion. The resulting attacks are often referred to as Distributed Denial-of-Service (DDoS) attacks, because of the distributed nature of the source of the attack. The term "swarming" is also used to denote the swarm-like fashion in which multiple agents (bots or people) simultaneously strike a common target (Arquilla & Ronfeldt, 2000). Most of the DoS attacks described in this chapter are of this nature.

The Electrohippies used their website to introduce another innovation in networked collaboration--collective decision making. During an international week of protest against genetically-modified foods in 2000, visitors to their website could vote on whether the final phases of the campaign, which included a virtual sit-in, should go forward. When the final vote was only 42% in favor, with 29% opposed and 29% undecided, they cancelled the rest of the campaign. However, future actions did not include an opportunity to vote, so the Electrohippies may have decided that they had yielded too much power to site visitors, likely including curious onlookers and persons associated with the target.

Cyber activists also use email as a means of attack. In 1997, for example, protestors bombarded the web-hosting company IGC with a flood of email (sometimes called "email bombing"), demanding that IGC pull the site of the *Euskal Herria Journal* on the grounds it supported the Spanish-based terrorist group ETA. The protestors also clogged IGC's website with bogus credit card orders. The effect of the attacks severely impacted IGC's ability to service other customers, leading them to give way to the protestors' demands (Denning, 2001, p. 270).

In what some intelligence authorities characterized as the first known attack by terrorists against a country's computer systems, an offshoot of the Liberation Tigers of Tamil Eelam (LTTE) claimed responsibility for "suicide email bombings" against Sri Lankan embassies. Calling themselves the Internet Black Tigers, the group swamped Sri Lankan embassies with about 800 emails a day over a two-week period in 1998. The messages read, "We are the Internet Black Tigers and we're doing this to disrupt your communications" (Denning, 1999, p. 69).

During the early days of cyber activism in the late 1990s, someone created a Hacktivism email list for persons interested in hacking and activism. Following discussions on the list about "jamming up" the Echelon global surveillance system operated by the US, UK, Canada, Australia, and New Zealand, October 21, 1999, was named Jam Echelon Day. On that day, activists were to send out email messages filled with subversive keywords such as "revolt," causing the messages to be snagged by Echelon's filters—thereby clogging the system with useless intercept data. Word spread around the Internet and generated media attention. But when the day came, the Hacktivism list, along with various political email lists, were the recipients of massive amounts of the nonsense email, leading the news service ZDNet to characterize it as a "spam farce" (Knight, 1999).

The Church of Scientology: Key Target for Cyber Activists

The Church of Scientology has been the target of cyber activists for years, often in response to the Church's efforts to censor leaked information about itself. In January 2008, cyber activists stepped up their assaults, launching Project Chanology to "expel the church from the Internet" and "save people from Scientology by reversing the brainwashing." The project, growing to about 9,000 people, used a DDoS attack to cripple the Scientology website for two weeks. It also published on the Web censored materials and personal information about Church leaders (Fritz, 2008).

The activists behind Project Chanology took advantage of the Internet's relative anonymity by using Anonymous accounts. Other activists, most notably the founders of EDT and the Electrohippies, have operated in the open, revealing their true names and taking responsibility for their actions. However, whereas the relatively small leadership of these groups have disclosed their identities and even spoken at conferences, the thousands of participants in their cyber operations have not.

The Role of Lycos Europe

Another leadership core that revealed its identity was Lycos Europe, an email service provider launching a campaign against spammers in 2004. Participants in the Make Love, Not Spam campaign installed a special screen saver generating a slow stream of traffic against websites used by spammers. The campaign claimed that 110,000 screensavers irritated 100,000 spam sites over a one-month period (Make Love Not Spam, 2004). It also generated negative publicity, as critics argued the participants were essentially spamming the spammers' websites.

Cautionary Note

Although this section has focused on activists deploying cyber attacks, it is important to emphasize that most activists *do not engage* in cyber attacks. Rather, they use the Internet to publish information about the issues, generate support, sponsor letter writing campaigns and petitions, and coordinate non-cyber activities such as meetings, marches, and street demonstrations.

ELECTRONIC JIHAD

Defined

Electronic jihad refers to cyber attacks conducted on behalf of al-Qa'ida and the global jihadist movement associated with it. This movement is held together largely through the Internet.

History of the Movement

The first appearance of an al-Qa'ida-associated hacker group occurred after the September 11, 2001, terrorist attacks, when GForce Pakistan announced the formation of the Al-Qaeda Alliance Online on a U.S. government website it defaced on October 17, 2001. Declaring that "Osama bin Laden is a holy fighter, and whatever he says makes sense," the group of Pakistani Muslim hackers posted a list of demands and warned that it planned to hit major U.S. military and British websites (McWilliams, 2001b). A subsequent message from the group announced that two other Pakistani hacking groups had joined the alliance: the Pakistan Hackerz Club and Anti India Crew. Collectively, the groups had already defaced hundreds of websites, often with political messages.

Although GForce expressed support for bin Laden, they distanced themselves from terrorism. In an October 27, 2001, defacement of a US military website, they proclaimed that they were "not a group of cyber terrorists." Condemning the attacks of September 11 and calling themselves "cyber crusaders," they wrote, "ALL we ask for is PEACE for everyone." This turned out to be one of their last recorded defacements. GForce Pakistan and all mention of the Al-Qaeda Alliance Online disappeared.

Other hackers, however, have emerged in their place, engaging in what is sometimes called "electronic jihad." Jihadist forums are used to distribute manuals and tools for hacking and to promote and coordinate cyber attacks, including a DoS attack against the Vatican website (triggered by Pope Benedict's comments about the Prophet Mohammad)--which mainly fizzled, and an "Electronic Battle of Guantanamo" attack against American stock exchanges and banks, canceled because the banks had been notified (Alshech, 2007; Gross & McMillan, 2006).

The al-Jinan forum has played a particularly active role, distributing a software tool called Electronic Jihad, used by hackers to participate in DoS attacks against target websites deemed harmful to Islam. The forum even gives awards to the most effective participants, where the objective is to "inflict maximum human, financial and morale damage on the enemy by using the Internet" (Bakier, 2007).

The al-Farouq forum has also promoted electronic jihad, offering a hacker library with information for disrupting and destroying enemy electronic resources. The library held keylogging software for capturing keystrokes and acquiring passwords on compromised computers, software tools for hiding or misrepresenting the hacker's Internet address, and disk and system utilities for erasing hard disks and incapacitating Windows-based systems. Postings on the forum in 2005 called for heightened electronic attacks against US and allied government websites (Pool, 2005a). On another jihadist forum, a posting in October, 2008, invited youths to participate in an 'electronic jihadist campaign' against US military systems by joining the Tariq Bin-Ziyad Brigades. The recently-formed group was looking to increase its ranks so it could be more effective (OSC, 2008).

In a February, 2006, report, the Jamestown Foundation reported that "most radical jihadi forums devote an entire section to [hacker warfare]." The al-Ghorabaa site, for example, contained information on penetrating computer devices and intranet servers, stealing passwords, and security. It also contained an encyclopedia on hacking websites and a 344-page book on hacking techniques, including a step-by-step guide for "terminating pornographic sites and those intended for the Jews and their supporters" (Ulph, 2006). The forum Minbar ahl al-Sunna wal-Jama'a (The Pulpit of the People of the Sunna) offered a hacking manual said to be written in a pedagogical style and discussed motives and incentives for computer-based attacks, including political, strategic, economic, and individual. The manual discussed three types of attack: (i) direct intrusions into corporate and government networks, (ii) infiltration of personal computers to steal personal information, and (iii) interception of sensitive information, such as credit card numbers in transit (Pool, 2005b).

Younis Tsoulis, who went by the codename Irhabi (Terrorist) 007, also promoted hacking, publishing a 74-page manual "The Encyclopedia of Hacking the Zionist and Crusader Websites" with hacking instructions and a list of vulnerable websites on a website he managed (Jamestown, 2008). Tsoulis was later arrested and sentenced to ten years in prison for inciting terrorist murder on the Internet.

Triggering Events for Electronic Jihad

Electronic jihad, like other acts of cyber protest, is often triggered by particular events. Publication of the Danish cartoons satirizing the Prophet Mohammad, for example, sparked a rash of cyber attacks as violence erupted on the streets in early 2006. By late February, Zone-h had recorded almost 3,000 attacks against Danish websites. In addition, the al-Ghorabaa site coordinated a 24-hour cyber attack against *Jyllands-Posten*, the newspaper that first published the cartoons, and other newspaper sites (Ulph, 2006). A video purporting to document a DoS attack against the *Jyllands-Posten* website was later released on the jihadist site 3asfh.com. The video was in the style of jihadist videos coming out of Iraq, showing that the hackers were emulating the publicity tactics of violent jihadists (Internet Haganah, 2006).

Jihadists often target websites used to actively oppose them. For example, a message posted to a Yahoo! group attempted to recruit 600 Muslims for jihad cyber attacks against Internet Haganah's website. The motive was retaliation against Internet Haganah's efforts to close down terrorist-related websites by reporting them to their service providers. Muslim hackers were asked to register to a Yahoo! group called Jehad-Op (Reynalds, 2004). According to the Anti-Terrorism Coalition (ATC), the jihad was organized by a group named Osama Bin Laden (OBL) Crew, also threatening attacks against the ATC website (ATC, 2004).

The use of electronic jihad to support al-Qa'ida is explicitly promoted in a book by Mohammad Bin Ahmad As-Sālim titled *39 Ways to Serve and Participate in Jihâd.* Initially published on al-Qa'ida's al-Farouq website in 2003 (Leyden, 2003), principle 34 in the book discusses two forms of "electronic *Jihâd*:" (i) discussion boards (for media operations) and (ii) hacking methods, about which the book writes: "this is truly deserving of the term 'electronic *Jihâd*,' since the term carries the meaning of force; to strike and to attack. So, whoever is given knowledge in this field, then he should not be stingy with it in regards to using it to serve the *Jihâd*. He should concentrate his efforts on destroying any American websites, as well as any sites that are anti-*Jihâd* and *Mujâhidîn*, Jewish websites, modernist and secular websites" (As-Sālim, 2003).

The Value of Inflicting Harm

Al-Qa'ida has long recognized the value of inflicting economic harm on the United States, and electronic jihad is seen as a tool for doing so. After the Electronic Battle of Gauntanomo was canceled, a message posted on an Islamist website stated how "disabling [sensitive economic American websites] for a few days or even for a few hours ... will cause millions of dollars worth of damage" (Alshech, 2007). A message on al-Jinan noted that hacking methods could "inflict the greatest [possible] financial damage" on their enemies.

According to Fouad Husseing, economically-damaging cyber attacks are part of al-Qa'ida's long-term war against the United States. In his book, *al-Zarqawi-al-Qaeda's Second Generation*, Husseing describes al-Qa'ida's seven-phase war as revealed through interviews of the organization's top lieutenants. Phase 4, scheduled for the period 2010-2013, includes conducting cyberterrorism against the U.S. economy (Hall, 2005).

Although damages from cyber attacks attributed to al-Qa'ida and associated hackers so far has been minor compared to the damages from al-Qa'ida's violent acts of terror, Husseing's book and other writings suggest that al-Qa'ida may be thinking bigger. A posting in a jihadist forum advocated attacking all the computer networks around the world, including military and telecommunication networks, in order to 'bring about the total collapse of the West' (Alshech, 2007). Of course, the idea of shutting down every single network is utter fantasy, so vision by itself does not translate into a threat.

PATRIOTIC HACKING

Defined

Patriotic or nationalistic hacking refers to networks of citizens and expatriates engaging in cyber attacks to defend their mother country or country of ethnic origin. Typically, patriotic networks attack the websites and email accounts of countries whose actions have threatened or harmed the interests of their mother country.

The cyber attacks against Estonia in 2007, for example, were triggered by the physical relocation of a Soviet-era war memorial, while those against Georgia in 2008 accompanied a military confrontation with Russia. Cyberspace provides a venue whereby patriotic hackers can vent their outrage with little effort and little risk. They can be armchair warriors, safe behind their computers. Through their online social networks, they become part of a cyber force larger than themselves—a force with greater impact than they could have alone, and one that provides cover for their individual acts.

History of Patriotic Hackers

Chinese hackers were among the first to form social networks of patriotic hackers. Beginning with the 1998 riots in Jakarta, Indonesia, when Indonesians committed atrocities against the Chinese living among them, a loose network of Chinese hackers came together under a nationalistic banner. The network, which Scott Henderson (2007) calls the Red Hacker Alliance, and others have called the Honker Union of China, was formed from such hacking groups as the Green Army and China Eagle Union. After gathering on Internet Relay Chat (IRC) channels to set a course of action against Indonesia, the hackers formed the Chinese Hacker Emergency Conference Center and launched coordinated cyber attacks, including web defacements and DoS attacks against Indonesian websites and government email boxes (Henderson, 2007, pp. 9-12).

According to Henderson (2007, p. 13), the Indonesian cyber attacks served as both the recruiting and training grounds for the alliance's next mission: attacks against US websites in retaliation for the accidental bombing of the Chinese Embassy in Belgrade during the 1999 Kosovo conflict. The Red Hacker Alliance published a manifesto expressing its patriotic mission and including quotes from Mao Zedong, such as "The country is our country; the people are our people; if we don't cry out, who will? If we don't do something, who will?" (Henderson, 2007, p. 14)

Following the embassy-related attacks, the Red Hacker Alliance engaged in a series of cyber attacks against foreign countries. These included attacks against Taiwan in 1999, following Taiwanese President Li Deng-Hui's advocacy for a "two-state-theory," and then in 2000, in conjunction with the Taiwanese elections. Attacks were also aimed at Japan in 2000, relating to Japan's handling of events concerning the Nanjing Massacre during WWII; in 2004, attacks were related to the disputed Diaoyu Islands; and in 2001, attacks were related to the US, following the collision of a US EP-3 reconnaissance plane with a Chinese F-8 fighter jet in late April, 2001, resulting in the fighter pilot's death and China's detaining the US aircrew after an emergency landing (Henderson, 2007).

Most of the attacks became two-sided cyber skirmishes, with hackers from both sides attacking targets associated with the other. Indeed, the 2001 strikes against the US may have been triggered as much by defacements of Chinese web sites in April, 2001, by a hacker perceived to be from the US--as by the spy plane incident itself. All in all, the incidents looked more like the acts of youthful hackers showing off their skills and expressing outrage than state-sponsored activity. Indeed, in 2002, the Chinese government asked their hackers to refrain from further attacks, as the anniversary of the 2001 attacks drew near (Hess, 2002).

By the time the 2001 spy plane incident had died down, the Red Hacker Alliance had grown to an estimated 50,000 to 60,000 members. But most of the members knew little about computer networks and hacking. The attacks were characterized as a "chicken-scratch game of a group of children," "a farcical 'patriotic show'," and the work of "Red Hackers who were totally clueless in terms of technology" (Henderson, 2007, pp. 44-45).

A network of patriotic US hackers also emerged over the spy plane incident. According to iDefense (2001b, p. 40), a coalition of hackers calling itself Project China formed and began defacing Chinese websites on May 1, 2001. The alliance was formed from several prominent hacking groups, including Hackweiser and World of Hell.

After the September 11, 2001, terrorist attacks and invasion of Afghanistan, the network of US hackers regrouped to avenge the attacks. Now called the Dispatchers, the patriotic hackers defaced several hundred websites associated with governments in the Middle East and Palestinian Internet service providers, and planned to hit targets in Afghanistan. Founded by Hackah Jak, a 21-year-old security expert from Ohio and former member of Hackweiser and Project China, the group of 60 hackers included members of World of Hell and even some non-US hackers (Graham, 2001; Peterson, 2001). The group seemed to quietly disappear, however, following appeals from industry leaders to refrain from hacking and the group's defacement of a website belonging to a company having offices in the World Trade Center (WTC) and losing employees on September 11, 2001 (Graham, 2001).

Another group of hackers going by the name "Young Intelligent Hackers Against Terrorism" (YIHAT) also surfaced after the September 11, 2001, attacks. Their objective was to disrupt al-Qa'ida's financial resources. However, claims that the group had penetrated bank accounts associated with Osama bin Laden and al-Qa'ida were unsubstantiated, and the group's website disappeared following cyber skirmishes with other hacking groups, most notably GForce Pakistan, the group of Pakistani hackers mentioned earlier in conjunction with their post September 11, 2001, web defacements and announcement of the Al Qaeda Alliance Online (McWilliams, 2001a, 2001c).

The Lack of U.S. Patriotic Hackers Post-2001

Since 2001, the United States has not seen a large and active network of patriotic hackers, perhaps because there has not been an international conflict or incident that has seriously threatened the US, or perhaps because Americans are simply not as nationalistic as the Chinese are. During the Iraq war (began in 2003), most of the cyber attacks originated with social activists and foreign hackers from China and elsewhere opposed to the war; however, there were not patriotic US hackers supporting it.

The Emergence of Patriotic Hackers in Other Countries

Patriotic hackers have emerged in other countries and regions, however. Pakistani and Indian hackers have been defacing each other's websites since the late 1990s over Kashmir and, more recently, in 2008 over the Mumbai terrorist attacks. In the early days, the Pakistan Hackerz Club (PHC), one of the other groups forming the Al Qaeda Alliance Online, was among the most prolific web defacement groups worldwide (Christenson, 1999). Armenian and Azerbaijani hackers similarly went after each other's websites in 2000 over the fighting in Nagorno-Karabakh, an ethnic Armenian enclave in Azerbaijan (Williams, 2000).

Israeli and Palestinian/Muslim hackers launched cyber attacks after the second intifada, or uprising, erupted in the Palestinian territories in late September, 2000, following a visit by Ariel Sharon to the Temple Mount and the murder of three Israeli soldiers. Hackers on both sides defaced each other's websites and launched DoS attacks.

By January 2001, over 40 hacker groups/individuals from 23 countries had hit the websites of eight governments, as well as numerous commercial sites, according to iDefense (2001a). Both GForce and PHC joined the loosely-formed network of Muslim hackers defacing Israeli sites. One defacement read: "GForce Declares a War against Israel?.... Ok, GForce Pakistan is back. We really planned not to come back to the defacing scene again, but once again our Muslim brothers needed us" (iDefense, 2001a).

A Cautionary Note

It is important to note that the cyber intifada illustrates that there is no hard line between electronic jihad and patriotic hacking. The attacks can be viewed both as electronic jihad by Muslim hackers against Israel and as patriotic hacking by Israeli and Palestinian hackers (and their external supporters) against each other. In addition, there is no hard line between jihadist and patriotic hacker networks. Groups such as GForce and PHC have used their skills to support the jihad as well as their own countries and other Muslim countries and territories.

Following the 2000 cyber intifada, hackers aligned with Israel or the Palestinians have engaged in repeated cyber skirmishes, often in conjunction with incidents taking place on the ground. Within 48 hours of Israel's bombing of Gaza in December, 2008, more than 300 Israeli websites had been defaced with anti-Israel (and anti-US) messages (Higgins, 2008). The hackers came from several countries, including Morocco, Syria, and Iran. Team Evil, a group of Moroccan hackers with a history of attacking Israeli websites, took over an Israeli domain name server and redirected Ynet's English news site and other websites to phony web pages condemning the Israeli strikes (Paz, 2009). For their part, an Israeli alliance called "Help Israel Win" developed and distributed a software tool for conducting DDoS attacks against Hamas-friendly sites like qudsnews.net and Palestine-info.info. According to the group, more than 8,000 people had downloaded and installed the Patriot software. With websites in Hebrew, English, Spanish, French, Russian and Portugese, the alliance claims to unite "the computer capabilities of many people around the world" (Shachtman, 2009).

The cyber attacks against Estonia in April/May, 2007, and in Georgia in August, 2008, put Russian hackers on the front page of news sites. However, patriotic Russians have engaged in cyber attacks since at least 1999, when the Russian Hackers Union defaced a US military website during the Kosovo war with anti-NATO messages. But with the Estonian attacks, the level of activity dramatically increased. Just before the 2008 Georgian cyber assault, Russian hackers attacked Lithuanian websites to protest a new law banning the display of Soviet emblems. They also issued a manifesto called "Hackers United Against External Threats to Russia," calling for a expansion of targets to include Ukraine, the rest of the Baltic states, and "flagrant" Western nations supporting the expansion of NATO (Krebs, 2008). Then, in January, 2009, the Russian hackers knocked Kyrgyzstan off the Internet (Keizer, 2009).

The Estonian and Georgian cyber assaults leveraged large social networks, as well as huge botnets of compromised computers scattered all over the world, mostly for DoS and DDoS attacks (Davis, 2007; Naraine & Danchev, 2008). Postings on Russian-language forums exhorted readers to defend the motherland and provided attack scripts to follow and target websites. The scripts, flooding targets with network traffic, allowed participants to join a loose network of cyber warriors knowing little or nothing about hacking. During the Georgian attacks, the Russian website stopgeorgia.ru offered several DoS tools and a list of 36 targets. According to one report, the site traced back to the Russian Business Network (RBN), a cybercrime network based in St. Petersburg, Russia (Georgia Update, 2008).

Psychological Analysis and Other Reasons for Patriotic Hacking

Rosanna Guadagno, Robert Cialdini, and Gadi Evron (2009) offer an interesting social- psychological analysis of the Estonian conflict. They posit that several factors contributed to the assault, including: (i) the loss of status of Estonia's ethnic Russian minority, following the collapse of the Soviet Union and Estonia gaining independence; (ii) the anonymity and resulting sense of depersonalization coming from online interaction; (iii) group membership and adherence to group norms; and (iv) rapid contagion through online forums. Because most Russian-language Internet users were participating in or endorsing the attacks, such behavior became normative and quickly spread.

Despite the ability of non-state actors to inflict considerable damage in cyberspace, many analysts see a government hand in nationalistic cyber attacks, for example, attributing the attacks against Estonia and Georgia to the Russian government. Stephen Blank (2008) of the US Army War College, for example, writes that "the computer attacks … and the other steps taken by Moscow against Estonia were acts sanctioned by high policy and reflected a coordinated strategy devised in advance of the removal of the Bronze Soldier from its original pedestal."

At the same time, there are good reasons to believe that the attacks were primarily, if not entirely, the work of non-state actors. First, some of the attacks have been traced to independent persons and to websites operated and frequented by independent persons. Second, non-state actors are capable of pulling off large-scale attacks such as these on their own. They do not need government resources, including funding. The attacks are cheap, and hackers outside the government have the tools and knowledge to launch them. Third, while the tactics used—including web defacements, web flooding, and botnets of compromised computer—are regularly used by non-state actors, there are good reasons why states would not engage in such attacks. They typically violate domestic crime statutes and cause considerable collateral damage, thereby, also violating law of war principles, such as necessity and proportionality. Fourth, states have other means of dealing with conflict; for example, diplomacy, sanctions, and military operations. Cyber attacks might be deployed as part of military operations, but they would more likely be precision strikes against military targets used for command and control, reconnaissance, and communications rather than mass attacks against civilian websites. However, it is possible that the Russian government played some role in the attacks, for example, by encouraging or condoning them.

Even when attacks can be traced to government computers, it would be presumptuous to conclude that they were launched by the state. The computers may have been compromised by hackers of any nationality. Even if individuals within the government were responsible for the attacks, they may have been operating on their own, not as agents of their government or under direction from their government. About 7.4% of the participants in a cyber attack against the Mexican Embassy's London website in June, 1999, for example, apparently had ".mil" addresses; that is, addresses assigned to the US Department of Defense. However, the attacks were not conducted by the Department of Defence. They were conducted by the Electronic Disturbance Theater (discussed earlier), having a history of attacking the websites of the US and Mexican governments, including the Department of Defence websites. The ".mil" participants likely visited the EDT website used to generate the attacks, becoming unwitting participants.

One participant in the Estonian attacks, Konstantin Goloskokov, was a commissar of the pro-Kremlin youth movement Nashi, but he said that he and a few friends had operated on their own initiative and not under the direction of the Russian government (Clover, 2009).

At least so far, non-state actors appear to be responsible for most cyber conflict, taking advantage of this new medium to conduct rapid, large-scale attacks at low cost.

CONCLUSION

Cyber conflict, at least so far, is predominantly a non-state activity. Networks of civilian cyber warriors come together to hack for a cause. Typically, the networks center around social activism (hacktivism), jihad (electronic jihad), or nationalism (patriotic hacking). Tools and tactics are adopted from those used by other hackers, while online forums provide the principal means of organization and support.

Although cyber attacks launched by non-state networks have been highly disruptive, they have not been lethal or even destructive. Nobody has died, and following an attack, services and data are restored. The attacks look more like the cyber-equivalent of street demonstrations than terrorism or warfare, though even street protests sometimes become destructive and deadly. When Estonia relocated its memorial, for example, riots broke out not only in cyberspace, but also on the streets, the latter leading to one death and 150 injuries (Fritz, 2008, p. 33). Similarly, the street violence that erupted over the Danish cartoons left 139 dead and 823 injured (Cartoon, 2006).

However, even if cyber conflict has not been particularly destructive, some of the attacks have inflicted substantial financial costs on their targets, owing to the disruption of services and the need to devote resources to defense and recovery. One Estonian bank targeted during the cyber assault was said to have lost at least $1 million (Landler & Markoff, 2007).

Whether cyber conflict will evolve to something more destructive is difficult to predict. Clearly, some jihadists would like to cause greater harm, though they currently lack the knowledge and skills to do so. Other non-state actors may also turn to more destructive cyber attacks, just as they turn to terrorism, insurgency, and other forms of physical violence.

Many critical infrastructures are vulnerable to cyber attacks that could be quite destructive, even deadly. Already, cyber attacks have caused raw sewage overflows, disabled emergency 911 services, and disrupted health care in hospitals. In addition, security researchers have demonstrated how cyber attacks could physically destroy electrical power generators (Meserve, 2007). Thus, in the presence of both motivated actors and vulnerable systems, cyber terrorism could morph from the largely theoretical threat it is today to something all too real.

Still, most activists are more interested in raising awareness about an issue and pressing for change rather than inflicting serious harm. For them, cyber conflict will retain its characteristic of being primarily disruptive. Exact tactics, however, will change as technology evolves and hacking along with it.

REFERENCES

Almeida, M. (2008). *Statistics report 2005-2007, March 5, 2008*. Retrieved March 18, 2008, from www.zone-h.org

Alshech, E. (2007). Cyberspace as a combat zone: The phenomenon of electronic jihad. *MEMRI Inquiry and Analysis Series, 329*. The Middle East Media Research Institute, February 7.

Arguilla, J., & Ronfeldt, D. (1993). Cyberwar is coming! *Comparative Strategy*, *12*, 141–165. doi:10.1080/01495939308402915

Arquilla, J., & Ronfeldt, D. (2000). *Swarming & the future of conflict*. Santa Monica, CA: RAND.

As-Sālim, M. (2003) *39 Ways to serve and participate in jihâd*. Retrieved June 30, 2008, from http://tibyan.wordpress.com/2007/08/24/39-ways-to-serve-and-participate-in-jihad/.

ATC. (2004). *ATC's OBL crew investigation*. Anti-TerrorismCoalition.

Attrition. (1996). *Attrition mirror*. Retrieved 1996 from http://attrition.org/mirror/attrition/1996.html#dec

Bakier, A. H. (2007). *Forum users improve electronic jihad technology*. Retrieved June 27, 2007, from http://www.jamestown.org/single/?no_cache=1&tx_ttnews%5Btt_news%5D=4256

Blank, S. (2008). Web war I: Is Europe's first information war a new kind of war? *Comparative Strategy*, *27*, 227–247. doi:10.1080/01495930802185312

Cartoon. (2006). *Cartoon body count*. Retrieved April 21, 2009, from http://web.archive.org/web/20060326071135/http://www.cartoonbodycount.com/

Cassell, D. (2000). *Hacktivism in the cyberstreets*. Retrieved May 30, 2000, from http://www.alternet.org/story/9223

Clover, C. (2009). Kremlin-backed group behind Estonia cyber blitz. *Financial Times (North American Edition)*, (March): 11.

CSI. (1998). Email attack on Sri Lanka computers. *Computer Security Alert*, *183*, 8.

Davis, J. (2007). *Web war one*. Retrieved September, 2007, from http://www.wired.com/images/press/pdf/webwarone.pdf

Denning, D. E. (1999). *Information warfare and security*. Reading, MA: Addison-Wesley.

Denning, D. E. (2001). Activism, hacktivism, and cyberterrorism . In Arquilla, J., & Ronfeldt, D. (Eds.), *Networks and netwars* (pp. 239–288). Santa Monica, CA: RAND.

Drogin, B. (1999). *Russians seem to be hacking into Pentagon*. Retrieved October 7, 1999, from http://www.sfgate.com/cgi-bin/article.cgi?f=/c/a/1999/10/07/MN58558.DTL

EDT. (2008). *EDT*. Retrieved December 17, 2008, from http://www.thing.net/~rdom/ecd/ecd.html

Electrohippies (2009). *The electrohippies call on people around the globe to celebrate World Intellectual Privateers Day 2009*. Retrieved April 13, 2009, from http://www.fraw.org.uk/ehippies

Fritz, J. (2008). How China will use cyber warfare to leapfrog in military competitiveness. *Culture Mandala, 8*(1), 28-80. Retrieved 2008 from http://epublications.bond.edu.au/cm/vol8/iss1/2/

Georgia Update. (2008). *Russian invasion of Georgia*. Retrieved October 9, 2008, from www.georgiaupdate.gov.ge

Graham, J. (2001). *Hackers strike Middle Eastern sites*. Retrieved September 26, 2001, from http://www.usatoday.com/tech/news/2001/09/19/hack-attack-launched.htm

Gross, G., & McMillan, R. (2006). Al-*Qaeda 'Battle of Guantanamo' cyberattack a no-show.* Retrieved December 1, 2006, from http://hostera.ridne.net/suspended.page/?currtag=12&currletter=2

Guadagno, R. E., Cialdini, R. B., & Evron, G. (2009). (in press). What about Estonia? A social psychological analysis of the first Internet war. *Cyberpsychology & Behavior*.

Hall, A. (2005). *Al-Qaeda chiefs reveal world domination design*. Retrieved August 24, 2005, from http://www.theage.com.au/news/war-on-terror/alqaeda-chiefs-reveal-world-domination-design/2005/08/23/1124562861654.html

Henderson, S. J. (2007). *The dark visitor: Inside the world of Chinese hackers*. Fort Leavenworth, KS: Foreign Military Studies Office.

Hess, P. (2002). *China prevented repeat cyber attack on US*. Retrieved October 29, 2002, from http://seclists.org/isn/2002/Oct/121

Higgins, K. J. (2008). *Hundreds of Israeli websites hacked in 'propaganda war.'* Retrieved December 31, 2008, from http://www.darkreading.com/security/attacks/showArticle.jhtml?articleID=212700313

iDefense. (2001a). *Israeli-Palestinian cyber conflict*. Fairfax, VA: Intelligence Services Report.

iDefense. (2001b). *US-China cyber skirmish of April-May 2001*. Fairfax, VA: Intelligence Operations Whitepaper.

Internet Haganah. (2006). *How the brothers attacked the website of Jyllands-Posten*. February 7. Retrieved October 21, 2008, from http://internet-haganah.com/harchives/005456.html

Jamestown. (2008). *Hacking manual by jailed jihadi appears on web*. Retrieved March 5, 2008, from http://www.jamestown.org/programs/gta/single/?tx_ttnews%5Btt_news%5D=4763&tx_ttnews%5BbackPid%5D=246&no_cache=1

Keizer, G. (2009). *Russian 'cybermilitia' knocks Kyrgyzstan offline*. Retrieved January 28, 2009, from http://www.computerworld.com/s/article/9126947/Russian_cybermilitia_knocks_Kyrgyzstan_offline

Knight, W. (1999). *Jam Echelon day descends into spam farce*. Retrieved October 22, 1999, from http://news.zdnet.co.uk/emergingtech/0,1000000183,2074601,00.htm

Krebs, B. (2008). *Lithuania weathers cyber attack, braces for round 2*. Retrieved July 29, 2008, from http://voices.washingtonpost.com/securityfix/2008/07/lithuania_weathers_cyber_attac_1.html

Landler, M., & Markoff, J. (2007). *Digital fears emerge after data siege in Estonia. RetrievedMay29, 2007*, from http://www.nytimes.com/2007/05/29/technology/29estonia.html

Leyden, J. (2003). *Al-Qaeda: The 39 principles of holy war*. Retrieved September 4, 2003, from http://www.israelnewsagency.com/Al-Qaeda.html

Make Love Not Spam. (2004). *Make Love Not Spam*. Retrieved April 3, 2009, from http://www.makelovenotspam.com/

McWilliams, B. (2001a). *Anti-terror hackers seek government blessing*. Retrieved October 17, 2001, from http://www.infowar.com/hacker/01/hack_101701b_j.shtml

McWilliams, B. (2001b). *Pakistani hackers deface US site with ultimatum*. Retrieved October 17, 2001, from http://lists.jammed.com/ISN/2001/10/0158.html

McWilliams, B. (2001c). *Pro-USA hackers target Pakistani defacement group*. Retrieved December 22, 2009, from http://faculty.vassar.edu/lenevare/91101/

Meserve, J. (2007). *Staged cyber attack reveals vulnerability in power grid*. Retrieved April 22, 2009, from http://www.cnn.com/2007/US/09/26/power.at.risk/index.html

Mutina, B. (2007). *Hacking incident goes on Czech TV*. Retrieved June 19, 2007, to www.zone-h.org

Naraine, R., & Danchev, D. (2008). *Zero Day: Coordinated Russia vs Georgia cyber attack in progress*. Retrieved August 11, 2008, from http://blogs.zdnet.com/security/?p=1670

Onley, D. S., & Wait, P. (2006). *Red storm rising*. Retrieved August 21, 2006, from http://www.gcn.com/Articles/2006/08/17/Red-storm-rising.aspx

OSC. (2008). *Jihadist forum invites youths to join 'electronic jihadist campaign.'* Open Source Center, October 6, 2008.

Parker, D. B. (1976). *Crime by computer*. New York: Scribner.

Paz, S. (2009). *Anti-Israel group wreaks havoc with Israeli web sites*. Retrieved January 4, 2009, from http://www.jpost.com/servlet/Satellite?cid=1230733155647&pagename=JPArticle%2FShowFull

Peterson, S. (2001). *Crackers prepare retaliation for terrorist attack*. Retrieved December 22, 2009, from http://www.gyre.org/news/explore/hacktivism?page=1

Pool, J. (2005a). *New web forum postings call for intensified electronic jihad against government websites*. Retrieved December 22, 2009, from http://www.itac-ciem.gc.ca/pblctns/tc_prsnts/2006-2-eng.asp

Pool, J. (2005b). *Technology and security discussions on the jihadist forums*. Retrieved December 22, 2009, from http://www.comw.org/tct/terrorinfowar.html

Reynalds, J. (2004). *Internet 'terrorist' using Yahoo to recruit 600 Muslims for hack attack*. Retrieved October 21, 2008, from http://www.mensnewsdaily.com/archive/r/reynalds/04/reynalds022804.htm

Schachtman, N. (2009). *Wage cyberwar against Hamas, surrender your PC*. Retrieved January 8, 2009, from http://www.wired.com/dangerroom/2009/01/israel-dns-hack/

Schwartau, W. (1996). *Information warfare* (2nd ed.). New York: Thunder's Mouth Press.

Ulph, S. (2006). *Internet mujahideen refine electronic warfare tactics*. Retrieved December 22, 2009, from http://www.jamestown.org/programs/gta/single/?tx_ttnews%5Btt_news%5D=666&tx_ttnews%5BbackPid%5D=239&no_cache=1

Vatis, M. (2001). Cyber terrorism and information warfare: Government perspectives. In Alexander, Y., & Swetnam, M. S. (Eds.), *Cyber terrorism and information warfare. Ardsley: Transnational Publishers, Inc.*

William, S. (2000). *Armenian and Azerbaijani hackers wage war on Internet.* Retrieved February 17, 2000, from http://www.hrea.org/lists/huridocs-tech/markup/msg00417.html

Chapter 10
Control Systems Security

Jake Brodsky
Washington Suburban Sanitary Commission, USA

Robert Radvanovsky
Infracritical, Inc., USA

ABSTRACT

With recent news media discussions highlighting the safety and integrity of the U.S. national power grid, questions have been raised by both political and executive-level management, specifically, as to the risks associated with our critical infrastructures. More specifically, the issue of concern is dealing with and addressing cyber vulnerability issues, threats and risks associated with an extremely complex and inter-twining series of dependencies arising from legacy industries established almost 100 years ago. Equally as important are the growing threats and risks to these environments resulting from their exposure to outside networks (such as the Internet), exposing critically vital and important cyber systems to just about everyone and anyone globally. This chapter highlights the importance of preventing hack attacks against SCADA systems, or Industrial Control Systems (abbreviated as ICS), as a means of protecting our critical infrastructures.

INTRODUCTION

This chapter highlights an important but seemingly under-represented area of attack for Black Hat hackers or terrorists' intending to cause harm to an industry's networks and/or to a nation's citizens. It provides an overview of a critical aspect of security that impacts end users and security personnel, alike. It also gives a review and discussion of the weaknesses of SCADA systems and the various ways they may be compromised. Suggested remedies for securing these systems are presented at the end of this chapter.

DOI: 10.4018/978-1-61692-805-6.ch010

What are Control Systems?

Generally speaking, most control systems are computer-based. Control systems are used by many infrastructures and industries to monitor and control sensitive processes and physical functions. Typically, control systems collect sensor measurements and operational data from the field, process and display this information, and relay control commands to local or remote equipment. In the electric power industry, they can manage and control the transmission and delivery of electric power, for example, by opening and closing circuit breakers and setting thresholds for preventive shutdowns. By employing integrated control systems, the oil and gas industry can control the refining operations on a plant site, remotely monitor the pressure and flow of gas pipelines, and control the flow and pathways of gas transmission. With water utilities, control systems can remotely monitor well levels, control pumps, monitor water flows, tank levels, and so on.

Control system functions vary from simple to complex, and many may be used to simply monitor processes running. For example, environmental conditions within a small office building would represent the simplest form of site monitoring, whereas managing most (or in most cases, all) activities for a municipal water system or a nuclear power plant would represent the complex form of site monitoring. Within certain industries, such as chemical and power generation, safety systems are typically implemented to mitigate a disastrous event if control and other systems fail.

It is important to note that control systems were not always computer-based. In fact, there are still many pneumatic control systems; some are analog systems (based upon operational amplifier circuits), some are mechanical feedback systems, and others are hydraulic systems. The motivation for migrating controls toward digital computing platforms was primarily driven by increasingly complex systems and a need for embedded diagnostics. For example, the set-point for many pressure-reducing valves is made by setting the position of a hydraulic pilot valve configuration.

Besides guarding against both physical attack and system failure, organizations may establish backup control centers that include uninterruptible power supplies and backup generators (Shea, 2003, 2004).

Types of Control Systems

There are two primary types of control systems: Distributed Control Systems (DCS) and Supervisory Control and Data Acquisition (SCADA) systems. Distributed Control Systems, typically used within single processes, a generating plant, or over a smaller geographic area or single-site location, usually work in a strictly real-time environment. The term "real-time" in this context means that the time it takes to transmit data, process it, and command a device is fast enough to be negligible. A DCS usually polls data regularly and deterministically.

Supervisory Control and Data Acquisition systems are typically used for larger-scaled environments that may be geographically dispersed in an enterprise-wide distribution operation. A SCADA system may be a real-time computing environment, or it may have "near real-time" features. A SCADA system tends to have a more irregular and less-deterministic polling strategy than the DCS. To illustrate, a utility company may use a DCS to generate power, but would utilize a SCADA system to distribute it (Shea, 2003, 2004).

Operators tend to see "open control loops" (meaning control systems with a human in charge) in a SCADA system; conversely, operators tend to see "closed control loops" (with automation in charge) in DCS systems. Moreover, the SCADA system communications infrastructure tends to be lower bandwidth and longer range, so the RTU (Remote Terminal Unit) in a SCADA system has local control schemes to handle that eventuality. In a DCS, networks tend to be highly reliable, high bandwidth campus LANs (Local Area Networks). The remote sites in a DCS can not only afford to send more data but they can afford to centralize the processing of that data.

What are the Components of a Control System?

A control system typically consists of a master control system, or central supervisory control and monitoring station, with one or more human-machine interfaces so that an operator may view displayed information about the remote sites and/or issue commands directly to the system. Typically, this is a device or station located at a site in which application servers and production control workstations are used to configure and troubleshoot other control system components. The central supervisory control and monitoring station is generally connected to local controller stations through a hard-wired network or to remote controller stations through a communications network that may be communicated through the Internet, a Public Switched Telephone Network (PSTN), or a cable or wireless network (such as radio, microwave, or wireless).

Each controller station may have a Remote Terminal Unit (RTU), a Programmable Logic Controller (PLC), a DCS controller, and/or other controllers that communicate with the supervisory control and monitoring station. The controller stations include sensors and control equipment that connect directly with the working components of the infrastructure (for example, pipelines, water towers, and power lines). Sensors take readings from infrastructure equipment, such as water or pressure levels, electrical voltage, and so on, sending messages to the controller.

The controller may be programmed to determine a course of action, send a message to the control equipment, or instruct it what to do (for example, to turn off a valve or dispense a chemical). If the controller is not programmed to determine a course of action, the controller communicates with the supervisory control and monitoring station before sending a command back to the control equipment. The control system may also be programmed to issue alarms back to the control operator when certain "conditions" are detected.

Handheld devices, such as Personal Digital Assistants (PDA), may be used to locally monitor controller stations. Because controller station technologies are becoming more intelligent and automated, they can communicate with the supervisory central monitoring and control station less frequently, requiring less human intervention—and, thus, fewer security concerns.

VULNERABILITY CONCERNS ABOUT CONTROL SYSTEMS

Historically, security concerns about control systems have been related primarily to protecting against physical attack. However, more recently, there has been a growing recognition that control systems are now vulnerable to cyber attacks from numerous sources, including hostile governments, terrorist groups, disgruntled employees who may have been passed, and other malicious intruders wanting to cause harm to property and/or persons.

In October 1997, the President's Commission on Critical Infrastructure Protection in the United States discussed the potential damaging effects on the nation's electric power, oil, and gas industries of successful attacks on control systems (Protecting America's Infrastructures, 1997). More recently in 2002, the National Research Council identified "the potential for attack on control systems," requiring "urgent attention" (National Research Council, 2002). And in February 2003, President Bush outlined his concerns over "the threat of organized cyber attacks capable of causing debilitating disruption to our nation's critical infrastructures, economy, or national security," noting that "disruption of these systems can have significant consequences for public health and safety" and emphasizing that the protection of control systems has become "a national priority" (National Strategy to Secure Cyberspace, 2003).

Several factors have contributed to the escalation of risk regarding control systems, noting the following as key concerns:

- The adoption of standardized technologies with known vulnerabilities.
- The connectivity of many control systems via, through, within, or exposed to unsecured networks, networked portals, or mechanisms connected to unsecured networks.
- Implementation constraints of existing security technologies and practices within the existing control systems infrastructure (and its architectures).
- The connectivity of insecure remote devices in their connections to control systems.
- The widespread availability of technical information about control systems, most notably via publicly available and/or shared networked resources, such as the Internet.

Recent known activities in 2009, affirmed President Obama, have indicated a serious concern about cyber security issues--not just those related to the Internet or Information Technology--but to a broader range of cyber-related issues, including Industrial Control Systems. Given this context, the U.S. federal government is not only investigating effective methods of securing the cyber aspects of critical infrastructures but has established various working groups to deal with these vulnerabilities (based on levels of importance and by sector).

Adoption of Standardized Technologies with Known Vulnerabilities

Historically, proprietary hardware, software, and network protocols made it rather difficult to understand how control systems operated, as information was not commonly or publicly known, was considered to be proprietary, and was, therefore, not susceptible to hacker attacks. Today, however, to reduce costs and improve performance, organizations have begun transitioning from proprietary systems to less expensive, standardized technologies utilizing and operating under platforms running operating systems such as Microsoft Windows, UNIX and/or LINUX, along with the common networking protocols used by the Internet. These widely-used standardized technologies have commonly known vulnerabilities; moreover, today, more sophisticated and effective exploitation tools are widely available over the Internet and are relatively easy to use. As a consequence, both the number of people with the knowledge to wage attacks and the number of systems subject to attack have increased dramatically.

Connecting Control Systems to Unsecured Networks

Corporate enterprises often integrate their control systems within their enterprise networks. This increased connectivity has significant advantages, including providing decision makers with access to real-time information, thus allowing site engineers and production control managers to monitor and control the process flow and the control of the entire system from within different points of the enterprise network. Enterprise networks are often connected to networks of strategic partners, as well as to the Internet. Control systems are, increasingly, using Wide Area Networks (WAN) and the Internet to transmit data to remote or local stations and individual devices. This convergence of control networks with public and enterprise networks potentially exposes the control systems to additional security vulnerabilities. Unless appropriate security controls are deployed within and throughout the enterprise and control system network, breaches in enterprise security may adversely impact operations.

Implementing Constraints of Existing Security Technologies

The use of existing security technologies as well as the use of strong user authentication and patch (or fix) management practices are typically *not* implemented in control systems; because control systems operate in real time, they are typically not designed with security in mind. Consequently, they have limited processing capabilities to accommodate or handle security measures or countermeasures. In addition, the software ingredients used to create control systems, being embedded, are usually not made known to end users. This reality makes it extremely difficult, even if there is a patch, to know that one exists and where it may apply.

Existing security technologies such as authorization, authentication, encryption, intrusion detection, and filtering of network traffic and communications require significantly increased bandwidth, processing power, and memory--much more than control system components may have or are capable of sustaining. The entire concept behind control systems is integrated systems technologies, which are small, compact, and relatively easy to use and configure. Because controller stations are generally designed to perform specific tasks, they use low-cost, resource-constrained microprocessors. In fact, some devices within the electrical industry still use the Intel 8088 processor, introduced decades earlier in 1978. Consequently, it is difficult to install existing security technologies without seriously degrading the performance of the control systems or requiring a complete overhaul of the entire control system infrastructure and its environment.

Control systems often exist in low-power environments, sometimes because they use solar power or because they need to be installed in environments where the risk of explosion is likely. This reality places constraints upon the processor speed. In fact, the embedded processors are often just fast enough to do the job at hand, with very little extra performance available to perform tasks such as asymmetric key validation.

Furthermore, complex password-controlling mechanisms may not always be used to prevent unauthorized access to control systems, partially because this process could hinder a rapid response to safety procedures during an emergency, or it could affect the performance of the overall environment. As a result, note experts, weak passwords that are easy to guess, are shared, and infrequently changed are reportedly common in control systems, including the use of default passwords or no password at all.

Current control systems are based on standard operating systems, as they are typically customized to support control system applications. Often, vendor-provided software patches are either incompatible or cannot be implemented without compromising service by shutting down "always-on" systems or affecting interdependent operations.

Insecure Connectivity to Control Systems and to Their Networks

Potential vulnerabilities in control systems are exacerbated by insecure connections, either within the corporate enterprise network or external to the enterprise or controlling station. Organizations often leave access links (such as dial-up modems to equipment and control information) "open" for remote diagnostics, maintenance, and examination of system status. Such links may not be protected with authentication or encryption, increasing the risk that an attempted external penetration could use these insecure connections to "break into" (known as hacking, or more correctly, cracking) remotely-controlled systems. Some control systems use wireless communications systems--especially vulnerable to attack—or leased lines passing through commercial telecommunications facilities. Neither method of communication has significant security features, and if there are any security measures implemented, they can be easily compromised. Without encryption to protect data as it flows through these insecure connections or authentication mechanisms to limit access, there is limited protection for the integrity of the information being transmitted; thus, the data may be subjected to interception, monitoring, and (eventual) penetration.

Publicly Available Information on Control Systems

Public information about critical infrastructures and control systems is available through widely available and public networks, such as the Internet. The risks associated with the availability of critical infrastructure information poses a serious threat to attack, as demonstrated by a George Mason University graduate student whose dissertation reportedly mapped every industrial sector connected via computer networks utilizing tools and materials publicly available on the Internet. Further, none of the data, the site maps, or the tools used were classified or sanitized. A prime example of publicly available information relates to the electric power industry, whereby open sources of information--such as product data, educational materials, and maps (though dated) --are available. They show line locations and interconnections currently being used. Additional information includes filings of the Federal Energy Regulation Commission (FERC), industrial publications on various subject matters pertaining to the electric power industry, and other materials — all of which are publicly available via the Internet.

As a result of this information state, foreign hacker web sites now contain varied information, openly and public disseminated throughout the Internet, pertaining to electrical and nuclear power systems, water systems, and transportation systems, often stating that this information is for "educational purposes only," disguising as an alleged engineering school (usually unconfirmed) or as some other allegedly legitimate educational institution or consortium. It comes as no surprise that many of these educational facilities are located within countries accused of attacking the United States' critical infrastructures (as demonstrated by recent news media articles from the Wall Street Journal) (Gorman, 2009; Wall Street Journal Blog, 2009).

ATTACK VECTORS: CONTROL SYSTEMS MAY BE VULNERABLE TO ATTACK

Entities or individuals with an intent to disrupt service may take one or more of the following methods to be successful in attacking control systems (GAO, 2004):

- Disrupt the operations of control systems by delaying or blocking the flow of information through the networks supporting the control systems, thereby denying availability of the networks to control systems operators and production control managers.
- Attempt, or succeed at, making unauthorized changes to programmed instructions within PLCs, RTUs, or DCS controllers to: change alarm thresholds or issue unauthorized commands to control station equipment, potentially resulting in damage to equipment (if tolerances have been exceeded); the premature shutdown of processes (shutting down transmission lines or causing cascading termination of service to the electrical grid); or disabling control station equipment.
- Send falsified information to control system operators, either to disguise unauthorized changes or to initiate inappropriate actions to be taken by them. Falsified information is sent and/or displayed to systems operators having them think that an alarmed condition has been triggered, resulting in their acting upon this falsified information, thus potentially causing "the actual event."
- Modify or alter control system software or firmware, so that the net effect produces unpredictable results (such as introducing a computer "time bomb" to go off at 12 midnight every night, thus partially shutting down some of the control systems,

causing a temporary brownout condition. (A "time bomb" is a forcibly-introduced piece of computer logic, or source code, causing certain courses of action to be taken when either an event or a triggered state has been activated.)
- Interfere with the operation and processing of safety systems; for example, tampering with or causing Denial of Service (DoS) to the control systems regulating the processing control rods within a nuclear power generation facility.

Furthermore, since many remote locations containing control systems (as part of, say, an enterprise DCS environment) are often unstaffed and may not be physically monitored through surveillance, the risk of threat remains. In fact, the threat may be higher if the remote facility is physically penetrated at its perimeter. Intrusion attempts can then be made to the control systems networks from within. In short, control systems are vulnerable to attacks of varying degrees--from telephone line sweeps ("wardialing") to wireless network sniffing ("wardriving") to physical network port scanning and to physical monitoring and intrusion.

CONSEQUENCES OF CONTROL SYSTEM COMPROMISES AND REAL-LIFE OCCURRENCES

Consequences of Control System Compromises

Some known consequences resulting from control system compromises are as follows:

- While computer network security is undeniably important, a control system that is compromised can have significant adverse impacts within the real-world, having far-reaching consequences not previously envisioned, or in areas affecting other industrial sectors (and their related infrastructures).
- Enterprise network security breaches can have severe financial consequences for industries, governments, and institutions; customer privacy can become compromised, resulting in a lack of consumer confidence; and computer systems needing to be rebuilt cause major productivity downturns and operational inefficiencies.
- A breach in the security of a control system can have a cascading effect upon other systems, either directly or indirectly connected to the compromised control system; property can be destroyed and innocent citizens can be hurt or killed (St. Sauver, 2004).

Real-Life Occurrences of Control Systems Attacks

A number of exploitations of control systems throughout the United States have been reported in the last decade. As a result of successful penetration attempts, intruders would be able to follow through on their intentions of causing harm to persons or property. Some examples follow:

- In 1998, during a two-week military exercise code-named Eligible Receiver, staff from the National Security Agency (NSA) used widely-available tools and software to simulate how sections of the United States' electrical power grid control system networks could be disabled through computer-based attacks. The simulated attempts were successful, demonstrating how within several days, portions of or the entire country's national power grid could have been rendered useless. The simulated attacks also demonstrated the impotency capabilities of the command-and-control elements within the United States Pacific Command (Ellis, 1998).

- In the spring of 2000, a former employee of an Australian company that develops manufacturing software applied for a job within the local government. After he was rejected, the disgruntled former employee reportedly used a radio transmitter device on numerous occasions to remotely access control systems of a sewage treatment system, releasing an estimated 264,000 gallons of untreated, raw sewage into nearby waterways (Ellis, 1998).
- A former employee of the Tehama Colusa Canal Authority (TCAA) was charged with installing unauthorized software and damaging computer equipment to divert water from the Sacramento River. The former employee was an electrical supervisor with the water authority, responsible for all of the computer systems throughout the organization. The individual faced 10 years in prison on charges that he "intentionally caused damaged without authorization to a protected computer." The Tehama Colusa Canal and the Corning Canal provide water for agriculture in central California and the city of Chico; they are both owned by the federal government (McMillan, 2007).
- Another disgruntled employee from an energy company allegedly temporarily disabled a computer system for detecting pipeline leaks for three oil derricks off the Southern Californian coast. Authorities expressed concern not only about the disruption of service caused by this attack but about the safety of the offshore platform personnel as well as the Southern California coastline and its wetlands (Kravets, 2009).

ISSUES IN SECURING CONTROL SYSTEMS

A significant challenge in effectively securing control systems environments and their networks include the following issues:

- Some of the technology has not yet been proven to be 100% effective. For example, is Intrusion Detection good enough to be an effective alarm for an operator to react to at, say, 2 AM? If alerted, what do the operators do with this information?
- How can one acquire and validate the precise time of day (for legal purposes) for a manhole deep underground?
- Because one cannot pull many of these devices from service for attack incidents, what forensic data can be used, then, for "evidence of malfeasance"?
- How can one patch and validate a control system without incurring significant logistical and monetary penalties?
- Can end-users and systems designers determine if, or when, dangerous vulnerabilities exist without exposing these vulnerabilities to the world-at-large?
- Is there a way to test products for security before deployment? Can this testing be done by an independent and trusted certification agency?
- Where and how can IT security practices be adapted to real-time Industrial Control Systems? More importantly, how can they be implemented *without* adversely affecting production or operations?
- How can one manage the radio spectrum in ways that are compatible with the need for availability and traceability?

Furthermore, anti-virus software often must be customized to handle a control system to avoid certain files for scanning--such as the log files, the HMI trend history files, and so forth. This requirement limits their utility in the field. Having an anti-virus utility scanning these files runs the risk of either having them automatically be removed by the anti-virus software (ascertaining that they are " infected"), or causing negative performance issues (such as slowing the HMI application within the HMI environment). Too, the SCADA and control systems industry has been operating in isolation for a many number of years and is now facing issues with patching and software/firmware version control.

Another very contentious issue is that of dealing with patching an embedded system, for embedded systems often include "smart" instruments, Programmable Logic Controllers (PLC), Remote Terminal Units (RTU), and Human Machine Interface (HMI) software. To complicate matters, these embedded systems components often have more software embedded within; for example, a PLC may have software that runs on an operating system (such as VxWorks) or an embedded version of Linux.

Also, vendors do not usually disclose what is in these devices to customers or end-users. The devices may well have an embedded version of a popular kernel, and there may well be known hacks against that kernel, too. In short, the end-users typically have no way of knowing if these vulnerabilities exist unless the vendor discloses such to them. That said, most customers take their vendors' trust in good faith.

Aside from this concern, even if the vendors and the end-users know of these problems, the reality is that most of these embedded devices cannot be remotely patched. Since many of them exist in hostile, isolated environment, the "windshield time" just to get to several hundred such sites makes patching an extremely expensive and time-consuming affair. In addition, unlike a typical office Information Technology environment, these patches must be validated and vetted before deployment, and in some critical cases, even at each site where it is deployed. In particular, patching a Safety Integration Level (SIL) application requires careful validation that safety systems work as designed both before and after the patch, for safety systems protect human life within the production environment.

Given these constraints, it should be apparent why office patching *policies* are toxic to most control systems. Simply stated, office applications are about "the data." While data can be restored in most cases, human lives and limbs lost or burns sustained as a result of an incident are another entirely different matter—and one of deep concern to nations and their citizens. Therefore, testing must be done very carefully to ensure the safety of everyone involved. It is imperative that new software is not casually deployed without a thorough and careful review and testing process.

Another complicating matter is that once employed software has passed the requisite safety checks, most industrial users are very reluctant to change it, unless there is a perceived significant cost-benefit to the end-user. Contrary to an ideal world where everyone in industry conforms to safety standards, there is simply no way that industrial users can update or patch control systems as frequently as most Information Technology (IT) departments would like.

Another critical issue concerns audits and forensics management—or more appropriately stated--a lack thereof. Most industrial control systems are designed to leave a log behind--and not a very good or verbose one, either. The log is usually validated when the system is commissioned or when significant work has been done to upgrade or modify that particular control system. Aside from these basic functions, there is little data recorded to provide "evidentiary proof" that a concerning event has transacted.

So, what does a law enforcement official do with these control system logs? Industrial Control Systems are "live systems," meaning that they can never be powered-off, usually for safety reasons. Unlike office systems, Industrial Control Systems are usually designed to operate large, high energy processes, so that removing them for study could be exceedingly dangerous or onerous. Large utilities for example, leverage their distribution SCADA systems so that they do not have to dispatch so many operators to every corner of the system. Before removing such a system, one would need to find many more operators and engineers to assist with the manual operations of the distribution system. This capability is not something that can be arranged quickly, or (perhaps more importantly from an organizational perspective) cost effectively. One of the major hurdles to operating manually is the lack of Highly Qualified Personnel (HQP) having sufficient training to handle manual operations. Some experts may argue that it is the control system itself that is to blame for this situation, for often they were sold with the purported notion that by using an Industrial Control System, a company could reduce labor costs, while increasing productivity. Acknowledging this point, many utilities today no longer have enough HQP on hand to run things manually for any significant length of time.

While most investigators can often acquire copies of the databases, key SCADA system files (such as the alarm logs), or key process data from individual instruments without causing much trouble to the operations, things can get tricky—particularly from a regulatory environment perspective. Most industries (in some form or another) are regulated, such that their regulatory requirements often insist on "continuous process monitoring," most times for safety reasons or concerns. For example, a lack of a Continuous Emissions Monitoring System could lead to the immediate shutdown of a furnace, because it is no longer "in compliance." Waste-water treatment plants, for example, have an effluent flow meter, which when disabled or if data is destroyed, will place the plant's certification in jeopardy. There are many more examples of this sort, but these examples should give readers a sense of present-day utility operational and compliance realities.

Furthermore, while it would be wise for law enforcement officials to meet with plant superintendents before incidents to discuss utility policies and procedures—accepting that the worst time for introductions is during a crisis--if history provides any guidelines, within the past 20 years, at least half of all industrial cyber incidents are known to have originated from disgruntled employees or contractors (note the earlier-cited Tehama Colusa Canal Authority incident). Furthermore, many incidents happen from sheer ignorance, and quite a few from negligence regarding repair and maintenance. A water treatment plant in Harrisburg, Pennsylvania, for example, suffered from an e-mail "bot" virus suspected to have been inadvertently brought in to the utility on a contractor's laptop (Ross, 2006).

SUGGESTED METHODS FOR SECURING CONTROL SYSTEMS

Several steps may be taken to address potential threats to control systems, including the following:

- Research and develop new security techniques to protect or enhance control systems; there are currently some open systems development efforts under way.
- Develop security policies, standards, and/or procedures that are implemented on, for, or with control systems' security in mind. Use of consensus standardization would provide a catalyst within the utility industry to invest in stronger and more sustainable security methods for control systems.
- If developing independent security policies, standards, and/or procedures are not applicable, implement similar security policies, standards, and/or procedures taken from a plethora of widely available Information Technology security good business practices. A good example might be the segmentation of control systems' networks with firewall network-based in-

trusion detection systems technologies, along with strong authentication practices.

- Define and implement a security awareness program for employees, contractors, and customers.
- Define and implement information-sharing capabilities promoting and encouraging the further development of more secure architectures and security technology capabilities and enhancements. Organizations can benefit from the education and distribution of corporate-wide information about security and the risks related to control systems, best practices, and methods (GAO, 2003).
- Define and implement effective security management programs and practices that include or take strongly into consideration control systems' security and management.
- Conduct periodic audits to test and ensure security technologies integrity is at expected levels of security. The findings of this audit should be reviewed with all necessary parties involved, mitigating the potential risk issues delineated in this chapter. The said audit should be based on standard risk assessment practices for mission-critical Business Units and their functional subunits (GAO, 1999).
- Define and implement logging mechanisms for forensics purposes.
- Define and implement mission-critical Business Continuity strategies and continuity plans within organizations and industries, ensuring safe and continued operations in the event of an unexpected interruption or attack. Elements of continuity planning typically include: (1) perform assessments against the target mission-critical Business Unit(s) for criticality of operations and identify supporting resources to mitigate ; (2) develop methods to prevent and minimize potential damage and interruption of service; (3) develop and document comprehensive continuity plans; (4) conduct periodic testing and evaluations of the continuity plans; these are similar to performing security audits but are specialized around disaster recovery and/or Business Continuity efforts of the control systems' environments; (5) make adjustments where necessary, or as needed (GAO, 2003).

SUGGESTED METHODS FOR IMPLEMENTING A MORE SECURED ENVIRONMENT FOR CONTROL SYSTEMS

As part of a sound methodology for safeguarding critical infrastructure control systems, here are some suggested methods to implement a more secured environment:

- Implement auditing controls over process systems; these systems are periodically audited.
- Develop policies, standards, and/or procedures that are managed and updated periodically.
- Assist in the development of secured architectures that can integrate with computer technologies today as well as 10 years into the future.
- Implement segments networks that are protected with firewalls and Intrusion Detection technology; periodically test intrusion attempts to ensure that security countermeasures are operating correctly.
- Develop a method for "exception" tracking.
- Develop and implement company-wide Incident Response Plans (IRP); IRP documentation should work with existing DRP (Disaster Recovery Plan) and BCP (Business Continuity Plan) documentation, in case of an outage.

CAN CONTROL SYSTEMS BE AUDITED WITHOUT ANY MAJOR CONCERNS?

Control systems can be audited, but some points of concern need to be addressed. First, developing methodologies with levels of awareness for corporate executives and managers such that state-of-the-art computer-based security mechanisms can be implemented for Industrial Control Systems is considered by many experts to be unconventional and very tricky. Second, Industrial Control Systems' auditing does not provide the same focus as computer-based security auditing. As noted throughout this chapter, Industrial Control Systems breaches involving real-life scenarios can result in loss of life, extreme financial or monetary losses, and loss of property (including real estate and assets such as chemical production facilities). Third, testing and evaluating control systems during a routine audit do not come without any risks. Though many audits may be similar to their counterparts from other infrastructure sectors, it is important to recognize that technical audits must be performed following a carefully-outlined set of guidelines performed by a certified or licensed technical professional who is knowledgeable in the areas of Industrial Control Systems and their safe and efficient operations.

FURTHER SUGGESTIONS FOR SAFEGUARDING INDUSTRI AL CONTROL SYSTEMS AGAINST COSTLY HACK ATTACKS

Develop Adequate Policies and Controlling Mechanisms for Crisis Management

To build better leverage within any given control systems environment, organizations need to develop adequate security policies, standards, and/or procedures for the control systems in advance of crises that: (1) set out and define a statement of goals and objectives for the safeguarding of the control system device, (2) delineate responsibilities for departments and groups in maintaining these goals and objectives over time, (3) designate a realistic number of Highly Qualified Personnel for supporting and responding to emergency or disaster conditions/situations when and if they arise, and (4) delineate in advance of potential crises acceptable responses, ensuring that there is a trained Incident Response Planning Team who will be the overseeing group when procedures are implemented in the event of threatening hack attacks or disaster situations.

Furthermore, to ensure that the policies and controlling mechanisms for crisis management continue to be valid and functional over time, "dry-run" or "table-top" exercises should be performed on a regular basis. Dry-run or table-top exercises are intended to provide an opportunity for communities to test their ability to respond to incidents. The exercises provide the opportunity to not only identify the appropriate response and coordination issues during a variety of incident scenarios but also determine vulnerabilities in the system. Following these exercises, improved business and safety decisions can be created to resolve those issues identified. A good business practice is to have security policies defined and implemented at a strategic, tactical level.

Segment the Control Systems Architecture from the Remainder of the Corporate Enterprise

In the development and implementation of a multiple-levelled network infrastructure, segmenting the control systems architecture from that of the remainder of the corporate enterprise network is highly advised. Effective usage of firewalls and Intrusion Detection technologies provide an almost granular level of protection and are part of sound safety and security business planning.

Essentially, the firewall acts as a lock on the door, but it is not the "burglar alarm." The Intrusion Detection system adds to the lock's protection by serving as an alarm. Practically speaking, network Intrusion Detection systems monitor any and all network traffic, identifying any unintended and/or malicious activity going on within, or through, the network. Since control systems network traffic patterns tend to be very repetitive and consistent, given their simplicity, the definition of network traffic matrices may be enough to determine what is accessing the control systems' networks.

Simpler architectures might be divided within a facility as follows: (1) all inter-networking and inter-layer network traffic flows through the firewall and Intrusion Detection systems areas, and (2) a single point of control is provided to oversee, manage, and maintain control of all network traffic in and out of areas involving control systems. Segmentation, as described, is probably the best method for ensuring that a control system is protected from unwanted intrusion.

THE ROLE OF THE U.S. CONTROL SYSTEMS SECURITY PROGRAM IN REDUCING CONTROL SYSTEM RISKS

The goal of the U.S. Department of Homeland Security National Cyber Security Division's (NCSD) Control Systems Security Program (CSSP) is to reduce control system risks within and across all critical infrastructure sectors by coordinating efforts among federal, state, local, and tribal governments, as well as control systems' owners, operators and vendors. The CSSP coordinates activities to reduce the likelihood of success and severity of impact of a cyber attack against critical infrastructure control systems through risk-mitigation activities. These risk-mitigation activities have resulted in the following tools (US-CERT, 2008):

- Catalogue of Control Systems Security: Recommendations for Standards Developers
- Control System Cyber Security Self-Assessment Tool (CS2SAT) (Lofty Perch, 2008)
- CSSP Documents
- Critical Infrastructure and Control Systems Security Curriculum
- Cyber Security Procurement Language for Control Systems
- Recommended Practices
- Training

The NCSD established the CSSP to guide a cohesive effort between government and industry to improve the security posture of control systems within the nation's critical infrastructure. The CSSP assists control systems vendors and asset owners/operators in identifying security vulnerabilities and developing measures to strengthen their security posture by reducing risk through sound mitigation strategies (US-CERT-2, 2008).

The CSSP has established the Industrial Control Systems Joint Working Group (ICSJWG) for federal stakeholders to provide a forum by which the federal government can communicate and coordinate its efforts to increase the cyber security of control systems in critical infrastructures. These efforts facilitate interaction and collaboration among federal departments and agencies regarding control systems cyber security initiatives (US-CERT-3, 2008).

The ICSJWG contains a team of Highly Qualified Personnel from various federal departments and agencies having roles and responsibilities in securing industrial control systems within the critical infrastructure of the United States. Since there are similar cyber security challenges from sector to sector, this collaboration effort benefits the nation by promoting and leveraging existing work and by maximizing the efficient use of resources (US-CERT-2, 2008).

The ICSJWG operates under the Critical Infrastructure Partnership Advisory Council (CIPAC) requirements. The ICSJWG acts a vehicle for communicating and partnering across all Critical Infrastructure and Key Resources Sectors (CIKR) between federal agencies and departments, as well as private asset owner/operators of industrial control systems. The longer-term goal is to enhance the facilitation and collaboration of the industrial control systems stakeholder community in securing CIKR by accelerating the design, development, and deployment of secure industrial control systems (US-CERT, 2009).

Further, the ICSJWG is connected with various stakeholders involved in industrial control systems, including participants from the international community, government, academia, the vendor community, owner/operators, and systems integrators. The ICSJWG is meant to serve as a sector-sponsored joint cross-sector working group operating under the auspices and in full compliance with the requirements of the CIPAC. Stakeholders participating in the ICSJWG are offered the opportunity to address efforts of mutual interest within various stakeholder communities, build upon existing efforts, reduce redundancies, and contribute to national and international CIKR security efforts (US-CERT, 2009, CIPAC, 2009).

The CSSP is partnering with members of the control community to develop and vet recommended practices, provide guidance in supporting the CSSP's incident response capability, and participate in leadership working groups to ensure the community's cyber security concerns are considered in emerging products and deliverables (US-CERT-3, 2008).

The CSSP aims to facilitate discussions between the federal government and the control systems vendor community, thereby establishing relationships meant to foster an environment of collaboration to address common control systems cyber security issues. The CSSP is also engaged in the development of a suite of tools, which when complete will provide asset owners and operators with the ability to measure the security posture of their control systems environments and to identify the appropriate cyber security mitigation measures to be implemented (US-CERT-3, 2008).

SCADA AND CONTROL SYSTEMS COMMUNITY CHALLENGES

One of the more interesting challenges facing industry and governments today is how to address security-related issues within the SCADA/control systems community and the sectors it supports, for SCADA/control systems enterprises do not operate in a context similar to that of its traditional Information Technology (IT) components. Probably one of the more significant aspects to SCADA is the scope dictating how issues are to be addressed.

One of the larger problems is that the forensics and evidentiary discovery practices are often associated with security management practices. Within control systems, these priorities are a little bit different from normalized systems, commonly listed as follows: (1) Safety, (2) Availability, and (3) Integrity.

IT-based architectures may be completely inverted from the priorities above, and thus, there appears to be a conflict between what and how SCADA/control systems operate, and, perhaps more importantly, how the corporation's enterprise defines its priorities. Several industries are currently attempting to reach a compromise by figuring out how both IT and SCADA environments can work together. Observationally, in some industries, such as nuclear power generation, these environments may never ever co-exist together.

Some of the highly concerning issues associated with control systems involve legacy architectures that are no longer being supported, utilizing equipment that cannot be taken offline immediately or easily, and posing serious operational and financial risks to the companies utilizing them. Unless these systems are interconnected with newer systems or are upgraded, there will be no easy methods of determining a plausible cause for any given intrusion event or incident. Moreover, beyond the company's control center, there is little forensic data to be found. The reality is that control center computers do not lend themselves to traditional forensics analysis unless they are taken offline and/or removed off-site. Given the nature of most control systems, if there exists an ongoing operational need, it may be very difficult to remove the servers in question for an extended forensics analysis.

THE FUTURE OF SCADA AND CONTROL SYSTEMS

Looking toward the future, control systems will have to be segmented and configured so that high- risk sections of control systems will have to be carefully protected. It is important to ensure that logging takes place in more than one part of control systems. When the gates of a dam are opened, there should be not only a digital signature of the operator who initiates the command at the Master Station from which it was sent, but also the signature of the operator at the Remote Terminal Unit where the command was executed.

Protocols such as IEC-60870 (Control Microsystems, 2009, Netted Automation, 2008) and DNP3 (DNP, 2005) have recently called for secure authentication features to increase protection of SCADA and control systems. [The latter can be found in IEC-62351 (UCI, 2009).]

The future holds much promise with standards, such as IEC-61850 (an object standard for substations), meant to be used with the telecommunications specifications in UCA2 (Mackiewicz, 2008). However, it involves an extremely complex undertaking that mixes many features into one layer. The Maintenance Management System, while a nice proposition for integrating SCADA data, may not be the best option to place on SCADA communications infrastructure, since one of these operational approaches is tactically significant, while the other is strategically significant.

Experts may want to consider novel ways of segmenting and separating traffic for security reasons. This undertaking could entail re-examining the lower layers of the communications infrastructure.

Since SCADA infrastructure needs to use a variety of ways to connect to remote stations, a key objective is to avoid having a common carrier disable a control system that it might depend on. In the future, multi-head RTU devices may be used in SCADA systems.

The future will likely also see the convergence of DCS and SCADA technologies. The SCADA concept originally grew from dealing with the constraints of high latency, low reliability and expensive bandwidth. DCS concepts, on the other hand, originally grew from the need to network everything to one central computer where everything could be processed all at once. Currently, DCS systems are getting "smarter" about how they distribute the functional pieces, and SCADA systems are handling closed loops more often as the communications infrastructure gets faster and more reliable. With continued evolution, these two system paradigms may converge into what is known as "the Programmable Automation Controller."

Finally, it is important to note that the languages of control systems in IEC-601131 are not well defined, providing an opportunity for experts to add certain features that might also include security. This move could assist greatly in auditing and protecting control systems processes.

CONCLUSION

Although SCADA and control systems security has been undergoing a continuous, evolutionary process since about the mid-1990s, the terrorist events of September 11, 2001, have brought increased awareness about security threats to

SCADA and control systems, particularly toward these devices and their architectures. Without their continuous operations, a Nation's economic and social well-being would be placed severely at risk, for citizens and governments, alike, depend upon these devices for their daily living and long-term sustainability. Life as we know it today would drastically alter if there were a massive attack against critical infrastructures, and nations would either revert back to pre-technological times or shift to something entirely different as a means of survival. For these reasons, present-day concerns by industry subject-matter experts on this topical issue should not be taken lightly.

REFERENCES

Blog Staff, W. S. J. (2009). *China denies hacking U.S. electricity grid.* Retrieved April 9, 2009, from http://blogs.wsj.com/digits/2009/04/09/china-denies-hacking-us-electricity-grid/

Control Microsystems. (2009). *DNP and IEC 60870-5 Compliance FAQ.*Retrieved December 1, 2009, from http://controlmicrosystems.com/resources-2/downloads/dnp3-iec-60870-5-compliance/

Critical Infrastructure Protection Advisory Council (CIPAC). (2009). *U.S. Department of Homeland Security, Critical Infrastructure Partnership Advisory Council FAQ.* Retrieved December 1, 2009, from http://www.dhs.gov/files/committees/editorial_0843.shtm

DNP Users Group. (2005). *DNP3 primary.* Retrieved March 20, 2005, from [REMOVED HYPERLINK FIELD]http://www.dnp.org/About/DNP3%20Primer%20Rev%20A.pdf

Ellis, S. (1998). *Computers are weapons in potential cyber attacks.* Retrieved 1998 from http://www.fas.org/irp/news/1998/08/98082502_ppo.html

Gorman, S. (2009). *Electricity grid in U.S.penetrated by spies.* Retrieved April 8, 2009, from http://online.wsj.com/article/SB123914805204099085.html

Kravets, D. (2009). *Feds: Hacker disabled offshore oil platforms leak-detection system, threat level.* Retrieved March 18, 2009, from http://www.wired.com/threatlevel/2009/03/feds-hacker-dis/

Lofty Perch. (2008). *Control system cyber security self-assessment tool, U.S. Department of Homeland Security, Control Systems Security Program (CSSP).* Retrieved 2008 from http://www.loftyperch.com/cs2sat.html

Mackiewicz, R. (2008). *Benefits of IEC 61850 networking, marketing subcommittee chair, UCA international users group, SISCO, Inc.* (2008). Retrieved December 13, 2009, from http://www.SISCOnet.com/

McMillan, R. (2007). *Insider charged with hacking California canal system.* Retrieved November 29, 2007, from http://www.computerworld.com/s/article/9050098/Insider_charged_with_hacking_California_canal_system?taxonomyName=storage

National Research Council. (2002). Making the nation safer: the role of science and technology in countering terrorism, *Report from the Committee on Science and Technology for Countering Terrorism.* Retrieved 2002 from http://www.nap.edu/openbook.php?record_id=10415&page=R1

Netted Automation. (2008). *Comparison of IEC 60870-5-101/-103/-104, DNP3, and IEC 60870-6-TASE.2 with IEC 61850 FAQ.* Retrieved 2008 from http://www.nettedautomation.com/news/n_51.html

Ross, B. (2006). *Hackers penetrate water system computers.* Retrieved October 30, 2006, from http://blogs.abcnews.com/theblotter/2006/10/hackers_penetra.html

Shea, D. (2003). *Resources, Science and Industry Division; The Library of Congress, CRS Report for Congress, Critical Infrastructure: Control Systems and the Terrorist Threat, CRS-RL31534*. January 20, 2004, from: http://www.fas.org/sgp/crs/homesec/RL31534.pdf

St. Sauver, J. (2004). *NLANR/Internet2 Joint Techs Meeting, University of Oregon Computing Center*. Retrieved July 24, 2004, from http://www.uoregon.edu/~joe/scada/SCADA-security.pdf.

The White House. (2003). *The National Strategy to Secure Cyberspace*. Retrieved February 2003, from http://georgewbush-whitehouse.archives.gov/pcipb/cyberspace_strategy.pdf

U.S. Computer Emergency Response Team (US-CERT). (2008). *U.S. Department of Homeland Security, Control systems Security Program (CSSP)*. Retrieved 2008 from http://www.us-cert.gov/control_systems

U.S. Computer Emergency Response Team (US-CERT). (2008). *FAQ about the Control Systems Security Program (CSSP)*. Retrieved 2008 from http://www.us-cert.gov/control_systems/csfaq.html

U.S. Computer Emergency Response Team (US-CERT). (2008). *U.S. Department of Homeland Security, Control Systems Security Program (CSSP)*. Retrieved 2008 from http://cipbook.infracritical.com/book3/chapter10/ch10ref14.pdf

U.S. Computer Emergency Response Team (US-CERT). (2009). *U.S. Department of Homeland Security, Control Systems Security Program (CSSP), industrial control systems joint working group FAQ*. Retrieved 2009 from http://www.us-cert.gov/control_systems/icsjwg/

U.S. General Accounting Office. (1999). *Federal Information System Controls Audit Manual, GAO/AIMD-12.19.6*. Retrieved January, 1999, from http://www.gao.gov/special.pubs/ai12.19.6.pdf

U.S General Accounting Office. (2003). *Homeland Security: Information sharing responsibilities, challenges and key management issues, GAO-03-1165T*. Retrieved September 17, 2003, from http://www.gao.gov/new.items/d031165t.pdf

U.S. General Accounting Office. (2003). *Critical infrastructure protection: Challenges for selected agencies and industry sectors, GAO-03-233*. Retrieved February 28, 2003, from http://www.gao.gov/new.items/d03233.pdf

U.S General Accounting Office. (2004). *Critical infrastructure protection: Challenges and effort to secure control systems, GAO-04-354*. Retrieved March 15, 2004, from http://www.gao.gov/new.items/d04354.pdf

Utility Consulting International (UCI). (2009). *Development of security standards for DNP, ICCP and IEC 61850 FAQ*. Retrieved 2009 from http://www.uci-usa.com/Projects/pr_List/Systems/CyberSecurity/Standards.html

Section 5

Policies, Techniques, and Laws for Protection

Chapter 11
Social Dynamics and the Future of Technology-Driven Crime

Max Kilger
Honeynet Project, USA

ABSTRACT

The future paths that cybercrime and cyber terrorism take are influenced, in large part, by social factors at work in concert with rapid advances in technology. Detailing the motivations of malicious actors in the digital world, coupled with an enhanced knowledge of the social structure of the hacker community, will give social scientists and computer scientists a better understanding of why these phenomena occur. This chapter builds upon the previous chapters in this book by beginning with a brief review of malicious and non-malicious actors, proceeding to a comparative analysis of the shifts in the components of the social structure of the hacker subculture over the last ten years, and concluding with a descriptive examination of two future cybercrime and national security-related scenarios likely to emerge in the near future.

INTRODUCTION

Some Opening Comments on the Future of Cybercrime and Cyber Terrorism

The future of cybercrime and cyber terrorism is not likely to follow some monotonic, simple deterministic path. The complex interplay of technology and social forces, as demonstrated in the previous chapters, reveals that this outcome will be anything but straightforward. However, this reality does not mean that through a better understanding of the social relationships between technology and humans, we cannot influence, at least partially, that future. In particular, social scientists have accumulated a significant body of knowledge on how various types of social processes--such as sentiment, status, social control and distributive justice, just to name a few – operate and interact to form our social world. We are now just beginning to gain a better understanding of how these processes are altered through the catalyst of digital technologies.

DOI: 10.4018/978-1-61692-805-6.ch011

It is hoped that through this understanding, we will build a better foundation from which to suggest how cybercrime and cyber terrorism may evolve over time. As social scientists, we have an obligation to share this understanding with others and, in particular, with our counterparts in the computer science and Information Technology (IT) security fields. These scientists and professionals approach the issues of cybercrime and cyber terrorism from a technological perspective, attempting to devise algorithms, encryption, authentication techniques, and strategic security platforms to protect networks and information systems from intrusion, data theft, and intentional damage. While many of these IT security researchers were initially resistant to considering bodies of knowledge outside of the traditional hard sciences, in the past five years there has been a shift in thought, reflecting a willingness to bring social science knowledge and research into consideration in their thinking. This recent change has also benefited social science researchers interested in people, technology, and issues such as cybercrime and cyber terrorism, because it has purposely exposed social scientists to IT scientists and their knowledge of technical systems and strategies.

Historically, the landscape of the IT security battlefield has been filled with technological weapons and defenses. Computer network defenders typically deploy a panoply of software and hardware tools--including (i) firewalls that restrict and control TCP/IP address and port traffic, (ii) intrusion detection systems that look for suspicious network traffic and unexpected program behavior, and (iii) anti-viral/spyware applications that scan files and memory for known virus signatures and exploits. IT security professionals spend a good deal of their time conducting very technical forensic analyses of compromised computer systems and attempting to reverse- engineer worms and other malware to see what their purpose and intended actions might be. The strategic nature of these efforts to defend computer networks and servers has typically almost always been reactive and from a temporal aspect, post hoc. IT security professionals normally have to wait until an exploit or threat has been uncovered before they can examine the threat and take preventative action.

The most common exception to this situation is when a security vulnerability in an application or operating system component is uncovered by IT security professionals, and a preventative patch is created and applied to the appropriate systems before individuals with malicious intent discover the vulnerability and take advantage of it.

It is evident from the current state of the IT security environment that there are a number of serious deficiencies in the current strategies used to combat cybercrime and cyber terrorism. Continuously fighting malicious actors and agents from what is mostly a post hoc, defensive posture is likely neither the most desirable nor optimal arrangement. Developing a more theoretical understanding of the reasons why individuals or groups develop and deploy exploits and malware, on the other hand, is one important pathway likely to enable IT security researchers and professionals to begin to emerge from their historically defensive posture.

This Chapter's Approach

The theoretical and empirical lessons learned from the previous chapters of this book are both relevant and valuable components of this strategy. This chapter builds upon those chapters by beginning with a brief review of the motivations of malicious and non-malicious online actors, then proceeding to a comparative analysis of the shifts in the components of the social structure of the hacker subculture over the last decade. This chapter concludes with a descriptive examination of two future cybercrime and national security-related scenarios likely to emerge in the near future. It is hoped that by providing a better understanding of the social-psychological and cultural forces at work within the hacking community, a more forward-looking and proactive strategy toward dealing with the current and emerging cybercrime and cyber terrorism threats can be developed.

THE PSYCHOLOGICAL AND SOCIAL-PSYCHOLOGICAL ASPECTS OF MALICIOUS ACTORS

The importance of the philosophy of "knowing your enemy "has historically been emphasized as a critical component of a successful outcome in conflict (Sun Tzu, cite1):

Remember, know the opponent and know yourself and you will not see defeat, even in a hundred conflicts. If you know yourself but not your opponent, then your chances of winning or losing are uncertain, and even your victories will be very costly. If you do not know yourself or your opponent, then you will be in mortal danger every step you take.

The task of "getting to know your enemy" in the digital world can be facilitated from a number of different, and most likely equally valuable, analysis levels. Rogers (2003) has examined online malicious actors from a moral choice and personality trait approach. He hypothesized that (1) online criminal actors would possess personality traits such as neuroticism and extraversion, and (2) they would utilize exploitive and manipulative behavior and have higher levels of hedonistic morality. Similarly, Shaw, Ruby and Post (1998) conducted research into the psychological and personality characteristics of individuals posing insider threats to information systems. They posited that social and personal frustration, computer "dependency", ethical flexibility, reduced loyalty, entitlement, and a lack of empathy contributed to the increased probability that an individual within an organization would commit criminal acts upon the internal information systems.

A more social-psychological analysis of mal-inclined individuals and groups can be found in Kilger, Stutzman, and Arkinet (2004). The authors cite the following motivations directing the actions of malicious actors and, to some extent, benign actors in the online world: (i) money, (ii) entertainment, (iii) ego, (iii) cause, (iv) entrance to social group (v) and status[1].

Money. In the early days of the Internet when it was considered a rare motivation, money has now become, from a numerical-distribution standpoint, the leading motivation for malicious behavior online. The number of vectors and strategies through which malicious actors and their agents attempt to compromise computer systems to obtain personal information and account passwords for financial gain has grown exponentially. Drive-by downloads (Provos, McNamee, Mavrommatis, Wang, & Modadugu, 2007), phishing and its variant spearphishing (Jagatic, Johnson, & Jakobsson, 2008; Watson, Holz, & Mueller, 2005), keyloggers (Heron, 2007), and man-in-the middle attacks are just a few of the techniques that have been developed.

Entertainment. Entertainment is a motivation that emerged early on in the emergence of digital technology. An early example of this motivation came from the phone phreaking world, where the legendary hacker John Draper (aka Captain Crunch) hacked his way through a series of phone systems around the world, just so he could speak into a telephone handset and hear his voice some seconds later after it had traveled around the world (Chisea, Ciappi, & Ducci, 2008). Other examples on the entertainment motivation include computer viruses written to spread some humorous message on computer screens around the world on a particular day or writing erroneous error information on computer monitors.

The entertainment motivation nearly disappeared for a number of years, but recently has found a renewed presence in at least one new form known as griefers. Griefers are individuals creating virtual identities or characters in online virtual worlds and guiding these virtual actors to perpetrate malicious acts on other unsuspecting virtual characters within the online world (Dibbell, 2008), often for the purposes of entertainment.

Ego. Ego is a motivation arising from the internal satisfaction that is achieved in getting a digital device to do exactly what one intended it to do. Shared by both malicious and IT security professionals, this motivation often involves getting a computer, router, or other digital device to execute some action it was not originally intended to do. The more difficult and complex the digital system, the greater the challenge to force it to undertake unintended actions and behaviors, and, consequently, the greater the psychological and social reward for succeeding.

The complex nature of information security systems--such as firewalls, intrusion detection systems, and their implied challenge that they have been created to keep people out-- makes an especially enticing target for malicious online actors. Ego has close connections to the idea of "mastery," one of the three subcultural components of the hacking community (Holt, 2007). "Mastery" refers to the extensive breadth and depth of technical knowledge an individual possesses that is necessary to understand and manipulate digital technologies in sophisticated ways.

Cause. Cause as a motivational factor for malicious actors is often a complex result of a one or more of the consequences of more macro-level geo-political, cultural, ideological, nationalistic, or religious forces. There are a number of potential objectives and courses of action available to a cause-oriented malicious online actor. One of these objectives involves the attempt to pressure a particular government, political party, military, commercial or non-governmental organization, or other collective entity to perform a specific act, make a statement that supports the actor's intended cause, or protest a specific act committed by another nation state.

The malicious actor may attempt to accomplish this objective in a number of different ways. One example would be to deface the website of the target organization or entity with messages denouncing the organization and promoting the message or cause that the actor supports. This kind of website defacement often follows some international incident, inciting the malicious actor to action. A good reaction to this reality was the website defacement of the United States Embassy in China, following the mistaken bombing of the Chinese embassy in Kosovo (Wu, 2007).

A second strategy sometimes deployed by a cause-motivated malicious actor is to illegally obtain information from the target's information system, likely to embarrass or expose the organization to criticism and then release the information to the public, usually over the web or through a major news organization.

A third, often more potentially serious action taken by a cause-motivated actor is to mount a direct attack upon the target organization's information or critical services infrastructure. These infrastructures might include military computer networks; control structures for electrical grids and water supply control systems; or industrial control systems embedded within industries utilizing hazardous materials as part of their production processes (for an example of an electrical grid attack, see Garrick, Stetkar, & Kilger, 2009). While much less common, this kind of attack could have devastating results and pose serious national security issues. This issue will be addressed later in this chapter, where the concept of the civilian cyber warrior is introduced.

Entrance to Social Group. Entrance to social group is a popular motivation for individuals seeking to build social ties with other malicious or non-malicious actors. Hacking groups tend to be fairly skill-homogenous, where technical skill and knowledge tend to be concentrated within members of the group's leadership (Kilger, Stutzman, & Arkin, 2004); non-leaders, in general, tend to be group members sharing somewhat lower levels of skills and expertise. Leaders in these hacking groups often serve as mentors for other less-skilled individuals within their group. This tendency toward status homogeneity within the group means that prospective members need to find a group that comes close to matching one's level of expertise as a precursor to attempting to join that hacking group.

A significant component to gaining entrance to a hacking group is to be able to demonstrate sufficient technical expertise, such that they would likely become a productive, contributing member of that group. Often this demonstration of skill involves the creation of a new exploit or a non-trivial enhancement of an already-existing one. Giving the exploit to one or more members of the group, in conjunction with a positive evaluation of the work by other members of the hacking group, presents the actor with the potential opportunity for acceptance and membership in the group and the positive reward of a newly acquired social identity.

The majority of entrance transitions to a hacking group involve consistent value orientations. That is, malicious hacking groups most often admit motivated newcomers already having a consistent history of developing and deploying malicious code. Similarly, non-malicious hacking groups usually only admit potential candidates with a solid history of non-malicious code development.

This reality is not always the case, however. The most common inconsistent transition taken from anecdotal evidence is the transition of a non-malicious actor into a maliciously motivated hacking group. There appears to be an asymmetrically stronger attraction to malicious hacking groups by non-malicious actors than the converse; that is, to turn Blackhat from White Hat seems much more attractive from a psychological sense than turning Whitehat from Blackhat. Migration of an actor with a history of maliciously motivated online actions to a group with non-malicious motivations appears to be somewhat less common, and often tends to occur later in the hacking career of the individual. This type of transition is often more difficult for the individual to successfully complete, due to serious trust issues arising between the non-malicious hacking group and the hacker appearing to be "switching sides."

Level of Status. The final motivation involves the level of status an individual possesses. Status plays an important part in guiding the attitudes and behaviors of online actors in the hacking community. The hacking community itself is considered a strong meritocracy (Kilger et al., 2004), based upon the knowledge, skill, and expertise in coding and understanding the technical aspects of computer networks, operating systems, and related digital devices. An actor's status can be evaluated at both a local level (e.g., within their social network or, more formally, within the immediate hacking group they belong to), as well as on a global level, where the actor can attempt to gain status and acknowledgement of one's expertise within the at-large hacking community scattered across the globe.

One method by which a malicious actor may gain status is by authoring a piece of elegant code overcoming a set of difficult technical or security obstacles. It must be clear that the malicious actor actually has authored the code. Hackers are sometimes questioned about various technical aspects of the code to ensure that the individual is the true author and did not misappropriate the code from somewhere on the Web. Failure to competently answer these questions can become a serious norm violation and, inevitably, lead to a loss of status for that actor. Depending upon the group's norms and the seriousness of the misrepresentation, the misappropriating hacker may be shunned or ejected from the hacking group and, thereafter, socially labeled as a "poser" to the hacker community at-large.

Another way malicious actors may gain status is to possess status-valued objects. These objects imparting status might include incontrovertible evidence that they have "rooted" (i.e., gained root access) to a particularly well-guarded computer network or server. Sometimes the possession of a sensitive private-sector, military file, or government document may be used in an attempt to enhance the status of a malicious online actor. However, often the individual attempting to claim status in this manner is challenged by others, usually by suggesting that the claimant has come across the document or file by some other less difficult means.

In any event, one of the interesting aspects of status-motivated acts is the necessary expenditure of status-valued objects: sharing an exploit with other hackers, revealing a software or hardware vulnerability that was uncovered but not previously known, or possessing and producting a status-valued document (i.e., stolen commercial, government, or military file) having sufficient provenance to imbue the malicious actor with additional status. In short, to enhance one's status in this manner, the hacker must usually disclose information.

The act of disclosing information often drains the status object itself of status—for once information is no longer "secret," it loses a significant portion of its value. Often, once the file or information is disclosed, it is then distributed by the members witnessing the disclosure to a much larger audience over the Internet, often resulting in the "zeroing out" of any status value remaining within the status object (i.e., file, code, image, etc.).

Summary Remarks

This discussion completes this section on descriptions involving the motivations of malicious online actors. The objective of this discussion was to acquaint the reader with a few of the possible explanations why individuals commit malicious acts in a digital environment. Significantly more research into this topic area is needed to provide both social and computer scientists with a better understanding of why cybercrime occurs.

CHANGES IN THE SOCIAL STRUCTURE OF THE HACKING COMMUNITY OVER TIME

The hacking community is a complex social community undergoing rapid evolutionary change. Much of its social structure and social components--such as social norms, values, and customs-- are influenced, to a very great extent, by digital technologies in constant flux. Often a cursory examination of this community results in the conclusion that it is a chaotic community with few norms, values, social structure, or organization.

The fact is that initial observations can be deceiving. A careful examination of the hacking community to the trained observer will reveal a complex social structure with strong norms and intra-group shared values. The community itself can be described as a strong meritocracy (Kilger et al., 2004), where the level of skill and expertise at areas such as programming, digital network protocols, and operating system internals strongly determine an individual's status position within both the local and the global hacking communities.

Additionally, as is common among newly-emerging social groups, the hacking community appears to be bound together mostly by mechanical solidarity (Durkheim, 1893), where associations appear to be more clan-based, and violations of norms by individuals often invite exaggerated responses from social control agents within the community.

Hacking Community: Counterculture or Subculture?

There has also been some disagreement about whether the hacking community is a counterculture or a subculture. Kilger and colleagues (2004), in their earlier work describing the social structure of the hacking community, considered it to be an example of a counterculture, because of the community's appearance to run strongly counter to the norms and values of traditional society. More recently, Holt (2007) classified the hacking community as a subculture rather than a counterculture, and it may be that there is now some truth in that assertion. As the hacking community has matured over time, there has been evidence of mainstream society, to some extent, culturally appropriating some of the norms, values, and styles of the hacking community. A number of recent popular movies and television programs (such as "Live Free or Die Hard" or "MI5" [Spooks in the UK]) have villains that are hackers, and while they are villains, they are "cool" bad guys, in some way interesting and attractive to movie and television audiences.

Another recent phenomenon providing support for this view is the gradual positive change in attitudes toward technologically-skilled individuals (e.g., "geeks" in pop culture terms) by members of mainstream society. These technology-focused individuals are no longer the social outcasts they once were some years ago but are now regarded by some traditional societal groups as "cool." Given this and other anecdotal evidence, there is some reason to believe that members of the hacking community are slowly becoming regarded not as members of a counterculture but rather members belonging to a subculture within traditional societal boundaries.

Barriers to Researchers Wishing to Study Hacker Communities

Whether counterculture or subculture, among the more difficult challenges in studying this community is the inability for researchers to collect adequate quantitative or qualitative data concerning hackers' activities, attitudes, goals, and objectives. The hacking community is under constant pressure from a number of hostile vectors, including local, state, and federal law enforcement, as well as from intelligence agencies from a number of countries around the world. This constant threat of surveillance and pursuit by governmental entities creates strong in-group and out-group boundaries and generates a rather strong sense of suspicion of individuals not belonging to their immediate hacking group. This sense of suspicion extends even to those who are true members of the hacking community at-large but who are not members of a person's immediate hacking group. Thus, researchers' gaining the trust of individuals within this community for the purpose of interviews or other data collection techniques is often difficult.

Fortunately, one of the traits of subcultures, especially newly-merging ones, is the propensity for members of that subculture to collaborate to develop a permanent recorded history of the important concepts, events, and persons holding special meaning for the subculture as a whole. Originating in 1975 at Stanford University, the Jargon File was for decades a repository for members of the hacking community to share concepts, historical moments, and important documents and to celebrate that individuals were shaping the nature of the hacking community. This repository was maintained and updated over the years in online form, but the document was eventually commercially published as <u>The Hackers Dictionary</u> (Raymond, 1996) and was maintained for only some years after that commercialization.

KILGER AND COLLEAGUES' 2004 STUDY OF THE JARGON FILE

Kilger and colleagues (2004) conducted a content analysis of the Jargon File (multiple unknown authors, 1994) to attempt to identify major components of the social structure of the hacking community. This analysis revealed that the words, phrases, and symbols in the Jargon File could be classified into 18 distinct thematic categories, including the following:[2]

1. Technical
2. Derogatory
3. History

Figure 1. Dimensions of the social structure of the hacking community. Note: Jargon File entry may be coded into multiple thematic categories

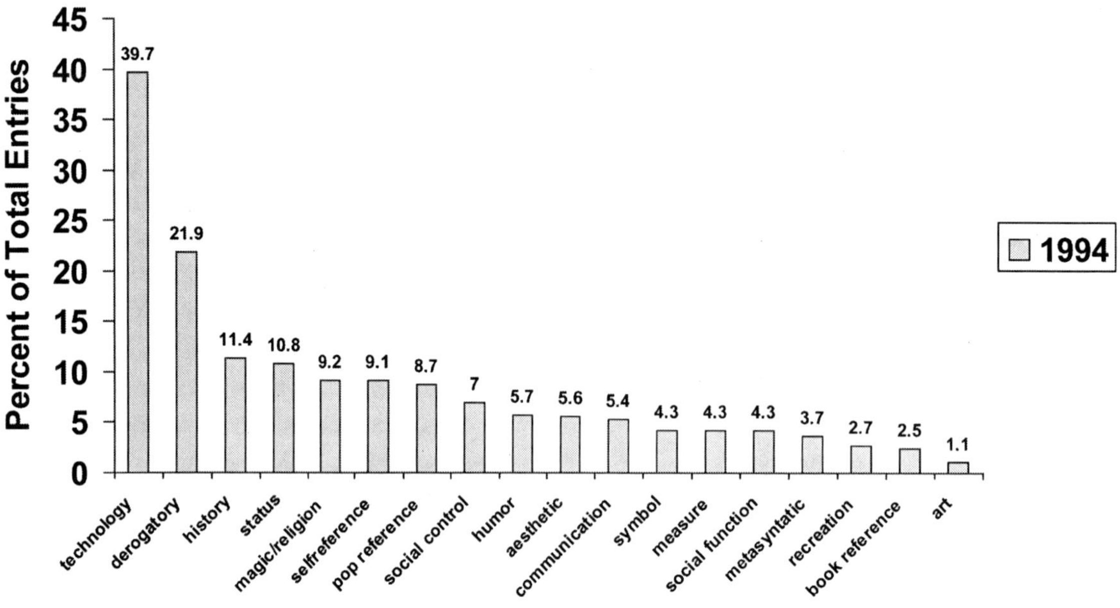

4. Status
5. Magic/Religion
6. Self-Reference
7. Popular Reference
8. Social Control
9. Humor
10. Aesthetic
11. Communication
12. Symbol
13. Measure
14. Social Function
15. Metasyntatic Variable
16. Recreation
17. Book Reference
18. Art

The emergence of this taxonomy of concepts, words, symbols, and phrases served to highlight themes within the social structure of the hacking community important to the community as a whole. These shared values give the researcher an idea of the social processes and elements operating within the community and help define its social structure. In addition to identifying a taxonomy of structural elements, the original content analysis of the Jargon File produced a frequency distribution of the thematic categories. This frequency distribution is displayed in Figure 1.

Thematic Categories That Emerged

The two simplest thematic categories emerging from the analysis are technology and history. As one would expect, the technology category is the most frequently encountered theme in entries in the original Jargon File analysis, with 39.7% of the entries classified within this dimension. Members of the hacking community, especially during the early years, needed a method by which they could memorialize and share details about technical discoveries with the rest of the community. Adding entries to the Jargon File describing technical objects, procedures, or challenges, to an extent, helped to serve this function.

The history category also makes sense as one of the more popular thematic categories (11.4%), because that was one of the critical functions of the Jargon File--to create a permanent historical record of the important dates, events, and people associated with the community. Given the virtual nature of the digital world, where most of its members did not live within physical proximity of each other, members of the hacking community could not effectively utilize other more traditional history-preserving strategies, such as oral histories or physically-shared documents, such as books. This reality is likely one reason why the Jargon File came into being.

The status category is also one of the most frequent entries (10.8%) in the Jargon File. This point should come as no surprise, due to the nature of the community as a strong meritocracy. Community members need to be able to somehow signal their status position within the community. The emergence of terms like "wizard" or "net.god" likely made their way into the vernacular of the hacking community to facilitate the communication of high status to other individuals.

The derogatory category turns out to be the second most frequently coded theme, with 21.9% of the entries coded with this tag. Entries coded as derogatory are typically objects rather than persons. In the quest to navigate complex operating systems, write sophisticated code, and understand the functions of intricate pieces of hardware, often members of the community are confronted by computer software or hardware operating systems not appearing to do what they are expected to do, or they do it poorly. This reality was especially prevalent in the early days of the digital revolution when software and hardware components were often experimental and with little or no documentation. Often the result of this situation was a tension between hacker and technology that eventually surfaced in the form of denigration of the very objects the hacker is working with and, thus, filling the Jargon Files with words and phrases of derision for these objects.

Social control entries (7% of entries) involve the specific denigration of other individuals thought to have violated some norm present within the social system of the hacking community. These entries typically cast targets as possessing extremely negative characteristics, and fellow members of the community become agents of social control utilizing these terms. Social control entries are also likely associated with the fact that the hacking community is a strong meritocracy existing within an environment where the exchange of status cues is often constrained by the fact that most actors are separated by geography. This lack of propinquity means that members must use more status cue-limiting communication channels, such as email, IRC, and webcam video calls. These constraints inhibit verbal and non-verbal cues transmitting information about an actor's position in a status hierarchy. When this status cue information is not available for actors to assess the status of others they are interacting with, often status conflicts result and social control processes are activated.

The final group of entries included: magic/religion[3], aesthetic, self- reference, communication, symbol, social function, and art. While each of these classes of entries is important, taken together, they form the core of the original zeitgeist of the hacker spirit. That is, these dimensions of the social structure of the hacking community hold forth some of the fundamental values of the community. The appreciation of "beautiful things" such as the *aesthetic* of elegantly-written code and the *art* that springs from the graphical representation of symbols of a complex mathematical algorithm are among these elements. This appreciation also includes the act of *self-referencing,* where members of the community describe their actions in terms of terms of "art within the field of computer science," "the imbuement of computer protocol *symbols* with rich social meaning," and "the application of computer processes to describe social relations (e.g., *social functions*) between themselves and other human actors." Finally, the use of *magic or religious* terms to describe phenomena they cannot otherwise explain all lie at the core of the original hacker social structure and hold a special place within the structure of the community.

A Note on the Complexity of the Structure and Community

One other important measure this analysis of the Jargon File brings to bear on the social structure of the hacker community is some basic quantification of the complexity of the structure and community itself. One unique characteristic of this analysis is that Jargon File entries were allowed to be encoded into as many categories as fit the coding rules. A consequence of this multiple-encoding procedure is that the percentages in Figure 1 add up to more than 100% and, in fact, sum to 157%. An observation made during the original coding procedures was that the more thematic categories an entry could be classified into, the more likely the definition of the entry in the Jargon File tended to be complex and more directly connected to the inner core of the social structure of the hacking community. Thus, the extent to which the sum of all category frequencies exceeds 100% corresponds to some simple measure of the complexity or depth of the social structure of the hacking community.

THE ORIGINAL ANALYSIS AS A CONTRIBUTION TO UNDERSTANDING THE SOCIAL STRUCTURE OF THE HACKING COMMUNITY

The original analysis of the Jargon File is an important contribution to the understanding of the social structure of the hacking community. However, the utility of this specific analysis can be extended. One of the benefits of the Jargon File as a social artifact is that it is a dynamic object modified by members of the hacking community over time, and it is hypothesized that these changes reflect shifts in the social structure of the hacking community itself. Over the years, the Jargon File has been extensively modified, in that it has had a number of entries removed, many more new entries added by various contributors, and others modified. This process has traditionally been overseen by individuals in the community who have taken it upon themselves to be the "official keeper" of the Jargon File.

The dynamic nature of the Jargon File suggests that a second content analysis of a more recent Jargon File, when paired with the original analysis, may shed some light on the nature of what some of those changes in the social structure of the hacking community might be. New thematic categories emerging from this second analysis may mean that there are new components to the social structure. Thematic categories disappearing or almost disappearing may suggest that this component of the social structure has lost most of its meaning for the community. Similarly, change in the frequency distribution may reflect the relative increase or decrease in importance of the element of the social structure component to the hacking community.

Follow-Up Content Analysis of the December 2003 Jargon File

The most recent revision of the Jargon File (revision 4.7.7, last revised December 2003) was obtained online (multiple unknown authors, 2003). A content analysis of this newer version was undertaken, using the same coding rules as were in effect for the original analysis. Particular attention was paid to the potential emergence of new thematic categories, and if during the course of the coding process a recurrent new theme emerged, it would be inserted into the coding protocol, and the previously-coded entries would be retroactively examined to see if any of them could be encoded into the new thematic category.

Figure 2. Dimensions of the Social Structure of the Hacking Community

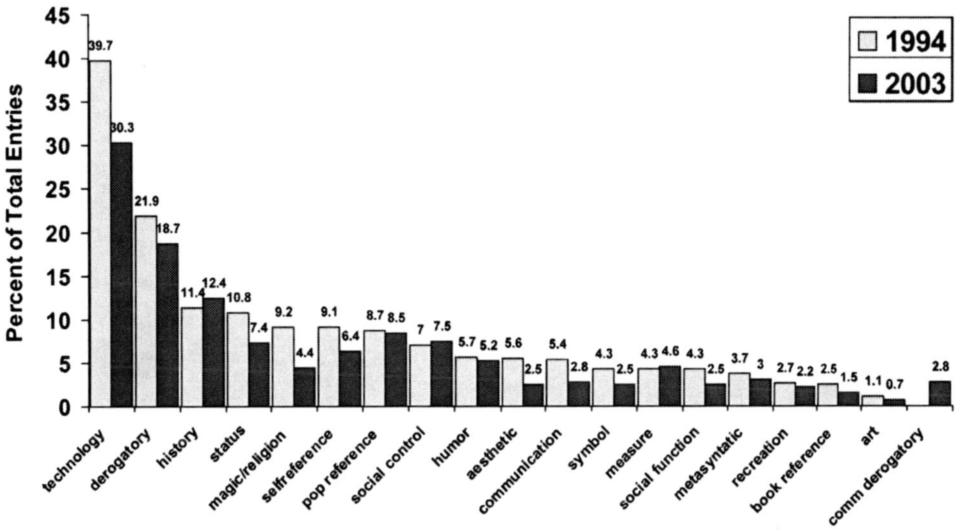

Approximately 2,307 terms were available for coding, and approximately 21% of these entries could not be coded in the first pass of the analysis. A second phase of the analysis consisted of a second pass through the entries initially coded as "uncodable" during the first pass to see if there were any pattern to these unclassifiable terms, leading one to establish a new thematic category and re-classify those terms into a new thematic category. This second pass did not yield any additional classes, but 1,816 entries were coded. Figure 2, below, contains both the 2003 coding results, as well as the original 1994 results for comparison.

A Closer Look at the Technology and History Classes. Following the previous example, let's examine the technology and history classes first. The most straightforward and expected result is that there is an increase in the number of history entries, what one might expect, given that the Jargon File functions as a historical record of the important events, dates, concepts, and people within the community. A more interesting result is the decline in the number of entries classified as "technical." It would seem logical there would be an increase in technological terms rather than a decrease, given the rate of advancement of digital technology. However, recall that one of the hypotheses about the function of the technology class was that it was used to memorialize and share knowledge about new technology. The information-sharing capabilities of the Internet have matured, and many more options for sharing information are available now then there were during the time of the original analysis. This fact may have made the Jargon File less of a desirable and efficient method by which to memorialize technology, thus explaining why the number of technology entries in the file has substantially decreased.

A Closer Look at Other Entry Drops. Derogatory, status, and social control entries also experienced drops in incidence between the two time periods of analysis. Some of this decline may be due to the increased opportunity to exchange verbal and non-verbal cues among members of the hacking community. First of all, 2003 marked the early years of Voice over Internet Protocol (VoIP) and webcam technologies--the kind of technologies allowing hacker communications to carry verbal and non-verbal cues previously missing in less rich communication channels, such as email or IRC channels.

Secondly, during the years between the analyses, there was a significant increase in the number of attendees and venues billed as "cons" or "hacker conferences." One of the indirect consequences of these meetings was that they allowed members of the hacking community to meet face-to-face to have discussions and, thereby, exchange extensive levels of verbal and non-verbal cues communicating status hierarchy positions.

A Closer Look at the Final Set of Categories. The final set of categories examined is the set consisting of magic/religion, aesthetic, self reference, communication, symbol, social function, and art. Recall that these categories together form "the zeitgeist" or "spiritual core" of the hacking community social structure. An examination of Figure 2 reveals that each of these classes declined in the period from 1994 to 2003, some decreasing in frequency appreciably. One possible hypothesis for this decline is that the original core values and norms of the hacking community present in 1994 have weakened significantly and may be quickly vanishing from the social structure binding the community together.

A further corroborating piece of evidence can also be found in the analysis of the social structure. Recall that one of the measures of the complexity and depth of the core values of the hacker community social structure was the extent to which entries in the Jargon File were coded to more than one thematic category. In the second 2003 analysis, if one sums the percentages in the graph, one will arrive at the figure of 1.23, a relative decrease of almost 22% from 1994. This observation further suggests that there are significant shifts occurring within the social structure of the hacker community, and these shifts may bring permanent changes in the way in the community sees the world and itself.

The conjecture that the original strength of the core spirit of the hacking community has deteriorated aligns to a significant extent with field observations collected over the years. The chapter author was present in Silicon Valley for a number of years during the birth of the digital revolution, spending a significant amount of time in the budding technology and hacking community. Many of these core components of the social structure of the hacker community had a strong visible presence during this time, recognized by the members themselves as core values and norms. More recent field observations by the author appear to confirm that the strength of these core values have declined appreciably. If this trend continues, there may come a time when these original core dimensions of the social structure of the hacking community disappear altogether.

A Closer Look at Two Final Questions. Two final questions remain to be answered in this analysis. First, Why is this shift in the social structure of the hacking community happening? One conjecture is that the approaching ubiquitous presence of digital computational devices is having some kind of normalizing effect on the relationship between people and technology. In simpler terms, now that computers are common household "appliances" present in the lives of most individuals in first-world countries, the "social" bond between person and machine is no longer as rare and unique as it was in the early days of the digital revolution, for sophisticated software and hardware are utilized by individuals in their everyday lives.

Another potential factor in the decline of the core values comprising the social structure of the hacking community may be the commercialization of the digital world. This new vision of the digital world that the hacking community inhabits as one full of potential to exploit for financial gain is anathema to the hackers. This new way of looking at the digital online world originates both from legitimate sources--such as media companies, commercial auction houses (e.g. Ebay), retailers, and others--as well as from illegitimate sources including cybercriminals utilizing the same expert knowledge of operating systems, networks, and programming languages to exploit other online users for financial gain through worms, exploits, phishing, and other strategies. Indeed, in the second analysis of the Jargon File only one new category emerged from the process: the commercial derogatory class. This class represents negative affect towards individuals involved in the digital world who are not technical experts but who seek to exploit the technology for financial gain; this class was present in 2.8% of the entries coded.

Second, the question remains, What does this "negative" observation mean in terms of malicious behavior--whether it be cybercrime, cyber terrorism, or some new emerging phenomenon. One potential consequence of the decline in the traditional core elements of the hacker social structure is the loss of control over the norms and values of individuals in the hacking community. The original character of the core elements of the social structure of the hacking community was such that it discouraged malicious behavior. In the early days of the digital revolution, when the core social structure elements were strongest, there were very strong norms against causing harm or damage to other machines and networks, formalized in a philosophy labeled "The Hackers Ethic" (MIT IHTFP, 1994). Note that this did not preclude illegal acts, such as compromising computer networks and servers, as long as the perpetrator did not damage the systems he (or she) explored. With the breakdown in the core social structure elements inhibiting these malicious behaviors, we are now seeing an exponential surge in the number and magnitude of cybercrime acts. Is the breakdown of the core responsible for this surge? It is difficult to say; however, this analysis has provided some initial food for thought in regard to this question.

FUTURE THREATS IN CYBERSPACE

The analysis in the preceding section has provided some initial empirical evidence corroborating that as technology continues to evolve, so does the social structure of the online hacking community, no matter whether the actors caught up in this digital revolution are malicious or non-malicious in nature. At the very beginning of this chapter, the idea was presented that for the IT security community to more successfully challenge the onslaught of worms, malware, exploits, and compromises, they were going to have to reassess its traditional reactive strategies and likely adopt a more proactive approach.

One of the key components to this shift in tactics suggested developing a better awareness of the motives of malicious actors, building a more comprehensive picture of the social structure of the hacking community and how it is changing over time, and, importantly, applying this knowledge to begin to build a threat matrix of cybercrime and cyber terrorism scenarios likely to emerge in the future. The discussion that follows explores two potential cyber scenarios that may be likely candidates for that forward-looking threat matrix, labeled as Scenario #1 and Scenario #2.

Scenario #1: Loosely-Coupled Criminal Enterprises

One phenomenon that may emerge is the loose coupling of online criminal enterprises with actors from more traditional offline criminal milieus. This collaboration of old and new criminal elements is hypothesized to be facilitated by technological- and non-technology-related changes in both the virtual and physical worlds. In this scenario, virtual criminal enterprises use cyberspace to identify and evaluate the value of prospective targets, extract money or other items of value from victims, and arrange for the coercive elements encouraging the cooperation of victims. Before we discuss in more detail how this virtual-to-traditional criminal intercourse actually takes place, it is useful to identify three elements at work that help facilitate these types of collaborative efforts.

First Key Element. The first element key to this scenario is the emergence of online payment systems like Paypal, originally designed to facilitate the transfer of funds to pay for purchases made online. Paypal allows the secure transfer of funds to and from a number of financial instruments, including credit cards or bank accounts, in 18 different currencies across 190 countries. Fund transfers can be made via a personal computer, or even a mobile phone. Other electronic fund-transfer systems, such as Hong Kong's Octopus card, originally designed for collecting fares on transportation systems, is now also being deployed as financial fund bearer instruments that can be utilized to make retail purchases and even serve as an access control card to physical facilities.

Online payment systems like Paypal are not restricted to the online purchase of products or services online. These services can also be used to move funds to and from individuals who have never met each other but have agreed to a transfer of a specific amount. While there are admonishments against the transfer of funds for illegal purposes in the terms of user agreements for online payment systems like Paypal, these terms of service are, to a great extent, unenforceable--unless one or more parties to the transaction files a complain, which in an illegal transaction, is highly unlikely.

The secure online movement of funds facilitates two key actions enabling commerce between virtual and more traditional criminal groups or organizations. First, it allows the movement of funds from a victim to the virtual criminal enterprise, without a physical exchange injecting substantially more risk to the perpetrators. While online payment systems do contain some security elements supposed to allow the identification of the parties involved in fund transfers, the opportunity for "money mules," the ability to quickly shuffle money through multiple accounts as well as other techniques can be deployed to obscure the true parties involved in the transaction. These circumstances dramatically reduce the risk of exposure of the virtual criminal enterprise.

Second Key Element. The second key element is that online payment systems facilitate the transfer of funds between the virtual criminal enterprise and the more traditional criminal individual or gang. This transfer allows a secure, lower-risk method for the virtual criminal enterprise to hire the services of more traditional criminals or gangs to "subcontract" the most hazardous components of criminal activity. The benefits of this type of arrangement will become clearer as the actual criminal scenario is laid out.

Third Key Element. The final element likely to foster this scenario is present in the physical rather than in the virtual world. This reality involves the immigration of nationals from other countries. The presence of foreign nationals in a country provides the opportunity for virtual criminal enterprises in other countries to enlist the assistance of individuals sharing cultural, religious, or nationalistic bonds making these individuals more likely to cooperate with virtual criminal organizations. In addition to these social and geo-political ties, there are also often additional pathways to gain the cooperation of foreign nationals in other countries, such as family members who have been left behind and are more susceptible to physical harm by members of the virtual criminal enterprise or their agents. As this scenario becomes more common, it may eventually become the case that immigration by some foreign nationals could be "sponsored" by the virtual criminal enterprise with the intention of exchanging emigration assistance for cooperation once in the host country.

How Loosely-Coupled Enterprises Might Work. Now that some of the precursors for this scenario have been laid out, we can proceed to the description of how loosely-coupled criminal enterprises might actually work. Imagine the existence of a virtual criminal enterprise located in country A. This enterprise likely consists of a number individuals having a meaningful division of labor in the organization. Some individuals are involved in target or victim prospecting; their job is to evaluate potential targets or victims for both value and risk and then select those having the maximum potential payoff for the estimated minimum level of risk to the virtual criminal enterprise. These "victim prospectors" utilize a number of online resources to estimate the value of potential victims. They may utilize informal resources, such as social network sites (e.g., myspace.com or facebook.com) to look for signs of expensive hobbies or material possessions. They may also utilize specialty websites, such as zillow.com, to obtain an estimate of the value of a home as an indicator of the net worth of an individual, or use career-oriented websites such as linkedin.com to obtain occupational information that can be used to estimate household income. More professional and substantial virtual criminal enterprises may resort to using online paid information search firms, or credit reporting firms to obtain information on potential victims.

Once the potential target has been identified, an email exchange is established between the virtual criminal enterprise and the victim, perhaps by an individual within the criminal enterprise skilled in gaining the trust of others. The endpoint of this exchange is the demand for money or other object(s) of value from the victim. This demand may be presented immediately or, more likely, the virtual criminal may engage in some sort of discussion, ruse, or story that engages, disarms, or compromises the victim, such that the probability the victim reports the demand to law enforcement is attenuated. Accompanying this demand in the email will also be a coercive statement. This statement typically threatens physical harm to the target, their family members, or other significant others if the demand is not met.

While the actual enactment of the coercive threat may not be necessary to extract funds from the victim, a threat with no probability of occurrence is likely, in the long run, to become ineffectual. This point is where the loose coupling of the virtual criminal enterprise with more traditional criminal gangs or individuals comes into play. The idea here is that the virtual criminal enterprise attempts to locate and identify more traditional criminal gangs or individuals in the online world. It is not uncommon for these more traditional gangs and individuals to have their own websites or social networking pages where they can be identified and contacted.

Once communication is made, then, initially, a series of exchanges between the two types of criminal entities take place. These initial exchanges serve to build trust and respect between the two parties. Once this rapport is secured between the two parties, negotiations can begin for the exchange of funds for the performance of the violent act upon the target of the virtual criminal enterprise. This point is where the key of secure online payment systems plays its part, allowing the virtual criminal enterprise the ability to securely pay these more traditional criminal "contractors" for their services. The use of online payment systems can also assist in obscuring the fund transfer trail so that law enforcement officials may have a difficult time tracing back the funds to a specific party. In addition, no physical exchange of funds has to take place, reducing the risk of apprehension of members of the virtual criminal enterprise, as well as reducing the risk of violence from the more traditional criminal elements they are contracting with, should something go wrong with the transaction.

The final outcome of this scenario depends upon the actions of the targets. If they comply with the demands of the virtual criminal enterprise and move the requested funds, then they receive a final email warning them that the coercive act will occur anyway if they notify law enforcement or attempt in anyway to track down members of the virtual criminal enterprise. If the target refuses to comply with the demand, the virtual criminal enterprise notifies its traditional criminal accomplices to carry out the coercive act.

As this cycle of crime repeats itself, these two types of criminal organizations, virtual and traditional, become loosely coupled in a series of mutually-beneficial but illegal activities. One of the advantages of this schema for the virtual criminal organization is that it can minimize the risk of apprehension by subcontracting the riskier components of the crime to the more traditional criminal elements. The virtual criminals can also utilize the Internet to assist them in remaining unidentified. If the virtual criminal enterprise locates itself in a country other than the one in which its victims reside, then this strategy also substantially reduces their risk. The difficulties in cross-national pursuit, issues of jurisdiction, extradition, and prosecution help ensure lower risk levels for the virtual criminal organization, especially if that organization resides in a country with lower levels of cybercrime expertise and enforcement, or where the level of governmental corruption makes apprehension a much less likely event.

Scenario #2: The Civilian Cyber Warrior

The motivation of cause, as mentioned earlier in this chapter, is a powerful one inspiring groups and individuals to use the Internet directly to promote their ideological stance. They may accomplish this through non-malicious means, such as establishing something as simple as a website. They may also promote their ideas through more malicious means, such as the commonly-used tactic of defacing the website of one's ideological opponent. Often the nature of these conflicts pits groups of like-minded individuals against the policies or tactics of a nation state --either their own or that of another country. Conflict between the individual and the state has long been a topic of sociological, political, and philosophical discussion.

Individual actions against a nation state can also be analyzed from an interpersonal cost/benefits perspective. Prior to the prevalence of the Internet, this cost/benefit ratio was skewed heavily toward the cost side of the equation. A pre-Internet hypothetical example will be illustrative here. Imagine you are a citizen of country A. Through the media you have become aware that Country B has committed some action you consider so immoral and reprehensible that you feel that you cannot conscientiously stand by without participating in some sort of act of protest. You proceed to write a personal letter to the president of country B, explaining to this nation's leader that this kind of conduct is unacceptable and should cease; you post the letter. Realistically, what are the chances your letter will actually have an effect? Essentially, nil.

You could escalate your behavior by traveling to the embassy of country B in the nearby metro area and join other citizens in a demonstration, protesting outside the embassy. Again, the probability that this civil protest changes the policies of country B is near zero, and the likely cost to you is arrest and detention by the civil authorities. Not a very satisfactory cost-to-benefit ratio here, either.

Escalating this example a bit further, you might decide you need to do something more drastic and effective. You withdraw your life savings, travel to country B, procure the raw materials to make a bomb, and target a government building. Here, the personal cost is likely to be very high. If you are fortunate, you may only be arrested, tried, and convicted to a long prison term before you even have the opportunity to act. You are also more likely to either be killed by country B's security or law enforcement services or meet your end in the actual explosion itself. Even if the attempt is successful and you manage to escape capture, the severe effects of the event are likely to be localized to a small geographic area. While the national focus via the media may be upon the affected local area, the scope of the actual physical damage remains very limited and the rest of country B remains essentially functionally intact and undamaged.

The above example illustrates how an individual, acting alone in the days prior to the Internet, was going to have a very difficult time on his/her own initiating an act of destruction upon a nation state having serious physical effects across a larger geographical area and having broad-based national consequences. Typically, acts of destruction having a more broad-based effect on a nation state require the training, coordination, and collaboration of groups of ideologically-driven individuals to carry out attacks against significant components of a nation state. These attacks are often planned out months or years in advance by a separate, smaller group of ideological and expertise-based leaders. These destructive events are most typically labeled "terrorist acts" and the plotters as well as the execution-level individuals are labeled "terrorists." What drives individuals to terrorist acts is a question of some importance, and there are efforts underway to provide a more complex, better understanding of the motivations involved (for example, see Hudson, 1999).

The disquieting fact now is that there is a convergence of significant changes in terms of the number of people today who have access to the Internet, changes in the fundamental aspects of the relationship between digital technology and the individual, and the wholesale deployment of digital technology into national critical infrastructures. What we will see in the discussion that follows is that the intersection of these phenomena is deeply concerning from an IT security and more national security standpoint.

Much of the nation's critical infrastructure--from electrical generation grids and water supply distribution to production of key materials such as gasoline and oil--is controlled by Supervisory Control and Data Acquisition (SCADA) systems that, in turn, often communicate via data communication lines that are either public or private but often modestly hardened or defended. Historically, these SCADA systems have been developed more with the objectives of reliability and cost effectiveness in mind rather than security, and until very recently, issues of security were still secondary considerations for most of the devices and software comprising these systems.

Until recently, there was little public attention paid to this potentially serious vulnerability. However, one example of a public "wake up call" for this threat was an experimental attempt to damage or destroy a commercial power generator conducted by a U.S. National Laboratory. While there was skepticism among many experts about the probabilities of a successful attack resulting in serious or disabling damage to the commercial generator, the result of the experiment was that the "red team" was, in fact, able to essentially destroy the generator without any physical access to it at all! The only access they needed was to be able to connect and communicate with the generator through a computer network. What heightened the seriousness of this threat was that the results of the test were supposed to have been kept secret, but somehow information managed to leak out and eventually reported in the press (Meserve, 2007).

The expansion of access to the Internet across the globe means that there is now a much higher probability that the command and control systems supervising a nation's critical infrastructures may be exposed to unauthorized access by individuals anywhere in the world where there is an Internet point of presence. Often the critical system itself need not be directly connected to the Internet; cyber attackers, many times, will conduct extensive reconnaissance of secondary systems connected to the actual target to find a secondary, "back door" method of entering, eventually compromising the targeted computer network. For example, hackers may attack and compromise a utility company's accounting or dispatch system, and then use the trust privileges of that system to gain "trusted" access to more critical computer systems within the utility company's network, such as a SCADA system.

As for the second component of this convergence--the potential change in the relationship between technology and the individual--let's now return to our discussion of conflict between the individual and the state. Remember that part of the pre-Internet analysis revealed that the personal cost-to-benefit ratio of an attack on a nation state was particularly high. In addition, the previous discussion demonstrated how it was highly unlikely that a single individual acting alone would be able to successfully deploy an attack having broad-based serious consequences beyond a small geographic area. Both of these elements have now changed significantly.

The presence of critical infrastructure control communications exposed directly on the public Internet, or the ability to reach SCADA systems controlling critical infrastructure elements through secondary and tertiary computer networks that are connected to the Internet, provides the opportunity for a single malicious individual to hack his/her way into critical systems from anywhere in the world where there is an Internet point of presence. This reality means that the scope of potential damage a single individual may inflict on a nation state is now significantly wider and significantly more serious. A single individual may no longer be limited to causing damage only within a small geographic or logistical area but may be able to affect large areas and significant portions of the population of a nation state.

In addition, the single, malicious individual is much less likely to be caught, because he/she does not need to be in close physical proximity to the target, thus lowering the expected personal cost of apprehension. The ability to act remotely from great distances also means that the risks of physical harm are also virtually eliminated. Also, a virtual attacker has the advantage of being able to hide behind a daisy chain of numerous compromised computers across the world, making it significantly more difficult to trace the origins of the attack. The personal cost of the act is further reduced, in that it is not necessary to own sophisticated computer equipment or expensive high speed access to the Internet; the simple combination of an old discarded computer and a primitive Internet dial-up account may be all that is needed. Finally, because it is now possible for a lone individual to initiate an effective wide-scale attack, the risk of exposure and apprehension due to the need to assemble a group of individuals--any one of whom might be a weak link in the security environment of the group--is now gone as well.

What this all means is that suddenly the personal cost-to-benefit ratio of an attack by a single, malicious individual has decreased exponentially. The result is that *possibly for the first time in history, a lone individual has the capability to* ***effectively*** *attack a nation state with minimal personal risk.* This is the key point of this scenario. The consequences of this change in the relationship between the individual and the state cannot be overestimated! It threatens to change a great deal of the power relationship between the individual and the state existing historically for a very long time.

This threat has not gone unnoticed by various nation states. In the past three or so years, there has been a quiet, urgent, and effective effort in much of the modernized world to "harden" and secure SCADA systems to control national critical infrastructures against cyber attacks. In addition, there has been a concerted effort on the part of the U.S. government to remove information from the Internet that might give malicious groups or individuals information or intelligence to assist them in an infrastructure attack.

Compare this current situation with one just five years ago, when the chapter author was challenged on the spot to come up with information useful to a cyber attack on the nation's electrical grid. Using a laptop computer and a simple public connection to the Internet, in just five minutes, the author was able to come up with an official government list of every publicly owned utility generator in the United States providing power to the U.S. electric grid, its physical location, make, model, generating capacity, and serial number. Given an additional ten minutes, the author was able to produce a report detailing for a Rocky Mountain public utility each of the critical components of its regional power grid and connections to other regional electrical grids, along with a comprehensive evaluation of the effects of the failure of each of the key components of the regional grid.

In summary, this scenario presents a clear and present serious threat to the safety and security of citizens of nations all over the world. It is likely only a matter of time before this kind of attack is attempted, and while the first attempts may not be successful, with experience and practice, a successful attack is a non-trivial possibility. Hopefully, the appropriate government agencies will continue to act quickly to reduce the likelihood of an attack of this nature.

CONCLUSION

This chapter has endeavored to meet three objectives. First, it has introduced the idea there is both theoretical and practical value in understanding the motivations of malicious actors in the digital environment. Whether viewed from a more traditional psychological point of view, a moral choice/personality trait viewpoint, or from a more social-psychological perspective, understanding the reasons and motivations prompting online actors to commit malicious acts is a key component in contributing to the objective of being able to predict the future path of cybercrime and cyber terrorism.

Second, a comparative analysis of the components of the social structure of the hacking community was presented at two points in time. Decomposing the social structure of a social group or community is normally a difficult task, and it is especially thorny when the community is not amenable to surveillance or data collection due to threats to its existence from outside entities, such as law enforcement and intelligence organizations. Also unusual and especially valuable is the fact that in this case the decomposition of a social structure had some empirical evidence to help support its claims. This analysis identified a number of key dimensions that comprise the social structure of the hacking community. Identifying these elements can provide the researcher with a significantly better understanding of the origins of attitudes, behaviors, values, and norms present in the hacking subculture, as well how this structure may be changing. This process, in turn, may assist researchers in evaluating potential shifts in the levels or nature of future cybercrime trends.

Third, two hypothetical future scenarios were presented. The first scenario involved a new form of cybercrime, where emerging virtual criminal enterprises utilize the Internet to identity victims and minimize their risk of apprehension or physical harm by forming loosely- coupled relationships with more traditional criminal gangs. The second scenario explored a cyber terrorism situation where, for the first time in history, a single individual could effectively attack a nation state with minimal personal risk.

Finally, it was the objective of this chapter to engage social scientists, computer scientists, and IT security specialists in a more productive exchange of theories, ideas, and strategies giving them a better understanding of the nature of cybercrime and cyber terrorism. Through a better understanding of the motivations, social structure, and threat scenarios relevant to the issues at hand, it is hoped that national policies and resources will be better directed to prevent the spread and severity of these types of events.

REFERENCES

Chisea, R., Ciappi, S., & Ducci, S. (2008). *Profiling hackers: The science of criminal profiling as applied to the world of hacking. now Your Enemy*. Danvers, MA: Auerbach Publications. doi:10.1201/9781420086942

Dibbell, J. (2008). *Mutilated furries, flying phalluses: Put the blame on griefers, the sociopaths of the virtual world.* Retrieved December 22, 2009, from http://www.wired.com/gaming/virtualworlds/magazine/16-02/mf_goons

Durkheim, E. (1947). *The division of labor in society*. Glencoe, IL: Free Press. (Original work published 1893)

Garrick., Stetkar, J., & Kilger, M. (2009). Terrorist attack on the national electrical grid. In J. Garrick (Ed.), *Quantifying and controlling catastrophic risks* (pp. 111-177). St. Louis, MO: Academic Press.

Heron, S. (2007). The rise and rise of keyloggers. *Network Security*, *7*, 4–6. doi:10.1016/S1353-4858(07)70052-1

Holt, T. (2007). Subcultural evolution? Examining the influence of on- and -off line experiences on deviant subcultures. *Deviant Behavior*, *28*(2), 171–198. doi:10.1080/01639620601131065

Hudson, R. (1999). *The sociology and psychology of terrorism: Who becomes a terrorist and why?*Washington, D.C: Federal Research Division, Library of Congress.

Jagatic, T., Johnson, N., & Jakobsson, M. (2008). Social phishing. *Communications of the ACM*, *50*(10), 94–100. doi:10.1145/1290958.1290968

Kilger, M., Stutzman, J., & Arkin, O. (2004). Profiling. *The Honeynet Project (2nd Ed.):Know your enemy*. Reading, MA: Addison Wesley Professional.

Meserve, J. (2007). Sources: Staged cyber attack reveals vulnerability in power grid. Retrieved December 22, 2009, from http://www.cnn.com/2007/US/09/26/power.at.risk/index.html

MIT IHTFP Hack Gallery. (1994). *The hacker ethic*. Retrieved from December 22, 2009, from http://hacks.mit.edu/misc/ethics.html

Multiple unknown authors (1994). *The Jargon File, version 3.1.0*. Retrieved December 22, 2009, from http://jargon-file.org/archive/

Multiple unknown authors (2003). *The Jargon File, version 4.4.7*. Retrieved December 22, 2009, from http://www.catb.org/~esr/jargon/html/index.html

Provos, N. McNamee, D., Mavrommatis, P., Wang, K., & Modadugu, N. (2007). *The ghost in the browser: Analysis of web-based malware*. USENIX Workshop on Hot Topics in Understanding Botnets, April 2007.

Raymond, E. (1996). *The new hackers dictionary*. Cambridge, MA: MIT Press.

Rogers, M. (2003). *Preliminary findings: Understanding criminal computer behavior: A Personality trait and moral Choice Analysis*. Retrieved December 22, 2009, from http://homes.cerias.purdue.edu/~mkr/

Shaw, E., Ruby, K., & Post, J. (1998). *The insider threat to insider information systems*. Retrieved December 22, 2009, from http://www.rand.org/pubs/conf_proceedings/CF163/CF163.appe.pdf

Tzu, S. (2002). *The Art of War: Sun Tzu's Classic: In plain English. With Sun Pin's The Art of Warfare*. San Jose, CA: Writer's Club Press.

Watson, D., Holz, T., & Mueller, S. (2005). Know your enemy: Phishing. Retrieved December 22, 2009, from http://www.honeynet.org/papers/phishing

Wu, X. (2007). *Chinese cyber nationalism: Evolution, characteristics and implications*. Lanham, MD: Lexington Books.

ENDNOTES

1 These motivations form the acronym MEEC-ES, an intentional play on words originating

from the acronym MICE, which historically has been used in the counterintelligence field to stand for money, ideology, compromise and ego – motivations typically associated with betraying one's country.

2 See Appendix A for descriptions of the original 18 thematic categories uncovered in the original content analysis of the Jargon File.

3 For the curious reader, a short but useful discussion of how magic and religion form an important part of the social structure of the hacker community, see Kilger et al (2004).

APPENDIX A

The following thematic categories emerged in the original analysis of the Jargon File (Kilger et al, 2004). Each of the categories below has a brief description and illustrative example.

- **Technical.** Having to do directly with some technical aspect of computer hardware, software, algorithm, or process. Example: *kamikaze packet,* a network packet where every option is set.
- **Derogatory.** A word or phrase used in a derogatory fashion toward a person or object. Example: *bagbiter,* software, hardware, or a programmer that has failed to perform to standards.
- **History.** A word or phrase referring to a specific event, person, or object in the past deemed to be of sufficient significance that the typical hacker would have some generalized knowledge about it. Example: *The Great Renaming,* the day in 1985 when a large number of newsgroups on USENET had their names changed for technical reasons.
- **Status.** A word or phrase used to note the status of or esteem with which a person, event, or object is viewed by others in the hacker community. Example: *net.god,* a person who has been using computer networks (USENET, etc.) for quite some time or personally knows one or more individuals of high status within the hacker and computer community. The term also traditionally implies expert technical skills.
- **Magic/Religion.** A word or phrase explicitly referring to magic or some individual, object, or event with paranormal powers or characteristics. It can also be a word or phrase implicitly or explicitly describing events that cannot normally be explained. Example: *incantation,* some obscure command or procedure that does not make sense but corrects some software or hardware problem.
- **Self-Reference.** There are two instances where this category applies. In the first instance, the word or phrase refers to a characteristic of a computer a person ascribes to themselves or another person. The second instance refers to the anthropomorphic practice of assigning human traits to computers. Example: *pop,* which refers both to an operation that removes the top of the stack of a computer register or to someone in a discussion suggesting that the level of detail of the conversation is too deep and should return to a more general level.
- **Popular Reference.** The use of popular culture concepts or characters in describing something in the social world of the computer hacker. Example: *Dr. Mbogo,* a professional person whom you would not want to consult about a problem. Taken from the original Addams Family television show, Dr. Mbogo was the family's physician who was portrayed as a witch doctor.
- **Social Control.** Words or phrases directly used in a social control process. Example: *flame,* an email message that holds its recipient up to ridicule.
- **Humor.** Words or phrases that are direct attempts at humor are put into this thematic category. Example: *Helen Keller mode,* a computer that is not responding to input and not producing any output.
- **Aesthetic.** An object, event, or process thought to have elegant qualities. Example: *indent style,* the practice of using a set of rules to make a computer program more readable.
- **Communication.** The use of computer terms in actual speech between two or more individuals. Example: *ACK,* a data communications term meaning that one computer acknowledges the communication of another computer. Also used by individuals in the hacker community in conversation to acknowledge a statement made by another.

- **Symbol.** Any symbol having meaning beyond its strict technical interpretation. Example: *bang,* the exclamation point symbol (!) that is used in email addresses and in computer languages.
- **Measure.** Any word or phrase denoting a certain level or unit of measure. Example: *byte,* a unit of memory consisting of 8 bits.
- **Social Function.** The deliberate use of a word or phrase by a hacker to describe some aspect of social interaction. Example: *lurker,* an individual who reads a newsgroup regularly but rarely or never contributes to it.
- **Metasyntatic Variable.** A letter or word standing for some variable quantity or characteristic. Example: "If we had done *x,* nothing bad would have happened," referring to the idea that if they had performed some specific yet unnamed action, then the unwanted event would not have happened.
- **Recreation.** Words or phrases referring to play or leisure activities. Example: *Hunt the wumpas,* a very early computer game played by hackers.
- **Book Reference.** A word or phrase referring to some specific book. Example: *Orange Book,* a U.S. government publication detailing computer security standards.
- **Art.** Words or phrases directly referring to some artistic element or object. Example: *twirling baton,* an animated graphic often found in early emails.

Chapter 12
The 2009 Rotman-TELUS Joint Study on IT Security Best Practices:
Compared to the United States, How Well is the Canadian Industry Doing?

Walid Hejazi
University of Toronto, Rotman School of Business, Canada

Alan Lefort
TELUS Security Labs, Canada

Rafael Etges
TELUS Security Labs, Canada

Ben Sapiro
TELUS Security Labs, Canada

ABSTRACT

This chapter describes the 2009 study findings in a series of annual studies that the Rotman School of Management at the University of Toronto in Ontario and TELUS, one of Canada's major Telecommunications companies, are committed to undertake to develop a better understanding of the state of IT Security in Canada and its relevance to other jurisdictions, including the United States. This 2009 study was based on a pre-test involving nine focus groups conducted across Canada with over 50 participants. As a result of sound marketing of the 2009 survey and the critical need for these study results, the authors focus on how 500 Canadian organizations with over 100 employees are faring in effectively coping with network breaches. In 2009, as in their 2008 study version, the research team found that organizations maintain that they have an ongoing commitment to IT Security Best Practices. However, with the 2009 financial crisis in North America and elsewhere, the threat appears to be amplified, both from outside the organization and from within. Study implications regarding the USA PATRIOT Act are discussed at the end of this chapter.

DOI: 10.4018/978-1-61692-805-6.ch012

INTRODUCTION

2008-2009: A Challenge for IT Security in Canada

In 2008, TELUS and the University of Toronto's Rotman School of Management jointly developed a study to provide clarity on the state of IT Security in Canada. Responses from 300 IT and security professionals allowed the study team to understand for the first time how Canada differs from the U.S. in terms of system vulnerability threats and how prepared Canada is to deal with those threats, in terms of people, process, and technology. The 2008 study was also meant to serve as an important data base that could be coordinated with study findings in other jurisdictions, such as in the U.S., where the annual Computer Security Institute's computer crime survey and findings are reported (CSI, 2008).

As a result of the authors' 2008 study undertaking in the Canadian domain, they discovered some key Best Practices of the top industry performers in terms of IT Security. These practices included a stronger focus on communication and risk management, a greater focus on protecting applications, and a commitment to optimizing budgets to reduce risks and to maintain business continuity when network breaches occur.

After concluding their 2008 study, the study team set a 2009 goal to validate and expand on their many useful findings, which they shared with colleagues in the IT Security sector. However, in late 2008, the Canadian economy experienced a serious crisis, with adverse impacts felt across all business sectors. The magnitude of that downturn forced the research team to rethink their approach to the 2009 study.

Before we get into the approach that we finally settled on, we first look at the 2009 U.S.-based Computer Security Institute key survey findings. We then ask the Question of, Given the annual Computer Security Institute (CSI) computer crime and security survey, Why undertake a separate Canadian study?

The U.S. Computer Security Institute (CSI) 2009 Key Study Findings

As noted, the CSI Computer Crime and Security Survey (CSI, 2009) is part of an annual undertaking describing what kinds of attacks U.S. IT Security respondents' organizations experienced over the previous 12 months, and how much these security incidents cost those organizations. The annual survey includes information about targeted attacks, incident response, and the impacts of both malicious and non-malicious insiders' exploits. It also contains details about how respondents' IT Security programs (including budgeting, policies, and tools) were implemented, respondents' satisfaction with their organizations' tools and budgets, and the effects of compliance with legal and "Best Practices" requirements.

During the tumultuous financial environment of 2009, some of the key findings of the 2009 CSI annual survey included the following (CSI, 2009):

- The IT Security respondents reported big jumps in the incidence of password sniffing, financial fraud, and malware infections.
- The average losses due to security incidents in 2009 were down from those in 2008—from $289,000 per respondent in 2008 to $234,244 per respondent in 2009.
- This decrease in cost was generally perceived by respondents to be a serious commitment by their organizations to maintaining industry "Best Practices" in terms of IT Security compliance.
- Generally, the survey respondents were satisfied but not overjoyed with the security techniques employed by their organizations.
- When asked what actions were taken following a security breach, 22% of the re-

spondents said that they notified individuals whose personal information was breached, and they provided new and improved services to users.

Why the Need for a Canadian IT Security Study?

Given these CSI findings for 2009, why undertake a separate Canadian study, such as the one described in this chapter? While there are other U.S. surveys considering the state of IT security (such as the *McAfee 2009Threat Predictions* and *McAfee Virtual Criminology Report: Cybercrime Versus Cyberlaw*), not one was focused exclusively on Canada. Following the Canadian study team's interactions with senior IT executives in 2007 and early 2008, it was clear to us that many industry and government leaders felt that existing studies were not accurately portraying the Canadian situation. Moreover, many felt that IT security strategies in Canada may differ from those in the U.S. because of the structural differences in the Canadian economy.

These differences in the environmental and legal contexts were noted between the United States and Canada:

- The US has a private healthcare system; Canada has a publicly-funded one.
- The US financial system is thousands of banks with fierce regulation and oversight; Canada has six large banks dominating the banking industry and operating under government charter.
- There are cultural differences in Canada with regard to government and the role that it should play as compared to the US.

Given these obvious differences—and more not mentioned here, the study team felt that Canadian attitudes toward IT Security and the approaches to managing security risk needed to be understood. For these reasons, we felt that a dedicated study focusing on Canadian inputs and issues was needed. With this mandate in mind, TELUS Security Labs and the Rotman School of Management at the University of Toronto began a joint-study in early 2008, with the expressed purpose of examining the state of IT security in Canada. The 2008 study sought to enhance the understanding of IT security from many dimensions, including, but not necessarily limited to vulnerabilities, preparedness, budgets, satisfaction, compliance, and "Best Practices."

The 2008 study was also unique in that it sought to understand the broader business context of IT Security. By focusing on how people, process, and technology interact to yield superior results, we discovered some key Best Practices of top performers. These practices included: (i) a stronger focus on communication and risk management, (ii) a greater focus on protecting applications, and (iii) a greater focus on how to optimize budgets.

Furthermore, the 2008 Rotman-TELUS Joint Study on IT Security Practices provided clarity on the state of IT Security in Canada and the dimensions in which Canada differed from the US. Equally as important, the study findings of the 2008 study actually led to many new Question s that needed answering—such as Question s involving the security of information systems and business applications; and newly emerging Question s about cloud computing, breaches, and countermeasures.

Upon concluding the 2008 study, the study team set a 2009 goal to validate and expand on our many findings, but something happened to change our focus. In late 2008, the economy experienced a serious crisis with lasting effects across all business sectors. The magnitude of the downturn forced us to rethink our approach to the 2009 study, for the financial crisis posed new Question s of its own. What would happen to budgets, staffing, outsourcing, technologies and initiatives? Could changes in these areas affect how well organizations could prevent and respond to threats and vulnerabilities?

THE 2009 ROTMAN-TELUS IT SECURITY STUDY APPROACH AND THIS CHAPTER'S FOCUS

Focus Group Study Phase and Discoveries

To ensure that our 2009 IT Security survey would bring to light the major effects of the financial crisis, we held eight focus groups across the country with over 50 security executives and practitioners. Their insight not only helped to shape our survey but gave us a much-needed context to interpret the 2009 results.

After our focus groups, we no longer wondered whether or not we would observe changes in security year-Over-year. That was a given. Rather, we focused our study on a better understanding of where the changes were occurring, and what impact those changes would have on Canadian government and organizations.

As it turns out, according to the focus group study phase, respondents said that the impacts were significant. Although organizations generally maintained their commitment to security, the crisis had amplified the threat, noted respondents both from the outside the enterprise and from within. As a result, the gap between "threat" and "preparedness" had grown significantly—in just one year.

Chapter's Focus

The balance of this chapter describes the purpose of the 2009 study, the types of enhancements the Canadian study team made to the study survey from 2008, the 59 items that appeared in the final 2009 survey, the respondents who participated in the study, and the respondents' reactions to these survey items. The chapter closes with concluding remarks on prevailing themes and makes comparisons to U.S. study findings and the USA Patriot Act.

Study Purpose

Collecting, storing, and processing information is an increasingly important activity for businesses, governments, and non-profit organizations. Therefore, securing that information is critical to the success of such enterprises. Real or perceived vulnerabilities in an IT Security system can undermine user confidence, discouraging clients from using the services of that organization or government agency. Conversely, an organization or government agency can leverage well-structured, effective, and secure IT systems as a competitive advantage in the marketplace, whether it be in the private or public sector. This 2009 IT Security Study, like its 2008 version, sought to understand how Canadian organizations and government agencies can secure their IT systems, thus enabling these safer and secure systems to provide a competitive advantage.

The 2009 Survey Items and Key Study Objectives

The 2009 study survey included 59 items, designed to examine the state of IT Security in Canada. As in the 2008 study version, the survey items included a number of primary dimensions for study, including perceived vulnerabilities, preparedness, budgets, satisfaction, compliance, and "Best Practices." Given the 2009 financial crisis, new Question s in our 2009 approach were considered, such as: What would happen to IT Security budgets, staffing, outsourcing, technologies, and initiatives? Could changes in these areas affect how well organizations and government agencies could prevent and respond to threats and vulnerabilities?

In short, the 2009 survey was enhanced to include items regarding how the current financial crisis affected the state of IT Security in Canada. It was our hope that the result of this study's findings would allow Canadian and other countries' IT Security executives and practitioners to better understand existing and coming IT Security trends and to be better able to formulate improved and Best Practices that would improve safety and security postures. All 59 items included in the 2009 study survey are presented in Appendix A of this chapter.

The 2009 Study Approach to Engage More Study Participants

Though the 2008 study analyzed the responses from 300 respondents in Canada across different geographies, industries and organization types, in 2009, the study team intensified our efforts so that we could increase the number of respondents and, thereby, improve the representation across Canada and from across several verticals. These efforts included the following:

- We hosted cross-country roundtable discussions with IT Security officers in Vancouver, Edmonton, Calgary, Toronto, Ottawa, and Montreal. These discussions were both specific to certain regions and to certain industry sectors, such as government, finance, energy, and utilities. These discussions were attended by representatives from all organizational levels, from security analysts and technical experts to senior vice-presidents and compliance officers.
- We presented extensively at IT Security conferences across Canada and collected feedback from attendees. We encouraged participation in our 2009 survey.
- We focused our resources on increasing general awareness so that potential respondents would understand the value of becoming more involved and sharing their honest perspectives with others in the IT Security field.
- To promote participation from all regions of Canada, we administered the survey and all communications in Canada's two official languages: English and French.

The 2009 Study Respondents

The study team's efforts to increase participation from relevant sectors appeared to pay off, as there was a 60% increase in responses from 2008, providing the study team with access to the views of 500 Canadian organization and government agencies having 100 employees or more.

The respondent profile was as follows:

- *Organization Type*: Government organizations were the most highly represented, with 35% of the respondent sample coming from this segment, followed by publicly traded companies at 31%. Private companies represented 27% of the sample, and not-for-profit organizations represented 6%.
- *Geography*. In all, 55% of the respondents were from Ontario, 16% were from Alberta, 12% were from Quebec, and 10% were from British Columbia. The aggregation of all other regions in Canada and organizations represented 7% of the sample.
- *Global Headquarters Location*: The majority—83% of the respondents—had their headquarters in Canada, 11% had headquarters in the United States, 4% had headquarters in Europe (including the United Kingdom), and the remaining 3% had headquarters in Asia and elsewhere.
- *Operational Reach*: When asked where the organization does significant business (with the option to mark more than one region), the bulk of respondents—96%--marked Canada. The balance was as follows: 41% marked the United States, 24% marked Europe, 13%, marked Japan, 19% marked Asia (excluding Japan), 14% marked Latin America, and 10% marked"other regions."
- *Annual Revenue Size or Budget Size for Government Organizations*: Organizations with less than $1 million Canadian dollars revenue size accounted for 1% of the

sample. Another 10% of the organizations had a revenue/budget of up to $24M, 11% had a revenue/budget between $25M and $99M, 14% had a revenue/budget between $100M and $499M, 8% had a revenue/budget between $500M and C$999M, 10% had a revenue/budget between $1B and $1.99B, 13% had a revenue/budget between $2B and $10B, and another 13% had a revenue/budget higher than $10B.
- *Number of employees*: Organizations with less than 100 employees represented 31% of the 2009 study respondents, 16% of the respondents had between 100 and 500 full-time staff, 7% of the respondents had between 500 and 999 full-time staff, 18% of the respondents had between 1,000 and 4,999 full-time staff, 6% of the respondents had between 5,000 and 9,999 full-time staff, 8% of the respondents had between 10,000 and 19,000 full-time staff, 6% of the respondents had between 20,000 and 49,999 full-time staff, and 9% of the respondents had more than 50,000 full-time staff.

It is important to note that though organizations with fewer than 100 employees participated in the 2009 survey, their responses were not included in some of the breakdown examinations. This separation was necessary to allow the analysis to be consistent with the 2008 study approach in order to capture year-Over-year trends. Moreover, small organizations have significantly different behavior patterns regarding IT Security approaches, as compared to medium- and large- organizations, sometimes adding elements of randomness to the analysis. The investigation of smaller organizations' security practices, therefore, will receive a separate, dedicated treatment in another report.

In short, the study team felt that this year's sample size of 500 organizationswas comparable with most North American and global surveys produced in the field of IT Security and IT risk management. To contextualize, we must consider the overall size of the Canadian economy against other countries. Canada's economy is approximately one-tenth the size of the US economy, and Canada is the smallest member of the G7 group. When we looked further at the number of 2009 survey respondents, we felt that the relative representation of Canadian IT and Security professionals was quite high. A strong willingness to cooperate in the study objectives was reflected in the high level of participation and discussions held with security officers in earlier focus groups and roundtable discussions across Canada.

Furthermore, the study team felt that there was good representation from IT Security Professionals across Canada. Professionals from all provinces and territories, except Prince Edward Island and the Northwest Territories, participated in the 2009 study. Also, representatives from 21 industry types, including the federal, provincial and municipal government levels were included. The study team concluded, therefore, that the diversity in the respondent population would allow us to understand how IT Security differed, tactically and strategically, by region, by experience level, and by industry.

The study team was also pleased with the range of respondent positions—with good representation from CEOs (9%) to Security Analysts (19%) or System Administrators (12%). About one-fifth, or 20% of the respondents, identified themselves as being a Director or higher position. The majority of respondents—59%—reported being a manager or individual contractor.

THE 2009 STUDY FINDING THEMES

This section details the key 2009 study themes, with details given in corresponding tables. The respondents' breakdown in responses for all 59 survey items is found in Appendix A.

Theme #1: 2009 Breaches Are Up Significantly, as are Annual Costs; Single-breach Costs Are Down

Breach measures are important because they reflect the hardest, most-impacting indicators telling how well an organization's IT Security program is performing. For 2009, we focused on three measures: (i) the number of breaches, (ii) the annual loss due to breaches, and (iii) individual breach costs.

For 2009, the study findings indicate that respondents reported a much higher number of breaches as compared to 2008, offset partially by lower costs per breach, resulting in higher annual costs. Specifically, annual losses from breaches increased to $834,149 per organization, up from $423,469 per organization in 2008. This finding increased most for government and private companies and increased minimally at publicly-held companies. See Table 1.

The average number of annual breaches reported increased to 11.3 per year, up from 3 per year in 2008. The government led in this category, while publicly-held organizations increased the least. See Table 2.

The cost per breach decreased across all types of organizations. For example, publicly- traded organizations reported a decreased breach cost of $75,014 in 2009, down from $213, 926 reported in 2008. See Table 3.

While the increase in reported breaches is significant, there is some good news. While threats are up, the rise is partially due to organizations having improved their capabilities to detect unknown IT Security events. Organizations are also improving their response to breaches, with an overall effect of lowering individual breach costs.

Table 1. Annual loss from breaches by organizational type

Organization Type	2009	2008
Private Company	$807,310	$293,750
Publicly Traded Company	$675,132	$637,500
Government	$1,004,799	$321,429

Table 2. Estimated number of annual breaches

Organization Type	2009	2008
Private Company	11.7	3.1
Publicly Traded Company	9.0	3.0
Government	13.4	3.5

Table 3. Estimated cost per breach

Organization Type	2009	2008
Private Company	$69,103	$94,758
Publicly Traded Company	$75,017	$213,926
Government	$74,985	$92,364

Table 4. Comparison of security breaches in Canada and in the U.S.

Breach Type	RT 2009 (CAN)	2008 CSI (U.S.)
Denial of service	16%	21%
Financial fraud	14%	12%
Web-site defacement	6%	6%
Theft of IP	7%	9%
Sabotage	3%	2%
Virus / malware	70%	50%
Abuse by employees / insiders	36%	44%
Abuse of wireless networks	15%	14%
Misuse of application	13%	11%
Bots	15%	20%
Password Sniffing	5%	9%

Theme #2: Canada Is Catching Up to the United States in Terms of Breaches

In 2008, the study team noted that Canada had caught up with the United States in terms of IT Security investment, driven by requirements to comply with Canadian regulations such as PCI (Payment Card Industry Data Security Standards; see Cloakware, 2009) and PIPEDA (Personal Information Privacy and Electronic Documents Act Compliance; see nCircle, 2009).

In 2009, Canada caught up to the United States in a less-than-desirable category. We compared our 2009 breach statistics with those from the United State's Computer Security Institute's (CSI) annual computer crime survey (2008). Our comparison showed that across most categories, Canadians reported the U.S.-equivalent or higher numbers in terms of breaches—with breaches caused by viruses and malware exceeding those reported in the United States. See Table 4.

Other examples where Canada's breach record was worse than that for the United States were as follows:

- Financial fraud (Canada 14% vs. U.S. 12%)
- Sabotage (Canada 3% vs. U.S. 2%)
- Virus /malware (Canada 70% vs. U.S. 50%)
- Wireless abuse (Canada 15% vs. U.S. 14%)
- Misuse of applications (Canada13% vs. U.S. 11%)

Theme #3: Most breaches Are Up--Led by Unauthorized Access by Employees

In 2009, the number of breaches in Canada increased in 12 of the 17 categories surveyed and decreased in three of the categories. See Table 5.

Furthermore, the five fastest-rising breach categories in Canada were as follows:

1. Unauthorized access to information by employees (up by 112%)
2. "Bots" within an organization (up by 88%)
3. Financial fraud (up by 88%)
4. Theft of proprietary information (up by 75%)
5. Laptop or mobile-device theft (up by 58%)

The five breach categories remaining constant in Canada or declining since 2008 were as follows:

1. Password sniffing (down by 17%)

Table 5. 2009 vs. 2008 Trend analysis on reported breaches

Type of Breach	2009	2008	% change
Virus/worms/spyware/malware/spam	70%	62%	13%
Laptop or mobile hardware device theft	53%	34%	56%
Financial fraud	14%	8%	75%
Bots (zombies) within the organization	15%	8%	88%
Phishing/pharming where your organization was fraudulently described as the sender	23%	27%	-15%
Denial of service attack	16%	17%	-6%
Sabotage of data or networks	3%	3%	0%
Unauthorized access to information by employees	36%	17%	112%
Extortion or blackmail (ransomware)	3%	2%	50%
Web-site defacement	6%	4%	50%
Loss of confidential customer/employee data	10%	8%	25%
Abuse of wireless network	15%	11%	36%
Password sniffing	5%	6%	-17%
Misuse of a corporate application	13%	10%	30%
Theft of proprietary information	7%	4%	75%
Identity theft	7%	6%	17%
Exploitation of your domain name server (DNS)	2%	2%	0%

2. Phishing and pharming (down by 15%)
3. Denial of Service attacks (down by 6%)
4. Sabotage of networks (no increase)
5. Exploiting DNS (no increase)

Theme #4: Insider Breaches Almost Doubled in 2009--Now Comparable to U.S. Rates

In 2008, Canadians respondents reported that about 17% of breaches were related to insider activity, while the U.S. statistic was about 60%. In 2009, this number increased to 36% in Canada and decreased to 44% in the U.S., based on the latest CSI survey.

Theme #5: Disclosure or Loss of Customer Data Remains Top Issue

To understand what drives Canadian IT Security programs and spending, we asked respondents to rank 10 prevailing IT Security issues. Their top five concerns for 2009 were as follows:

- Disclosure or loss of confidential data
- Compliance with Canadian regulations and legislation
- Business continuity and disaster recovery
- Loss of strategic corporate information
- Employee understanding and compliance with security policies.

Theme #6: Organizations Cite Damage to Brand as Biggest Breach Concern

Canadian organizations continue to report damage to brand as the most significant impact of a system breach. Organizational respondents cited the following as their top five *costs* associated with breaches:

1. Damage to brand or reputation
2. Lost time due to disruption
3. Lost customers
4. Regulatory actions
5. Litigation.

Theme #7: Growing Threat Has Rendered Most Security Budgets Inadequate

In 2009, the average Canadian security budget was 7% of the overall IT budget. Top-performing respondents said their companies spent at least 10% on IT Security, and several spent 15% or more of their IT budget on security. Spending alone, however, did not guarantee a better posture.

In 2008, we found that a budget of at least 5% correlated with "high satisfaction" in security posture. In 2009, we found that" high satisfaction" with security performance *required at least a 15% investment.* This upward shift is mirrored by a significant increase in number of breaches, suggesting that the effect of IT Security budgets, often planned a year in advance, is highly sensitive to sudden and major changes to the threat environment.

Theme #8: Budgets Were Reduced by 1/10th Due to the Financial Crisis

The financial crisis that began late in 2008 and intensified during 2009 prompted organizations to make several fiscal adjustments. According to the 2009 study respondents, the financial crisis had adversely impacted their IT Security program, mostly in budgets and outsourcing. See Table 6.

We observed that:

- Respondents reported an average IT Security budget decrease of 10%
- 25% of the respondents reported a budget increase in 2009.
- 20% of the respondents reduced their reliance on outsourcers and contractors.
- 75% of the respondents reported no changes to headcount.

Overall, the budgets adjustments were challenging, but not severe. Had it been any other year, affirmed respondents, the impact might have been minor or negligible. *It is important to note that in 2009, the significant surge in the number*

Table 6. Response to the 2009 financial crisis, by organization type

Effect of 2009 Crisis on Security Budgets	Government	Private	Public
Severe Budgetary Cuts: 50% to 100% of the original budget for contracts or projects related to security and privacy was cut.	4%	13%	12%
Major Budgetary Cuts: 25% to 49% of the original budget for contracts or projects related to security and privacy was cut.	6%	11%	15%
Moderate Budgetary Cuts: 10% to 24% of the original budget for contracts or projects related to security and privacy was cut.	15%	21%	23%
Minor Budgetary Cuts: Less than 10% of the original budget for contracts or projects related to security and privacy was cut.	42%	29%	38%
Minor Budgetary Increase: original budget increased by less than 10% for contracts or projects related to security and privacy.	27%	21%	10%
Moderate Budgetary Increase: original budget increased by 10% to 24% for contracts or projects related to security and privacy.	6%	3%	2%
Major Budgetary Increase: original budget increased by 25% to 49% for contracts or projects related to security and privacy.	0%	3%	0%
Average Budgetary Impact	4.6% (Cut)	6.6% (Cut)	10.8% (Cut)

of breaches served to magnify the effects of the budgetary adjustments.

Theme #9: Organizations Rewarding Formal Education More Than Certifications

Notwithstanding the just-cited budgetary adjustments, the Canadian IT Security profession is well compensated. Nearly half (46%) of the 2009 respondents earned more than $100,000 annually, falling into our high-earner category. High earners were most prevalent in IT Security, Communications and Media, Finance and Insurance, and Government. Within the high earners, we found a wide range of salaries. For example, Directors averaged $132,000 nationally, the government sector averaged $118,000 nationally, and the Finance, IT, and Communications averaged close to $160,000 nationally.

For high earners, formal education paid more than IT Security certifications and experience, alone. Similar to our 2008 study results, high earners were much more likely to have a university degree, and twice as likely to have a business degree. IT Security professional designations like the CISA and CISM still appear to command a modest premium but much less so than a business degree.

Theme #10: The Earnings Gap Between Government and the Private Sector Could Lead to Brain-Drain

In 2008, we observed that the potential for a migration of talent from the Canadian government to the Private Sector was a possibility because of a large compensation gap. This gap was slightly larger in 2009. About 35% of the IT Security professionals working in government earned over $100,000 per year, compared to 47% of those working in private companies and 57% of those employed by publicly-traded companies.

Theme #11: High-performing Security Programs Have Strong Governance and Education

A higher satisfaction with IT Security posture continues to be driven by a greater focus and investment on process. In 2009, education was a new driver for performance. Organizations using educational programs to promote awareness of IT Security risks *were almost twice as likely* to be highly satisfied with their IT security posture.

Other links between governance and high performance included the following:

- The adoption of business-level IT Security metrics increased the perceived value of the IT Security function by 47%.
- Awareness programs for staff and third parties were associated with a 45%-to-55% higher satisfaction with IT Security posture.
- Organizations linking staff evaluations to IT Security goals (i.e., accountability) were twice as likely to be high performers as those not conducting the link.

Theme #12: Regulatory Compliance Regarding Privacy

Regulatory compliance was, by far, the most relevant driver for IT Security budgets, and the implementation of IT Security and risk management programs in Canada. The Canadian landscape was also influenced by the U.S. regulatory framework, but it is still distinct. Canada's approach to Privacy issues is more closely aligned with the Commonwealth countries than to the United State's approach.

For example, Canada' PCI-DSS (Payment Card Industry Data Security Standards) validation requirements and deadlines are handled differently from those in the United States and Europe, and Canada's health care system is governed by very

Table 7. Regulatory priorities in 2008 and 2009 by ownership type

	Government		Private		Public	
	2008	2009	2008	2009	2008	2009
Sarbanes Oxley (US)	4	8	4	6	3	3
Bill 198	6	5	3	5	4	4
Privacy Act	1	1	1	1	1	1
Canadian Bank Act	8	8	6	8	7	7
Personal Information Protection and Electronic Documents Act (PIPEDA)	2	2	2	2	2	2
PCI-DSS	5	3	5	3	5	5
Other Industry Regulations (FFIEC, NERC, FERC, PHIPA, HIPAA)	3	4	7	4	6	6
Breach Notification Laws	7	7	9	7	8	8
Special Information Security Laws	6	6	8	8	9	9

specific requirements for safeguarding Privacy in health records.

The importance of regulations varied by organization type, with a clearly Canadian focus toward Privacy concerns. See Table 7.

Moreover, the awareness of regulatory requirements was not only driven by Canadian Privacy laws, for 83% of the 2009 study respondents indicated that their decision-makers have an adequate, good, or very good understanding of the IT Security requirements for compliance regarding the regulations and legislation affecting their organizations. This trend was stable and consistent with the 2008 study findings. A breakdown of ownership type shows the public companies leading in this regard, with 92% of respondents reporting high levels of understanding and commitment from senior management regarding compliance.

Theme #13: Application Security Practices Are Not Keeping Up With Evolving Threats

In our 2008 study, we found that the top performers invested more in application Security and were much less likely to experience several classes of breaches. In 2009, we focused on how Canadian organizations secure their applications and learned that:

- More than half of the respondents gave some consideration to IT Security in their development lifecycles.
- The focus in Canada is predominantly toward after-the-fact IT Security activities, such as testing, rather than embracing the proactive concept of "Build it Secure."

Table 8. Testing type ranked by contribution to satisfaction

Testing Type	Ranking
Automated Code Review	1
Manual Code Review	2
Manual Penetration Testing	3
Automated Vulnerability Testing	4

Based on the reported increase in application-related breaches, attempts to secure applications, noted the 2009 respondents, are falling behind. Moreover, they affirmed that organizations seem to be focused on testing application Security with certain types of testing—those yielding better results. Respondents further indicated that they were most satisfied with code reviews as a tool for identifying application Security issues. See Table 8.

According to the respondents, this important finding surfaced in the 2009 study: Organizations using *independent testing teams with direct access to management* were the most effective in addressing application Security issues. See Table 9.

Theme #14: On-shore Security Outsourcing Increased

Our 2008 report linked IT Security outsourcing to better satisfaction with IT Security posture. This year, we speculated that the 2009 financial crisis might accelerate a movement to outsourcing, yet it grew marginally. See Table 10.

Still, in 2009, we did observe a few important differences from 2008. For example:

- Slightly more organizations were willing to outsource (62% in 2009, versus 60% in 2008); those who do are outsourcing a greater percentage of their IT Security budget.
- Privacy concerns were driving a policy shift favoring outsourcing IT Security to Canadian service providers.
- Publicly-traded companies were more willing to outsource to "the best-value provider," regardless of location.

Overall, the use of IT Security outsourcing continues to mature in Canada. Respondents were spending more of their IT budgets to procure services such as security testing and perimeter security. As in 2008, organizations outsourcing

Table 9. Testing entity versus experienced breaches

Testing Team	Authority (Access to Senior Management.)	Independence (Degree of Separation from Development)	Likelihood of application-related breaches
Internal Development Team	Lowest	Lowest	49%
Internal Security Team	Low	Low	41%
Internal Audit Team	High	High	19%
External Audit Team	Highest	Highest	14%
External Security Consultant/Contractor	Varies	Varies	35%

Table 10. IT Security outsourcing policy

Does your organization have a policy regarding outsourcing of information security services to a third party?	2008	2009
We do not allow outsourcing of IT Security	40%	38%
We only outsource to Canadian companies	17%	24%
We allow outsourcing of Security to other countries where we do business	12%	6%
We outsource to the best value provider; location is not a major factor in our decision	18%	22%
We only allow outsourcing to countries with laws and regulations that are as stringent as those in Canada	13%	12%

Table 11. Percentage of insider breaches by outsourcing practices

Outsourcing part of Security	% of Insider Breaches
Yes	31%
No	35%

security were *less likely* to report a breach. See Table 11.

Theme #15: Cloud Security Concerns Similar to Classic Outsourcing; It's About Trust

An emerging trend in IT is the use of cloud- or utility-based computing to provide services and infrastructure to the business at an optimized cost. Despite the cost advantages and the clear-cost pressures imposed by the 2009 financial crisis, organizations will not rush to adopt cloud technologies until policy and governance concerns are more fully addressed. The top three concerns with Security services in the cloud were cited by respondents as being the following:

1. Location of the data.
2. Connecting "business-critical systems" to Security mechanisms outside the full control of the business.
3. Technical challenges associated with IT Security in multi-tenant environments.

The 2009 respondents were least concerned about application availability, suggesting that the alternate method of providing service is more accepted in terms of performance. Overall, cloud computing was viewed similarly to outsourcing; that is, similar trust issues must be satisfied prior to adoption.

Theme #16: Technology Investments Focus on Fighting Malware

Our 2009 study surveyed respondents on 23 technologies looking at current adoption, future plans, and satisfaction. One key finding was that in response to the continued threats of viruses, malware, and bots. Organizations seemed to be focusing their resources where breaches were highest: Malware. We observed an increased investment in the following technologies:

- e-mail security (ranked 1st in usage)
- Anti-virus (ranked 2nd in usage)
- Patch management (ranked 4th in usage)
- Content and malware filtering (ranked 5th, up 6 spots from 2008)
- Vulnerability detection and management (ranked 9th, up 7 spots from 2008)

Theme #17: Organizations Favor Protecting Applications Versus Fixing Them

Although malware-related breaches were on the rise in 2009, so were targeted attacks. Unlike 2008, organizations were starting to pay more attention to protecting applications and the proprietary data they hold. In 2009, the use of technologies preventing or deterring application-level attacks had increased. These technologies included the following:

- Two-factor authentication
- Web application firewalls
- Database encryption
- Public Key Infrastructure

Technologies aimed at fixing application flaws were used less often in 2009. Application security assessment tools, in fact, had the third lowest satisfaction level, according to respondents (21st out 23 technologies), likely due to a lack of skill sets and Highly Qualified staffing to remediate applications.

Theme #18: Insider Threats Are Up, Low Satisfaction Is Holding Up Investment

Given the surge in insider breaches, we expected technologies aimed at detecting and preventing internal abuse to be more common in 2009. Not so, according to our 2009 study findings. In some cases, the use of these technologies decreased, while in other cases, the use of these technologies gained marginally.

Several detective technologies seemed to have low satisfaction levels in common. According to our focus group interactions, technologies automating detection but not response can overburden IT Security teams. In 2009, IT Security staffing increases were uncommon, and organizations struggled with deploying more detective technologies. These technologies included the following:

- Data leakage prevention (ranked 23rd in satisfaction)
- Log management (ranked 22nd in satisfaction)
- Security information and event management (ranked 20th in satisfaction)
- Wireless intrusion prevention (ranked 19th in satisfaction)
- Network based access control (ranked 18th in satisfaction)

CONCLUSION

A Summary of the Top Performers' Capabilities to Overcome Difficulties in the Current Economic and High-Risk Environment

With the threat landscape evolving, Canadian organizations were finding it difficult to maintain their IT Security posture in 2009, especially with the financial challenges. In 2009, top performers in the IT industry overcame these difficulties by:

- Managing the complete breach life-cycle, ensuring that improvements in detection and remediation are accompanied by improvements in prevention.
- Developing flexible IT Security programs, with strong core capabilities and the ability to adjust to a rapidly-changing threat environment.
- Increasing focus on education and awareness across IT, development, and employees to ensure that Security risks and responsibilities are understood by all.
- Balancing technology spending with staffing to ensure that lack of resources does not impede deploying and using much-needed technologies to guard against crackers wanting to own the networks and cause harm.

The 2009 findings also reflect emerging concerns among IT Security specialists around the globe, including cloud Security and managing data in the cloud. Study results from other jurisdictions can shed light on additional "Best Practices," given these concerns. Comparing other nation's IT Security "Best Practices," as we did with the U.S. findings regarding the CSI survey, can help diversify present-day and future remedies to combat IT Security risks, thereby minimizing harms caused by crackers—both insiders and outsiders.

Moreover, as we have learned from our 2008 and 2009 study approaches, study teams comprised of IT Security experts, as well as academics from Business and other Social Science disciplines, can offer a much needed multi-dimensional approach to improving the study design and analysis of study findings.

Before closing this chapter, we would like to have a brief discussion regarding the USA PATRIOT Act and the 2009 study findings, for the latter piece of U.S. legislation has profound implications for Privacy in Canada. When an organization outsources any dimension of its IT Security, there is a risk that the information the outsourcing provider has access to will be provided to a third party. This risk has increased dramatically with the passage of the USA PATRIOT Act of 2001, where American companies and their affiliates may be required by the Act to turn this information over to the U.S. Department of Homeland Security. This requirement, in our view, can potentially alter the outsourcing decisions and compliance posture of Canadian organizations, as it can be seen as putting organizations at odds with their obligations under Canadian Privacy laws.

The PATRIOT Act of 2001, also known as the USA PATRIOT Act, was passed in the United States in response to the September 11, 2001, terrorist attacks. The longer title means "Uniting and Strengthening America by Providing Appropriate Tools Required to Intercept and Obstruct Terrorism." The Act's stated intent was to deter and punish terrorist acts in the United States and elsewhere and to enhance law enforcement investigation tools. Though U.S. federal courts have found some provisions of the Act to be unconstitutional--and despite continuing public controversy and concerns from within U.S. borders and outside of them--the law was renewed in March, 2006. (Schell & Martin, 2006)

In our 2009 survey study findings, the respondents noted that a decision was made to focus on the broader topic of geographies having legislation compatible with Canadian requirements. This focus was selected for two main reasons, noted the Canadian respondents: (1) With the growth of cloud computing, Canadian companies have a broader number of options for using external service providers, be they "in-the-cloud" co-location and hosting data centers or in the more traditional ones. (2) The USA PATRIOT Act has not been amended to account for this new reality, remaining the same on the legislative books as when it was first adopted in 2001.

The exploration of cloud computing concerns and outsourcing policies suggests that compatible legislation is prominent, as evidenced by 67% of all Canadian organizations willing to outsource but reporting some concern about the country the outsourcing occurs in. In addition, nearly 40% of the 2009 study respondents reported specific concerns about legislative compatibility (see Q. 29 in Appendix A).

Moreover, according to our earlier 2008 survey data findings, Canadian organizations perceived some degree of risk from the USA PATRIOT Act and USA Homeland Security requirements. Relevant to our 2008 survey findings, about 39% of the total respondent sample answered that the USA PATRIOT Act poses a "serious" or "very serious" concern. Canadian government respondents indicated the most concern with the USA PATRIOT Act, with almost half (47%) indicating at least "serious concern." Publicly-traded companies followed closely behind at 45% of the respondents having strong concern, while privately-held Canadian organizations were much less concerned, with fewer than a third of the respondents indicating significant concerns about the Act.

Combining the 2008 and 2009 Canadian study findings, there clearly is a call for discussions between IT Security professionals in the United States and those in Canada regarding this issue. The concerns of Canadian business with the USA PATRIOT Act--coupled with Canadian policies toward outsourcing—suggest that U.S. data mining centers will in the present and into the future continue to find difficulty attracting and maintaining Canadian customers.

REFERENCES

Cloakware. (2009). *Achieve PCI compliance: Privileged password management*. Retrieved December 22, 2009, from http://www.cloakware.com/cloakware-ds/whitepapers/security-compliance/intro-pci.php

CSI (Computer Security Institute). (2008). *2008 CSI computer crime and security survey*. Retrieved December 23, from https://my.infotex.com/article.php?story=20090206075608135

CSI (Computer Security Institute). (2009). *CSI computer crime and security survey 2009*. Retrieved December 23, 2009, from http://www.gocsi.com/2009survey/;jsessionid=JQ4RMAELQDPWPQE1GHOSKH4ATMY32JVN

nCircle. (2009). *PIPEDA Compliance*. Retrieved December 23, 2009, from http://www.ncircle.com/index.php?s=solution_regcomp_PIPEDA-Compliance&source=adwords&kw=pipeda&gclid=CJHNxLDl7Z4CFVw55QodnTEAKg

Schell, B., & Martin, C. (2006). *Webster's New World Hacker Dictionary*. Indianapolis, IN: Wiley Publishing Company.

APPENDIX A

Survey Questions

Question 1. What is the ownership/legal structure of your organization

Government organization	35%
Not-for-profit organization	6%
Private Company	27%
Publicly Traded Company	31%

Question 2. Which industry does your organization belong to? Pick one only, choose main revenue source if more than one applies.

Information - Publishing, Broadcasting, Communications and IT	14%
Finance and Insurance	14%
Professional, Scientific, and Technical Services	6%
Municipal Government	13%
Educational Services	7%
Other Services (except Public Administration)	5%
Retail Trade	5%
Federal Government	6%
Health Care and Social Assistance	6%
Provincial Government	6%
Manufacturing, Discrete	3%
Transportation and Warehousing	3%
Construction	2%
Mining	3%
Manufacturing, Process	2%
Administrative and Support Services	1%
Agriculture, Forestry, Fishing and Hunting	2%
Utilities	1%
Accommodation and Food Services	1%
Management of Companies and Enterprises	1%
Wholesale Trade, Durable Goods	0%
Arts, Entertainment, and Recreation	0%
Real Estate and Rental and Leasing	1%
Waste Management and Remediation Services	0%

Question 3. What region of Canada are you located in?

Ontario	55%
Alberta	16%
Quebec	12%
British Columbia	10%
USA	2%
Nova Scotia	1%
International	2%
Manitoba	1%
Saskatchewan	1%
New Brunswick	1%
Prince Edward Island	0%
Northwest Territories	0%

Question 4. Where is the global headquarters of your organization located?

Canada	83%
USA	11%
Europe (including UK)	4%
Other	1%
Asia (excluding Japan)	1%
Japan	1%

Question 5. Where does your organization do significant business?

Canada	96%
USA	41%
Europe (including UK)	24%
Japan	13%
Asia (excluding Japan)	19%
Latin America	14%
Other	10%

Question 6. How many employees does your organization have?

1,000-2,499	17%
50,000 or More	16%
2,500-4,999	15%
10,000-19,999	14%
20,000-49,999	11%
5,000-9,999	11%
500-749	8%
750-999	5%
Don't know	3%

Question 7. How large is your organization based on annual revenue for last year? (If government organization, please choose your organization's total budget)

$1 million – $24 million	10%
< $1 million	1%
Don't know	20%
$100 million – $499 million	14%
$2 billion – $10 billion	13%
> $10 billion	13%
$25 million – $99 million	11%
$1 billion – $1.99 billion	10%
$500 million – $999 million	8%

Question 8. What percentage of your employees works away from the office 25% or more of the time and accesses your network remotely? (Either wired or wirelessly)?

1-5%	34%
6-10%	24%
50% +	6%
11-15%	14%
16-25%	11%
0%	3%
26-50%	8%

Question 9. How many workstations (laptops/desktops) does your organization have as a percent of total employees?

More than 100%	26%
91-100%	26%
81-90%	8%
71-80%	7%
< 10%	4%
41%-50%	5%
51-60%	6%
21-30%	5%
61-70%	6%
11-20%	4%
31-40%	4%

Question 10. Please choose the job title that most closely matches your own

Manager of IT or Security	29%
Other	21%
Security Analyst	19%
System Administrator	12%
Director	8%
Chief Executive Officer	1%
VP of IT or Security or Risk Management	2%
Chief Technology Officer	2%
Chief Security Officer	3%
Chief Information Officer	2%
Chief Information Security Officer	1%

Question 11. Geographically, what is your scope of responsibility in security

Local or regional responsibility	39%
All of the organization's activities globally	29%
All the organizations activities in Canada only	12%
Responsibility for Canadian headquarters	8%
Other	7%
Responsible for North America (Canada and USA only)	3%
Responsible for Canada and International (USA excluded)	3%

Question 12. In your current role, which of the following functions do you perform?

Security Operations	54%
IT / Security Audit	61%
Policy Development	56%
Forensics / Incident Handling	40%
Risk Management	51%
Mgmt, Security Programs	46%
Security Architecture	50%
Secure Development	28%
Physical Security	25%
Regulatory Compliance	40%
Identity and Access Mgmt	47%
Privacy	33%
Loss Prevention	29%
None of the above	9%

Question 13. How long have you been in IT security?

10 years or more	32%
4-6 years	23%
1-3 years	18%
7-9 years	17%
< 1 year	9%

Question 14. What is the level of the staff turnover in your security organization currently?

Very low – it is rare that someone leaves our group	38%
Low – staff generally stay for more than 5 years	31%
Medium – staff generally stay for 3 to 5 years	25%
High – Staff generally stay for 1-3 years	5%
Very high – Staff generally stay for less than a year	1%

Question 15. Do you have any formal IT certifications, degrees or diplomas?

CISSP	32%
CISM	8%
CISA	10%
Privacy	2%
Business Continuity / Disaster Recovery	4%
SANS Systems Administration Networking and Security	9%
Degree, Computer Science / Engineering	30%
Degree, Economics / Finance / Business	11%
Degree, not in business or technology	11%

Question 16. Which range contains your current annual salary (including any bonuses)?

$100,000 – $119,999	22%
$80,000 – $89,999	13%
$70,000 – $79,999	12%
$90,000 – $99,999	9%
$120,000 – $139,999	8%
$60,000 – $69,999	7%
$140,000 – $159,999	4%
$50,000 – $59,999	4%
$160,000 – $179,999	3%
> $200,000	2%
$40,000 – $49,999	2%
< $40,000	1%
$180,000 – $199,999	1%
I prefer not to answer this Question	11%

Question 17. Where is the Information security policy for your Canadian operations determined?

Asia (excluding Japan)	0%
Canadian Headquarters	61%
Don't know	4%
Europe (including the UK)	0%
Local Canadian operations	28%
USA	7%

Question 18. Does your organization have a dedicated information security officer (i.e. CISO, CSO, or equivalent in government)?

No	44%
Yes	56%

Question 19. What is the management level of the highest ranking person responsible for information security?

Director-level	31%
Manager-level	27%
Vice President level	22%
Senior Manager	8%
Team lead	6%
Don't know	4%
Other	2%
Not applicable	1%

Question 20. Where does your highest ranking person responsible for information security report to?

IT	54%
CEO	26%
Other	10%
Finance	7%
Risk Management	3%
HR	1%

Question 21. Which areas is the information security function accountable for?

Audit	51%
Compliance	71%
Risk Management	62%
IT Security (network and applications)	94%
Physical Security	35%
Loss Prevention	38%
Safety	22%
Business Continuity / Disaster Recovery	56%

Question 22. Do any of the following government regulations or industry regulations with respect to information security affect your organization? Check all that apply

Sarbanes-Oxley (SOX)	31%
Bill 198 (Canadian Sarbanes-Oxley equivalent)	35%
Privacy Act (Canada or USA)	70%
Canadian Bank Act	15%
Personal Information Protection and Electronic Documents Act (PIPEDA) (Canada)	70%
Payment Card Industry (PCI- DSS)	43%
Other Industry-specific regulations (FFIEC, NERC, FERC, PHIPA, HIPAA)	29%
Breach disclosure laws	21%
Special information security laws	15%
Don't know	10%

Question 23. How well do key security decision-makers in your organization understand the information security requirements to comply with the regulations/legislation affecting your organization? Pick one

Our understanding of the requirements is very limited.	8%
We have a good understanding of the legislated/ regulated security requirements that we need to comply with.	30%
We have a very good understanding of the legislated/regulated security requirements that we need to comply with.	28%
We have an adequate understanding of the requirements.	25%

Question 24. How efficiently does your organization manage different compliance requirements (check the one that matches closest to your situation)?

Don't know	13%
We have not yet analyzed our regulatory compliance obligations.	12%
We understand our compliance obligations and we treat each regulation as a separate project / set of requirements.	40%
We understand our regulatory obligations and search for projects or approaches that enable compliance with different requirements.	35%

Question 25. Does your organization formally measure its IT staff against specific information security objectives (i.e., does their compensation depend in part on achieving security objectives)?

Don't Know	18%
No	61%
Yes	21%

Question 26. How often does your organization communicate about security issues, threats and policies to its workforce (including employees, students and long-term contractors)? Pick the ONE frequency that most closely matches

At least once a month	11%
At least once a quarter	16%
At least once every two weeks	5%
At least once per year	25%
At least twice per year	8%
Don't know	5%
Less than once per year	12%
Never	3%
Upon hiring only	13%

Question 27. Assessing information security risk involves establishing the value of business assets (data, software, hardware), understanding which threats they are vulnerable to, and understanding how well current security measures protect these assets. How often does your organization assess its security risks (including external or internal audits)? Pick one

Don't know	15%
Every 6 months	11%
Every two years	7%
Every year	21%
Less than once every two years	11%
Monthly	10%
More often than once per month	8%
Never	4%
Quarterly	12%

Question 28. What share of your organization's information security budget is spent on outsourced security services? Pick one

21% to 40%	4%
41% to 60%	4%
61% to 80%	0%
Don't know	31%
More than 80%	4%
None	24%
Up to 20%	32%

Question 29. Which of the following functions do you currently outsource?

Security programme development / management	11%
Management of firewalls	20%
Management of web application firewalls	16%
Management of network intrusion prevention systems	20%
Monitoring of security events (SIEM)	14%
Collection of security logs (log mgmt)	16%
Management of virtual private networks	6%
Management of local area networks	19%
Management of desktops	18%
Management of servers / applications (on premise)	16%
Management of servers / applications (in datacenter)	18%
Security testing of networks and infrastructure	37%
Testing of software and applications (including web)	25%
Backups	16%

Question 30. Does your organization have a policy regarding outsourcing of information security services to a third party?

We allow outsourcing of security to other countries where we do business	6%
We do not allow outsourcing of IT security	39%
We only allow outsourcing to countries with laws and regulations that are as stringent as those in Canada	12%
We only outsource to Canadian companies	24%
We outsource to the best value provider; location is not a major factor in our decision	20%

Question 31. To what extent is your organization concerned about the following regarding the provisioning of information security services through cloud computing (Security as a Service, Security in the Cloud)?

Concerns	AverageConcern
We are concerned about the location of our data	23%
We are concerned with the level of security in a multi-tenant environment	16%
We are concerned with the ability to remove/recover our data from the cloud	13%
We are concerned that our availability needs cannot be met with a cloud-based service	11%
We are concerned about our ability to audit the environment for compliance with our security needs	14%
We are concerned about our ability to perform forensic analysis on cloud security systems in the event of a breach	12%
We are concerned about connecting business critical systems to security mechanisms outside our full control	21%

Question 32. How many applications does your organization have?

> 1000	13%
1-4	6%
5-9	9%
10-25	15%
26-50	11%
51-100	16%
101-500	26%
501-1000	4%

Question 33. How often do you perform the following types of testing on Applications for your critical applications?

	Never	Yearly	Quarterly	Monthly	Weekly
Frequency of Manual Penetration Testing	33%	38%	16%	4%	8%
Frequency of Automated Vulnerability Testing	24%	23%	23%	15%	15%
Frequency of Manual Source Code Review?	54%	21%	10%	6%	9%
Frequency of Automated Code Review?	60%	15%	12%	5%	8%

Question 34. Who performs the majority of your application testing? (Please check all that apply.)

Internal security team	29%
Internal development team	32%
Internal audit team	11%
External audit team	8%
External security consultants	18%
Don't know	7%

Question 35. What role does security play in your software development lifecycle? (Please check all that apply.)

Security starts with the requirements analysis phase	27%
Security starts with the design phase	17%
Security is integrated at the coding phase	17%
Security is tested for after coding is complete	22%
Security is tested after being promoted to production	16%
Security is tested on ad-hoc basis as needed	22%
Don't know	8%
Security testing is not part of our development practices	10%

Question 36. What percent of your applications are developed in-house?

0%	5%
1 - 20%	29%
21 - 40%	16%
41 - 60%	14%
61 - 80%	13%
81 - 100%	13%
Don't know	8%

Question 37. Approximately how many full time equivalent staff (FTEs) does your organization devote to IT security (including IT security operations, audit and policy functions)?

0 FTEs	9%
1 FTE	21%
2-4 FTEs	22%
5 to 10 FTEs	16%
11 to 25 FTEs	4%
26 to 50 FTEs	5%
Don't know	10%
More than 50 FTEs	11%

Question 38. Rate the effectiveness of the following strategies in obtaining funding for information security projects and initiatives from your organization's business leaders?

Strategy	AverageCon-cern
Explaining the nature and magnitude of the risk	17%
Explaining the nature and magnitude of the threat	15%
Demonstrating Return on Investment (revenue increase, cost reduction)	17%
Demonstrating how the initiative links to business strategy	16%
Demonstrating how the initiative meets compliance requirements	20%
Demonstrating need to follow industry best practices	12%
Demonstrating the need to meet the internal policies and security objectives	19%

Question 39. Approximately what percent of your security staff are contractors? (including IT security operations, audit and policy functions)?

< 2%	53%
2 - 4%	18%
5 - 10%	9%
11 - 15%	7%
16 - 25%	4%
26 - 50%	6%
More than 50%	3%

Question 40. What percentage of your organization's revenue/funding is spent on IT?

< 1%	6%
1% - 2%	19%
3% - 4%	11%
5% - 6%	9%
7% - 9%	1%
10% -15%	8%
16% - 25%	4%
Don't know	34%
More than 25%	6%

Question 41. Approximately what share of the IT budget is spent on security?

< 1%	12%
1% - 2%	11%
3% - 4%	11%
5% - 6%	12%
7% - 9%	5%
10% -15%	9%
16% - 25%	5%
Don't know	30%
More than 25%	3%

Question 42. How important are the following in driving your organization's IT security investment?

Legislation / Regulations	60%
Security breaches that have occurred in our organization	42%
Security breaches that have occurred at competitors, clients, suppliers' or affiliate organizations	25%
Media reporting of security breaches	33%
Increased concern over risk management, potential losses	41%
Increased risk from increased activities by employees such as: use of wireless devices, remote access, instant messaging, etc.	46%
See security as a potential competitive advantage	21%
Clients demanding better IT / information security from us	30%

Question 43. Was your IT Security budget affected by the 2009 global financial crisis?

Major Budgetary Cuts: 25% to 49% of the original budget for contracts or projects related to security and privacy was cut.	10%
Major Budgetary Increase: original budget increased by 25% to 49% for contracts or projects related to security and privacy.	1%
Minor Budgetary Cuts: Less than 10% of the original budget for contracts or projects related to security and privacy was cut.	36%
Minor Budgetary Increase: original budget increased by less than 10% for contracts or projects related to security and privacy.	19%
Moderate Budgetary Cuts: 10% to 24% of the original budget for contracts or projects related to security and privacy was cut.	20%
Moderate Budgetary Increase: original budget increased by 10% to 24% for contracts or projects related to security and privacy.	5%
Severe Budgetary Cuts: 50% to 100% of the original budget for contracts or projects related to security and privacy was cut.	8%
Very Significant Budgetary Increase: original budget increased by 50% to 100% for contracts or projects related to security and privacy.	1%

Question 44. If the level of your outsourcing was affected by the 2009 global financial crisis, please choose the main reason

Don't know	26%
No, outsourcing was not impacted in our organization	48%
We increased our outsourcing relationships to reduce headcount	4%
We increased our outsourcing relationships to reduce operating expenses	2%
Yes, our outsourcing relationships were impacted but not significantly	10%
Yes, we were asked to reduce our outsourcing relationships significantly	12%

Question 45. Did the 2009 global financial crisis cause your organization to re-consider staffing decisions related to security or privacy? (Check all that apply)

Yes, we had to lay off full time security personnel	5%
Yes, we had to lay off part-time security personnel, contractors or consultants	5%
No staffing changes caused by the 2009 financial downturn	38%
Yes, we increased our full time security personnel	2%
Don't know	10%

Question 46. If you suffered a breach, what is your confidence level that you would be able to detect it?

High	26%
Low	19%
Moderate	41%
Very High	5%
Very Low	8%

Question 47. Did your organization experience and identify any of the following types of information security breaches in the past 12 months? Check all that apply

Virus/worms/spyware/malware/spam	70%
Laptop or mobile hardware device theft	53%
Financial fraud	14%
Bots (zombies) within the organization	15%
Phishing/Pharming where your organization was fraudulently described as the sender	23%
Denial of service attack	16%
Sabotage of data or networks	3%
Unauthorized access to information by employees	36%
Extortion or blackmail (ransomware)	3%
Website defacement	6%
Loss of confidential customer/employee data	10%
Abuse of wireless network	15%
Password Sniffing	5%
Misuse of a corporate application	13%
Theft of proprietary information	7%
Identity Theft	7%
Exploitation of your domain name server (DNS)	2%

Question 48. How many Security breaches do you estimate your organization has experienced in the past 12 months?

1	6%
2 – 5	33%
6 – 10	9%
11 – 25	7%
26 – 50	3%
51 – 100	2%
Don't know	23%
More than 100	2%
None	14%

Question 49. How many Privacy breaches do you estimate your organization has experienced in the past 12 months?

1	7%
2 – 5	19%
6 – 10	6%
11 – 25	5%
26 – 50	2%
51 – 100	1%
Don't know	31%
More than 100	1%
None	32%

Question 50. How often do you test your Security Incident Response process (or equivalent)?

Annually	25%
Don't know	22%
Monthly	9%
Never / We don't have an Security Incident Response process	35%
Quarterly	8%

Question 51. Please estimate what percentage of security breaches come from insiders of the organization

6% to 10%	5%
11% to 20%	6%
21% to 40%	9%
41% to 60%	10%
61% to 80%	7%
81% to 100%	9%
Don't know	31%
None	13%
Up to 5%	11%

Question 52. What types of costs would your organization be most concerned about if there was a major information security breach? Please rank the options below

Breach Cost	Average
Damage to Brand reputation or image	28%
Lost Time due to Disruption	17%
Personal Accountability	9%
Litigation	14%
Regulatory Action	15%
Lost Customers	13%
Cost of New Equipment / Services Required	8%
Cost to Compensate Customers / Damaged Parties	11%
Loss of Market Valuation (share price)	9%

Question 53. Please estimate the total dollar value of losses that your company has experienced due to all breaches (including those not formally disclosed) over the past 12 months?

$1 million - $2.9 million	3%
$3 million - $4.9 million	2%
$100,000 to $249,999	4%
$250,000 to $499,999	2%
$500,000 - $999,999	11%
< $100,000	24%
$0	14%
Don't know	40%

Question 54. How concerned is your organization about each of the following issues?

Managing Risks from Third-Parties, i.e. business partners, suppliers and collaborators	8%
Managing Security of Wireless and Mobile Devices	10%
Disclosure / Loss of Confidential Customer Data	21%
Compliance with Canadian Regulations and Legislation	17%
Compliance with USA or Other Foreign Regulations and Legislation	9%
Accountability of User Actions and Access	10%
Employees Understanding and Complying with Security Policies	11%
Business Continuity / Disaster Recovery	16%
Loss of Strategic Corporate Information	13%
Managing data in the cloud (cloud computing)	4%

Question 55. Please indicate the status of the following initiatives in your organization

Security Initiative	Not Interested	Evaluating	Planning	Deploying	In Place
Security awareness program for general employees	21%	22%	15%	7%	35%
Security awareness program specific to IT staff	25%	12%	18%	3%	43%
Security awareness program specific to developers and architects	44%	10%	15%	0%	31%
Linking general IT staff's performance evaluations to security objectives	53%	10%	24%	1%	12%
Creating business-level security metrics	38%	23%	24%	5%	11%
Security awareness programs for customers	43%	15%	22%	7%	13%
Requiring suppliers, business partners or other third parties agree to organization's security policy	35%	10%	26%	3%	25%
Integration of security into software/ application development	35%	18%	9%	3%	35%
Requiring suppliers, business partners or other third parties to agree to organization's privacy policy	38%	21%	10%	4%	27%
Security training for third parties (contractors, volunteers, co-op)	56%	18%	7%	6%	13%
Mandatory tests after security awareness training	54%	16%	12%	3%	15%
Criminal background checks for all IT and Security staff	40%	25%	9%	1%	25%
Creating a security policy	12%	18%	19%	4%	47%
Creating a privacy policy	12%	18%	15%	3%	52%

Question 56. What specific technologies do you currently use and how satisfied are you with their effectiveness?

Technology	Do not use	Not at all satisfied	Not quite satisfied	Satisfied	More than satisfied	Very Satisfied
IPSEC based VPN	18%	1%	7%	40%	22%	30%
SSL VPN	19%	1%	5%	41%	26%	28%
Anti-Virus	1%	4%	9%	36%	26%	25%
Email Security (anti-spam, anti-malware)	0%	3%	10%	35%	29%	23%
Public Key Infrastructure	37%	3%	11%	47%	18%	21%
Storage / Hard Disk Encryption	35%	2%	14%	46%	21%	17%
Email Encryption	50%	5%	10%	51%	19%	15%
Database Encryption	46%	5%	14%	43%	26%	11%
URL / Content Filtering	14%	6%	15%	37%	24%	17%
Identity and Access Management	26%	4%	27%	36%	22%	10%
Network based Access Control (NAC via network)	55%	9%	17%	42%	24%	9%
Endpoint Security (NAC via desktop)	50%	7%	14%	40%	27%	12%
Firewalls	2%	3%	6%	31%	32%	28%
Web Application Firewalls	39%	5%	14%	40%	22%	20%
Log Management	26%	15%	29%	31%	15%	10%
Security Information & Event management (SIEM)	42%	12%	24%	38%	15%	12%
Network Intrusion Prevention / Detection	23%	5%	19%	41%	22%	14%
Wireless Intrusion prevention (WIPS)	56%	6%	28%	38%	18%	11%
Application Security Assessment Tools (web/code)	47%	10%	26%	39%	14%	12%
Two-factor authentication (tokens, smart-cards)	35%	3%	13%	37%	24%	23%
Vulnerability Scanning / Vulnerability management	26%	6%	21%	36%	25%	12%
Patch Management	8%	7%	15%	41%	22%	16%
Data Leakage Prevention	53%	12%	27%	43%	10%	8%

Question 57. What specific technologies will you deploy for IT security in the next 12 months? Please check your level of deployment

Technology	No deployment (1)	Technical Evaluation (2)	Pilot (3)	Limited Deployment (4)	Full Deployment (5)
IPSEC based VPN	51%	4%	1%	10%	33%
SSL VPN	39%	7%	1%	15%	38%
Anti-Virus	32%	3%	2%	5%	58%
Email Security (anti-spam, anti-malware)	35%	6%	3%	5%	52%
Public Key Infrastructure	52%	11%	4%	14%	19%
Storage / Hard Disk Encryption	42%	14%	7%	18%	20%
Email Encryption	46%	18%	8%	15%	13%
Database Encryption	58%	11%	9%	10%	12%
URL / Content Filtering	38%	10%	5%	13%	34%
Identity and Access Management	38%	16%	9%	14%	22%
Network based Access Control (NAC via network)	40%	17%	10%	15%	18%
Endpoint Security (NAC via desktop)	51%	13%	10%	6%	19%
Firewalls	37%	3%	3%	7%	51%
Web Application Firewalls	47%	10%	6%	12%	25%
Log Management	38%	15%	11%	13%	23%
Security Information & Event management (SIEM)	47%	12%	9%	16%	16%
Network Intrusion Prevention/Detection	37%	9%	5%	17%	32%
Wireless Intrusion prevention (WIPS)	53%	16%	7%	10%	14%
Application Security Assessment Tools (web/code)	53%	17%	9%	9%	12%
Two-factor authentication (tokens, smartcards)	46%	14%	6%	9%	25%
Vulnerability Scanning / Vulnerability management	40%	13%	8%	13%	27%
Patch Management	37%	7%	5%	11%	41%
Data Leakage Prevention	53%	9%	9%	10%	9%

Question 58. How do you feel about your organization's overall IT and information security situation?

About the same as last year	34%
Improved somewhat from last year	41%
Improved substantially compared to last year	18%
Much worse than last year	1%
Not sure	4%
Somewhat worse than last year	2%

Question 59. How satisfied are you with your organization's overall IT security posture?

Not sure	2%
Not very satisfied	13%
Satisfied	43%
Somewhat dissatisfied	31%
Very satisfied	12%

Compilation of References

Agnew, R. (1994). The techniques of neutralization and violence. *Criminology, 32*, 555–580. doi:10.1111/j.1745-9125.1994.tb01165.x

Agnew, R. (1992). Foundation for a general strain theory of crime and delinquency. *Criminology, 30*(1), 47–87. doi:10.1111/j.1745-9125.1992.tb01093.x

Ahrens, F. (2006, June 15). U.S. joins industry in piracy war: Nations pressed on copyrights. *The Washington Post*, A01.

Akers, R. L., Krohn, M. D., Lanza-Kaduce, L., & Radosevich, M. (1979). Social learning and deviant behavior: A specific test of a general theory. *American Sociological Review, 44*, 636–655. doi:10.2307/2094592

Akers, R. L. (2000). *Criminological theories: Introduction, evaluation, and application*. Los Angeles: Roxbury Publishing Company.

Akers, R. L. (1991). Self-control theory as a general theory of crime. *Journal of Quantitative Criminology, 7*, 201–211. doi:10.1007/BF01268629

Akers, R. L. (1998). *Social learning and social structure: A general theory of crime and deviance*. Boston: Northeastern University Press.

Akers, R. L., & Lee, G. (1996). A longitudinal test of social learning theory: Adolescent smoking. *Journal of Drug Issues, 26*, 317–343.

Akers, R. L., & Jensen, G. F. (2006). The empirical status of social learning theory of crime and deviance: The past, present, and future . In Cullen, F. T., Wright, J. P., & Blevins, K. R. (Eds.), *Taking stock: The status of criminological theory*. New Brunswick, NJ: Transaction Publishers.

Allison, S. F. H., Schuck, A. M., & Learsch, K. M. (2005). Exploring the crime of identity theft: prevalence, clearance rates, and victim/offender characteristics. *Journal of Criminal Justice, 33*, 19–29. doi:.doi:10.1016/j.jcrimjus.2004.10.007

Almeida, M. (2008). *Statistics report 2005-2007, March 5, 2008*. Retrieved March 18, 2008, from www.zone-h.org

Alshech, E. (2007). Cyberspace as a combat zone: The phenomenon of electronic jihad. *MEMRI Inquiry and Analysis Series, 329*. The Middle East Media Research Institute, February 7.

Anderson, C. A. (2004). An update on the effects of playing violent video games. *Journal of Adolescence, 27*, 113–122. doi:10.1016/j.adolescence.2003.10.009

Anderson, A. (2000). *Snake Oil, Hustlers and Hambones: The American Medicine Show*. Jefferson, NC: McFarland.

Anderson, C. (2006). *The Long Tail: Why the Future of Business is Selling Less of More*. New York: Hyperion.

Andersson, L., & Trudgill, P. (1990). *Bad language*. Oxford, UK: Blackwell.

APACS. (2006) *Fraud: The Facts 2006*, APACS, at http://www.cardwatch.org.uk/publications.asp?sectionid=all&pid=76&gid=&Title=Publications.

Arguilla, J., & Ronfeldt, D. (1993). Cyberwar is coming! *Comparative Strategy, 12*, 141–165. doi:10.1080/01495939308402915

Arneklev, B. J., Grasmick, H. G., Tittle, C. R., & Bursik, R. J. (1993). Low self-control and imprudent behavior. *Journal of Quantitative Criminology, 9*, 225–247. doi:10.1007/BF01064461

Arquilla, J., & Ronfeldt, D. (2000). *Swarming & the future of conflict*. Santa Monica, CA: RAND.

Arthur, C. (2005) 'Interview with a link spammer', *The Register*, 31 January, at www.theregister.co.uk/2005/01/31/link_spamer_interview/.

As-Sālim, M. (2003) *39 Ways to serve and participate in jihâd*. Retrieved June 30, 2008, from http://tibyan.wordpress.com/2007/08/24/39-ways-to-serve-and-participate-in-jihad/.

ATC. (2004). *ATC's OBL crew investigation*. Anti-TerrorismCoalition.

Attrition. (1996). *Attrition mirror*. Retrieved 1996 from http://attrition.org/mirror/attrition/1996.html#dec

Bailey, T., Le Couteur, A., Gorresman, I., Bolton, P., Simonoff, E., Yuzda, E., & Rutter, M. (1995). Autism as a strongly genetic disorder: Evidence from a British twin study. *Psychological Medicine*, *25*, 63–77. doi:10.1017/S0033291700028099

Bakier, A. H. (2007). *Forum users improve electronic jihad technology*. Retrieved June 27, 2007, from http://www.jamestown.org/single/?no_cache=1&tx_ttnews%5Btt_news%5D=4256

Ball, L. D. (1985). Computer crime. In F. Tom (Ed.), *The information technology revolution* (pp. 532-545). Oxford, UK: Basil Blackwell and Cambridge, MA: MIT Press.

Barclay, G., Tavares C., Kenny, S., Siddique, A. & Wilby, E. (2003). International Comparisons of Criminal Justice Statistics 2001. *Home Office Statistics Bulletin, May 6, 2001*.

Barnard, J., Harvey, V., Prior, A., & Potter, D. (2001). *Ignored or ineligible? The reality for adults with autistic spectrum disorders*. London: National Autistic Society.

Baron-Cohen, S., Bolton, P., Wheelwright, S., Short, L., Mead, G., Smith, A., & Scahill, V. (1998). Autism occurs more often in families of physicists, engineers, and mathematicians. *Autism*, *2*, 296–301. doi:10.1177/1362361398023008

Baron-Cohen, S., Wheelwright, S., Skinner, R., Martin, J., & Clubley, E. (2001). The Autism-spectrum quotient (AQ): Evidence from Asperger syndrome/high-functioning autism, males and females, scientists and mathematicians. *Journal of Autism and Developmental Disorders*, *31*, 5–17. doi:10.1023/A:1005653411471

Bates, M. (2001). Emerging trends in information brokering . *Competitive Intelligence Review*, *8*(4), 48–53. doi:10.1002/(SICI)1520-6386(199724)8:4<48::AID-CIR8>3.0.CO;2-K

Bayley, D. H. (1991). *Forces of order: Modern policing in Japan*. Berkeley, CA: University of California Press.

Bayley, D. H. (2006). *Changing the guard: Developing democratic police abroad*. New York: Oxford University Press.

Bayley, D. H., & Shearing, C. D. (1996). The future of policing. *Law & Society Review*, *30*(3), 585–606. doi:10.2307/3054129

BBC (2001) 'Warning over Nigerian mail scam', *BBC News Online*, 10 July, at news.bbc.co.uk/hi/english/uk/newsid_1431000/1431761.stm

Bednarz, A. (2004). *Profiling cybercriminals: A promising but immature science*. Retrieved May 03, 2008, from http://www.networkworld.com/supp/2004/cybercrime/112904profile.html

Behar, R. (1997). Who's reading your e-mail? *Fortune*, *147*, 57–70.

Ben Yehuda, N. (1986). The sociology of moral panics: Toward a new synthesis. *The Sociological Quarterly*, *27*(4), 495–513. doi:10.1111/j.1533-8525.1986.tb00274.x

Bennett, R. R., & Bennett, S. B. (1983). Police personnel levels and the incidence of crime: A cross-national investigation. *Criminal Justice Review*, *8*(31), 32–40. doi:10.1177/073401688300800206

Benson, M. L., & Moore, E. (1992). Are white-collar and common offenders the same? An empirical and theoretical critique of a recently proposed general theory of crime. *Journal of Research in Crime and Delinquency*, *29*(3), 251–272. doi:10.1177/0022427892029003001

Benson, M. L., & Simpson, S. S. (2009). *White-collar crime: An opportunity perspective*. Oxford, UK: Taylor & Francis.

Benson, M. L. (1996). Denying the guilty mind: Accounting for involvement in a white-collar crime . In Cromwell, P. (Ed.), *In their own words, criminals on crime* (pp. 66–73). Los Angeles: Roxbury Publishing Company.

Bequai, A. (1990). *Computer-related crime*. Strasburg, Germany: Council of Europe.

Bequai, A. (1987). *Technocrimes*. Lexington, MA: Lexington.

Beveren, J. V. (2001). A conceptual model of hacker development and motivations. *The Journal of Business*, *1*, 1–9.

Biddle, P., England, P., Peinado, M., & Willman, B. (2002). The darknet and the future of content distribution. *ACM Workshop on Digital Rights Management 2002*.

Blake, R. (1994). *Hackers in the mist*. Chicago, IL: Northwestern University.

Blank, S. (2008). Web war I: Is Europe's first information war a new kind of war? *Comparative Strategy*, *27*, 227–247. doi:10.1080/01495930802185312

Blenkenship, L. (1986). *The hacker manifesto: The conscience of a hacker*. Retrieved May 4, 2009, from http://www.mithral.com/~beberg/manifesto.html

Blitstein, R. (2007). *Experts fail government on cybersecurity*. Retrieved January 2, 2007, from http://www.ohio.com/business/12844007.html

Blog Staff, W. S. J. (2009). *China denies hacking U.S. electricity grid*. Retrieved April 9, 2009, from http://blogs.wsj.com/digits/2009/04/09/china-denies-hacking-us-electricity-grid/

Bloom-Becker, J. (1986). *Computer crime law reporter*. Los Angeles: National Center for Computer Crime Data.

Bollen, K. A. (1989). *Structural equations with latent variables*. New York: Wiley.

Bollen, K. A., & Lennox, R. (1991). Conventional wisdom on measurement: a structural equation perspective. *Psychological Bulletin*, *110*, 305–314. doi:10.1037/0033-2909.110.2.305

Bollen, K. A., & Ting, T. (2000). A tetrad test for causal indicators. *Psychological Methods*, *15*, 3–22. doi:10.1037/1082-989X.5.1.3

Bossler, A. M., & Holt, T. J. (2009). On-line activities, guardianship, and malware infection: An examination of routine activities theory. *International Journal of Cyber Criminology*, *3*, 400–420.

Boudreau, M. C., Gefen, D., & Straub, D. W. (2001). Validation in information systems research: A state-of-the-art assessment. *Management Information Systems Quarterly*, *11*(1), 1–16. doi:10.2307/3250956

Braithwaite, J. (1985). White collar crime. *Annual Review of Sociology*, *11*, 1–25. doi:10.1146/annurev.so.11.080185.000245

Braithwaite, J. (1989). *Crime, shame and reintegration*. Cambridge, UK: Cambridge University Press.

Brenner, S. J., & Schwerha, J. J. (2004). Introduction-cybercrime: A note on international issues. *Information Systems Frontiers*, *6*(2), 111–114. doi:10.1023/B:ISFI.0000025779.42497.30

Brezina, T. (2000). Are deviants different from the rest of us? Using student accounts of academic cheating to explore a popular myth. *Teaching Sociology*, *28*, 71–78. doi:10.2307/1319424

Bryant, C. D. (1984). Odum's concept of the technicways: Some reflections on an underdeveloped sociological notion. *Sociological Spectrum*, *4*, 115–142. doi:.doi:10.1080/02732173.1984.9981714

Burris, S. C. (2004). Governance, micro-governance and health. *Temple Law Review*, *77*, 335–361.

Burris, S. C., Drahos, P., & Shearing, C. (2005). Nodal governance. *Australian Journal of Legal Philosophy*, *30*, 30–58.

Buzzell, T., Foss, D., & Middleton, Z. (2006). Explaining use of online pornography: A test of self-control theory and opportunities for deviance. *Journal of Criminal Justice and Popular Culture*, *13*, 96–116.

Cabinet Office. (2009) *Cyber Security Strategy of the United Kingdom: safety, security and resilience in cyber space*, http://www.cabinetoffice.gov.uk/media/216620/css0906.pdf

Caldwell, R. (1990). Some social parameters of computer crime. *Australian Computer Journal*, *22*, 43–46.

Caldwell, R. (1993). University students' attitudes toward computer crime: A research note. *Computers & Society*, *23*, 11–14. doi:10.1145/174256.174258

Caminada, M., Van de Riet, R., Van Zanten, A., & Van Doorn, L. (1998). Internet security incidents, a survey within Dutch organizations. *Computers & Security*, *17*(5), 417–433. doi:10.1016/S0167-4048(98)80066-7

Cards International. (2003) 'Europe "needs mag-stripe until US adopts chip"', *epaynews.com*, 28 July, at www.epaynews.com/ index.cgi?survey_&ref_browse&f_view&id_1059392963622215212&block_.(no longer available online)

Cartoon. (2006). *Cartoon body count*. Retrieved April 21, 2009, from http://web.archive.org/web/20060326071135/http://www.cartoonbodycount.com/

Casey, E. (2004). *Digital evidence and computer crime: Forensic science, computers and the internet* (2 ed.). San Diego, CA and London, UK: Academic Press.

Cassell, D. (2000). *Hacktivism in the cyberstreets*. Retrieved May 30, 2000, from http://www.alternet.org/story/9223

Castells, M. (1996). The rise of the network society.: *Vol. 1. The information age: Economy, society and culture*. Cambridge, MA: Blackwell Publishers.

Chambliss, W. J. (1975). Toward a political economy of crime. *Theory and Society*, *2*(2), 149–170. doi:10.1007/BF00212732

Chan, J. B. L. (1997). *Changing police culture: Policing in a multicultural society*. New York: Cambridge University Press. doi:10.1017/CBO9780511518195

Chandler, A. (1996). The changing definition and image of hackers in popular discourse. *International Journal of the Sociology of Law*, *24*, 229–251. doi:10.1006/ijsl.1996.0015

Cheng, J. (2009). *Judge: 17,000 illegal downloads don't equal 17,000 lost sales. Retrieved onFebruary13, 2009*, from http://arstechnica.com/tech-policy/news/2009/01/judge-17000-illegal-downloads-dont-equal-17000-lost-sales.ars

Chirillo, J. (2001). *Hack attacks revealed: A complete reference with custom security hacking toolkit*. New York: John Wiley & Sons.

Chisea, R., Ducci, D., & Ciappi, S. (2008). *Profiling hackers: The science of criminal profiling as applied to the world of hacking*. Boca Raton, FL: Auerbach Publications. doi:10.1201/9781420086942

Chisea, R., Ciappi, S., & Ducci, S. (2008). *Profiling hackers: The science of criminal profiling as applied to the world of hacking. now Your Enemy*. Danvers, MA: Auerbach Publications. doi:10.1201/9781420086942

Clark, T. L. (1986). Cheating terms in cards and dice. *American Speech*, *61*, 3–32. doi:.doi:10.2307/454707

Clinard, M. B., & Quinney, R. (1973). *Criminal behavior systems: A typology*. New York: Holt, Rinehart and Winston.

Cloakware. (2009). *Achieve PCI compliance: Privileged password management*. Retrieved

Clough, B., & Mungo, P. (1992). *Approaching zero: Data crime and the computer underworld*. London: Faber and Faber.

Clover, C. (2009). *Kremlin-backed group behind Estonia cyber blitz.* Retrieved March 16, 2009, from http://www.ft.com/cms/s/0/57536d5a-0ddc-11de-8ea3-0000779fd2ac.html

Cluley, G. (2009). *Regarding Gigabyte.* Retrieved March 25, 2009, fromhttp://www.theregister.co.uk/2009/03/26/melissa_virus_anniversary/comments/

Cohen, L., & Felson, M. (1979). Social change and crime rate trends: A routine activity approach. *American Sociological Review, 44*, 588–608. doi:10.2307/2094589

Coleman, E. G., & Golub, A. (2008). Hacker practice: Moral genres and the cultural articulation of liberalism. *Anthropological Theory, 8*, 255–277. doi:10.1177/1463499608093814

Coleman, J. W. (1987). Toward an integrated theory of white-collar crime. *American Journal of Sociology, 93*(2), 406–439. doi:10.1086/228750

Coleman, J. W. (1995). Constructing white-collar crime: Rationalities, communication, power. *American Journal of Sociology, 100*(4), 1094–1096. doi:10.1086/230631

Coleman, E. G., & Golub, A. (2008). Hacker practice: Moral genres and the cultural articulation of liberalism. *Anthropological Theory, 8*, 255–277. doi:10.1177/1463499608093814

Computer Security Institute (CSI). (2007). *Computer Crime and Security Survey.* Retrieved March 2007 from http://www.cybercrime.gov/FBI2006.pdf

Computer Security Institute and Federal Bureau of investigations. (2006). *CSI/FBI Computer crime and security survey.* Retrieved 2006 from http://i.cmpnet.com/gocsi/db_area/pdfs/fbi/FBI2006.pdf

Conger, A. J. (1974). A revised definition for suppressor variables: A guide to their identification and interpretation. *Educational and Psychological Measurement, 34*, 35–46. doi:10.1177/001316447403400105

Control Microsystems. (2009). *DNP and IEC 60870-5 Compliance FAQ.*Retrieved December 1, 2009, from http://controlmicrosystems.com/resources-2/downloads/dnp3-iec-60870-5-compliance/

Cooper, J., & Harrison, D. M. (2001). The social organization of audio piracy on the internet. *Media Culture & Society, 23*, 71–89. doi:.doi:10.1177/016344301023001004

Copes, J. H. (2003). Societal attachments, offending frequency, and techniques of neutralization. *Deviant Behavior, 24*, 101–127. doi:10.1080/01639620390117200

Corbin, J., & Strauss, A. (1990). Grounded theory research: Procedures, canons, and evaluative criteria. *Qualitative Sociology, 13*, 3–21. doi:.doi:10.1007/BF00988593

Craig, S. G. (1984). The deterrent impact of police: An examination of a locally provided public service. *Journal of Urban Economics, 21*(3), 298–311. doi:10.1016/0094-1190(87)90004-0

Critical Infrastructure Protection Advisory Council (CIPAC). (2009). *U.S. Department of Homeland Security, Critical Infrastructure Partnership Advisory Council FAQ.* Retrieved December 1, 2009, from http://www.dhs.gov/files/committees/editorial_0843.shtm

Croall, H. (1992). *White-collar crime.* Philadelphia and Buckingham, PA: Open University Press.

Cromwell, P., & Thruman, Q. (2003). The devil made me do it: Use of neutralizations by shoplifters. *Deviant Behavior, 24*, 535–550. doi:10.1080/713840271

Cromwell, P. (Ed.). (1999). *In their own words, criminals on crime.* Los Angeles: Roxbury Publishing Company.

Cronan, T. P., Foltz, C. B., & Jones, T. W. (2006). Piracy, computer crime, and IS misuse at the university. *Communications of the ACM, 49*, 85–90. doi:10.1145/1132469.1132472

CSI (Computer Security Institute). (2008). *2008 CSI computer crime and security survey.* Retrieved December 23, from https://my.infotex.com/article.php?story=20090206075608135

CSI (Computer Security Institute). (2009). *CSI computer crime and security survey 2009*. Retrieved December 23, 2009, from http://www.gocsi.com/2009survey/;jsessionid=JQ4RMAELQDPWPQE1GHOSKH4ATMY32JVN

CSI. (1998). Email attack on Sri Lanka computers. *Computer Security Alert, 183*, 8.

Curran, K., Morrissey, C., Fagan, C., Murphy, C., O'Donnell, B., & Firzpatrick, G. (2005). Monitoring hacker activity with a honeynet. *International Journal of Network Management, 15*(2), 123–134. doi:10.1002/nem.549

Curry, G. D., & Decker, S. H. (2007). *Confronting gangs: Crime and community* (2nd ed.). Oxford, UK: Oxford University Press.

Cyber911 Emergency. (2009). *What is the profile of a typical cyberstalking/harassment victim?* Retrieved May 8, 2009, from http://www.wiredsafety.org/cyberstalking_harassment/csh7.html

Dabney, D. A. (1995). Neutralization and deviance in the workplace: Theft of supplies and medicines by hospital nurses. *Deviant Behavior, 16*, 313–331. doi:10.1080/01639625.1995.9968006

D'Arcy, J. P. (2007). *The misuse of information systems: The impact of security countermeasures*. New York: Lfb Scholarly Pub.

Davis, J. (2007). *Web war one*. Retrieved September, 2007, from http://www.wired.com/images/press/pdf/webwarone.pdf

December 22, 2009, from http://www.cloakware.com/cloakware-ds/whitepapers/security-compliance/intro-pci.php

DeLamater, J. (1978). On the nature of deviance . In Farrel, R. A., & Lynn Swigert, V. (Eds.), *Social deviance*. Philadelphia, PA: J.B. Lippincott.

Denning, D. (1998). *Information warfare and security*. Reading, MA: Addison-Wesley.

Denning, D. E. (1999). *Information warfare and security*. Reading, MA: Addison-Wesley.

Denning, D. E. (2001). Activism, hacktivism, and cyberterrorism . In Arquilla, J., & Ronfeldt, D. (Eds.), *Networks and netwars* (pp. 239–288). Santa Monica, CA: RAND.

Denning, D. E. (1990). *Concerning hackers who break into computer security systems*. Paper presented at the 13th National Computer Security Conference, October 1-4, Washington, D.C.

Derogatis, L., Lipman, R., Covi, L., Rickels, K., & Uhlenhuth, E. H. (1974). The Hopkins Symptom Checklist (HSCL): A self-report symptom inventory. *Behavioral Science*, (19): 1–15. doi:10.1002/bs.3830190102

Dewan, R., Friemer, M., & Gundepudi, P. (1999). Evolution of the internet infrastructure in the twenty-first century: The role of private interconnection agreements. In *Proceedings of the 20th International Conference on Information Systems*, Charlotte, North Carolina, (pp.144-154).

Dibbell, J. (2008). *Mutilated furries, flying phalluses: Put the blame on griefers, the sociopaths of the virtual world*. Retrieved December 22, 2009, from http://www.wired.com/gaming/virtualworlds/magazine/16-02/mf_goons

Dowland, P. S., Furnell, S. M., Illingworth, H. M., & Reynolds, P. L. (1999). Computer crime and abuse: A survey of public attitudes and awareness. *Computers & Security, 18*(8), 715–726. doi:10.1016/S0167-4048(99)80135-7

Drogin, B. (1999). *Russians seem to be hacking into Pentagon*. Retrieved October 7, 1999, from http://www.sfgate.com/cgi-bin/article.cgi?f=/c/a/1999/10/07/MN58558.DTL

Dubrin, A. J. (1995). *Leadership: Research Findings, Practice, and Skills*. Boston, MA: Houghton Mifflin Co.

Duff, L., & Gardiner, S. (1996). Computer crime in the global village: Strategies for control and regulation--in defence of the hacker. *International Journal of the Sociology of Law, 24*(2), 211–228. doi:10.1006/ijsl.1996.0014

Dumond, R. W. (1992). The sexual assault of male inmates in incarcerated settings. *International Journal of the Sociology of Law, 2*, 135–157.

Dupont, B. (2006). Power struggles in the field of security: Implications for democratic transformation . In Wood, J., & Dupont, B. (Eds.), *Democracy, Society and the Governance of Security* (pp. 86–110). New York: Cambridge University Press. doi:10.1017/CBO9780511489358.006

Dupont, B., & Mulone, M. (2007). *Airport security: A different kind of alliance.* Paper presented at the American Society of Criminology Annual Meeting on November 14-17, 2007, in Atlanta, GA.

Durkheim, E. (1947). *The division of labor in society.* Glencoe, IL: Free Press. (Original work published 1893)

Edelhertz, H. (1975). *The nature, impact and prosecution of white collar crime.* Washington, DC: LEAA.

EDT. (2008). *EDT.* Retrieved December 17, 2008, from http://www.thing.net/~rdom/ecd/ecd.html

Ehlers, S., & Gillberg, C. (1993). The epidemiology of Asperger syndrome: A total population study. *Journal of Child Psychology and Psychiatry, and Allied Disciplines, 34,* 1327–1350. doi:10.1111/j.1469-7610.1993.tb02094.x

Einat, T., & Einat, H. (2000). Inmate argot as an expression of prison subculture: The Israeli case. *The Prison Journal, 80,* 309–325. doi:.doi:10.1177/0032885500080003005

Electrohippies (2009). *The electrohippies call on people around the globe to celebrate World Intellectual Privateers Day 2009.* Retrieved April 13, 2009, from http://www.fraw.org.uk/ehippies

Elliott, D. S., Huizinga, D., & Menard, S. (1989). *Multiple problem youth.* New York: Springer-Verlag.

Ellis, S. (1998). *Computers are weapons in potential cyber attacks.* Retrieved 1998 from http://www.fas.org/irp/news/1998/08/98082502_ppo.html

Engdahl, O. (2008). The role of money in economic crime. *The British Journal of Criminology, 48*(2), 154–170. doi:10.1093/bjc/azm075

Erickson, J. (2008). *Hacking: The art of exploitation* (2 ed.). San Francisco, CA: No Starch Press.

Ericson, R. V., & Haggerty, K. D. (1997). *Policing the risk society.* Toronto, ON: University of Toronto Press.

Europe, M. T. B. (2009). *Autism genes discovery suggests biological reasons for alteredneural development.* Retrieved May 8, 2009, from http://www.mtbeurope.info/news/2009/905020.htm

Farrell, N. (2007). *Hacker mastermind has Asperger syndrome.* Retrieved December 3, 2007, from http://www.theinquirer.net/inquirer/news/1038901/hacker-mastermind-asperger

Fay, J. (2005) 'WTO rules in online gambling dispute', *The Register*, 8 April, at www.theregister.co.uk/2005/04/08/wto_online_gambling/.

Finch, E. (2002) 'What a tangled web we weave: identify theft and the internet', in Y. Jewkes (ed.), *dot.cons: Crime, Deviance and Identity on the Internet*, Cullompton: Willan, 86–104.

Finch, E. and Fafinski, S. (2010) *Identity Theft*, Cullompton: Willan

Finney, S. J., & DiStefano, C. (2006). Nonnormal and categorical data . In Hancock, G. R., & Mueller, R. O. (Eds.), *Structural equation modeling: A second course.* Greenwhich, CT: Information Age Publishing.

Flora, D. B., Finkel, E. J., & Foshee, V. A. (2003). Higher order factor structure of a self-control test: Evidence from confirmatory factor analysis with polychoric correlations. *Educational and Psychological Measurement, 63,* 112–127. doi:10.1177/0013164402239320

Forester, T., & Morrison, P. (1994). *Computer ethics: Cautionary tales and ethical dilemmas in computing.* London: MIT Press.

Forsyth, C. (1986). Sea daddy: An excursus into an endangered social species. *Maritime Policy and Management: The International Journal of Shipping and Port Research, 13*(1), 53–60.

Fox, M. (2009). Autism: Brain development: Gene could be link to 15 per cent of cases. *The Globe and Mail*, April 30, p. L6.

Franklin, J., Paxson, V., Perrig, A., & Savage, S. (2007). An inquiry into the nature and cause of the wealth of internet miscreants. Paper presented at CCS07, October 29-November 2, 2007 in Alexandria, VA.

Frieder, L., & Zittrain, J. (2006) 'Spam works: evidence from stock touts and corresponding market activity', *Working Paper, Krannert School of Management and Oxford Internet Institute*, 25 July, at www.ssrn.com/abstract_920553.

Friedrichs, D. O. (1996). *Trusted criminals in contemporary society*. Belmont, CA: Wadsworth Publishing Company.

Friedrichs, D. O. (2002). Occupational crime, occupational deviance, and workplace crime: Sorting out the difference. *Criminal Justice, 2*, 243–256.

Fritz, J. (2008). How China will use cyber warfare to leapfrog in military competitiveness. *Culture Mandala, 8*(1), 28-80. Retrieved 2008 from http://epublications.bond.edu.au/cm/vol8/iss1/2/

Furnell, S. M., & Warren, M. J. (1999). Computer hacking and cyber terrorism: The real threats in the new millennium. *Computers & Security, 18*, 28–34. doi:10.1016/S0167-4048(99)80006-6

Furnell, S. (2002). *Cybercrime: Vandalizing the information society*. Boston, MA: Addison-Wesley.

Garfinkel, H. (1978). Conditions of successful degradation ceremonies . In Farrell, R. A., & Swigert, V. L. (Eds.), *Social deviance* (pp. 135–142). Philadelphia, PA: J.B. Lippincott Company.

Garrick., Stetkar, J., & Kilger, M. (2009). Terrorist attack on the national electrical grid. In J. Garrick (Ed.), *Quantifying and controlling catastrophic risks* (pp. 111-177). St. Louis, MO: Academic Press.

Geis, G. (2000). On the absence of self-control as the basis for a general theory of crime: A critique. *Theoretical Criminology, 4*, 35–53. doi:10.1177/1362480600004001002

Geis, G. (1992). White-collar crime: What is it? In Kip, S., & Weisburd, D. (Eds.), *White-collar crime reconsidered* (pp. 31–52). Boston, MA: Northeastern University Press.

Gentile, D. A., Lynch, P. J., Linder, J. R., & Walsh, D. A. (2004). The effects of violent video game habits on adolescent hostility, aggressive behaviors, and school performance. *Journal of Adolescence, 27*, 5–22. doi:10.1016/j.adolescence.2003.10.002

Georgia Update. (2008). *Russian invasion of Georgia*. Retrieved October 9, 2008, from www.georgiaupdate.gov.ge

Gibbs, J. J., & Giever, D. M. (1995). Self-control and its manifestations among university students: An empirical test of Gottfredson and Hirschi's general theory. *Justice Quarterly, 12*, 231–255. doi:10.1080/07418829500092661

Gibson, C., & Wright, J. (2001). Low self-control and coworker delinquency: A research note. *Journal of Criminal Justice, 29*, 483–492. doi:10.1016/S0047-2352(01)00111-8

Gilbora, N. (1996). Elites, lamers, narcs and whores: Exploring the computer underground . In Cherny, L., & Weise, E. R. (Eds.), *Wired women: Gender and new realities in cyberspace*. Seattle, WA: Seal Press.

Gleeson, S. (2008). *Freed hacker could work for police*. Retrieved July 16, 2008, from http://www.nzherald.co.nz/nz/news/article.cfm?c_id=1&objectid=10521796

Glessner, J. T., Wang, K., Cai, G., Korvatska, O., Kim, C. E., Wood, S., et al. (2009). *Autism genome-wide copy number variation reveals ubiquitin and neuronal genes*. Retrieved on April 28, 2009, from http://dx.doi.org/10.1038/nature07953

Globerman, S. (1988). Addressing international product piracy. *Journal of International Business Studies, 19*(3), 497–504. doi:10.1057/palgrave.jibs.8490384

Goodin, D. (2007). *TJX breach was twice as big as admitted, banks say*. Retrieved March 27, 2008, from http://www.theregister.co.uk/2007/10/24/tjx_breach_estimate_grows/

Gordon, L. A., Loeb, M. P., Lucyshyn, W., & Richardson, R. (2005). *Computer crime and security survey*: Retrieved December 22, 2009, from http://www.cpppe.umd.edu/Bookstore/Documents/2005CSISurvey.pdf

Gordon, S. (1994). The generic virus writer. In *Proceedings of the International Virus Bulletin Conference*. Jersey, Channel Islands, pp.121-138.

Gordon, S. (2000). *Virus writers: The end of innocence*? Retrieved 2000 from http://www.research.ibm.com/antivirus/SciPapers/VB2000SG.pdf

Gordon, S., & Ma, Q. (2003). *Convergence of virus writers and hackers: Fact or fantasy*. Cupertine, CA: Symantec Security White paper.

Gordon-Larsen, P., Nelson, M. C., & Popkin, B. M. (2005). Meeting national activity and inactivity recommendations: Adolescence to adulthood. *American Journal of Preventive Medicine*, *28*, 259–266.

Gorman, S. (2009). *Electricity grid in U.S.penetrated by spies*. Retrieved April 8, 2009, from http://online.wsj.com/article/SB123914805204099085.html

Goss, A. (2001) 'Jay Cohen's brave new world: the liability of offshore operators of licensed internet casinos for breach of United States' anti-gambling laws', *Richmond Journal of Law & Technology*, 7 (4): 32, at http://jolt.richmond.edu/v7i4/article2.html.

Gottfredson, M. R., & Hirschi, T. (1990). *A general theory of crime*. Stanford, CA: Stanford University Press.

Gould, P. (1991). Dynamic structures of geographic space. In S.D. Brunn, S. D. & T.R. Leinbach (Ed.) *Collapsing space and time: Geographic aspects of communication and information* (pp. 3-30). London, UK: Harper Collins Academic.

Grabosky, P. N. (2001). Virtual criminality: Old wine in new bottles? *Social & Legal Studies*, *10*, 243–249.

Grabosky, P. (2004). The global dimension of cybercrime. *Global Crime*, *6*(1), 146–157. doi:10.1080/1744057042000297034

Graham, J. (2001). *Hackers strike Middle Eastern sites*. Retrieved September 26, 2001, from http://www.usatoday.com/tech/news/2001/09/19/hack-attack-launched.htm

Granovsky, Y. (2002) 'Yevroset tainted by gray imports', *The Moscow Times*, 9 July: 8, at www.themoscowtimes.com/stories/2002/07/09/045.html.

Grasmick, H. G., Tittle, C. R., Bursik, R. J. Jr, & Arneklev, B. J. (1993). Testing the core empirical implications of Gottfredson and Hirschi's general theory of crime. *Journal of Research in Crime and Delinquency*, *30*, 5–29. doi:10.1177/0022427893030001002

Grecs. (2008). *ShmooCon 2008 infosec conference event*. Retrieved April 25, 2008, from http://www.novainfosecportal.com/2008/02/18/shmoocon-2008-infosec-conference-event-saturday/

Green, G. S. (1990). *Occupational crime*. Chicago, IL: Nelson-Hall.

Gross, G., & McMillan, R. (2006). Al-*Qaeda 'Battle of Guantanamo' cyberattack a no-show.* Retrieved December 1, 2006, from http://hostera.ridne.net/suspended.page/?currtag=12&currletter=2

Groves, R. M., Fowler, F. J., Couper, M. P., & Lepkowski, J. M., Singer, E., & Tourangeau, R. (2004). *Survey methodology*. Hoboken, NJ: Wiley.

Guadagno, R. E., Cialdini, R. B., & Evron, G. (2009). (in press). What about Estonia? A social psychological analysis of the first Internet war. *Cyberpsychology & Behavior*.

Hafner, K., & Markoff, J. (1993). *Cyberpunk: Outlaws and hackers on the computer frontier*. London: Corgi Books.

Halbert, D. (1997). Discourses of danger and the computer hacker. *The Information Society*, *13*, 361–374. doi:10.1080/019722497129061

Halderman, J. A., & Felton, E. W. (2006). Lessons from the Sony CD DRM episode. *Proceedings from the 15th USENIX Security Symposium*, July 31-August 4, 2006, Vancouver, B.C.

Hall, A. (2005). *Al-Qaeda chiefs reveal world domination design*. Retrieved August 24, 2005, from http://www.theage.com.au/news/war-on-terror/alqaeda-chiefs-reveal-world-domination-design/2005/08/23/1124562861654.html

Hall, C. (2005) 'Internet fuels boom in counterfeit drugs', *Sunday Telegraph*, 16 August, at http://www.telegraph.co.uk/news/uknews/3322447/Internet-fuels-boom-in-counterfeit-drugs.html.

Halliday, M. A. K. (1977). Language structure and language function . In Lyons, J. (Ed.), *New Horizons in Linguistic Structure* (pp. 140–165). Harmondsworth, UK: Penguin.

Hamm, M. S. (1993). *American skinheads: The criminology and control of hate crime*. Westport, CT: Praeger.

Hannemyr, G. (1999). Technology and pleasure: Considering hacking constructive. *Firstmonday, Peer-Reviewed Journal on the Internet, 4.*

Hauben, M., & Hauben, R. (1997). *Netizens: On the history and impact of usenet and the internet*. Los Alamitos, CA: IEEE Computer Society Press.

Hawes, J. (2009). *E-crime survey 2009*. Retrieved May 3, 2009, from http://www.securingourecity.org/resources/pdf/E-CrimeSurvey2009.pdf

Henderson, S. J. (2007). *The dark visitor: Inside the world of Chinese hackers*. Fort Leavenworth, KS: Foreign Military Studies Office.

Hensley, C., Wright, J., Tewksbury, R., & Castle, T. (2003). The evolving nature of prison argot and sexual hierarchies. *The Prison Journal*, *83*, 289–300. doi:. doi:10.1177/0032885503256330

Herbert, S. (1999). The end of the territorial sovereign state? The Case of Criminal Control in the United States. *Political Geography*, *18*, 149–172. doi:10.1016/S0962-6298(98)00080-8

Heron, S. (2007). The rise and rise of keyloggers. *Network Security*, *7*, 4–6. doi:10.1016/S1353-4858(07)70052-1

Hess, P. (2002). *China prevented repeat cyber attack on US*. Retrieved October 29, 2002, from http://seclists.org/isn/2002/Oct/121

Higgins, G. E. (2005). Can low self-control help with the understanding of the software piracy problem? *Deviant Behavior*, *26*, 1–24. doi:10.1080/01639620490497947

Higgins, G. E. (2006). Gender differences in software piracy: The mediating roles of self-control theory and social learning theory. *Journal of Economic Crime Management*, *4*, 1–30.

Higgins, G. E. (2007). Digital piracy, self-control theory, and rational choice: An examination of the role of value. *International Journal of Cyber Criminology*, *1*, 33–55.

Higgins, G. E., Fell, B. D., & Wilson, A. L. (2006). Digital piracy: Assessing the contributions of an integrated self-control theory and social learning theory using structural equation modeling. *Criminal Justice Studies*, *19*, 3–22. doi:10.1080/14786010600615934

Higgins, G. E., Fell, B. D., & Wilson, A. L. (2007). Low self-control and social learning in understanding students' intentions to pirate movies in the United States. *Social Science Computer Review*, *25*, 339–357. doi:10.1177/0894439307299934

Higgins, G. E., Wolfe, S. E., & Marcum, C. (2008). Digital piracy: An examination of three measurements of self-control. *Deviant Behavior*, *29*, 440–460. doi:10.1080/01639620701598023

Higgins, K. J. (2008). *Hundreds of Israeli websites hacked in 'propaganda war.'* Retrieved December 31, 2008, from http://www.darkreading.com/security/attacks/showArticle.jhtml?articleID=212700313

Hinduja, S. (2007). Neutralization theory and online software piracy: An empirical analysis. *Ethics and Information Technology*, *9*, 187–204. doi:10.1007/s10676-007-9143-5

Hinduja, S. (2001). Correlates of Internet software piracy. *Journal of Contemporary Criminal Justice*, *17*(4), 369–382. doi:10.1177/1043986201017004006

Hirschi, T. (1969). *Causes of delinquency*. Berkeley, CA: University of California Press.

Hirschi, T., & Gottfredson, M. R. (1993). Commentary: Testing the general theory of crime. *Journal of Research in Crime and Delinquency*, *30*, 47–54. doi:10.1177/0022427893030001004

Hirschi, T., & Gottfredson, M. R. (Eds.). (1994). *The generality of deviance*. New Brunswick, NJ: Transaction Publishers.

Hirschi, T., & Gottfredson, M. R. (2000). In defense of self-control. *Theoretical Criminology*, *4*, 55–69. doi:10.1177/1362480600004001003

Hirschi, T., & Gottfredson, M. R. (1994). The generality of deviance . In Hirschi, T., & Gottfredson, M. R. (Eds.), *Generality of deviance* (pp. 1–22). New Brunswick, NJ: Transaction.

Hollinger, R. C. (1993). Crime by computer: Correlates of software piracy and unauthorized account access. *Security Journal*, *4*, 2–12.

Hollinger, R. C. (1991). Hackers: Computer heroes or electronic highwaymen. *Computers & Society*, *2*, 6–17. doi:10.1145/122246.122248

Hollinger, R. C., & Lanza-Kaduce, L. (1988). The process of criminalization: The case of computer crime laws. *Criminology*, *26*(1), 101–126. doi:10.1111/j.1745-9125.1988.tb00834.x

Hollinger, R. C. (1992). Crime by computer: Correlates of software piracy and unauthorized account access. *Security Journal*, *2*, 2–12.

Holt, T. J. (2007). Subcultural evolution? Examining the influence of on- and off-line experiences on deviant subcultures. *Deviant Behavior*, *28*, 171–198. doi:10.1080/01639620601131065

Holt, T. J., & Bossler, A. M. (2009). Examining the applicability of lifestyle-routine activities theory for cybercrime victimization. *Deviant Behavior*, *30*, 1–25. doi:10.1080/01639620701876577

Holt, T. J., & Blevins, K. R. (2007). Examining sex work from the client's perspective: Assessing johns using online data. *Deviant Behavior*, *28*(3), 333–354. doi:. doi:10.1080/01639620701233282

Holt, T. J., & Graves, D. C. (2007). A Qualitative Analysis of Advanced Fee Fraud Schemes. *The International Journal of Cyber-Criminology*, *1*(1), 137–154.

Holt, T. J., & Lampke, E. (2010). Exploring stolen data markets on-line: Products and market forces. *Forthcoming in Criminal Justice Studies*, *33*(2), 33–50. doi:. doi:10.1080/14786011003634415

Holt, T. J. (2009). Lone hacks or group: Examining the social organization of computer hackers . In Schmalleger, F. J., & Pittaro, M. (Eds.), *Crimes of the Internet*. Upper Saddle River, NJ: Prentice Hall.

Holt, T. J., & Kilger, M. (2008). *Techcrafters and makecrafters: A comparison of two populations of hackers*. 2008 WOMBAT Workshop on Information Security Threats Data Collection and Sharing. Pp. 67-78.

Holtfreter, K., Slyke, S. V., Bratton, J., & Gertz, M. (2008). Public perceptions of white-collar crime and punishment. *Journal of Criminal Justice*, *36*(1), 50–60. doi:10.1016/j.jcrimjus.2007.12.006

Honeynet Research Alliance. (2003). Profile: Automated Credit Card Fraud, *Know Your Enemy Paper* series. Retrieved June 21, 2005, from http://www.honeynet.org/papers/profiles/cc-fraud.pdf

Howell, B. A. (2007). Real-world problems of virtual crime . In Balkin, J. M., Grimmelmann, J., Katz, E., Kozlovski, N., Wagman, S., & Zarsky, T. (Eds.), *Cybercrime: Digital cops in a networked environment*. New York: New York University Press.

Hu, L., & Bentler, P. M. (1999). Cutoff criteria for fit indexes in covariance structure analysis: Conventional criteria versus new alternatives. *Structural Equation Modeling*, *6*, 1–55. doi:10.1080/10705519909540118

Hudson, R. (1999). *The sociology and psychology of terrorism: Who becomes a terrorist and why?* Washington, D.C: Federal Research Division, Library of Congress.

Huey, L. (2002). Policing the abstract: Some observations on policing cyberspace. *Canadian Journal of Criminology, 44*(3), 248–254.

Hughes, L. A., & DeLone, G. J. (2007). Viruses, worms, and Trojan horses: Serious crimes, nuisance, or both? *Social Science Computer Review, 25*, 79–98. doi:10.1177/0894439306292346

Hughes, B. G. R. (2003). *Understanding our gifted and complex minds: Intelligence, Asperger's Syndrome, and learning disabilities at MIT*. Retrieved July 5, 2007, from http://alum.mit.edu/news/WhatMatters/Archive/200308/

Humble, C. (2005) 'Inside the fake Viagra factory', *Sunday Telegraph*, 21 August, at http://www.telegraph.co.uk/news/uknews/3322770/Inside-the-fake-Viagra-factory.html.

Humphries, M. (2008). *Teen hacker Owen Walker won't be convicted*. Retrieved July 17, 2008, from http://www.geek.com/articles/news/teen-hacker-owen-walker-wont-be-convicted-20080717/

IC3. (2009) 2008 *Internet Crime Report*, Internet Crime Complaint Center, at www.ic3.gov/media/annualreport/2008_IC3Report.pdf

IFAW. (2005) *Born to be Wild: Primates are Not Pets*, London: International Fund for Animal Welfare, at http://www.ifaw.org/Publications/Program_Publications/Wildlife_Trade/Campaign_Scientific_Publications/asset_upload_file812_49478.pdf.

Ingram, J. R., & Hinduja, S. (2008). Neutralizing music piracy: An empirical examination. *Deviant Behavior, 29*, 334–366. doi:10.1080/01639620701588131

Internet Haganah. (2006). *How the brothers attacked the website of Jyllands-Posten*. February 7. Retrieved October 21, 2008, from http://internet-haganah.com/harchives/005456.html

Jagatic, T., Johnson, N., & Jakobsson, M. (2008). Social phishing. *Communications of the ACM, 50*(10), 94–100. doi:10.1145/1290958.1290968

Jaishankar, K. (2007). Cyber criminology: Evolving a novel discipline with a new journal. *International Journal of Cyber Criminology, 1*(1), 1–6.

James, L. (2005). *Phishing Exposed*. Rockland, MA: Syngress.

Jamestown. (2008). *Hacking manual by jailed jihadi appears on web*. Retrieved March 5, 2008, from http://www.jamestown.org/programs/gta/single/?tx_ttnews%5Btt_news%5D=4763&tx_ttnews%5BbackPid%5D=246&no_cache=1

Jesilow, P., Pontell, H. M., & Geis, G. (1996). How doctors defraud medicaid: Doctors tell their stories . In Cromwell, P. (Ed.), *In their own words, criminals on crime* (pp. 74–84). Los Angeles: Roxbury Publishing Company.

Jewkes, Y. (2006). *Comment on the book 'cyber crime and society by Majid Yar*. Retrieved September 09, 2007, from http://www.sagepub.co.uk/booksProdDesc.nav?prodId=Book227351

Johansson, J. (2008) 'Anatomy of a malware scam: The evil genius of XP Antivirus 2008', *The Register*, 22 August, at www.theregister.co.uk/2008/08/22/anatomy_of_a_hack/print.html

Johnson, B. D., Bardhi, F., Sifaneck, S. J., & Dunlap, E. (2006). Marijuana argot as subculture threads: Social constructions by users in New York City. *The British Journal of Criminology, 46*, 46–77. doi:.doi:10.1093/bjc/azi053

Johnson, B. (2008). *Nato says cyber warfare poses as great a threat as a missile attack*. Retrieved May 02, 2008, from http://www.guardian.co.uk/technology/2008/mar/06/hitechcrime.uksecurity

Johnson, B. (2009, April 27). *Pirate bay: Industry lawyers' websites attacked*. Retrieved April 28, 2009, from http://www.guardian.co.uk/technology/2009/apr/27/pirate-bay-law-firms-attack

Johnston, L., & Sharing, C. (2003) *Governing security: Explorations in policing and justice*. New York: Routeledge.

Jordan, T., & Taylor, P. (1998). A sociology of hackers. *The Sociological Review*, *46*(4), 757–780. doi:10.1111/1467-954X.00139

Jordan, T., & Taylor, P. (2004). *Hacktivism and cyberwars: Rebels with a cause?* London, UK: Routledge.

Kaplan, C. D., Kampe, H., & Farfan, J. A. F. (1990). Argots as a code-switching process: A case study of sociolinguistic aspects of drug subcultures . In Jacobson, R. (Ed.), *Codeswitching as a Worldwide Phenomenon* (pp. 141–157). New York: Peter Lang.

Katz, J. (1988). *Seductions of crime: Moral and sensual attractions in doing evil.* New York: Basic Books.

Kavur, J. (2009). *Mafiaboy speech a standing room only affair.* Retrieved April 9, 2009, from http://www.itworldcanada.com/Pages/Docbase/ViewArticle.aspx?title=&ID=idgml-88fa73eb-2d00-4622-986d-e06abe0916fc&lid

Keizer, G. (2009). *Russian 'cybermilitia' knocks Kyrgyzstan offline.* Retrieved January 28, 2009, from http://www.computerworld.com/s/article/9126947/Russian_cybermilitia_knocks_Kyrgyzstan_offline

Kilger, M., Stutzman, J., & Arkin, O. (2004). Profiling. *The Honeynet Project (2nd Ed.): Know your enemy*. Reading, MA: Addison Wesley Professional.

Kirk, J. (2007). Estonia recovers from massive denial-of-service attack. *InfoWorld, IDG News Service*. Retrieved May 17, 2007, from http://www.infoworld.com/article/07/05/17/estonia-denial-of-service-attack_1.html

Kleinrock, L. (2004). The internet rules of engagement: Then and now. *Technology and Society*, *24*, 193–207. doi:10.1016/j.techsoc.2004.01.015

Klick, J., & Tabarrok, A. (2005). Using terror alert levels to estimate the effect of police on crime. *The Journal of Law & Economics*, *48*, 267–279. doi:10.1086/426877

Kline, R. B. (2005). *Principles and practice of structural equation modeling*. New York: The Guilford Press.

Klockars, C. B. (1974). *The professional fence.* New York: Free Press.

Knight, W. (1999). *Jam Echelon day descends into spam farce.* Retrieved October 22, 1999, from http://news.zdnet.co.uk/emergingtech/0,1000000183,2074601,00.htm

Kravets, D. (2009). *Feds: Hacker disabled offshore oil platforms leak-detection system, threat level.* Retrieved March 18, 2009, from [REMOVED HYPERLINK FIELD]http://www.wired.com/threatlevel/2009/03/feds-hacker-dis/

Kravetz, A. (2002) 'Qatari national taken into federal custody in wake of terrorist attacks allegedly committed credit card fraud', *Peoria Journal Star*, 29 January.

Krebs, B. (2008). *Lithuania weathers cyber attack, braces for round 2.* Retrieved July 29, 2008, from http://voices.washingtonpost.com/securityfix/2008/07/lithuania_weathers_cyber_attac_1.html

Krohn, M. D., Skinner, W. F., Massey, J. L., & Akers, R. L. (1985). Social learning theory and adolescent cigarette smoking: A longitudinal study. *Social Problems*, *32*, 455–473. doi:10.1525/sp.1985.32.5.03a00050

Lakhani, K. R., & Wolf, R. G. (2003). *Why hackers do what they do: Understanding motivation and effort in free/open source software projects*. SSRN.

Landler, M., & Markoff, J. (2007). *Digital fears emerge after data siege in Estonia. RetrievedMay29, 2007*, from http://www.nytimes.com/2007/05/29/technology/29estonia.html

Landreth, B. (1985). *Out of the inner circle: A hacker's guide to computer security*. Bellevue, WA: Microsoft Press.

Langton, L., Piquero, N. L., & Hollinger, R. C. (2006). An empirical test of the relationship between employee theft and self-control. *Deviant Behavior*, *27*, 537–565. doi:10.1080/01639620600781548

Lasica, J. D. (2005). *Darknet: Hollywood's war against the digital generation*. Hoboken, NJ: John Wiley & Sons.

Lee, G., Akers, R. L., & Borg, M. J. (2004). Social learning and structural factors in adolescent substance use. *Western Criminology Review*, *5*, 17–34.

Lerman, P. (1967). Argot, symbolic deviance, and subcultural delinquency. *American Sociological Review*, *32*, 209–224. doi:.doi:10.2307/2091812

Levene, T. (2003) 'The artful dodgers', Guardian, 29 November, at *money.guardian.co.uk*/scamsandfraud/story/0,13802,1095616,00.html.

Levi, M. (2000). *The Prevention of Plastic and Cheque Fraud: A Briefing Paper*. London: Home Office Research, Development, and Statistics Directorate.

Levi, M. (2006). The Media Construction of Financial White-Collar Crimes. *The British Journal of Criminology*, *46*(6), 1037–1057. doi:10.1093/bjc/azl079

Levy, S. (1994). *Hackers: Heroes of the computer revolution*. Harmondsworth, UK: Penguin.

Lewis, E., & Anthony, D. (2005, August 12). Social Networks and Organizational Learning During a Crisis: A Simulated Attack on the Internet Infrastructure. Paper presented at the annual meeting of the American Sociological Association, Marriott Hotel, Loews Philadelphia Hotel, Philadelphia, PA

Leyden, J. (2002) 'Online gambling tops Internet card fraud league', *The Register*, 28 March, at www.theregister.co.uk/content/23/24633.html.

Leyden, J. (2003). *Al-Qaeda: The 39 principles of holy war*. Retrieved September 4, 2003, from http://www.israelnewsagency.com/Al Qaeda.html

Leyden, J. (2004) 'WTO rules against US gambling laws', *The Register*, 11 November., at www.theregister.co.uk/2004/11/11/us_gambling_wto_rumble/.

Leyden, J. (2006) 'Slobodan Trojan poses as murder pics', *The Register*, 15 March, at www.theregister.co.uk/2006/03/15/slobodan_trojan/.

Liedtke, M. (2005) 'Click fraud' threatens online advertising boom, *Legal Technology*, 14 February.

Loader, I. (1999). Consumer culture and the commodification of policing and security. *Sociology*, *33*(2), 373–392.

Loader, B. D. (1997). The governance of cyberspace: Politics, technology, and global restructuring. In Loaderv, B. D. (Ed.), *The governance of cyberspace: Politics, technology and global Restructuring* (pp. 1–19). New York, NY: Routledge. doi:10.4324/9780203360408_chapter_1

Loeber, R., & Stouthamer-Loeber, M. (1986). Family factors as correlates and predictors of juvenile conduct problems and delinquency . In Tonry, M., & Morris, N. (Eds.), *Crime and justice: An annual review of research* (*Vol. 7*). Chicago, Ill.: University of Chicago Press.

Lofland, J., & Lofland, L. H. (1995). *Analyzing social settings: A guide to qualitative observation and analysis* (3rd ed.). Belmont, CA: Wadsworth Publishing.

Lofty Perch. (2008). *Control system cyber security self-assessment tool, U.S. Department of Homeland Security, Control Systems Security Program (CSSP)*. Retrieved 2008 from http://www.loftyperch.com/cs2sat.html

Longshore, D., Chang, E., Hsieh, S. C., & Messina, N. (2004). Self-control and social bonds: A combined control perspective on deviance. *Crime and Delinquency*, *50*, 542–564. doi:10.1177/0011128703260684

Lord, C., Rutter, M., & Le Couteur, A. (1994). Autism diagnostic interview—Revised. *Journal of Autism and Developmental Disorders*, *24*, 659–686. doi:10.1007/BF02172145

Lucas, A. M. (2005). The work of sex work: Elite prostitutes' vocational orientations and experiences. *Deviant Behavior*, *26*, 513–546. doi:.doi:10.1080/01639620500218252

Mackiewicz, R. (2008). *Benefits of IEC 61850 networking, marketing subcommittee chair, UCA international users group, SISCO, Inc.* (2008). Retrieved December 13, 2009, from http://www.SISCOnet.com/

Make Love Not Spam. (2004). *Make Love Not Spam*. Retrieved April 3, 2009, from http://www.makelovenotspam.com/

Mann, D., & Sutton, M. (1998). NetCrime. More change in the organisation of thieving. *The British Journal of Criminology*, *38*(2), 210–229.

Manning, P. K. (2006). Two cases of American anti-terrorism . In Wood, J., & Dupont, B. (Eds.), *Democracy, society and the governance of security* (pp. 52–85). New York: Cambridge University Press. doi:10.1017/CBO9780511489358.005

Marron, D. B., & Steel, D. G. (2000). Which countries protect intellectual property? The case of software piracy. *Economic Inquiry*, *38*(2), 159–174.

Maruna, S., & Copes, J. H. (2005). What have we learned from five decades of neutralization research? *Crime and Justice: An Annual Review of Research*, *32*, 221–320.

Marx, G. T. (1997). Some conceptual issues in the study of borders and surveillance. In E. Zureik, E. & M.B. Salter (Ed.), *Global surveillance and policing: Borders, security, identity* (pp. 11-35). Portland, OR: Willan Publishing.

Masters, G. (n.d.). *Majority of adolescents online have tried hacking*. Retrieved May 18, from http://www.securecomputing.net.au/News/145298,majority-of-adolescents-online-have-tried-hacking.aspx

Mativat, F., & Tremblay, P. (1997). Counterfeiting credit cards: Displacement effects, suitable offenders, and crime wave patterns. *The British Journal of Criminology*, *37*(2), 165–183.

Matza, D. (1964). *Delinquency and drift*. New York: John Wiley and Sons, Inc.

Matza, D. (1969). *Becoming deviant*. Upper Saddle River, NJ: Prentice-Hall, Inc.

Maurer, D. W. (1981). *Language of the underworld*. Louisville, KY: University of Kentucky Press.

McEwen, T. J. (1989). *Dedicated computer crime units*. Washington, DC: National Institute of Justice.

McGinn, D. (2009). Asperger's parents resist name change. *The Globe and Mail*, November 4, pp. L1, L5.

McKenzie, H. (2007, July 31). *Faking it: Piracy poses headache for Olympics*. Retrieved October 26, 2007, from http://www.cnn.com/2007/WORLD/asiapcf/07/24/olympics.piracy/index.html

McMillan, R. (2007). *Insider charged with hacking California canal system*. Retrieved November 29, 2007, from http://www.computerworld.com/s/article/9050098/Insider_charged_with_hacking_California_canal_system?taxonomyName=storage

Melbin, M. (1978). Night as frontier. *American Sociological Review*, *43*, 3–22. doi:.doi:10.2307/2094758

Meserve, J. (2007). *Staged cyber attack reveals vulnerability in power grid*. Retrieved April 22, 2009, from http://www.cnn.com/2007/US/09/26/power.at.risk/index.html

Meyer, G., & Thomas, J. (1990). The baudy world of the byte bandit: A postmodernist interpretation of the computer underground . In Schmalleger, F. (Ed.), *Computers in criminal justice*. Bristol, IN: Wyndham Hall.

Meyer, G. R. (1989). *The social organization of the computer underground*. Master of Arts Thesis. Dekalb, IL: Northern Illinois University.

Michalowski, R. J., & Pfuhl, E. H. (1991). Technology, property, and law - the case of computer crime. *Crime, Law, and Social Change*, *15*(3), 255–275.

Miller, D., & Slater, D. (2000). *The Internet: An ethnographic approach*. New York, NY: Berg.

Miller, D., & Slater, D. (2000). *The internet: An ethnographic approach*. New York: Berg.

Minor, W. W. (1981). Techniques of neutralization: A re-conceptualization and empirical examination. *Journal of Research in Crime and Delinquency*, *18*, 295–318. doi:10.1177/002242788101800206

MIT IHTFP Hack Gallery. (1994). *The hacker ethic*. Retrieved from December 22, 2009, from http://hacks.mit.edu/misc/ethics.html

Mitnick, K. D., & Simon, W. L. (2005). *The art of intrusion: The real stories behind the exploits of hackers, intruders & deceivers*. New York: John Wiley and Sons.

Mitnick, K. D., Simon, W. L., & Wozniak, S. (2002). *The art of deception: Controlling the human element of security*. New York: John Wiley and Sons.

Mittelstaedt, M. (2007). Researcher sees link between vitamin D and autism. *The Globe and Mail*, July 6, p. L4.

Modine, A. (2009) 'Sports site sues Facebook for click fraud: RootZoo files class-action complaint', *The Register*, 14 July, at www.theregister.co.uk/2009/07/14/rootzoo_sues_facebook_for_click_fraud/

Morphy, E. (2004). *MPAA steps up fight against piracy*. Retrieved October 24, 2007, from http://www.newsfactor.com/story.xhtml?story_title=MPAA-Steps-Up-Fight-Against-Piracy&story_id=25800

Morris, R. G., & Blackburn, A. G. (2009). Cracking the code: An empirical exploration of social learning theory and computer crime. *Journal of Criminal Justice*, *32*, 1–32.

Morris, R. G., & Higgins, G. E. (2009). (in press). Neutralizing potential and self-reported digital piracy: A multi-theoretical exploration among college undergraduates. *Criminal Justice Review*, *34*. doi:10.1177/0734016808325034

Morris, R. G., Copes, J., & Perry-Mullis, K. (2009). (in press). Correlates of currency counterfeiting. *Journal of Criminal Justice*. doi:.doi:10.1016/j.jcrimjus.2009.07.007

Morris, R. G., & Johnson, M. C. (2009). Sedentary activities, peer behavior, and delinquency among American youth. *University of Texas at Dallas*. Working Paper.

Muhlhausen, D. B., & Little, E. (2007). *Federal law enforcement grants and crime rates: No connection except for waste and abuse*. Retrieved October 10, 2007, from http://www.heritage.org/Research/Crime/upload/bg_2015.pdf

Mulhall, R. (1997). Where have all the hackers gone? A study in motivation, deterrence,and crime displacement. Part I—Introduction and methodology. *Computers & Security*, *16*(4), 277–284. doi:10.1016/S0167-4048(97)80190-3

Multiple unknown authors (2003). *The Jargon File, version 4.4.7*. Retrieved December 22, 2009, from http://www.catb.org/~esr/jargon/html/index.html

Muthén, L. K., & Muthén, B. O. (2007). *Mplus user's guide* (4th ed.). Los Angeles, CA: Muthén & Muthén.

Mutina, B. (2007). *Hacking incident goes on Czech TV*. Retrieved June 19, 2007, to www.zone-h.org

Naraine, R., & Danchev, D. (2008). *Zero Day: Coordinated Russia vs Georgia cyber attack in progress*. Retrieved August 11, 2008, from http://blogs.zdnet.com/security/?p=1670

Nash, J. M. (2002). *The geek syndrome*. Retrieved May 6, 2002, from http://www.time.com/time/covers/1101020506/scaspergers.html

National Research Council. (2002). Making the nation safer: the role of science and technology in countering terrorism, *Report from the Committee on Science and Technology for Countering Terrorism*. Retrieved 2002 from http://www.nap.edu/openbook.php?record_id=10415&page=R1

Naughton, J. (2000). *A brief history of the future: The origins of the internet*. London, UK: Phoenix.

NCIRC. (2008). *NATO opens new centre of excellence on cyber defense*. Retrieved May 03, 2008, from http://www.nato.int/docu/update/2008/05-may/e0514a.html

nCircle. (2009). *PIPEDA Compliance*. Retrieved December 23, 2009, from http://www.ncircle.com/index.php?s=solution_regcomp_PIPEDA-Compliance&source=adwords&kw=pipeda&gclid=CJHNxLDl7Z4CFVw55QodnTEAKg

Nelken, D. (1994). *White-collar crime*. Aldershot, MA: Dartmouth.

Nelson, M. C., & Gordon-Larsen, P. (2006). Physical activity and sedentary behavior patterns are associated with selected adolescent health risk behaviors. *Pediatrics*, *117*, 1281–1290. doi:10.1542/peds.2005-1692

Netted Automation. (2008). *Comparison of IEC 60870-5-101/-103/-104, DNP3, and IEC 60870-6-TASE.2 with IEC 61850 FAQ*. Retrieved 2008 from http://www.nettedautomation.com/news/n_51.html

Newman, O. (1973). *Defensible space: Crime prevention through urban design*. New York: Macmillan Publishing.

Newman, G., & Clarke, R. (2003). *Superhighway robbery: Preventing e-commerce crime*. Cullompton, UK: Willan Press.

Newsted, P. R., Chin, W., Ngwenyama, O., & Lee, A. (1996, December 16-18). *Resolved: surveys have outlived their usefulness in IS research.* Paper presented at the Seventeenth International Conference on Information Systems, Cleveland, OH.

NFSA. (2009) *The National Fraud Strategy A new approach to combating fraud*, The National Fraud Strategic Authority, at http://www.attorneygeneral.gov.uk/News-Centre/News/Documents/NFSA_STRATEGY_AW_Web%5B1%5D.pdf

Nhan, J. (2008). Criminal justice firewalls: Prosecutorial decision-making in cyber and high-tech crime cases . In Jaishankar, K. (Ed.), *International perspectives on crime and justice*. Oxford, UK: Cambridge Scholars Publishing.

Nhan, J., & Huey, L. (2008). Policing through nodes, clusters and bandwidth: The role of network relations in the prevention of and response to cyber-crimes . In Leman-Langlois, S. (Ed.), *Techo-crime: Technology, crime, and social control*. Portland, OR: Willan Press.

Nhan, J., & Bachmann, M. (2009). The challenges of cybercriminological research . In Maguire, M., & Okada, D. (Eds.), *Critical Issues of Crime and Criminal Justice*. Washington D.C., London: Sage.

Nickerson, C. (2008). Mutual Suppression: Comment on Paulhus et al. (2004). *Multivariate Behavioral Research*, *43*, 556–563. doi:10.1080/00273170802490640

Nuwere, E., & Chanoff, D. (2003). *Hacker cracker: A journey from the mean streets of Brooklyn to the frontiers of cyberspace*. New York: HarperCollins Publishers.

O'Harrow, R. (2001) 'Identity thieves thrive in information age: rise of online data brokers makes criminal impersonation easier', *Washington Post*, 31 May, at http://www.encyclopedia.com/doc/1P2-438258.html.

Odum, H. (1937). Notes on technicways in contemporary society. *American Sociological Review*, *2*, 336–346. doi:.doi:10.2307/2084865

Ogburn, W. (1932). *Social change*. New York: Viking Press.

Ogilvie, M. (2007). New genetic link to autism. *Toronto Star*, February 19, pp. A1, A12.

Onley, D. S., & Wait, P. (2006). *Red storm rising*. Retrieved August 21, 2006, from http://www.gcn.com/Articles/2006/08/17/Red-storm-rising.aspx

OSC. (2008). *Jihadist forum invites youths to join 'electronic jihadist campaign*.' Open Source Center, October 6, 2008.

Parizo, E. B. (2005). *Busted: The inside story of "Operation Firewall*." Retrieved January 18, 2006, from http://searchsecurity.techtarget.com/news/article/0,289142,sid14_gci1146949,00.html

Parker, F. B. (1972). Social control and the technicways. *Social Forces*, *22*(2), 163–168. doi:.doi:10.2307/2572684

Parker, D. B. (1976). *Crime by computer*. New York: Scribner.

Parker, D. B. (1989). *Computer crime: Criminal justice resource manual*. (2th ed.). Standfor, CA: Stanford Research Institute (SRI) International.

Paulhus, D. L., Robins, R. W., Trzesniewski, K. H., & Tracy, J. L. (2004). Two replicable suppressor situations in personality research. *Multivariate Behavioral Research*, *39*, 303–328. doi:10.1207/s15327906mbr3902_7

Payne, B. K., & Chappell, A. T. (2008). Using student samples in criminological. research. *Journal of Criminal Justice Education*, *19*, 177–194. doi:10.1080/10511250802137226

Paz, S. (2009). *Anti-Israel group wreaks havoc with Israeli web sites*. Retrieved January 4, 2009, from http://www.jpost.com/servlet/Satellite?cid=1230733155647&pagename=JPArticle%2FShowFull

Pearce, F. (1976). *Crimes of the Powerful – Marxism, Crime and Deviance*. London: Pluto Press.

Peterson, S. (2001). *Crackers prepare retaliation for terrorist attack.* Retrieved December 22, 2009, from http://www.gyre.org/news/explore/hacktivism?page=1

Piquero, N. L., Tibbetts, S. G., & Blankenship, M. B. (2005). Examining the Role of Differential Association and Techniques of Neutralization in Explaining Corporate Crime. *Deviant Behavior, 26*, 159–188. doi:10.1080/01639620590881930

Piquero, A., & Tibbetts, S. (1996). Specifying the direct and indirect effects of low self control and situational factors in offenders' decision making: Toward a more complete model of rational offending. *Justice Quarterly, 13*, 481–510. doi:10.1080/07418829600093061

Piquero, A. R., MacIntosh, R., & Hickman, M. (2000). Does self-control affect survey response? Applying exploratory, confirmatory, and item response theory analysis to Grasmick et al.'s self-control scale. *Criminology, 38*, 897–929. doi:10.1111/j.1745-9125.2000.tb00910.x

Piquero, A. R., & Rosay, A. B. (1998). The reliability and validity of Grasmick et al.'s self-control scale. A comment on Longshore et al. *Criminology, 36*, 157–174. doi:10.1111/j.1745-9125.1998.tb01244.x

Pontell, H. N., & Rosoff, S. M. (2009). White-collar delinquency. *Crime, Law, and Social Change, 51*(1), 147–162. doi:10.1007/s10611-008-9146-0

Powell, A. (2002). *Taking responsibility: Good practice guidelines for services: Adultswith Asperger syndrome.* London, UK: National Autistic Society.

Pratt, T. C., & Cullen, F. T. (2000). The empirical status of Gottfredson and Hirschi's general theory of crime: A meta-analysis. *Criminology, 38*, 931–964. doi:10.1111/j.1745-9125.2000.tb00911.x

Primoratz, I. (2004). *Terrorism: The philosophical issues.* New York: Palgrave Macmillan.

Provos, N. McNamee, D., Mavrommatis, P., Wang, K., & Modadugu, N. (2007). *The ghost in the browser: Analysis of web-based malware.* USENIX Workshop on Hot Topics in Understanding Botnets, April 2007.

Quayle, E., & Taylor, M. (2002). Child pornography and the internet: Perpetuating a cycle of abuse. *Deviant Behavior, 23*, 331–361. doi:.doi:10.1080/01639620290086413

Quinn, J. F., & Forsyth, C. J. (2005). Describing sexual behavior in the era of the Internet: A typology for empirical research. *Deviant Behavior, 26*, 191–207. doi:.doi:10.1080/01639620590888285

Raymond, E. S. (Ed.). (1996). *The new hacker's dictionary.* Cambridge, MA: The MIT Press.

Raymond, E. (1996). *The new hackers dictionary.* Cambridge, MA: MIT Press.

Reed, G. E., & Yeager, P. C. (1996). Organizational offending and neoclassical criminology: Challenging the reach of A General Theory of Crime . *Criminology, 34*, 357–382. doi:10.1111/j.1745-9125.1996.tb01211.x

Research, I. B. M. (2006). *Global security analysis lab: Factsheet. IBM Research.* Retrieved January 16, 2006, from http://domino.research.ibm.com/comm/pr.nsf.pages/rsc.gsal.html

Reuters (2005) 'Microsoft, Nigeria fight e-mail scammers', *e-week.com*, 14 October, at www.eweek.com/article2/0,1895,1871565,00.asp.

Reynalds, J. (2004). *Internet 'terrorist' using Yahoo to recruit 600 Muslims for hack attack.* Retrieved October 21, 2008, from http://www.mensnewsdaily.com/archive/r/reynalds/04/reynalds022804.htm

Richardson, R. (2008). *CSI computer crime and security survey.* Retrieved December 16, 2009, from http://www.cse.msstate.edu/~cse2v3/readings/CSIsurvey2008.pdf

Richardson, T. (2005) 'BT cracks down on rogue diallers', *The Register*, 27 May, at www.theregister.co.uk/2005/05/27/rogue_bt_diallers/.

Rogers, M., Smoak, N. D., & Liu, J. (2006). Self-reported deviant computer behavior: A big-5, moral choice, and manipulative exploitive behavior analysis. *Deviant Behavior, 27*, 245–268. doi:10.1080/01639620600605333

Rogers, J. (2007). *Gartner: victims of online phishing up nearly 40 percent in 2007*. Retrieved January 2, 2008, from http://www.scmagazineus.com/Gartner-Victims-of-online-phishing-up-nearly-40-percent-in-2007/article/99768/

Rogers, M. (2003). *Preliminary findings: Understanding criminal computer behavior: A Personality trait and moral Choice Analysis*. Retrieved December 22, 2009, from http://homes.cerias.purdue.edu/~mkr/

Rogers, M. K. (2001). A social learning theory and moral disengagement analysis of criminal computer behavior: An exploratory study. (PhD dissertation), University of Manitoba, Canada.

Roher, E. (2006). Cyber bullying: A growing epidemic in schools. *OPC Register*, *8*, 12–15.

Rosoff, S. M., Pontell, H. N., & Tillman, R. H. (2002). *Profit without honor* (2nd ed.). Englewood-Cliffs, NJ: Prentice-Hall.

Ross, B. (2006). *Hackers penetrate water system computers*. Retrieved October 30, 2006, from http://blogs.abcnews.com/theblotter/2006/10/hackers_penetra.html

Rothman, M., & Gandossy, R. F. (1982). Sad tales: The accounts of white-collar defendants and the decision to sanction. *Pacific Sociological Review*, *4*, 449–473.

Rotter, J. B. (1954). *Social learning and clinical psychology*. Englewood Cliffs, NJ: Prentice-Hall. doi:10.1037/10788-000

Roush, W. (1995). Hackers: Taking a byte out of computer crime. *Technology Review*, *98*, 32–40.

Rowland, G. (2004). Fast-moving and slow-moving institutions. *Studies in Comparative International Development*, *38*, 109–131. doi:10.1007/BF02686330

Rupnow, C. (2003) 'Not "made of money" ', *Wisconsin Leader-Telegram*, 23 April, at www.xpressmart.com/thebikernetwork/scam.html.

Rupp, W. T., & Smith, A. D. (2004). Exploring the impacts of P2P networks on the entertainment industry. *Information Management & Computer Security*, *12*(1), 102–116. doi:10.1108/09685220410518865

Rutherford, M.D., Baron-Cohen, S., & Wheelwright, S. (2002). Reading the mind in the voice: A study with normal adults and adults with Asperger syndrome and high functioning autism. *Journal of Autism and Developmental Disorders, 3)*, 189-194.

Sandars, N. K. (1972). *The Epic of Gilgamesh: An English Version with an Introduction*. Harmondsworth: Penguin Classics.

Satchwell, G. (2004). *A Sick Business: Counterfeit medicines and organised crime*. Lyon: Interpol.

Schachtman, N. (2009). *Wage cyberwar against Hamas, surrender your PC*. Retrieved January 8, 2009, from http://www.wired.com/dangerroom/2009/01/israel-dns-hack/

Schell, B. H., Dodge, J. L., & Moutsatos, S. (2002). *The Hacking of America: Who's Doing It, Why, and How*. Westport, CT: Quorum Books.

Schell, B. H., & Martin, C. (2006). *Webster's New World Hacker Dictionary*. Indianapolis, IN: Wiley.

Schell, B. H. (2007). *Contemporary world issues: The internet and society*. Santa Barbara, CA: ABC-CLIO.

Schell, B. H., & Martin, C. (2004). *Contemporary world issues: Cybercrime*. Santa Barbara, CA: ABC-CLIO.

Schlegel, K. (2000). Transnational crime: Implications for local law enforcement. *Journal of Contemporary Criminal Justice*, *16*(4), 365–385. doi:10.1177/1043986200016004002

Schneider, J. L. (2005). Stolen-goods markets: Methods of disposal. *The British Journal of Criminology*, *45*, 129–140. doi:.doi:10.1093/bjc/azh100

Schoepfer, A., Carmichael, S., & Piquero, N. L. (2007). Do perceptions of punishment vary between white-collar and street crimes? *Journal of Criminal Justice*, *35*(2), 151–163. doi:10.1016/j.jcrimjus.2007.01.003

Schwartau, W. (1996). *Information warfare* (2nd ed.). New York: Thunder's Mouth Press.

Scott, M. B., & Lyman, S. M. (1968). Accounts. *American Sociological Review*, *33*, 46–62. doi:10.2307/2092239

Shaw, E. D., Post, J. M., & Ruby, K. G. (1999). *Inside the mind of the insider*. www.securitymanagement.com, December, pp. 1-11.

Shaw, E., Ruby, K., & Post, J. (1998). *The insider threat to insider information systems*. Retrieved December 22, 2009, from http://www.rand.org/pubs/conf_proceedings/CF163/CF163.appe.pdf

Shea, D. (2003). *Resources, Science and Industry Division; The Library of Congress, CRS Report for Congress, Critical Infrastructure: Control Systems and the Terrorist Threat, CRS-RL31534*. January 20, 2004, from: http://www.fas.org/sgp/crs/homesec/RL31534.pdf

Shearing, C. D., & Wood, J. (2003). Nodal governance, democracy, and the new 'denizens.'. *Journal of Law and Society*, *30*(3), 400–419. doi:10.1111/1467-6478.00263

Sieber, U. (1986). *The International handbook on computer crime*. Oxford, UK: John Wiley.

Sijtsma, K. (2009). On the use, misuse, and the very limited usefulness of Cronbach's alpha. *Psychometrika*, *1*, 107–120. doi:10.1007/s11336-008-9101-0

Silverman, D. (2001). *Interpreting qualitative data: Methods for analyzing talk, text, and interaction* (2nd ed.). Thousand Oaks, CA: SAGE Publications.

Simpson, S. S. (1987). Cycles of illegality: Antitrust violations in corporate America. *Social Forces*, *65*(4), 943–963. doi:10.2307/2579018

Simpson, S. S., & Piquero, N. L. (2002). Low self-control, organizational theory, and corporate crime. *Law & Society Review*, *36*, 509–548. doi:10.2307/1512161

Siwek, S. E. (2006). *The true cost of motion picture piracy to the U.S. economy*. Retrieved September 20, 2007, from http://www.ipi.org/ipi%5CIPIPublications.nsf/PublicationLookupFullText/E274F77ADF58BD08862571F8001BA6BF

Siwek, S. E. (2007). *The true cost of sound recording piracy to the U.S. economy*. Retrieved September 20, 2007, from http://www.ipi.org/ipi%5CIPIPublications.nsf/PublicationLookupMain/D95DCB90F513F7D78625733E005246FA

Skinner, W. F., & Fream, A. M. (1997). A social learning theory analysis of computer crime among college students. *Journal of Research in Crime and Delinquency*, *34*, 495–518. doi:10.1177/0022427897034004005

Skolnick, J. H., & Fyfe, J. J. (1993). *Above the law: Police and the excessive use of force*. New York: The Free Press.

Skorodumova, O. (2004). Hackers as information space phenomenon. *Social Sciences*, *35*, 105–113.

Smith, R. G., Grabosky, P., & Urbas, G. (2004). *Cyber criminals on trial*. New York: Cambridge University Press. doi:10.1017/CBO9780511481604

Sockel, H., & Falk, L. K. (2009). Online privacy, vulnerabilities, and threats: A manager's perspective . In Chen, K., & Fadlalla, A. (Eds.), *Online consumer protection: Theories of human relativism*. Hershey, PA: Information Science Reference. doi:10.4018/978-1-60566-012-7.ch003

Sophos. (2004). Female virus-writer Gigabyte,arrested in Belgium, Sophos comments.Retrieved February 16, 2004, from http://www.sophos.com/pressoffice/news/articles/2004/02/va_gigabyte.html

St. Sauver, J. (2004). *NLANR/Internet2 Joint Techs Meeting, University of Oregon Computing Center*. Retrieved July 24, 2004, from http://www.uoregon.edu/~joe/scada/SCADA-security.pdf.

Staff, J., & Uggen, C. (2003). The fruits of good work: Early work experiences and adolescent deviance. *Journal of Research in Crime and Delinquency*, *40*, 263–290. doi:10.1177/0022427803253799

Stallman, R. (2002). *Free software, free society: Selected essays of Richard M. Stallman*. Boston: Free Software Foundation.

Steele, G. Jr, Woods, D. R., Finkel, R. A., Crispin, M. R., Stallman, R. M., & Goodfellow, G. S. (1983). *The hacker's dictionary*. New York: Harper and Row.

Steffensmeier, D. (1989). On the causes of "white-collar" crime: An assessment of Hirschi and Gottfredson's claims. *Criminology*, *27*(2), 345–358. doi:10.1111/j.1745-9125.1989.tb01036.x

Sterling, B. (1992). *The hacker crackdown: Law and disorder on the electronic frontier*. London, UK: Viking.

Stewart, J. K. (1990). *Organizing for computer crime: Investigation and prosecution*. Medford, MA: Davis Association.

Stohl, M. (2006). Cyber terrorism: a clear and present danger, the sum of all fears, breaking point or patriot games? *Crime, Law, and Social Change*, *46*, 223–238. doi:10.1007/s10611-007-9061-9

Sturgeon, W. (2004). Alleged Belgian virus writer arrested. Retrieved February 17, from http://news.cnet.com/Alleged-Belgian-virus-writer-arrested/2100-7355_3-5160493.html

Sutherland, E. H. (1940). White-collar criminality. *American Sociological Review*, *5*(1), 1–12. doi:10.2307/2083937

Sutherland, E. (1949). *White Collar Crime*. New York: Dryden.

Sykes, G. M., & Matza, D. (1957). Techniques of neutralization: A theory of delinquency. *American Sociological Review*, *22*, 664–670. doi:10.2307/2089195

Sykes, G. M., & Matza, D. (1957). Techniques of neutralizations: A theory of delinquency. *American Sociological Review*, *22*(6), 664–670. doi:10.2307/2089195

Szalavitz, M. (2009). Asperger's theory does about-face. *Toronto Star*, May 14, 2009, pp. L1, L3.

Tappan, P. W. (1947). Who is the criminal? *American Sociological Review*, *12*, 96–102. doi:10.2307/2086496

Tavani, H. (2000). Defining the boundaries of computer crime: Piracy, break-ins, and sabotage in cyberspace. *Computers & Society*, *30*, 3–9. doi:10.1145/572241.572242

Tavani, H. T., & Grodzinsky, F. S. (2005). Threat to democratic ideals in cyberspace. *Technology and Society Magazine, IEEE*, *24*(3), 40–44. doi:10.1109/MTAS.2005.1507539

Taylor, P. A. (1999). *Hackers: Crime and the digital sublime*. New York: Routledge. doi:10.4324/9780203201503

Taylor, R. W., Caeti, T. J., Loper, D. K., Fritsch, E. J., & Liederbach, J. (2006). *Digital crime and digital terrorism*. Upper Saddle River, NJ: Pearson.

Taylor, P. A. (2000). Hackers - cyberpunks or microserfs . In Thomas, D., & Loader, B. (Eds.), *Cybercrime: law enforcement, security and surveillance in the information age*. London, UK: Routledge.

Taylor, P. A. (1999). *Hackers: Crime in the digital sublime*. New York: Routledge. doi:10.4324/9780203201503

The White House. (2003). *The National Strategy to Secure Cyberspace*. Retrieved February 2003, from http://georgewbush-whitehouse.archives.gov/pcipb/cyberspace_strategy.pdf

Thomas, D. (2002). *Hacker culture*. Minneapolis, MN: University of Minnesota Press.

Thomas, D. (2002). *Notes from the underground: Hackers as watchdogs of industry*. Retrieved April 20, 2009, from http://www.ojr.org/ojr/business/1017969515.php

Thomas, J. (2005). *Intellectual property theft in Russia increasing dramatically: U.S. officials warns of "rampant piracy and counterfeiting*". Retrieved October 24, 2007, from http://usinfo.state.gov/ei/Archive/2005/May/19-415943.html

Thomas, R., & Martin, J. (2006). The underground economy: Priceless. *:login, 31*(6), 7-16.

Tittle, C. R., Ward, D. A., & Grasmick, H. G. (2003). Self-control and crime/deviance: Cognitive vs. behavioral measures. *Journal of Quantitative Criminology*, *19*, 333–365. doi:10.1023/B:JOQC.0000005439.45614.24

Tombs, S., & Whyte, D. (2003). Unmasking the Crimes of the Powerful . *Critical Criminology*, *11*(3), 217–236. doi:10.1023/B:CRIT.0000005811.87302.17

Treverton, G. F., Matthies, C., Cunningham, K. J., Goulka, J., Ridgeway, G., & Wong, A. (2009). *Film piracy, organized crime, and terrorism*. Retrieved April 20, 2009, from http://www.rand.org/pubs/monographs/2009/RAND_MG742.pdf

Turgeman-Goldschmidt, O. (2005). Hackers' accounts: Hacking as a social entertainment. *Social Science Computer Review*, *23*, 8–23. doi:10.1177/0894439304271529

Turgeman-Goldschmidt, O. (2008). The rhetoric of hackers' neutralizations . In Schmalleger, F., & Pittaro, M. (Eds.), *Crimes of the Internet* (pp. 317–335). Englewood-Cliffs, NJ: Prentice-Hall.

Turkle, S. (1984). *The second self: Computers and the human spirit*. New York, NY: Simon and Schuster.

Tzelgov, J., & Stern, I. (1978). Relationships between variables in three variable linear regression and the concept of suppressor. *Educational and Psychological Measurement*, *38*, 325–335. doi:10.1177/001316447803800213

Tzu, S. (2002). *The Art of War: Sun Tzu's Classic: In plain English. With Sun Pin's The Art of Warfare*. San Jose, CA: Writer's Club Press.

U.S General Accounting Office. (2003). *Homeland Security: Information sharing responsibilities,challenges and key management issues, GAO-03-1165T*. Retrieved September 17, 2003, from http://www.gao.gov/new.items/d031165t.pdf

U.S General Accounting Office. (2004). *Critical infrastructure protection: Challenges and effort to secure control systems, GAO-04-354*. Retrieved March 15, 2004, from http://www.gao.gov/new.items/d04354.pdf

U.S. Computer Emergency Response Team (US-CERT). (2008). *FAQ about the Control Systems Security Program (CSSP)*. Retrieved 2008 from http://www.us-cert.gov/control_systems/csfaq.html

U.S. Computer Emergency Response Team (US-CERT). (2008). *U.S. Department of Homeland Security, Control Systems Security Program (CSSP)*. Retrieved 2008 from http://cipbook.infracritical.com/book3/chapter10/ch10ref14.pdf

U.S. Computer Emergency Response Team (US-CERT). (2008). *U.S. Department of Homeland Security, Control systems Security Program (CSSP)*. Retrieved 2008 from http://www.us-cert.gov/control_systems

U.S. Computer Emergency Response Team (US-CERT). (2009). *U.S. Department of Homeland Security, Control Systems Security Program (CSSP), industrial control systems joint working group FAQ*. Retrieved 2009 from http://www.us-cert.gov/control_systems/icsjwg/

U.S. General Accounting Office. (1999). *Federal Information System Controls Audit Manual, GAO/AIMD-12.19.6*. Retrieved January, 1999, from http://www.gao.gov/special.pubs/ai12.19.6.pdf

U.S. General Accounting Office. (2003). *Critical infrastructure protection: Challenges for selected agencies and industry sectors, GAO-03-233*. Retrieved February 28, 2003, from http://www.gao.gov/new.items/d03233.pdf

Uchida, C. D. (1997). The development of the American police: An historical overview. In R.D. Dunham, R. D., & G.P. Alpert (Ed.) *Critical issues in policing: Contemporary readings 3rd ed.* (pp. 13-35). Prospect Heights, IL: Waveland Press.

Ulph, S. (2006). *Internet mujahideen refine electronic warfare tactics*. Retrieved December 22, 2009, from http://www.jamestown.org/programs/gta/single/?tx_ttnews%5Btt_news%5D=666&tx_ttnews%5BbackPid%5D=239&no_cache=1

Upitis, R. B. (1998). From hackers to Luddites, game players to game creators: Profiles of adolescent students using technology. *Journal of Curriculum Studies*, *30*(3), 293–318. doi:10.1080/002202798183620

USDOJ. (2004) 'Computer programmer arrested for extortion and mail fraud scheme targeting Google, Inc.', *US Department of Justice press release*, 18 March, at http://www.justice.gov/criminal/cybercrime/bradleyArrest.htm.

Utility Consulting International (UCI). (2009). *Development of security standards for DNP, ICCP and IEC 61850 FAQ*. Retrieved 2009 from http://www.uci-usa.com/Projects/pr_List/Systems/CyberSecurity/Standards.html

Vamosi, R. (2008). *Second of 11 alleged TJX hackers pleads guilty*. Retrieved October 1, 2008, from http://news.cnet.com/8301-1009_3-10048507-83.html?tag=mncol

Van Doorn, L. (1992). Computer break-ins: A case study. Vrige Universiteit, Amsterdam, *NLUUG Proceedings*, October.

Vance, R. B. (1972). Howard Odum's technicways: A neglected lead in American sociology. *Social Forces, 50*, 456–461. doi:.doi:10.2307/2576788

Vatis, M. (2001). Cyber terrorism and information warfare: Government perspectives . In Alexander, Y., & Swetnam, M. S. (Eds.), *Cyber terrorism and information warfare. Ardsley: Transnational Publishers, Inc.*

Voiskounsky, A. E., & Smyslova, O. V. (2003). Flow-based model of computer hackers' motivation. *Cyberpsychology & Behavior, 6*, 171–180. doi:10.1089/109493103321640365

Wall, D. S. (2008). Cybercrime, media, and insecurity: The shaping of public perceptions of cybercrime. *International Review of Law Computers & Technology, 22*, 45–63. doi:10.1080/13600860801924907

Wall, D. S. (2007). *Cybercrime: The transformation of crime in the information age*. Cambridge: Polity.

Wall, D. S. (2005). The Internet as a conduit for criminal activity . In Pattavina, A. (Ed.), *Information technology and the criminal justice system* (pp. 78–94). Thousand Oaks, CA: Sage.

Wall, D. S. (2001). Cybercrimes and the internet . In Wall, D. S. (Ed.), *Crime and the internet* (pp. 1–17). New York: Routledge.

Wall, D. S. (2002) DOT.CONS: *Internet Related Frauds and Deceptions upon Individuals within the UK*, Final Report to the Home Office, March (unpublished).

Walters, G. D. (2002). *Criminal belief systems: An integrated-interactive theory of lifestyles*. Westport, CT: Greenwood Publishing Group.

Warr, M. (2002). *Companions in crime: The social aspects of criminal conduct*. Cambridge, MA: Cambridge University Press.

Wasserman, S., & Faust, K. (1994). *Social network analysis: Methods and applications*. New York: Cambridge University Press.

Watson, D., Holz, T., & Mueller, S. (2005). Know your enemy: Phishing. Retrieved December 22, 2009, from http://www.honeynet.org/papers/phishing

Weisburd, D., Waring, E., & Chayat, E. F. (2001). *White-collar crime and criminal careers*. Cambridge, MA: Cambridge University Press. doi:10.1017/CBO9780511499524

Weisburd, D., Wheeler, S., Waring, E., & Bode, N. (1991). *Crimes of the Middle Classes: White-Collar Offenders in the Federal Courts*. New Haven, CT: Yale University Press.

Weisburd, D., & Schlegel, K. (1992). Returning to the mainstream . In Kip, S., & Weisburd, D. (Eds.), *White-collar crime reconsidered*. Boston, MA: Northeastern University Press.

Welsh, B. C., & Farrington, D. P. (2002). Crime prevention effects of closed circuit television: A systematic review. Retrieved October 10, 2007, from http://www.homeoffice.gov.uk/rds/pdfs2/hors252.pdf

Welsh, B. C., & Farrington, D. P. (2006). Closed-circuit television surveillance. In B.C. Welsh & D.P. Farrington (Ed.) *Preventing crime: What works for children, offenders, victims, and places* (pp. 193-208). Dordrecht, NL: Springer.

WHO. (2004) *Report of Pre-eleventh ICDRA Satellite Workshop on Counterfeit Drugs*, Madrid, Spain, 13–14 February, at http://www.who.int/medicines/services/counterfeit/Pre_ICDRA_Conf_Madrid_Feb2004.pdf

William, S. (2000). *Armenian and Azerbaijani hackers wage war on Internet*. Retrieved February 17, 2000, from http://www.hrea.org/lists/huridocs-tech/markup/msg00417.html

Willott, S., Griffin, C., & Torrance, M. (2001). Snakes and ladders: Upper-middle class male offenders talk about economic crime. *Criminology*, *39*(2), 441–466. doi:10.1111/j.1745-9125.2001.tb00929.x

Wilson, B., & Atkinson, M. (2005). Rave and straightedge, the virtual and the real: Exploring online and offline experiences in Canadian youth subcultures. *Youth & Society*, *36*, 276–311. doi:10.1177/0044118X03260498

Wilson, J. Q. (1993). *Performance measures for the criminal justice system. Article prepared for the U* (pp. 153–167). Washington, DC: S. Department of Justice, Bureau of Justice Assistance. Bureau of Justice Statistics.

Wilson, M. I., & Corey, K. (2000). *Information tectonics: Space, place, and technology in an electronic age*. West Sussex, UK: John Wiley and Sons Ltd.

Wong, S. L., & Leatherdale, S. T. (2009). Association between sedentary behavior, physical activity, and obesity: Inactivity among active kids. *Preventing Chronic Disease*, *6*, 1–13.

Woo, Hyung-jin, Kim, Yeora & Dominick, Joseph (2004). Hackers: Militants or Merry Pranksters? A content analysis of defaced web pages. *Media Psychology*, *6*(1), 63-82.

Wood, J. (2006). Research and innovation in the field of security: A nodal governance view . In Wood, J., & Dupont, B. (Eds.), *Democracy, society and the governance of security* (pp. 217–240). New York: Cambridge University Press. doi:10.1017/CBO9780511489358.011

Wood, J., & Font, E. (2004, July 12-13). *Is "community policing" a desirable export? On crafting the global constabulary ethic*. Paper presented at the workshop on Constabulary Ethics and the Spirit of Transnational Policing. Oñati, Spain.

Woodbury-Smith, M. R., Robinson, J., Wheelwright, S., & Baron-Cohen, S. (2005).. . *Journal of Autism and Developmental Disorders*, *35*, 331–335. doi:10.1007/s10803-005-3300-7

Wright, J. P., & Cullen, F. T. (2004). Employment, peers, and life-course transitions. *Justice Quarterly*, *21*, 183–205. doi:10.1080/07418820400095781

Wu, X. (2007). *Chinese cyber nationalism: Evolution, characteristics and implications*. Lanham, MD: Lexington Books.

Yar, M. (2006). *Cybercrime and society*. Thousand Oaks, CA: Sage.

Yar, M. (2005). Computer hacking: Just another case of juvenile delinquency? *Howard Journal of Criminal Justice*, *44*, 387–399. doi:10.1111/j.1468-2311.2005.00383.x

Yar, M. (2005). The novelty of 'cybercrime': An assessment in light of routine activity theory. *European Journal of Criminology*, *2*(4), 407–427. doi:10.1177/147737080556056

Young, R., Zhang, L., & Prybutok, V. R. (2007). Hacking into the minds of hackers. *Information Systems Management*, *24*, 271–28. doi:10.1080/10580530701585823

Young, K. S. (1996). Psychology of computer use: XL. Addictive use of the Internet: A case that breaks the stereotype. *Psychological Reports*, *79*, 899–902.

Zuckerman, M. J. (2001). *Kevin Mitnick & Asperger syndrome?* Retrieved March 29, 2001, from http://www.infosecnews.org/hypermail/0103/3818.html

About the Contributors

Thomas J. Holt is an Assistant Professor at Michigan State University in the Department of Criminal Justice. Previously, he was at the University of North Carolina at Charlotte. He has a doctorate in criminology and criminal justice from the University of Missouri—Saint Louis. His research focuses on computer crime, cyber crime, and the role that technology and the Internet play in facilitating all manner of crime and deviance. Dr. Holt has authored several papers on the topics of hacking, cyber crime, and deviance that have appeared in journals such as *Deviant Behavior* and the *International Journal of Comparative and Applied Criminal Justice*. He is also a member of the editorial board of the *International Journal of Cyber Criminology*.

Bernadette H. Schell, the founding dean of the Faculty of Business and Information Technology at the University of Ontario Institute of Technology in Canada, is currently the President' Advisor on Cybercrime. She has authored four books on the topic of hacking: *The Hacking of America: Who's Doing It, Why, and How* (2002); *Contemporary World Issues: Cybercrime* (2004); *Webster's New World Hacker Dictionary* (2006); and *Contemporary World Issues: The Internet and Society* (2007). She has also written numerous journal articles on topics related to violence in society and is the author of three books dealing with stress-coping in the workplace (1997), the stress and emotional dysfunction of corporate leaders (1999), and stalking, harassment, and murder in the workplace (2000).

* * *

Michael Bachmann is Assistant Professor of Criminal Justice at Texas Christian University. He received his Ph.D. in Sociology from the University of Central Florida in 2008 and his M.A. in Social Sciences from University of Mannheim, Germany in 2004. Dr. Bachmann specializes in the investigation of computer and high tech crimes. His research focuses primarily on the social dimensions behind technology-driven crimes. He is the author of several book chapters and journal articles on cyber-crime and cyber-criminals.

Adam M. Bossler is an Assistant Professor of Justice Studies at Georgia Southern University. He received his Ph.D. in criminology and criminal justice from the University of Missouri - St. Louis. His research interests include testing criminological theories that have received little empirical testing, examining the application of traditional criminological theories to cybercrime offending and victimization, exploring law enforcement readiness for cybercrime, and evaluating policies and programs aimed at reducing youth violence.

Jacob Brodsky has a background of over 23 years of experience working on just about every aspect of SCADA and industrial control systems, including assembly language firmware coding, ladder logic programming, systems programming for many platforms and languages, and has a significant telecommunications background including FDM and Digital Microwave radio engineering, component level repair of radio equipment, radio path engineering, WAN and LAN design. He has written SCADA protocol drivers, and re-engineered process instrumentation and control problems. As a register, as well as a graduate from The Johns Hopkins University in 1990 with a Bachelor's Degree in Electrical Engineering, Jake's education has given him clear insight and fundamental and vast knowledge on the development and implementation of industrial control systems in the field. Mr. Brodsky is a voting member of the DNP3 Technical Committee, a contributing member of ISA-99, and a member of the American Water-Works Association.

George W. Burruss is an Assistant Professor in the Center for the Study of Crime, Delinquency & Corrections at Southern Illinois University at Carbondale. He received his Ph.D. in criminology and criminal justice from the University of Missouri – St. Louis. He does research on criminal justice organizations, including juvenile courts and the police. He has published articles in *Justice Quarterly*, *Policing*, and *Journal of Criminal Justice.*

Dorothy E. Denning (PhD) is Distinguished Professor of Defense Analysis at the Naval Postgraduate School, where her current research and teaching encompasses the areas of conflict and cyberspace; trust, influence and networks; terrorism and crime; and information operations and security. She is author of *Information Warfare and Security* and has previously worked at Georgetown University, Digital Equipment Corporation, SRI International, and Purdue University.

Rafael Etges is the Director for Risk Management Practices for TELUS Security Labs, Canada, and Program Director for Governance, Risk and Compliance at TELUS Security Solutions. Rafael brings 15 years of consulting experience at major consulting groups in South and North America. Rafael has extensive experience in corporate and IT governance, IT security policy development, IT security program management, and auditing. He is a subject matter expert on several security control frameworks (ISO 17799/27001, CobiT, COSO, ITIL, PCI DSS) and regulations (Sarbanes Oxley, Bill 198, PIPEDA, and international privacy laws).

Alessandra Garbagnati is a law student at the University of California, Hastings College of Law. Her area of specialization includes intellectual property and cyber law. She externed for Justice Richard McAdams at the California Court of Appeals during her first summer. Ms. Garbagnati also received her undergraduate degrees in Criminology, Law & Society and Psychology & Social Behavior at the University of California, Irvine. She plans on working in a corporate law firm upon completion of her J.D. in 2011.

Orly Turgeman-Goldschmidt (PhD) is in the Interdisciplinary Department of Social Sciences at Bar-Ilan University in Ramat Gan, Israel.

Walid Hejazi (PhD) is a Professor of Business Economics at the Rotman School of Management at the University of Toronto, where he regularly teaches Canada's current and future business leaders in the MBA and Executive MBA programs. He has published extensively in more than forty business journals and publications. In keeping with the spirit of Rotman, Walid balances his research activities by helping many of Canada's leading organizations leverage research to decide new strategies and initiatives. Recently, he assisted several large retail chains find new ways to understand their market data, providing them with perspectives allowing them to optimize their business activities. Walid has also consulted for several branches of Canadian government, on diverse themes such as the competitiveness of the Canadian economy and international trade. He is currently editor-in-chief of a study being prepared by the Department of Foreign Affairs measuring the economic benefits of Canada's partnership with the European Union.

Max Kilger is a profiler as well as a member of the board of directors for the Honeynet Project. As a social psychologist his research interests focus on the relationships between people and technology. In particular his research focuses on the motivations of individuals and groups in gaining non-traditional access to computer networks and resources. He is the co-author of several book chapters on profiling. He was a member of a National Academy of Engineering counterterrorism committee providing advice and counsel to Congress and other relevant federal entities. He is a frequent national and international speaker at information security forums.

Alan LeFort is currently the Managing Director for TELUS Security Labs, Canada, a research organization focused on helping more than 50 of the world's leading security companies identify and eradicate critical threats and vulnerabilities. Alan also acts as a senior advisor to several of the top security companies, providing guidance on their market strategy and their product roadmaps. Additionally, he heads up the product management team at TELUS for security products and services--including managed services, technology integration, and professional services. Prior to joining TELUS, Alan has held senior roles in software development, product management, and IT operations. He has also taught several security courses at the professional learning centre at the University of Toronto's Faculty of Information Studies.

June Melnychuk (BA) is a Teaching Assistant and Lab Instructor for the Faculty of Criminology, Justice and Policy Studies and for the Faculty of Business and Information Technology at the University of Ontario Institute of Technology, Canada. She was the recipient of the 2008-2009 Teaching Assistant Award, as nominated by the students. She is completing a Masters of Arts degree in Criminal Justice at the University of the Fraser Valley in British Columbia, Canada.

Robert G. Morris (PhD) is an Assistant Professor of Criminology at the University of Texas in Dallas. He studies the etiology of crime, with a specific interest in fraud and cybercrime, as well as issues surrounding the social response to crime. His recent work has appeared in *Criminal Justice Review, Journal of Criminal Justice, Journal of Crime and Justice, Deviant Behavior, Criminal Justice & Popular Culture, Criminal Justice Studies*, and *Criminal Justice Policy Review.*

Johnny Nhan is assistant professor of criminal justice at Texas Christian University. He obtained his Ph.D. in Criminology, Law and Society from the University of California, Irvine in 2008. He has written on various issues in cybercrime, including piracy, policing, and spam. His research interests include hacker culture, cyber law, and white-collar crime.

Bob Radvanovsky has knowledge about our Nation's critical infrastructures, publishing numerous articles regarding 'critical infrastructure protection' ('CIP'). He has established awareness programs through his company, Infracritical, with professional accreditation and educational institutions, specifically on critical infrastructure protection and assurance. This includes establishing the SCADASEC mailing list for control systems security discussions, is a participating subject-matter expert with DHS's Transportation Security Administration's *Transportation Systems Sector Cyber Working Group* (TSS-CWG) and DHS's Control Systems Security Program's (CSSP) *Industrial Control Systems' Joint Working Group* (ICSJWG), and is co-chairperson of the International Society of Automation (ISA) *ISA-99 WG10: Security Program Operations and Metrics* (to be integrated into the ANSI/ISA99.00.02-2009 standard).

Ben Sapiro is the Research Director with TELUS Security Labs, Toronto, responsible for Security Practices. Ben brings over ten years as a security consultant with global clients in North America, Europe, the Middle East and Asia. Ben's security experience includes security audits, ethical hacking, infrastructure work, threat modeling, secure development, secure architecture, social engineering, and application testing. Ben contributes to community efforts on emerging cloud security standards and XML-based security reporting languages.

David S. Wall (BA, MA, M Phil, PhD, FRSA, AcSS) is Professor of Criminal Justice and Information Society at the University of Leeds in the UK. He conducts research and teaches in the fields of criminal justice and information technology (Cybercrime), policing, cyber law and Intellectual Property crime. He has published a wide range of articles and books on these subjects, including: *Cybercrime: The Transformation of Crime in the Information Age* (2007), *Crime and Deviance in Cyberspace* (2009), *Cyberspace Crime* (2003), *Crime and the Internet* (2001) and *The Internet, Law and Society* (2000). He has also published a range of books and articles within the broader field of criminal justice, including *Policy Networks in Criminal Justice* (2001), *The British Police: Forces and Chief Officers* (1999), *The Chief Constables of England and Wales* (1998), *Access to Criminal Justice* (1996), and *Policing in a Northern Force* (1991).

Index

T

U

V

W

Z

Breinigsville, PA USA
24 September 2010

245912BV00002B/3/P

9 781616 928056